D0025285

Selected Works
of Angelina Weld Grimké

THE SCHOMBURG LIBRARY OF
NINETEENTH-CENTURY BLACK WOMEN WRITERS

Henry Louis Gates, Jr.
General Editor

Titles are listed chronologically; collections that
include works published over a span of years are listed according to
the publication date of their initial work.

Phillis Wheatley, *The Collected Works of Phillis Wheatley*
Six Women's Slave Narratives: M. Prince; Old Elizabeth;
    M. J. Jackson; L. A. Delaney; K. Drumgoold; A. L. Burton
Spiritual Narratives: M. W. Stewart; J. Lee; J. A. J. Foote;
    V. W. Broughton
Ann Plato, *Essays*
Collected Black Women's Narratives: N. Prince; L. Picquet;
    B. Veney; S. K. Taylor
Sojourner Truth, *Narrative of Sojourner Truth; A Bondswoman
    of Olden Time, With a History of Her Labors and Correspondence
    Drawn from Her "Book of Life"*
Frances E. W. Harper, *Complete Poems of Frances E. W. Harper*
Charlotte Forten Grimké, *The Journals of Charlotte Forten Grimké*
Two Biographies by African-American Women: J. Brown; F. A. Rollin
Mary Seacole, *Wonderful Adventures of Mrs. Seacole in Many Lands*
Eliza Potter, *A Hairdresser's Experience in High Life*
Harriet Jacobs, *Incidents in the Life of a Slave Girl*
Collected Black Women's Poetry, Volumes 1–4: M. E. Tucker;
    A. I. Menken; M. W. Fordham; P. J. Thompson;
    C. A. Thompson; H. C. Ray; L. A. J. Moorer; J. D. Heard; E. Bibb;
    M. P. Johnson; Mrs. H. Linden
Elizabeth Keckley, *Behind the Scenes. Or, Thirty Years a Slave,
    and Four Years in the White House*
C. W. Larison, M.D., *Silvia Dubois, A Biografy of the Slav
    Who Whipt Her Mistres and Gand Her Fredom*

Katherine Davis Chapman Tillman, *The Works of Katherine Davis Chapman Tillman*

Mrs. A. E. Johnson, *Clarence and Corinne; or, God's Way*

Octavia V. Rogers Albert, *The House of Bondage: or Charlotte Brooks and Other Slaves*

Emma Dunham Kelley, *Megda*

Anna Julia Cooper, *A Voice From the South*

Frances E. W. Harper, *Iola Leroy, or Shadows Uplifted*

Ida B. Wells-Barnett, *Selected Works of Ida B. Wells-Barnett*

Amanda Smith, *An Autobiography: The Story of the Lord's Dealings with Mrs. Amanda Smith the Colored Evangelist*

Mrs. A. E. Johnson, *The Hazeley Family*

Mrs. N. F. Mossell, *The Work of the Afro-American Woman*

Alice Dunbar-Nelson, *The Works of Alice Dunbar-Nelson*, Volumes 1–3

Emma D. Kelley-Hawkins, *Four Girls at Cottage City*

Olivia Ward Bush-Banks, *The Collected Works of Olivia Ward Bush-Banks*

Angelina Weld Grimké, *Selected Works of Angelina Weld Grimké*

Pauline E. Hopkins, *Contending Forces: A Romance Illustrative of Negro Life North and South*

Short Fiction by Black Women, 1900–1920: P. E. Hopkins; A. W. Grimké; A. B. Scales; G. F. Stewart; G. Mossell; R. D. Todd; G. H. D. Browne; F. B. Williams; M. L. Burgess-Ware; K. D. Sweetser; L. Plummer; E. E. Bulkley; F. Nordstrom; G. E. Tompkins; M. K. Griffin; J. Fauset; L. B. Dixon; A. Dunbar-Nelson; M. Jones; A. McCrary; E. E. Butler; H. G. Ricks; A. F. Ries; L. A. Pendleton; E. M. Harrold; A. S. Coleman

Pauline Hopkins, *The Magazine Novels of Pauline Hopkins*

Effie Waller Smith, *The Collected Works of Effie Waller Smith*

Hallie Q. Brown, *Homespun Heroines and Other Women of Distinction*

Jean Fagan Yellin and Cynthia D. Bond (Comps.), *The Pen Is Ours: A Listing of Writings by and about African-American Women before 1910. With Secondary Bibliography to the Present*

Selected Works

of

Angelina Weld Grimké

Edited by
CAROLIVIA HERRON

❧ ❧ ❧

❧ ❧ ❧

New York   Oxford
OXFORD UNIVERSITY PRESS
1991

Oxford University Press

Oxford   New York   Toronto
Delhi   Bombay   Calcutta   Madras   Karachi
Petaling Jaya   Singapore   Hong Kong   Tokyo
Nairobi   Dar es Salaam   Cape Town
Melbourne   Auckland

and associated companies in
Berlin   Ibadan

Library of Congress Cataloging-in-Publication Data
Grimké, Angelina Weld, 1880–1958.
Selected works of Angelina Weld Grimké /
edited by Carolivia Herron.
p.   cm.—(The Schomburg library of nineteenth-century Black women writers)
ISBN 0-19-506199-3
1. Afro-Americans—Literary collections.   I. Herron, Carolivia.
II. Title.   III. Series.
PS3513.R744A6   1991
818'.5209—dc20   90-23230

2 4 6 8 10 9 7 5 3 1

Printed in the United States of America
on acid free paper

PUBLISHER'S NOTE

FOREWORD TO THE
SCHOMBURG SUPPLEMENT

Henry Louis Gates, Jr.

The enthusiastic reception by students, scholars, and the general public to the 1988 publication of the Schomburg Library of Nineteenth-Century Black Women Writers more than justified the efforts of twenty-five scholars and the staff of the Black Periodical Literature Project to piece together the fragments of knowledge about the writings of African-American women between 1773 and 1910. The Library's republication of those writings in thirty volumes—ranging from the poetry of Phillis Wheatley to the enormous body of work that emerged out of the "Black Woman's Era" at the turn of this century—was a *beginning* for the restoration of the written sensibilities of a group of writers who confronted the twin barriers of racism and sexism in America. Through their poetry, diaries, speeches, biographies, essays, fictional narratives, and autobiographies, these writers transcended the boundaries of racial prejudice and sexual discrimination by recording the thoughts and feelings of Americans who were, at once, black *and* female. Taken together, these works configure into a literary tradition because their authors read, critiqued, and revised each other's words, in textual groundings with their sisters.

Indeed, by publishing these texts together as a "library," and by presenting them as part of a larger discourse on race and gender, we hoped to enable readers to chart the formal specificities of this tradition and to trace its origins. As a whole, the works in the Schomburg Library demonstrate that the contemporary literary movement of African-American women writers is heir to a legacy that was born in 1773, when Phillis Wheatley's *Poems on Various Subjects, Religious and Moral* first unveiled the mind of a black woman to the world. The fact that the Wheatley volume has proven to be the most popular in the Schomburg set is a testament to her role as the "founder" of both the black American's and the black woman's literary tradition.

Even before the Library was published, however, I began to receive queries about producing a supplement that would incorporate works that had not been included initially. Often these exchanges were quite dramatic. For instance, shortly before a lecture I was about to deliver at the University of Cincinnati, Professor Sharon Dean asked me if the Library would be reprinting the 1859 autobiography of Eliza Potter, a black hairdresser who had lived and worked in Cincinnati. I had never heard of Potter, I replied. Did Dean have a copy of her book? No, but there *was* a copy at the Cincinnati Historical Society. As I delivered my lecture, I could not help thinking about this "lost" text and its great significance. In fact, after the lecture, Dean and I rushed from the building and drove to the Historical Society, arriving just a few moments before closing time. A patient librarian brought us the book, and as I leafed through it, I was once again confronted with the realization that so often accompanied the research behind the Library's first thirty volumes—the exciting, yet poignant awareness that there probably exist *dozens* of works like Potter's, buried in research libraries, waiting only to be uncovered through an accident of contiguity like that which placed Sharon Dean in Cincinnati, roaming the shelves of its Historical Society. Another scholar wrote to me about work being done on the poet Effie Waller Smith. Several other scholars also wrote to share their research on other authors and their works. A supplement to the Library clearly was necessary.

Thus we have now added ten volumes, among them Potter's autobiography and Smith's collected poetry, as well as a narrative by Sojourner Truth, several pamphlets by Ida B. Wells-Barnett, and two biographies by Josephine Brown and Frances Rollin. Also included are books consisting of various essays, stories, poems, and plays whose authors did not, or could not, collect their writings into a full-length volume. The works of Olivia Ward Bush-Banks, Angelina Weld Grimké, and Katherine Davis Chapman Tillman are in this category. A related volume is an anthology of short fiction published by black women in the *Colored American Magazine* and *Crisis* magazine—a collection that reveals the shaping influence which certain periodicals had upon the generation of specific genres within the black women's literary tradition. Both types of collected books are intended to kindle an interest in still another series of works that bring together for the first time either the complete *oeuvre* of one writer or that of one genre within the periodical press. Indeed, there are several authors whose collected works will establish them as major forces in the nineteenth- and early twentieth-century black women's intellectual community. Compiling, editing, and publishing these volumes will be as important a factor in constructing the black women's literary tradition as has been the republication of books long out of print.

Finally, the Library now includes a detailed bibliography of the writings of black women in the nineteenth and early twentieth centuries. Prepared by Jean Fagan Yellin and Cynthia Bond, this bibliography is the result of years of research and will serve as an indispensable resource in future investigations of black women writers, particularly those whose works appeared frequently throughout the nineteenth century in the principal conduit of writing for black women *or* men, the African-American periodical press.

The publication of this ten-volume supplement, we hope, will make a sound contribution toward reestablishing the importance of the creative works of African-American women and reevaluating the relation of these works not only to each other but also to African-American *and* American literature and history as a whole. These works are invaluable sources for readers intent upon understanding the complex interplay of ethnicity and gender, of racism and sexism—of how "race" becomes gendered and how gender becomes racialized—in American society.

FOREWORD
In Her Own Write

Henry Louis Gates, Jr.

One muffled strain in the Silent South, a jarring chord and a vague and uncomprehended cadenza has been and still is the Negro. And of that muffled chord, the one mute and voiceless note has been the sadly expectant Black Women, ...

The "other side" has not been represented by one who "lives there." And not many can more sensibly realize and more accurately tell the weight and the fret of the "long dull pain" than the open-eyed but hitherto voiceless Black Woman of America.

. . . as our Caucasian barristers are not to blame if they cannot *quite* put themselves in the dark man's place, neither should the dark man be wholly expected fully and adequately to reproduce the exact Voice of the Black Woman.

—ANNA JULIA COOPER
A Voice From the South (1892)

The birth of the African-American literary tradition occurred in 1773, when Phillis Wheatley published a book of poetry. Despite the fact that her book garnered for her a remarkable amount of attention, Wheatley's journey to the printer had been a most arduous one. Sometime in 1772, a young African girl walked demurely into a room in Boston to undergo an oral examination, the results of which would determine the direction of her life and work. Perhaps she was shocked upon entering the appointed room. For there, perhaps gathered in a semicircle, sat eighteen of Boston's most notable citizens. Among them were John Erving, a prominent Boston merchant; the Reverend Charles Chauncy, pastor of the Tenth Congregational Church; and John Hancock, who would later gain fame for his signature on the Declaration of Independence. At the center of this group was His Excellency, Thomas Hutchinson, governor of Massachusetts, with Andrew Oliver, his lieutenant governor, close by his side.

Why had this august group been assembled? Why had it seen fit to summon this young African girl, scarcely eighteen years old, before it? This group of "the most respectable Characters in *Boston*," as it would define itself, had assembled to question closely the African adolescent on the slender sheaf of poems that she claimed to have "written by herself." We can only speculate on the nature of the questions posed to the fledgling poet. Perhaps they asked her to identify and explain—for all to hear—exactly who were the Greek and Latin gods and poets alluded to so frequently in her work. Perhaps they asked her to conjugate a verb in Latin or even to translate randomly selected passages from the Latin, which she and her master, John Wheatley, claimed that she "had made some Progress in." Or perhaps they asked her to recite from memory key passages from the texts of John Milton and Alexander Pope, the two poets by whom the African claimed to be most directly influenced. We do not know.

We do know, however, that the African poet's responses were more than sufficient to prompt the eighteen august gentlemen to compose, sign, and publish a two-paragraph "Attestation," an open letter "To the Publick" that prefaces Phillis Wheatley's book and that reads in part:

> We whose Names are under-written, do assure the World, that the Poems specified in the following Page, were (as we

verily believe) written by Phillis, a young Negro Girl, who was but a few Years since, brought an uncultivated Barbarian from *Africa,* and has ever since been, and now is, under the Disadvantage of serving as a Slave in a Family in this Town. She has been examined by some of the best Judges, and is thought qualified to write them.

So important was this document in securing a publisher for Wheatley's poems that it forms the signal element in the prefatory matter preceding her *Poems on Various Subjects, Religious and Moral,* published in London in 1773.

Without the published "Attestation," Wheatley's publisher claimed, few would believe that an African could possibly have written poetry all by herself. As the eighteen put the matter clearly in their letter, "Numbers would be ready to suspect they were not really the Writings of Phillis." Wheatley and her master, John Wheatley, had attempted to publish a similar volume in 1772 in Boston, but Boston publishers had been incredulous. One year later, "Attestation" in hand, Phillis Wheatley and her master's son, Nathaniel Wheatley, sailed for England, where they completed arrangements for the publication of a volume of her poems with the aid of the Countess of Huntington and the Earl of Dartmouth.

This curious anecdote, surely one of the oddest oral examinations on record, is only a tiny part of a larger, and even more curious, episode in the Enlightenment. Since the beginning of the sixteenth century, Europeans had wondered aloud whether or not the African "species of men," as they were most commonly called, *could* ever create formal literature, could ever master "the arts and sciences." If they could, the argument ran, then the African variety of humanity was fundamentally related to the European variety. If not, then it seemed clear that the African was destined by nature to be a slave. This was the burden shouldered by Phillis Wheatley when she successfully defended herself and the authorship of her book against counterclaims and doubts.

Indeed, with her successful defense, Wheatley launched two traditions at once—the black American literary tradition *and* the black woman's literary tradition. If it is extraordinary that not just one but both of these traditions were founded simultaneously by a black woman—certainly an event unique in the history of literature—it is also ironic that this important fact of common, coterminous literary origins seems to have escaped most scholars.

That the progenitor of the black literary tradition was a woman means, in the most strictly literal sense, that all subsequent black writers have evolved in a matrilinear line of descent, and that each, consciously or unconsciously, has extended and revised a canon whose foundation was the poetry of a black woman. Early black writers seem to have been keenly aware of Wheatley's founding role, even if most of her white reviewers were more concerned with the implications of her race than her gender. Jupiter Hammon, for example, whose 1760 broadside "An Evening Thought. Salvation by Christ, With Penitential Cries" was the first individual poem published by a black American, acknowledged Wheatley's influence by selecting her as the subject of his second broadside, "An Address to Miss Phillis Wheatly [*sic*], Ethiopian Poetess, in Boston," which was published in Hartford in 1778. And George Moses Horton, the second African American to publish a book of poetry in English (1829), brought out in 1838 an edition of his *Poems By A Slave* bound together with Wheatley's work. Indeed, for fifty-six years, between 1773 and 1829, when Horton published *The Hope of Liberty*, Wheatley was the *only* black person to have published a book of imaginative literature in English. So central was this black woman's role in the shaping of the

African-American literary tradition that, as one historian has maintained, the history of the reception of Phillis Wheatley's poetry *is* the history of African-American literary criticism. Well into the nineteenth century, Wheatley and the black literary tradition were the same entity.

But Wheatley is not the only black woman writer who stands as a pioneering figure in African-American literature. Just as Wheatley gave birth to the genre of black poetry, Ann Plato was the first African American to publish a book of essays (1841) and Harriet E. Wilson was the first black person to publish a novel in the United States (1859).

Despite this pioneering role of black women in the tradition, however, many of their contributions before this century have been all but lost or unrecognized. As Hortense Spillers observed as recently as 1983,

> With the exception of a handful of autobiographical narratives from the nineteenth century, the black woman's realities are virtually suppressed until the period of the Harlem Renaissance and later. Essentially the black woman as artist, as intellectual spokesperson for her own cultural apprenticeship, has not existed before, for anyone. At the source of [their] own symbol-making task, [the community of black women writers] confronts, therefore, a tradition of work that is quite recent, its continuities, broken and sporadic.

Until now, it has been extraordinarily difficult to establish the formal connections between early black women's writing and that of the present, precisely because our knowledge of their work has been broken and sporadic. Phillis Wheatley, for example, while certainly the most reprinted and discussed poet in the tradition, is also one of the least understood. Ann Plato's seminal work, *Essays* (which includes biographies and poems), has not been reprinted since it was published a century and a half ago. And Harriet Wilson's *Our Nig,* her

compelling novel of a black woman's expanding consciousness in a racist Northern antebellum environment, never received even *one* review or comment at a time when virtually
all works written by black people were heralded by abolitionists as salient arguments against the existence of human slavery. Many of the books reprinted in this set experienced a
similar fate, the most dreadful fate for an author: that of
being ignored then relegated to the obscurity of the rare book
section of a university library. We can only wonder how
many other texts in the black woman's tradition have been
lost to this generation of readers or remain unclassified or
uncatalogued and, hence, unread.

This was not always so, however. Black women writers
dominated the final decade of the nineteenth century, perhaps
spurred to publish by an 1886 essay entitled "The Coming
American Novelist," which was published in *Lippincott's
Monthly Magazine* and written by "A Lady From Philadel-
phia." This pseudonymous essay argued that the "Great
American Novel" would be written by a black person. Her
argument is so curious that it deserves to be repeated:

> When we come to formulate our demands of the Coming
> American Novelist, we will agree that he must be native-
> born. His ancestors may come from where they will, but we
> must give him a birthplace and have the raising of him.
> Still, the longer his family has been here the better he will
> represent us. Suppose he should have no country but ours,
> no traditions but those he has learned here, no longings apart
> from us, no future except in our future—the orphan of the
> world, he finds with us his home. And with all this, suppose
> he refuses to be fused into that grand conglomerate we call
> the "American type." With us, he is not of us. He is origi-
> nal, he has humor, he is tender, he is passive and fiery, he
> has been taught what we call justice, and he has his own
> opinion about it. He has suffered everything a poet, a dra-

matist, a novelist need suffer before he comes to have his lips anointed. And with it all he is in one sense a spectator, a little out of the race. How would these conditions go towards forming an original development? In a word, suppose the coming novelist is of African origin? When one comes to consider the subject, there is no improbability in it. One thing is certain,—our great novel will not be written by the typical American.

An atypical American, indeed. Not only would the great American novel be written by an African American, it would be written by an African-American *woman:*

> Yet farther: I have used the generic masculine pronoun because it is convenient; but Fate keeps revenge in store. It was a woman who, taking the wrongs of the African as her theme, wrote the novel that awakened the world to their reality, and why should not the coming novelist be a woman as well as an African? She—the woman of that race—has some claims on Fate which are not yet paid up.

It is these claims on fate that we seek to pay by publishing The Schomburg Library of Nineteenth-Century Black Women Writers.

This theme would be repeated by several black women authors, most notably by Anna Julia Cooper, a prototypical black feminist whose 1892 *A Voice From the South* can be considered to be one of the original texts of the black feminist movement. It was Cooper who first analyzed the fallacy of referring to "the Black man" when speaking of black people and who argued that just as white men cannot speak through the consciousness of black men, neither can black *men* "fully and adequately . . . reproduce the exact Voice of the Black Woman." Gender and race, she argues, cannot be conflated, except in the instance of a black woman's voice, and it is this voice which must be uttered and to which we must listen. As Cooper puts the matter so compellingly:

It is not the intelligent woman vs. the ignorant woman; nor the white woman vs. the black, the brown, and the red,—it is not even the cause of woman vs. man. Nay, 'tis woman's strongest vindication for speaking that *the world needs to hear her voice*. It would be subversive of every human interest that the cry of one-half the human family be stifled. Woman in stepping from the pedestal of statue-like inactivity in the domestic shrine, and daring to think and move and speak,—to undertake to help shape, mold, and direct the thought of her age, is merely completing the circle of the world's vision. Hers is every interest that has lacked an interpreter and a defender. Her cause is linked with that of every agony that has been dumb—every wrong that needs a voice.

It is no fault of man's that he has not been able to see truth from her standpoint. It does credit both to his head and heart that no greater mistakes have been committed or even wrongs perpetrated while she sat making tatting and snipping paper flowers. Man's own innate chivalry and the mutual interdependence of their interests have insured his treating her cause, in the main at least, as his own. And he is pardonably surprised and even a little chagrined, perhaps, to find his legislation not considered "perfectly lovely" in every respect. But in any case his work is only impoverished by her remaining dumb. The world has had to limp along with the wobbling gait and one-sided hesitancy of a man with one eye. Suddenly the bandage is removed from the other eye and the whole body is filled with light. It sees a circle where before it saw a segment. The darkened eye restored, every member rejoices with it.

The myopic sight of the darkened eye can only be restored when the full range of the black woman's voice, with its own special timbres and shadings, remains mute no longer.

Similarly, Victoria Earle Matthews, an author of short stories and essays, and a cofounder in 1896 of the National Association of Colored Women, wrote in her stunning essay,

"The Value of Race Literature" (1895), that "when the literature of our race is developed, it will of necessity be different in all essential points of greatness, true heroism and real Christianity from what we may at the present time, for convenience, call American literature." Matthews argued that this great tradition of African-American literature would be the textual outlet "for the unnaturally suppressed inner lives which our people have been compelled to lead." Once these "unnaturally suppressed inner lives" of black people are unveiled, no "grander diffusion of mental light" will shine more brightly, she concludes, than that of the articulate African-American woman:

> And now comes the question, What part shall we women play in the Race Literature of the future? . . . within the compass of one small journal ["Woman's Era"] we have struck out a new line of departure—a journal, a record of Race interests gathered from all parts of the United States, carefully selected, moistened, winnowed and garnered by the ablest intellects of educated colored women, shrinking at no lofty theme, shirking no serious duty, aiming at every possible excellence, and determined to do their part in the future uplifting of the race.
>
> If twenty women, by their concentrated efforts in one literary movement, can meet with such success as has engendered, planned out, and so successfully consummated this convention, what much more glorious results, what wider spread success, what grander diffusion of mental light will not come forth at the bidding of the enlarged hosts of women writers, already called into being by the stimulus of your efforts?
>
> And here let me speak one word for my journalistic sisters who have already entered the broad arena of journalism. Before the "Woman's Era" had come into existence, no one except themselves can appreciate the bitter experience and sore

disappointments under which they have at all times been
compelled to pursue their chosen vocations.

If their brothers of the press have had their difficulties to
contend with, I am here as a sister journalist to state, from
the fullness of knowledge, that their task has been an easy
one compared with that of the colored woman in journalism.

Woman's part in Race Literature, as in Race building, is
the most important part and has been so in all ages. . . . All
through the most remote epochs she has done her share in
literature. . . .

One of the most important aspects of this set is the republication of the salient texts from 1890 to 1910, which literary
historians could well call the "Black Woman's Era." In addition to Mary Helen Washington's definitive edition of
Cooper's *A Voice From the South,* we have reprinted two novels by Amelia Johnson, Frances Harper's *Iola Leroy,* two
novels by Emma Dunham Kelley, Alice Dunbar-Nelson's two
impressive collections of short stories, and Pauline Hopkins's
three serialized novels as well as her monumental novel,
Contending Forces—all published between 1890 and 1910.
Indeed, black women published more works of fiction in these
two decades than black men had published in the previous
half century. Nevertheless, this great achievement has been
ignored.

Moreover, the writings of nineteenth-century African-
American women in general have remained buried in obscurity, accessible only in research libraries or in overpriced and
poorly edited reprints. Many of these books have never been
reprinted at all; in some instances only one or two copies are
extant. In these works of fiction, poetry, autobiography, bi-
ography, essays, and journalism resides the mind of the
nineteenth-century African-American woman. Until these
works are made readily available to teachers and their students,
a significant segment of the black tradition will remain silent.

Oxford University Press, in collaboration with the Schomburg Center for Research in Black Culture, is publishing thirty volumes of these compelling works, each of which contains an introduction by an expert in the field. The set includes such rare texts as Johnson's *The Hazeley Family* and *Clarence and Corinne*, Plato's *Essays*, the most complete edition of Phillis Wheatley's poems and letters, Emma Dunham Kelley's pioneering novel *Megda*, several previously unpublished stories and a novel by Alice Dunbar-Nelson, and the first collected volumes of Pauline Hopkins's three serialized novels and Frances Harper's poetry. We also present four volumes of poetry by such women as Henrietta Cordelia Ray, Adah Menken, Josephine Heard, and Maggie Johnson. Numerous slave and spiritual narratives, a newly discovered novel—*Four Girls at Cottage City*—by Emma Dunham Kelley (-Hawkins), and the first American edition of *Wonderful Adventures of Mrs. Seacole in Many Lands* are also among the texts included.

In addition to resurrecting the works of black women authors, it is our hope that this set will facilitate the resurrection of the African-American woman's literary tradition itself by unearthing its nineteenth-century roots. In the works of Nella Larsen and Jessie Fauset, Zora Neale Hurston and Ann Petry, Lorraine Hansberry and Gwendolyn Brooks, Paule Marshall and Toni Cade Bambara, Audre Lorde and Rita Dove, Toni Morrison and Alice Walker, Gloria Naylor and Jamaica Kincaid, these roots have branched luxuriantly. The eighteenth- and nineteenth-century authors whose works are presented in this set founded and nurtured the black women's literary tradition, which must be revived, explicated, analyzed, and debated before we can understand more completely the formal shaping of this tradition within a tradition, a coded literary universe through which, regrettably, we are only just beginning to navigate our way. As Anna Cooper said nearly one hundred years ago, we have been blinded by the loss of sight in one eye and have therefore been unable to detect the full *shape* of the African-American literary tradition.

Literary works configure into a tradition not because of some mystical collective unconscious determined by the biology of race or gender, but because writers read other writers and *ground* their representations of experience in models of language provided largely by other writers to whom they feel akin. It is through this mode of literary revision, amply evident in the *texts* themselves—in formal echoes, recast metaphors, even in parody—that a "tradition" emerges and defines itself.

This is formal bonding, and it is only through formal bonding that we can know a literary tradition. The collective publication of these works by black women now, for the first time, makes it possible for scholars and critics, male and female, black and white, to *demonstrate* that black women writers read, and revised, other black women writers. To demonstrate this set of formal literary relations is to demonstrate that sexuality, race, and gender are both the condition and the basis of *tradition*—but tradition as found in discrete acts of language use.

A word is in order about the history of this set. For the past decade, I have taught a course, first at Yale and then at Cornell, entitled "Black Woman and Their Fictions," a course that I inherited from Toni Morrison, who developed it in the mid-1970s for Yale's Program in Afro-American Studies. Although the course was inspired by the remarkable accomplishments of black women novelists since 1970, I gradually extended its beginning date to the late nineteenth century, studying Frances Harper's *Iola Leroy* and Anna Julia Cooper's *A Voice From the South*, both published in 1892. With the discovery of Harriet E. Wilson's seminal novel, *Our Nig* (1859), and Jean Yellin's authentication of Harriet Jacobs's brilliant slave narrative, *Incidents in the Life of a Slave Girl* (1861), a survey course spanning over a century and a quarter emerged.

But the discovery of *Our Nig,* as well as the interest in nineteenth-century black women's writing that this discovery generated, convinced me that even the most curious and diligent scholars knew very little of the extensive history of the creative writings of African-American women before 1900. Indeed, most scholars of African-American literature had never even read most of the books published by black women, simply because these books—of poetry, novels, short stories, essays, and autobiography—were mostly accessible only in rare book sections of university libraries. For reasons unclear to me even today, few of these marvelous renderings of the African-American woman's consciousness were reprinted in the late 1960s and early 1970s, when so many other texts of the African-American literary tradition were resurrected from the dark and silent graveyard of the out-of-print and were reissued in facsimile editions aimed at the hungry readership for canonical texts in the nascent field of black studies.

So, with the help of several superb research assistants—including David Curtis, Nicola Shilliam, Wendy Jones, Sam Otter, Janadas Devan, Suvir Kaul, Cynthia Bond, Elizabeth Alexander, and Adele Alexander—and with the expert advice of scholars such as William Robinson, William Andrews, Mary Helen Washington, Maryemma Graham, Jean Yellin, Houston A. Baker, Jr., Richard Yarborough, Hazel Carby, Joan R. Sherman, Frances Foster, and William French, dozens of bibliographies were used to compile a list of books written or narrated by black women mostly before 1910. Without the assistance provided through this shared experience of scholarship, the scholar's true legacy, this project would not have been conceived. As the list grew, I was struck by how very many of these titles that I, for example, had never even heard of, let alone read, such as Ann Plato's *Essays,* Louisa Picquet's slave narrative, or Amelia Johnson's two novels, *Clarence and Corinne* and *The Hazeley Family.* Through our research with the Black Periodical Fiction and Poetry Project (funded by NEH and the Ford Foundation), I also realized that several novels by black women, including three works of fiction by Pauline Hopkins, had been serialized in black periodicals, but had never been collected and published as books. Nor had the several books of poetry published by black women, such as the prolific Frances E. W. Harper, been collected and edited. When I discovered still another "lost" novel by an African-American woman (*Four Girls at Cottage City,* published in 1898 by Emma Dunham Kelley-Hawkins), I decided to attempt to edit a collection of reprints of these works and to publish them as a "library" of black women's writings, in part so that I could read them myself.

Convincing university and trade publishers to undertake this project proved to be a difficult task. Despite the commercial success of *Our Nig* and of the several reprint series of women's works (such as Virago, the Beacon Black Women Writers Series, and Rutgers' American Women Writers Series), several presses rejected the project as "too large," "too limited," or as "commercially unviable." Only two publishers recognized the viability and the import of the project and, of these, Oxford's commitment to publish the titles simultaneously as a set made the press's offer irresistible.

While attempting to locate original copies of these exceedingly rare books, I discovered that most of the texts were housed at the Schomburg Center for Research in Black Culture, a branch of The New York Public Library, under the direction of Howard Dodson. Dodson's infectious enthusiasm for the project and his generous collaboration, as well as that of his stellar staff (especially Diana Lachatanere, Sharon Howard, Ellis Haizip, Richard Newman, and Betty Gubert), led to a joint publishing initiative that produced this set as part of the Schomburg's major fund-raising campaign. Without Dodson's foresight and generosity of spirit, the set would not have materialized. Without William P. Sisler's masterful editorship at Oxford and his staff's careful attention to detail, the set would have remained just another grand idea that tends to languish in a scholar's file cabinet.

I would also like to thank Dr. Michael Winston and Dr. Thomas C. Battle, Vice-President of Academic Affairs and the Director of the Moorland-Spingarn Research Center (respectively) at Howard University, for their unending encouragement, support, and collaboration in this project, and Esme E. Bhan at Howard for her meticulous research and bibliographical skills. In addition, I would like to acknowledge the aid of the staff at the libraries of Duke University, Cornell University (especially Tom Weissinger and Donald Eddy), the Boston Public Library, the Western Reserve Historical Society, the Library of Congress, and Yale University. Linda Robbins, Marion Osmun, Sarah Flanagan, and Gerard Case, all members of the staff at Oxford, were extraordinarily effective at coordinating, editing, and producing the various segments of each text in the set. Candy Ruck, Nina de Tar, and Phillis Molock expertly typed reams of correspondence and manuscripts connected to the project.

I would also like to express my gratitude to my colleagues who edited and introduced the individual titles in the set. Without their attention to detail, their willingness to meet strict deadlines, and their sheer enthusiasm for this project, the set could not have been published. But finally and ultimately, I would hope that the publication of the set would help to generate even more scholarly interest in the black women authors whose work is presented here. Struggling against the seemingly insurmountable barriers of racism *and* sexism, while often raising families and fulfilling full-time professional obligations, these women managed nevertheless to record their thoughts and feelings and to *testify* to all who dare read them that the will to harness the power of collective endurance and survival is the will to write.

The Schomburg Library of Nineteenth-Century Black Women Writers is dedicated in memory of Pauline Augusta Coleman Gates, who died in the spring of 1987. It was she who inspired in me the love of learning and the love of literature. I have encountered in the books of this set no will more determined, no courage more noble, no mind more sublime, no self more celebratory of the achievements of all African-American women, and indeed of life itself, than her own.

A NOTE FROM
THE SCHOMBURG CENTER

Howard Dodson

The Schomburg Center for Research in Black Culture, The
New York Public Library, is pleased to join with Dr. Henry
Louis Gates and Oxford University Press in presenting The
Schomburg Library of Nineteenth-Century Black Women
Writers. This thirty-volume set includes the work of a generation of black women whose writing has only been available previously in rare book collections. The materials reprinted in twenty-four of the thirty volumes are drawn from
the unique holdings of the Schomburg Center.

A research unit of The New York Public Library, the
Schomburg Center has been in the forefront of those insti-
tutions dedicated to collecting, preserving, and providing ac-
cess to the records of the black past. In the course of its two
generations of acquisition and conservation activity, the Center has amassed collections totaling more than 5 million items.
They include over 100,000 bound volumes, 85,000 reels
and sets of microforms, 300 manuscript collections containing some 3.5 million items, 300,000 photographs and extensive holdings of prints, sound recordings, film and video-
tape, newspapers, artworks, artifacts, and other book and
nonbook materials. Together they vividly document the history
and cultural heritages of people of African descent worldwide.

Though established some sixty-two years ago, the Center's
book collections date from the sixteenth century. Its oldest
item, an Ethiopian Coptic Tunic, dates from the eighth or
ninth century. Rare materials, however, are most available
for the nineteenth-century African-American experience. It

is from these holdings that the majority of the titles selected for inclusion in this set are drawn.

The nineteenth century was a formative period in African-American literary and cultural history. Prior to the Civil War, the majority of black Americans living in the United States were held in bondage. Law and practice forbade teaching them to read or write. Even after the war, many of the impediments to learning and literary productivity remained. Nevertheless, black men and women of the nineteenth century persevered in both areas. Moreover, more African Americans than we yet realize turned their observations, feelings, social viewpoints, and creative impulses into published works. In time, this nineteenth-century printed record included poetry, short stories, histories, novels, autobiographies, social criticism, and theology, as well as economic and philosophical treatises. Unfortunately, much of this body of literature remained, until very recently, relatively inaccessible to twentieth-century scholars, teachers, creative artists, and others interested in black life. Prior to the late 1960s, most Americans (black as well as white) had never heard of these nineteenth-century authors, much less read their works.

The civil rights and black power movements created unprecedented interest in the thought, behavior, and achievements of black people. Publishers responded by revising traditional texts, introducing the American public to a new generation of African-American writers, publishing a variety of thematic anthologies, and reprinting a plethora of "classic texts" in African-American history, literature, and art. The reprints usually appeared as individual titles or in a series of bound volumes or microform formats.

The Schomburg Center, which has a long history of supporting publishing that deals with the history and culture of Africans in diaspora, became an active participant in many of the reprint revivals of the 1960s. Since hard copies of original printed works are the preferred formats for producing facsimile reproductions, publishers frequently turned to the Schomburg Center for copies of these original titles. In addition to providing such material, Schomburg Center staff members offered advice and consultation, wrote introductions, and occasionally entered into formal copublishing arrangements in some projects.

Most of the nineteenth-century titles reprinted during the 1960s, however, were by and about black men. A few black women were included in the longer series, but works by lesser known black women were generally overlooked. The Schomburg Library of Nineteenth-Century Black Women Writers is both a corrective to these previous omissions and an important contribution to African-American literary history in its own right. Through this collection of volumes, the thoughts, perspectives, and creative abilities of nineteenth-century African-American women, as captured in books and pamphlets published in large part before 1910, are again being made available to the general public. The Schomburg Center is pleased to be a part of this historic endeavor.

I would like to thank Professor Gates for initiating this project. Thanks are due both to him and Mr. William P. Sisler of Oxford University Press for giving the Schomburg Center an opportunity to play such a prominent role in the set. Thanks are also due to my colleagues at The New York Public Library and the Schomburg Center, especially Dr. Vartan Gregorian, Richard De Gennaro, Paul Fasana, Betsy Pinover, Richard Newman, Diana Lachatanere, Glenderlyn Johnson, and Harold Anderson for their assistance and support. I can think of no better way of demonstrating than in this set the role the Schomburg Center plays in assuring that the black heritage will be available for future generations.

CONTENTS

Selected Works
of Angelina Weld Grimké

INTRODUCTION

Carolivia Herron

The Angelina Weld Grimké Collection at the Moorland-Spingarn Research Center of Howard University includes a note in Grimké's hand that lists the titles of a projected collection of poetry. The list begins with the poem "An Epitaph," which depicts the futility and despair of the narrator who longs first for joy, then for love, and is answered with pain and death. The poem is presented in three stanzas, the last of which unites the themes of death, lost love, repudiation of life, and despair. The typescript of the poem has many changes of pronoun—from *I* to *she* and from *me* to *her*—suggesting that Grimké debated between the closeness of the perspective and the participation of the narrator with the subject of the poem. The last stanza reads:

> And now I lie quite straight, and still and plain;
> Above my heart the brazen poppies flare,
> But I know naught of love, or joy, or pain;—
> Nor care, nor care.

Somewhat illegible, the list of poems moves through titles suggesting happiness and familial comfort ("Lullaby") and ends with "To Joseph Lee," an obituary poem that was published by the *Boston Evening Transcript* (11 Nov. 1908) and that commemorates an African-American caterer and civil rights advocate in Boston.

Grimké's projected volume thus moves from inner death

3

to outer death, from the metaphorical death and repudiation of the love of one who loves too much to the literal death of a publicly mourned figure in a communal occasion of grief. The first poem not only records the failure of love for the narrator, but also masks the fact that the love Grimké preferred to receive, the love she missed, was probably that of a woman in a lesbian relationship. Critics such as Gloria Hull in *Color, Sex, and Poetry,* and Barbara Christian in *Black Feminist Criticism,* have discussed the hidden lesbian life of Angelina Weld Grimké as it affects her poetry. A large percentage of the Grimké poetic canon is indeed a record of her attempt to love and be loved by another woman. Many of these poems, such as "Another Heart Is Broken," "Naughty Nan," and "Caprichosa," are here published for the first time.

"To Joseph Lee," however, is an example of a small percentage of Grimké's poetry that was written for occasions of celebration or commemoration. Among these are "To My Father Upon His Fifty-Fifth Birthday," "Two Pilgrims Hand in Hand," and "To the Dunbar High School." In addition, Grimké wrote and published several poems, such as "Tenebris" and "Beware Lest He Awakes," that portray the African-American experience of racial pride, as well as reaction against and revenge for lynching and other racist acts within the United States.

Although it is an extremely powerful theme when presented in her poetry, the subject of lynching is minor in terms of the number of poetic references to it. We may say that the three major themes in Grimké's poetry are lost love, commemoration of famous people, and African-American racial concerns, but we must acknowledge that racial concerns constitute less than five percent of her total output of poetry.

Most of the poems speak of love, death, and grief through narrative personae that are not explicitly identified with the interests of African Americans and that are often quite frankly white and male. "My Shrine," for example, is narrated by a standard nineteenth-century (male) persona who expresses his idealized love for a woman on a pedestal.

In contrast, the entire corpus of Grimké's fiction, nonfiction, and drama focus almost exclusively on lynching and racial injustice. These works take on African-American cultural grief rather than personal grief as their thematic focus, and they express great outrage over the lynching of African Americans in the South, over the failure of Northern whites to band together and demand an end to the crimes, and over racial injustice in general. In one story, "Jettisoned," Grimké also investigates the repercussions of passing for white in the African-American community.

Lynching is a particularly affecting theme in Grimké's play *Rachel* (1920). The play depicts the effects of lynching on the desire to live and the attraction toward genocide for members of the African-American community. The theme of lynching extends to her fiction as well, appearing in such stories as "The Closing Door," "Goldie," and "Blackness."

Angelina Weld Grimké was named for her white great aunt, Angelina Grimké Weld. As a young woman, Weld, along with her sister, Sarah Grimké, left South Carolina in the early nineteenth century to avoid participating directly in the ownership of slaves. The two sisters settled in Hyde Park, Massachusetts, and became well-known abolitionists and advocates of women's rights. Angelina Grimké eventually married the abolitionist Theodore Weld. Several years after the Civil War, the two sisters discovered and acknowledged their mulatto nephews, Archibald and Francis, and accepted them into their home. The young men were two of the three sons born to Angelina and Sarah's brother, Henry Grimké, and his slave, Nancy Weston. Francis married Charlotte Forten. Archibald married a white woman, Sarah Stanley, and their only child was Angelina Weld Grimké.

Angelina was born on February 27, 1880, in Boston and lived most of her life with her father to whom she was extremely attached emotionally. Soon after Angelina's birth, her mother left the Grimké household. Information concerning Sarah Stanley Grimké is scant, but it appears that she was confined in some manner for mental aberration or physical incapacity. In a letter written to Angelina when she was seven years old, Sarah speaks of wanting to return to visit her daughter, of hearing her cry out "Mamma" in her dreams. "I dream about you very often. The other night—I thought—I saw you out in a large cornfield. . . . Do you ever dream of Mamma?—Some time I shall be able to come to you in my *Shadow Body* and really *see* you. How would you like that? And *some* time we will be together again." [1]

In spite of (or because of) Angelina's great affection for her father, he seems to have been the source of some restriction and oppression in her own sexual self-consciousness as a lesbian. It is clear that she decided to forgo the expression of her lesbian desires in order to please her father, and in her poem written to commemorate his fifty-fifth birthday she describes what she would have been without him in terms of a great horror and scandal avoided. Love letters to named and unnamed women appear in Grimké's papers as early as her fourteenth year, and an exchange of letters with Mamie Burrill in 1896, when Grimké was sixteen years old, makes definite reference to a prior love affair. Burrill writes to Grimké, "Angie, do you love me as you used to?" Grimké's draft letter of response answers:

> My own darling Mamie, If you will allow me to be so familiar to call you such. I hope my darling you will not be offended if your ardent lover calls you such familiar names. . . . Oh Mamie if you only knew how my heart beats when I think of you and it yearns and pants to gaze, if only for one second upon your lovely face. If there were any trouble in this wide and wicked world from which I might shield you how gladly would I do it if it were even so great a thing as to lay down my life for you. I know you are too young now to become my wife, but I hope, darling, that in a few years you will come to me and be my love, my wife! How my brain whirls how my pulse leaps with joy and madness when I think of these two words, "my wife."[2]

Grimké was educated at Fairmont Grammar School in Hyde Park (1887–1894), Carleton Academy in Northfield, Minnesota (1895), Cushing Academy in Ashburnham, Massachusetts, and Girls' Latin School in Boston, and in 1902 she took a degree in physical education at the Boston Normal School of Gymnastics (now Wellesley College). That same year she began her teaching career as a gym teacher at Armstrong Manual Training School in Washington, D.C., but in 1907, after much tension with the principal of Armstrong, she transferred to the more academic M Street High School (later Dunbar High School) where she taught English. Grimké was always more academic than vocational in her interest, and there is some question as to why she took a degree in physical education in the first place. Perhaps as a closeted lesbian she found physical education attractive because it provided sublimated contact with women.

Grimké retired from teaching and moved to New York City in 1926 where she died on June 10, 1958. Most of her works were written between 1900 and 1920. The drama *Rachel* is her only published book prior to this volume, but she published some of her poetry, fiction, and nonfiction (reviews and biographical sketches) in many prominent journals, particularly *Opportunity*, and in newspapers and many anthologies.

The present volume includes approximately one-third of the poetry, one-half of the short stories, and a small sampling of the nonfiction found in Grimké's papers at the Moorland-Spingarn Research Center. A republication of *Rachel* is also included. Almost all of the nonfiction is still in holograph, as are perhaps another two hundred poems, the incomplete play *Mara* (which also centers on lynching), and many unfinished short stories.

When focusing on death, women as objects of desire, lost love, motherhood, and children, the emotive import of Grimké's poems is overwhelmingly that of despair. In the poem "The Garden Seat," for example, the narrator recalls a love tryst with a woman who has died:

> And then I stole up all noiseless and unseen,
> And kissed those eyes so dreamy and so sad—I
> Ah God! if I might once again see all
> Thy soul leap in their depths as then
> So hungry with long waiting and so true,
> I clasp thee close within my yearning arms
> I kiss thine eyes, thy lips, thy silky hair,
> I felt thy soft arms twining round my neck,
> Thy bashful, maiden, kisses on my cheek
> My whole heart leaping 'neath such wondrous joy—
> And then the vision faded and was gone

And I was in my lonely, darkened, room,
The old-time longing surging in my breast,
The old-time agony within my soul
As fresh, as new, as when I kissed thy lips
So cold, with frenzy begging thee to speak,
Believing not that thou wert lying dead.

Grimké's poem "Death" examines death abstractly as a philosophy of an afterlife and is more hopeful than her poems that describe the death of loved ones.

When the lights blur out for thee and me,
    And the black comes in with a sweep,
I wonder—will it mean life again,
    Or sleep?

Such philosophical investigations of death removed from expressions of lost love are rare, however. In "Where Phillis Sleeps" Grimké writes, "Dear one, I lie upon thy grave, my tears like rain are falling," and in "One Little Year," she writes, "Quite hopeless, now, my lips refuse to pray—/ For thou art dead." The poem "Thou Art So Far, So Far" is one of many that depict lost love due not to death but to the unapproachable nature of the beloved:

Thou art to me a lone, white, star,
That I may gaze on from afar;
But I may never, never, press
My lips on thine in mute caress, . . .

The poem "My Shrine" is Grimké's prime example of poems that depict women as ideal objects of desire:

The idol that I placed
Within this modest shrine
Was but a maiden small,

But yet divinely pure,
And there I humbly knelt
Before those calm, grey, eyes, . . .

In this poem Grimké takes the persona of a male, "Behold the one he loves!," presumably to divert attention from the lesbian implications of the poem. "Caprichosa" emphasizes a sexual rather than an ideal interest in a woman, and the narrator does not take on a male persona:

Little lady coyly shy
With deep shadows in each eye
Cast by lashes soft and long,
Tender lips just bowed for song,
And I oft have dreamed the bliss
Of the nectar in one kiss. . . .

Grimké's most significant statement about motherhood is unconsciously embedded within her poem "To My Father Upon His Fifty-Fifth Birthday." While the poem purports to praise her father's help and strength, it actually focuses on diminutive images of him as an infant incapable of sustaining himself:

. . . This day on which a new-made mother watched
You lying in her arms, your little head against
Her breast; and as you lay there, tiny wriggling mass, . . .

The description of her father as a "tiny wriggling mass" surely is not calculated to glorify his strength and has uncomfortable phallic implications as well. She goes on to describe her grandmother's new experience of motherhood in nursing her father. And the exclamation point is given not to a celebration of the child (her father), but to a glorification of the mother (her grandmother): "Ah, gift of Motherhood!" The poem then elaborates on the virtues of women and mothering. It is here that Grimké refers to what her life would have been like without her father (and presumably without having to restrict her lesbian inclinations):

> . . . What were I, father dear, without thy help?
> I turn my eyes away before the figure and
> Rejoice; and yet your loving hands have moulded me; . . .

Through her father's assistance, Grimké repudiates her own self-molding and takes her dependent imprint from him. Finally, after depicting the care he has given her through her life, Grimké gives her father her highest compliment, "You have been a gentle mother to your child." That is, the best she can say about her father is that he is almost a mother.

This poem gives the impression that Grimké and her father had no major disagreements in their lives, but that is belied by the opening passage in Grimké's first diary, started in July 1903 to record a lost love involvement with an unnamed person. "My father and I have been having a hard time tonight over you, dear. I guess he is right and I shall try to give you up." Earlier in this entry, she writes, "I suppose I was a fool and oh how I wish that I had a mother!" Grimké's inability to portray her father as an adult male in her poem celebrating his fatherhood reveals her ambivalent feelings toward this man whose approval she could not live without but whose moralistic dicta appear to have greatly restricted her own sexual expression.

The theme of children is almost as significant as the theme of mothers in Grimké's poetry and is usually linked, as in "The Black Child," with portrayals of the ways in which African Americans suffer oppression at the hands of whites. "The Black Child" uses the image of a black baby playing in sunlight and then in shadow as an affecting extended metaphor of black life and external oppression. The poem opens:

> I saw a little black child
> Sitting in a gold circle of sunlight;
> And in his little black hand,
> He had a little black stick,
> And he was beating, beating,
> With his little black stick,
> The sunlight all about him,
>   And laughing, laughing.

By elaborating on this scene through the passage of the day, and by refusing to explain or interpret it, Grimké increases the poignancy for the reader who alternately sees the poem as a metaphor of black life or as a realistic image of a black child playing. The image is so well formed, and the impulse to delight in it so strong, that the reader almost hopes the poem is simple realistic truth to enjoy and appreciate without confronting the psychic and sociological shadow that alters and subverts the lives of black children.

> And he sat in the gold circle of sunlight
> Kicking with his little feet,
> And wriggling his little toes,
> And beating, beating
> The sunlight all about him, . . .

The shadow eases upon the black child slowly until at the end of the poem he is beating not the light but the shadows. In another poem about a black child, "Lullaby [(2)]," Grimké includes her only attempt to write black diction in verse. She is not, in this instance, adept in the use of black diction, but the content of the poem reveals her attitude toward the limited possibilities available to black adults in the United States:

> Ain't you quit dis laffin' yet?
> Don' you know de sun's done set?
> Wan' me kiss dis li'l han'?

> Well, well, laf de w'ile you can,
> You won' laf w'en you'se a man,
> Dere! Dere! Sleep! Sleep!

Grimké's fiction is more stark in portraying the horror, the accents, and the future of black children. An infant is smothered in "The Closing Door," and in "Goldie" and "Blackness," an unborn child is cut from the womb of a lynched woman, revealing the full horror of African-American life in the United States.

Grimké wrote a few poems presenting her overall world view and background philosophy. Among these are "Life [(1)]" and "The Puppet-Player." In "Life [(1)]," for example, human beings are out of control of the destiny of their lives and overwhelmed by the "Ocean, boundless, infinite" of life:

> Thou ne'er hast known nor dead nor living
> One single braggart man as master. . . .
>
> And some are lost on rocks relentless;
> And some are drowned mid storms tremendous, . . .
> The waters close again impenetrably:—
> Each one must make his way alone—
> And this is Life!

"The Puppet-Player" is even more pessimistic and ascribes conscious and evil intention to the power that controls the world:

> Sometimes it seems as though some puppet-player
> A clenchéd claw cupping a craggy chin,
> Sits just beyond the border of our seeing,
> Twitching the strings with slow, sardonic grin.

Other poems directly examine the value of life for the narrator. "Epitaph on a Living Woman" describes the annihilation of emotion and joy for the speaker: "There were tiny flames in her eyes,/ Her mouth was a flame,/ And her flesh. . . . ./ Now she is ashes." "Life [(2)]" is Grimké's only acknowledgment in verse that the narrator's life, in spite of its grim sadness, has at least been more dynamic than other people's:

> What though I die mid racking pain,
> And heart seared through and through by grief,
> I still rejoice for I, at least, have lived.

By contrast, a rare poetic encounter with hope and joy is found in "A Mood":

> Up mocking, teasing, little, hill;
> Past dancing, glancing, little, rills,
> And up or down to left or right
> The same compelling, wild, delight!

"The Visitor" is Grimke's only poem in which the narrator repudiates rather than longs for death:

> I beg you come not near!
> See! Though I am so proud
> I'll fall upon my knees,
> And beg, and pray, of you
> To spare this little soul!

Some of Grimké's poems use such forms as the sonnet, the triolet, and the roundel. Sonnets are particularly solemn forms for Grimké, who uses them to commemorate the life of the philanthropist Mary Porter Tileston Hemenway in "Two Sonnets to Mrs. Hemenway," and to represent stern authoritarian sentiments about God in "As We Have Sowed":

> I
> As we have sowed so shall we also reap;
> And it were sweet indeed if blossoms fair

Grow from the seeds to scent the sunlit air,
But oh! How sad if weeds that hide and creep
Grow in their stead to prick and sting our feet.
Too soon we'll meet the Master on our path,
And in His deep sad eyes we'll feel the wrath
Of justice or the thrill of praises sweet.
I do but pray within this humble breast,
That little flowers may blossom on my way,
But yet so pure they change the night to day,
I beg that one more fair than all the rest
So please the Master that with glad surprise
He proudly plucks it, smiling in my eyes.

II

As we have sowed so shall we also reap:—
How sweet if by our path the blossoms fair
Grow from the seeds to scent the sunlit air;
But Oh! How sad if weeds that hide and creep
Grow in their stead to prick and sting our feet.
We know not when the Master passing by
May pause, nor when from out his deep sad eye
May leap the flame of wrath or praises sweet
The sweetest flowers are those not proudly drest,
But little ones that brighten all the way,
They are so pure and white. For me I pray
That one white flower more pure than all the rest
May burst in blossom 'neath the Master's eyes,
That only He may know the sacrifice.

In the first of these sonnets, the Master plucks the narrator's most beautiful flower, and in the second the narrator's one white flower bursts into bloom as an expression of her sacrifice. The stern taskmaster in the poem is surely an extension of Grimké's own father, who often chastised her verbally for her inadequacies and demanded that she fulfill all the restraining public roles that were expected of an educated middle-class African-American woman of her time.

"A Triolet," on the other hand, with its repeated line "Molly raised shy eyes to me," is an expression of joy in lesbian affection:

> Molly raised shy eyes to me,
>   On an April day;
> Close we stood beneath a tree;
> Molly raised shy eyes to me,
> Shining sweet and wistfully,
> Wet and yet quite gay;
> Molly raised shy eyes to me,
>   On an April day.

The roundel "Vigil" inhabits the intersection between hope and despair. The narrator repeatedly insists that her departed loved one will return—"You will come back"—but these words are surrounded by such a strong hint of impending hopelessness—"But if it will be bright or black"—that the act of hope appears to be merely the subterfuge of holding back despair:

> You will come back, sometime, somehow;
> But if it will be bright or black
> I cannot tell; I only know
>   You will come back.
>
> Does not the spring with fragrant pack
> Return unto the orchard bough?
> Do not the birds retrace their track?
>
> All things return. Some day the glow
> Of quick'ning dreams will pierce your lack;
> And when you know I wait as now
>   You will come back.

For the most part, Grimké uses the poetic rhythms and styles characteristic of Anglo-American poetry as a whole.

The African-American distinctiveness of her work is most visible in content and plot rather than in style. In those works dealing directly with the problem of being black in the United States, she attempts to tear down the master's house by using the master's tools. That is, she calls on the moral conscience of white Americans to correct and improve their relationship with their black fellow citizens. This mode of expression is particularly evident in her play *Rachel*. In fact, in an essay about the play, Grimké declared that *Rachel* had been written to educate whites and to correct their attitudes about lynching and its effects on African Americans.

Variously called *The Pervert*, *The Daughter*, and *Blessed Are the Barren* before receiving the title *Rachel*, the play is about a young African-American woman who prefers to forgo both marriage and motherhood so as not to provide whites with more black people to destroy through lynching and other racial atrocities. Indeed, the play may be said to encourage a form of self-genocide of African-American people. Although Grimké attempts to justify this attitude in terms of the cruelties that African Americans are forced to endure in the United States, it is probable that in this plot she is using a psychic energy that repudiates heterosexuality on a personal level to accentuate her passion for annihilating the marital and familial expectations in African-American culture. Her denial of the possibility and hopefulness of heterosexual union appears more explicitly in "The Laughing Hand," a short story that does not have African-American characters. In this story, a young woman is forced to break her engagement to her fiancé because he has contracted cancer and has suffered a disfiguring and silencing operation in which his tongue is cut out. This castration of language is more than an expression of the impossibility of heterosexual union; it may also comment on Grimké's closeted sexuality. Unendurable marriage is also the subject of the short story "The Drudge," whose white characters are of a lower economic class than those in "The Laughing Hand." Here a beaten, oppressed wife manages to get some control over her husband by refusing to accommodate herself to his adultery.

Grimké is essentially appalled at her incapacity to have a lover in this world. And she is appalled at the restricted world that the United States allows for its African-American citizens. Her inner astonishment at her failure to find sexual and romantic companionship, and her outer astonishment at finding herself in a world that denigrates her value because she is a black woman, combine to give terrifying but effective power to stories like "The Closing Door," "Goldie," "Blackness," and "Black Is, As Black Does," all of which, like *Rachel*, take lynching as their theme. Two of the stories, "The Closing Door," and "Goldie," were published in the *Birth Control Review* to encourage black women not to have children.

Although Grimké's consciousness of African-American culture is restricted primarily to plot, one large exception to this rule appears in "Jettisoned," a story written almost entirely in African-American English. It is probably not accidental that this short story, which adopts African-American style more overtly than do her other works, is the only one with an optimistic ending, though to get to that point her characters go through hell with problems of poverty, threatened suicide, and the pain of having relatives who pass for white.

Grimké's most radical works on African-American culture, including the short stories on lynching and the poems "Trees," "Surrender," "The Black Finger," "Tenebris," and "Beware Lest He Awakes," all lean toward a refusal to accept the given conditions of being black in the United States. But probably because of publication restrictions, these works often stop just short of demanding unapologetic revenge for acts against African-American people.

The poem "Beware Lest He Awakes," for example, has three versions, and Grimké's changes, when compared with the published text, reveal that she may have been coerced into making revisions in order for the poem to be published. The original statement of the poem, that African Americans would eventually wake up and take revenge for the actions against them, was changed from the definite statement, "Beware when he awakes" to the more suppositional, "Beware lest he awakes." Thus the final version leads us to believe that the African-American people may or may not wake up and take revenge. Further, the line "Beware lest he awakes," which in the earlier versions ("Beware when he awakes") ends the two stanzas and thereby gains greater importance than any other portion of the poem, is—in the published version—buried in the middle of the first verse. Though it still ends the poem, the line's message has nevertheless been diffused.

Similarly, the short story "Goldie," which is a revised version of "Blackness," ends with the statement that the African-American man who takes revenge for lynching is himself lynched as well: "And Victor Forrest died, as the other two had died, upon another tree." "Blackness," however, implies that the vindicator escapes safely: "I have reason, to believe, he escaped. But I have never heard from him or seen him since." Although this unnamed vindicator must leave his position in the North to escape the retribution of Southerners who come after him, we are given to understand that, with the money he has saved and with support from friends, he is able to live a life in another country or community and is not hunted to the death. Evidently, the revised story, "Goldie," was more palatable to, and therefore deemed more publishable by, the *Birth Control Review* whose subscribers were more likely to accept fiction that encouraged African Americans not to have children in order to avoid having them lynched. The same subscribers, who were primarily white, would probably not have been willing to read about African Americans successfully taking revenge for lynching. In addition, Grimké leaves the successful revenge taker unnamed, perhaps to imply that he is still at large, still among us, and therefore his name must be protected.

Finally, Angelina Weld Grimké places herself within the tradition of African-American writers who are interested in identifying what is distinctive about African-American literary works. In her "Remarks on Literature," she describes the coming black literary genius in these words:

> In preparation of the coming of this black genius I believe there must be among us a stronger and a growing feeling of race consciousness, race solidarity, race pride. It means a training of the youth of to-day and of to-morrow in the recognition of the sanctity of all these things. Then perhaps, some day, somewhere black youth, will come forth, see us clearly, intelligently, sympathetically, and will write about us and then come into his own.

Grimké herself is a participant in this coming genius, which is the forerunner of contemporary and emerging African-American artistic excellence. The oppressive stance of having to assume a white male narrative persona in her poetry in order to accommodate the "freedom" to describe sexual interest and encounters with other women gave Grimké profound information about the strategies of being closeted through concerns of race, gender, and sexual preference. The two major themes of her writings, the desire for romantic and sexual companionship and the desire for social and political equity for African Americans, give her work the import, if not the discrete form, of the blues—that musical and poetic cultural form which is the repository for African-American heroic anguish over love, lost love, and political disenfranchisement. The blues, whether in form or content or both, may indeed be characterized as the African-American epic song, and Grimké sings that song as an artist creating through the triple cultural blows of being black, female, and lesbian.

Much of her work has been rigorously ignored. Most of the poems were too lesbian and too sentimental for audiences during and after the Harlem Renaissance. Her fiction, on the other hand, was too stark in its unflinching descriptions of the violence of lynching. Indeed, the directness of her scenes of violence were unknown in African-American fictional literature prior to the work of Richard Wright. Further, her short stories with their promulgation of racial self-genocide have been too politically and emotionally threatening for African Americans and others to receive and accept. As Toni Morrison writes in the conclusion to *Beloved,* a more recent tale of infanticide, "This is not a story to pass on." Thus it is a painful gift to participate in the self-investigation this work has required of me; it is an honor finally to assist in passing on this story that was not to be passed on.

NOTES

I thank those who have helped me compile this book: Georgia Carol Johnson Herron, Oscar Smith Herron, the Moorland-Spingarn Research Center of Howard University, Lynda Blumenthal, Gloria Hull, Martha Nadell, Klaus Kirschbaum, Cassandra F. Richard, Henry Louis Gates, Jr., Esme Bahn, Laura Purdom, Karen Jefferson, Thomas Battle, Randall Burkett, Rosemary Crockett, Dorothy Porter, Lolita Roland, Noah Feldman, Marcelyn Dallis, Chris Sturr, Barbara Christian, Penny Codrington, Erlene

Stetson, Barbara Johnson, Helen Vendler, Patsy Yaeger, Marjorie Garber, Barbara Lewalski, Phyllis Keller, Werner Sollors, Bettina Brandt, Josine Shapiro, Brenda Walker, the students of Comparative Literature 171 at Harvard, the Summer Institute of the Classical Association of New England, the Western Herrons (Smitty, Theresa, Joseph, and Jeffrey), the Bunting Institute of Radcliffe College, the Beinecke Library of Yale University, the Folger Shakespeare Library, the Library of Congress, the Daughters of Bilitis of Cambridge, Massachusetts, Carlton College, Harvard University, Mount Holyoke College, Jonathan Edward Kolb, and Cheryl L. Abbott. My work on this text is dedicated to Marquita Vilette Lightfoot.

1. Sarah Stanley Grimké, letter to Angelina Weld Grimké, 15 July 1887, Angelina Weld Grimké Collection, Moorland-Spingarn Research Center, Howard University, box 38-5, folder 92.

2. Angelina Weld Grimké, letter to Mamie Burrill, 1896, Angelina Weld Grimké Collection, box 38-13, folders 1 and 2.

TEXTUAL NOTE

Unless otherwise indicated, texts are taken from typescript and holograph copies in the Angelina Weld Grimké Collection at the Moorland-Spingarn Research Center of Howard University, hereafter cited as MSRC. All of the poems in typescript have been included; selected poems in holograph have been included by criteria of completeness and legibility. Combined, the poems have been arranged to follow thematically Grimké's own ordering of a projected volume of twenty-three titles.

The drama section includes Grimké's only published play, *Rachel* (1920).

Since it is impossible to determine the chronology of Grimké's fiction, the stories appearing in this volume have been placed in the order used at the Moorland-Spingarn Research Center. This order separates "Goldie" from its earlier version, "Blackness."

The order of the nonfiction section is roughly by genre, beginning with Grimké's diary entries, continuing with her comments about her own drama and fiction, and ending with a book review, an article on her father, and her "Remarks on Literature."

For the most part, I have retained Grimké's format and punctuation in the text, although spacing, dashes, and single and double quotation marks have been standardized. Obvious typographical errors, misspellings, and some minor mistakes in capitalization and word choice have also been corrected. Otherwise, brackets enclose my editorial additions. Braces enclose exact rendering from Grimké's text; in the footnotes for the poetry section, that rendering—e.g., a holograph revision—occasionally appears in boldface type when presented in the larger context of a sentence that is otherwise unchanged. Indecipherable words are represented by question marks in brackets.

In addition, I have attempted whenever possible to identify, in my introduction or in footnotes, the various people that Grimké mentions in her writings, particularly in her poetry and diary entries. There are, however, a number of individuals whose identity I have been unable to determine at this time.

Finally, a listing of those works of Grimké's (including titles not in this volume) that have been published can be found in the Selected Bibliography in Appendix A.

POETRY

❧ ❧ ❧

THE GARDEN SEAT

I stood again within the garden old
Around whose edges grew the tall green box;
I saw again the winding, narrow, paths
So gay along their sides with pink sea shells;
I saw the holly-hocks so tall and prim
The humble sun-flower bowing 'neath the sun,
The mignonette and gay geranium,
The heliotrope and baby's breath so pure;
I saw the summer house with roses overgrown,
The quaint, old, bench whereon we used to sit
Day-dreaming hand in hand of times to come,
And on the bench I saw thee idly sit
The distaff at thy side all silent stood
(Thy listless hands forgetful of their stint)
Thy fair, dear, head was tilted slightly back
Against the bench's quaint and aged side,
Thine eyes half-closed, and sweet lips gravely set,
And then I stole up all noiseless and unseen,
And kissed those eyes so dreamy and so sad—I
Ah God! if I might once again see all
Thy soul leap in their depths as then
So hungry with long waiting and so true,
I clasp thee close within my yearning arms
I kiss thine eyes, thy lips, thy silky hair,
I felt thy soft arms twining round my neck
Thy bashful, maiden, kisses on my cheek,
My whole heart leaping 'neath such wondrous joy—

The poetry collected in this section represents approximately one-third of all poems in typescript and holograph in the Angelina Weld Grimké Collection, MSRC, box 38-10, folders 150–174. Only about thirty of the poems have ever been published (see Appendix A, Selected Bibliography).

And then the vision faded and was gone
And I was in my lonely, darkened, room
The old-time longing surging in my breast,
The old-time agony within my soul
As fresh, as new, as when I kissed thy lips
So cold, with frenzy begging thee to speak,
Believing not that thou wert lying dead.

———

Yes, lying dead these many, weary, years;
And when I push my darkened casement wide,
And gaze beyond the sleeping town of Life
Unto that town of Death upon the hill,
I see with streaming tears that vainly fall,
The plain, white, stone, that marks the spot she sleeps.

WHEN THE GREEN LIES
OVER THE EARTH

I

When the green lies over the earth, my dear,
A mantle of witching grace;
When the smile and the tear of the young child year
Dimple across its face,
And then flee. When the wind all day is sweet
With the breath of growing things;
When the wooing bird lights on restless feet
And chirrups and trills and sings
      To his lady-love
      In the green above;
Then oh! my dear, when the youth's in the year,
Yours is the face that I long to have near,
      Yours is the face, my dear.

But the green is hiding your curls, my dear,
Your curls so shining and sweet;
And the gold-hearted daisies this many a year
Have bloomed and bloomed at your feet,
And the little birds just above your head
With their voices hushed, my dear,
For you have sung and have prayed and have plead
This many, many a year.
And the blossoms fall.
On the garden wall,
And drift like snow on the green below.
But the sharp thorn grows
On the budding rose,
And my heart no more leaps at the sunset glow.
For oh! my dear, when the youth's in the year,
Yours is the face that I long to have near,
Yours is the face, my dear.

WHERE PHILLIS SLEEPS[1]

The fair enchantress of the skies smiles on the rippling river,
Along each bank the dark trees stand, and gently shake and
    shiver
With every passing wind. A bird its homeward way is
    winging,
And softly o'er the gloomy hills, a distant bell is ringing.
The World, upon the dreamy breast of Sleep, her head is
    bending,
While I, a soul alone, my melancholy way am wending
    To where the patient willow weeps
    Upon the grave where Phyllis sleeps.

1. Grimké uses two spellings, Phillis and Phyllis, in the typescript of
this poem.

Alone! For e'en the sobbing leaves rub cheek against the
    other,
And brother, mingling fear with tear, gives sympathy to
    brother.
Alone! For e'en the startled birds awakened by the weeping
Soothe each other with sweet chirps, and soon again are
    sleeping.
Alone! There is no loving heart, no falt'ring hand to need
    me,
Then wherefore linger on the path? So on my feet and lead
    me
        To where the patient willow weeps
        Upon the grave where Phyllis sleeps.

Dear one, I lie upon thy grave, my tears like rain are
    falling,
My breaking heart, my yearning soul in vain thy name are
    calling.
Poor little tired head, whose sunny curls I used to treasure!
Poor little tired feet, that learned all but too soon to measure
The distance to the door! And still those tender eyes so
    pleading
Can never see that all the pathways of my life are leading
        To where the patient willow weeps
        Upon the grave where now she sleeps.

IN MEMORIAM[2]
[TO KEEP THE MEMORY OF
CHARLOTTE FORTEN GRIMKÉ (1)][3]

Stíll áre there wónders óf the dárk and dáy:
The múted shrílling óf shy thíngs at níght,
   So smáll benéath the stárs and moón;
The peáce, dream-fráil, but pérfect whíle the líght
   Lies sóftly ón the leáves at noón.
     These áre, and thése will bé
       Untó etérnitý[4];
But shé who lóved them wéll has góne awáy.[5]

2. Typescript: {In Memorian.}. This poem is a late draft of "To Keep the Memory of Charlotte Forten Grimké," which follows. The original sheet has holograph markings of revisions, accents, mathematical computations, and a pattern of numbering lines or counting stress or syllabic line composition that I am unable to interpret. The lines of stanza 1 are numbered 8, 10, 12, 10, 12, 16, 22, with the last line having no number. The lines of stanzas 2 and 4 are numbered 8, 10, 12, 10, 12, 16, 22, and 8. The lines of stanza 3 were originally numbered like those of stanzas 2 and 4 but were changed to 5, 11 (blurred), 11 (blurred), 10, 12, 15, 22, and 8. I have retained stress marks in this version.

3. Charlotte Forten Grimké (1837–1914) was Angelina's aunt and a prominent abolitionist and advocate of women's rights. She and her husband, Francis Grimké, were also Angelina's legal guardians from 1894 to 1898 while Angelina's father, Archibald, served as consul to Santo Domingo.

4. Holograph revision: {**Until** eternity}. In footnotes such as this, the entire line is given to present the revision in context, with the revision itself boldfaced.

5. Stress mark is over the letter {w} but is probably meant to be written [awáy].

2[6]

Each dáwn, while yét the éast is veíléd gréy,[7]
The bírds aboút her window wáke and síng,
    And fár awáy, each dáy, some lárk
I knów, is sínging whére the grásses swíng,
    Some róbin cálls and cálls at dárk.
        These áre, and thése will bé
          Untíl etérnity;
But shé who lóved them wéll has góne awáy.[8]

The wíld flowers thát she lóved down greén ways stráy;
Her róses líft their wístful búds at dáwn,
    But nót for éyes that lóved them bést;
Ónly her líttle pánsies áre all góne,
    Sóme lying sóftly ón her breást.
        But flówers will bé[9]
          Untíl etérnity;
Though shé who lóved them bést has góne awáy.[10]

4

Whére has she góne? And whó is thére to sáy?
But thís we knów, her géntle spírit móves
    And ís where beaúty néver wánes;
Far, fár indeéd it ís from thóse she lóves;
    And tó us hére, ah! shé remáins
        A lóvely mémory

---

6. Typescript has {&} corrected to {2} in holograph.

7. Mark over {éd} of {veiléd} indicates ending is pronounced and does not indicate stress.

8. {Eternity} is written in holograph after this stanza.

9. Two holograph revisions: {And other flowers . . .}, {And flowers with bud will be}.

10. Holograph revision: {But she who loved them well has. . . .}.

To áll etérnity.[11]
She cáme, she lóved, and thén she wént awáy.[12]

TO KEEP THE MEMORY OF
CHARLOTTE FORTEN GRIMKÉ [(2)] [13]

Still are there wonders of the dark and day;
The muted shrilling of shy things at night,
So small beneath the stars and moon;
The peace, dream-frail, but perfect while the light
Lies softly on the leaves at noon.
These are, and these will be
Until Eternity;
But she who loved them well has gone away.

Each dawn, while yet the east is veiléd grey,
The birds about her window wake and sing;
And far away each day some lark
I know is singing where the grasses swing;
Some robin calls and calls at dark.
These are, and these will be
Until Eternity;
But she who loved them well has gone away.

The wild flowers that she loved down green ways stray;
Her roses lift their wistful buds at dawn,
But not for eyes that loved them best;
Only her little pansies are all gone,
Some lying softly on her breast.

11. Holograph revision: {(Unto Until) (To all) eternity.}.
12. Written in holograph below this line: {Perchance by other streams, and other groves}.
13. This is the final version of "In Memoriam," immediately preceding.

And flowers will bud and be
Until Eternity;
But she who loved them well has gone away.

Where has she gone? And who is there to say?
But this we know: her gentle spirit moves
And is where beauty never wanes,
Perchance by other streams, mid other groves;
And to us here, ah! she remains
A lovely memory,
Until Eternity;
She came, she loved, and then she went away.

NEVERMORE

I

Baby mine. Oh baby mine!
  Shall I see those eyes of thine
  Seriously on me bent,
  Ever wise, but innocent
          Nevermore?
  Shall I hear thy tiny feet
  In their ceaseless, tireless, beat
          Nevermore?
  Shall I hear thy joyous cries
  Gurgling o'er some new surprise,
  Artless with thy baby art
  Making music in my heart
          Nevermore?

II

Shall I wake to find thee prest
Close against my mother breast,

See thee smiling in thy sleep
Dreamful, an angel blest, and deep,
　　　　Nevermore?
Shall I hear thy prattle dear
Faltering secrets in my ear
　　　　Nevermore?
Shall I kiss away thy tears,
Drive away thy baby fears,
At thy feet my homage pay,
Live for thee from day to day,
　　　　Nevermore?

ONE LITTLE YEAR

But yester-year I laughed the livelong day
　　　　And night, my dear;
So happy, then, my lips forgot to pray,—
　　　　For thou wert here.

But now I weep the livelong night and day
　　　　On bitter bed;
Quite hopeless, now, my lips refuse to pray—
　　　　For thou art dead.

VIGIL
——
(A ROUNDEL)

You will come back, sometime, somehow;
But if it will be bright or black
I cannot tell; I only know
　　　　You will come back.

Does not the spring with fragrant pack
Return unto the orchard bough?
Do not the birds retrace their track?

All things return. Some day the glow
Of quick'ning dreams will pierce your lack;
And when you know I wait as now
        You will come back.

EPITAPH
ON
A LIVING WOMAN [14]

There were tiny flames in her eyes,
Her mouth was a flame,
And her flesh. . . . .
    Now she is ashes.

AN EPITAPH [15]

1

I plead for joy from star-wake until sun [16]
Then whitely tense I waited,—not in vain.
One came, slow came, with eyes enmisted, dun;
    And left me,—pain.

14. The words {On a Living Woman} are an emendation to the typescript in holograph.
15. Throughout the typescript of this poem, there are revisions in holograph changing {I} to {she} and {me} to {her}.
16. Holograph revision: {prayed} instead of {plead} in this line and in the first line of stanza 2.

2

I plead for love, the love men know but keep
So ill. I waited, waited with bound breath.
One came with eyes repellant, chill, and deep,
            And dealt me death.

3

And now I lie quite straight, and still and plain;
Above my heart the brazen poppies flare,[17]
But I know naught of love, or joy, or pain;—
            Nor care, nor care.[18]

TO
CLARISSA SCOTT DELANEY[19]

1

She has not found herself a hard pillow
            And a long hard bed,
A chilling cypress, a wan willow
            For her gay young head . . . . .
            These are for the dead.

2

Does the violet-lidded twilight die
            And the piercing dawn
And the white clear noon and the night-blue sky . . . .
            When they are gone?

17. Holograph revision: {flaunting poppy flares}.
18. Holograph revision: {*Nor* cares, *nor* cares.}.
19. Clarissa Scott Delaney (1901–1927) was a graduate of Wellesley College (from which Grimké herself graduated in 1902) and was Grimké's teaching colleague at Dunbar High School.

3 [20]

Does the shimmering note
In the shy, shy throat
Of the swaying bird?

4

O, does children's laughter
Live not after
It is heard?

5

Does the dear, dear shine upon dear, dear things
In the eyes, on the hair,
On waters, on wings . . . .
Live no more anywhere?

6

Does the tang of the sea, the breath of frail flowers,
    Of fern crushed, of clover,
Of grasses at dark, of the earth after showers
    Not linger, not hover?

7

Does the beryl in tarns, the soft orchid in haze,
The primrose through tree-tops, the unclouded jade
Of the north sky, all earth's flamings and russets and grays
    Simply smudge out and fade?

8

And all loveliness, all sweetness, all grace,
All the gay questing, all wonder, all dreaming,
They that cup beauty that veiled opaled vase,
Are they only the soul of a seeming?

9

O, hasn't she found just a little, thin door
And passed through and closed it between?

---

20. Stanzas 3 and 4 were originally typed as one stanza. Typescript
separates stanza into two parts with holograph markings.

O, aren't those her light feet upon that light floor,
. . . . That her laughter . . . . . O, doesn't she
    lean
As we do to listen? . . . . O, doesn't it mean
        She is only unseen, unseen?

DESPAIR

Oh empty, eyes that cannot weep!
Oh preying, pain that will not sleep!
On haunted heart all scarred and sore,
And raging 'neath the grief it bore!
Oh heavy, head that still must think
Though poised upon the fatal brink!
Oh weeks, and months of misery!
Oh woe is me! Oh woe is me!

———

And once the world was fleeting fair
Without a cross, without a care;
And thou, oh life! how glowing sweet
Thou mad'st the path before my feet:
And thou, white, Hope, thou too did'st rise,
And kissing visions on my eyes,
I saw again the sun-lit skies
With every growing sweet surprise.

———

You two, to me, were very dear
And I shall never, never fear[21]
Your flying feet, nor fondly see
Your loving faces, happy, free,
Again go forward laughingly.

21. Typescript: The word {fear} should probably be emended to [hear].

You lie all still and waxen white,
No more aware if it be night,
No more aware of swift alarms—
Asleep within the other's arms.
Therefore I beg with panting breath
Come thou to me, thou, white-faced, Death.

———

Ah! Come and woo me for thine own
Thou wild, wierd, woman, silent, lone,
And fix me with thy wide, strange, eyes
Forever mystical and wise;
And kiss me with thy cold, white, lips
Till all my swooning being sips
Of ecstacy undreamed, unknown,
And crush me till thy arms have grown
Around me, let there slowly creep
A numbness everlasting, deep,
And let me sleep, ah! let me sleep.

GRASS FINGERS

Touch me, touch me,
Little cool grass fingers,
Elusive, delicate grass fingers.
With your shy brushings,
Touch my face—
My naked arms—
My thighs—
My feet.
Is there nothing that is kind?
You need not fear me.
Soon I shall be too far beneath you,

For you to reach me, even,
With your tiny, timorous toes.

(TO DR. GEORGE F. GRANT)[22]

———

HUSHED BY THE HANDS OF SLEEP

I

Hushed by the hands of Sleep,
    By the beautiful hands of Sleep.
Very gentle and quiet he lies,
With a little smile of sweet surprise,
Just softly hushed at lips and eyes,
    Hushed by the hands of Sleep,
        By the beautiful hands of Sleep.

II

Hushed by the hands of Sleep,
    By the beautiful hands of Sleep.
Death leaned down as his eyes grew dim,
And his face, I know, was not strange, not grim,
But oh! it was beautiful to him.
    Hushed by the hands of Sleep,
        By the beautiful hands of Sleep.

22. A dentist, Grant graduated from Harvard University Dental School
in 1870. He was employed as an instructor and was renowned for bridge-
work. He was also an inventor and patented a golf tee on 12 December
1899.

DEATH [(1)] [23]

When the lights blur out for thee and me,
    And the black comes in with a sweep,
I wonder—will it mean life again,
    Or sleep?

LIFE OR SLEEP?
[DEATH (2)]

When the lights blur out for thee and me;
    And the dark comes in with a sweep;
I wonder, will it mean life again,—
    Or sleep?

AT THE END [24]

Thus may it be with me,
    When at the dusk His call
Rings through the silences
    Into my window tall:—

I may arise and go
    Down where the purple bay
Breathes through the mist; cut loose;—
    Put from the shore's cold gray;—

23. "Death" is a slight revision of "Life or Sleep?," which follows. There is also a copy of this poem entitled "At the End" in the Grimké papers. This additional copy has a revision in holograph {for you and me} to the typescript {for thee and me}. Grimké used the title "At the End" for another poem as well, which follows.

24. See note 23 to "Death [(1)], another version of which was also entitled "At the End."

Slip mid the tang of spray
    Where thwart the deeps on deeps,[25]
Straight 'neath a moon of gold,
    Golden a pathway creeps.

Then may sleep hush my heart,
    Sweet as the croon of sea,
Soft as the mist is soft:—
    Thus may it be with me.

TWO SONNETS
TO MRS. HEMENWAY
(On Seeing Her Picture)[26]

I

Dear lady with thy silken hair so white,
And placid smile soft trembling on thy cheek,
Thine eyes a queenly nature do bespeak,
And one that never feared to aid the Right.
Thy hands (that now are still forevermore),
How patiently upon thy lap they rest
Perchance, so they may grant some meek request,
And shed light where there was none before.
And when the twilight shades of Death drew near
Enfolding every form in deepening black

---

25. Holograph revision: {Where o'er the}.
26. Mary Porter Tileston Hemenway (1820–1894) was a philanthropist from New York City and Boston who, after the death of her husband, invested her money and effort in the education of Southern blacks and poor whites. Hampton and Tuskegee Institutes were among the recipients of her donations.

Each little good thou did'st came smiling back,
And sang thy noble praises sweet and clear:
Thus, wafted up mid songs that never cease,
Thou cam'st, at last, to lands of endless peace.

II

Sweet lady of the silken snowy hair,
Whose tiny tendrils cling about thy face
Loving full well their gentle resting-place:
Calm eyes, serene beyond compare,
A mother's patient ones, that understand,
Because the lips of love have kissed them wide,
And made of thee a woman deified,
And one, who proudly held the humblest hand.
Thy tender mouth, that smiles from out the frame
So full of sympathy and peace divine,
That we can see thy saintly spirit shine
As brightly gleaming as an altar flame:—
Smile on, sweet saint! Thy mission still fulfill,
For though we leave, we see thee smiling still.

FOR THE CANDLE-LIGHT

The sky was blue, so blue that day
    And each daisy white, so white,
O, I knew that no more could rains fall grey
    And night again be night.

        . . . . .

I *knew*, I *knew*. Well, if night is night,
    And the grey skies greyly cry.
I have in a book for the candle light,
    A daisy dead and dry.

THE CAPTIVE

I

Little plaintive, singing bird,
You who never, never, heard
The songs that breathe of Freedom's joy,
And happiness without alloy,
Captive in a gilded home
You may never, never, roam
Without its prison-bars so fair,
You may never drink the air,
Balmy with the scents of flowers,
Dewy with the breaths of showers:
You may only sing, and sing,
But not upon the soaring wing.
Are you happy little friend?
Know you peace that has no end?
Then why is it when you sing
Your throbbing trill too quickly bring
The burning tears and sobbing sighs,
That all unbidden swiftly rise,
       Sadly rise,
And overflow we know not why?

II

Tell me, does your little heart
Beating in this world apart
Long for woods of dancing green,
Woods that you have never seen?
Does it long for friends and love
Mid the feathered flocks that rove
Gayly from sweet clime to clime
Knowing nought of grief or time?
Do those wings so frail and soft

Long to soar on clouds aloft,
Cleaving with glad whirrs the air,
Darting here and darting there?
Is that why your perfect song
Brings a host and growing throng
Of sad thoughts so grave and deep,
That we can do naught but weep?
Is that how your little heart
Bears the aching, stinging, smart
Of its yearning, longing pain?
Do you guess that it is vain
                    All in vain,
Little plaintive, singing, bird?

LIFE [(1)]

Thou Ocean, boundless, infinite,
In power irresistible,
In vastness grandly awful,
Omnipotent and kingly
Thou ne'er hast known nor dead nor living
One single braggart man as master.
Spirit of eternal motion
Above whose darkling pathless depths
There never sits the bird of silence
Motionless, maddening, songless!
As oft it sits a monarch lonely
Amidst the wilds of wildernesses maiden,
Thou master absolute o'er every
Green-eyed, tireless, lion-billow,
Who flings his name upon the breezes,

And roaring rushes up the seashore
With jaws wide-oped in avid longing,
But e'er returns unsatisfied.

———

And we unknowing little pigmies
With hearts aglow and ideas lofty
Begin our barques preparing,
And where the limpid skies are swooning
Upon the throbbing bosom of the Ocean
We see the star of our ideal,
Its spirit beckoning and smiling;—
And then with compass ever starward
We sail away but never guessing,
That those from whom we gladly parted
We probably shall never see again.
And some of us are lost before
We leave behind the harbor's shelter,
And some, because they fritter time
Away, forget they have a star,
And starve to death mid vanities;
And some are lost on rocks relentless;
And some are drowned mid storms tremendous,
And those who watched their guiding star
So patiently, so tirelessly,
Behold the nearer their advance,
The farther its retreat beyond
Their grasp, a flaming will-o-wisp!
And worst of all for those who are
To follow upon the waiting shore
With faces all alike with joy sublime,
We cannot leave one single warning,
For just as soon as we have passed beyond

The waters close again impenetrably:—
Each one must make his way alone—
And this is Life!

LIFE [(2)] [27]

When I have watched the people crawling by
So haggard-visaged, and so wrinkled-browed,
With eyes that see naught save the greedy ground,
With ears that hear naught save their toiling feet,
To whom there can exist no other world
Besides the one of Commonplace and Real,
Where Fancy's idle beams ne'er fleck the gloom
With dancing, changing, lights of flitting dreams,
I do rejoice, for I, with all my woes
May see the sights and hear the sounds they miss,
For I may see the beauty in a cloud
Or tiny flower or slender blade of grass,
May watch the tree-tops whispering with the winds,
The slanting rain drops greyed by solemn skies,
And find insistent joyousness in all;
May speechless stand before some landscape grand,
Where mountains lift their regal heads in peace,
Enwrapped at morn and frail, sheer, robes of mist,
Enwrapped at even in voluptuous garb,
For I may hear the songs of little things,
The cricket, locust, tree-toad and the bird,
That sings within the woods at summer dawns
And twitters sleepily at summer dusks;

27. Grimké placed the initials W.A.G. at the end of the typescript of
this poem, reversing the initial letters of her given names to form a
pseudonym.

For I may hear the yearnings of the soul
Within the voice or throbbing violin
Until the ear so wrung by chords of joy
Comes nigh to bursting in delicious pain;
For I may feel the fierceness of great love
With all its agony and rare delights,
Its dire despair and lightning heights of joy.
What though I die mid racking pain,
And heart seared through and through by grief,
I still rejoice for I, at least, have lived.

LITTLE WANDERER

I

Little bird, try your wings,
It is day;
You will learn many things—
Fly away.

II

Little bird, when the west
Makes you yearn
For the hush and the nest,—
Then return.

MY SHRINE

I built a shrine one day
Within my inmost heart
And draped it not with words
And thoughts of gaudy weave
To catch the shallow crowd,

But with white words of truth.
I placed it not upon
The public-way but in
A spot retired and sweet,
Where I might go alone
The candle that I placed
Upon its sacred steps
Were not of dazzling grace,
Nor burned with light so bright,
That one who passed afar
Might step with widened eyes,
And say mid loud guffaw,
"Behold the one he loves!"
The idol that I placed
Within this modest shrine
Was but a maiden small,
But yet divinely pure,
And there I humbly knelt
Before those calm, grey, eyes,
Full oft throughout the night,
And oft at moments sweet,
Purloined throughout the day,
And all the loving words
I never dared to speak
Gushed through my silent lips
An unsealed fountain strong,—
They were not flowery words
For I ne'er had the gift
To speak in fragrant speech,
But still they had this grace,
They came from out my soul.

———

Sweet idol of my life,
One, little, saintly, maid,

Who keeps my actions pure,
And makes me see the best
In all the sinning world
Through her grave, thoughtful, eyes:—
Ah sweet! Cannot you guess
The idol at my shrine?

THOU ART SO FAR, SO FAR

I

Thou art to me a lone, white, star,
That I may gaze on from afar;
But I may never, never, press
My lips on thine in mute caress,
E'en touch the hem of thy pure dress,—
Thou art so far, so far.

II

Thou livest in a world apart
Created by thy sinless heart;—
There lilies white, and tall, and fair,
Are growing, glowing everywhere,
In gardens wonderful and rare,—
Thou art so far, so far.

III

A sinner, I may only stand,
Without thy white heart's border-land,
And kneeling humbly worship thee,
And kneeling humbly pray for thee,
And kneeling humbly long for thee,—
Thou are too far, too far.

A THRICE-TOLD TALE

I
Pansies for dreams,—
Dead dreams:
Dead, though with dew ashine;
Dead, though they were divine;
Dead, in this hand of mine;
Dreams of the Dawn,—
Soon gone.

II
Roses for love,—
Lost love:
Lost, in an hour of pain;
Lost, mid the heart's blood rain;
Lost, though we smile again;
Love of the Noon,—
O'er soon.

III
Lilies for sleep,—
Sweet sleep;
Sweet, when the dreams are done;
Sweet, when the love is gone;
Sweet, for the eyes of one;
Sleep at the end,
My friend.

THE VISITOR

Goodbye, sweet earth, goodbye!
I would that I might see
The sun rise once again

Within the dim, grey, east
I would that I might die
With his white beams upon
My face, and in my heart,—
But no—'twere better so,
That I should meet Grey Death
Amidst the shades of night,
For I have never walked
Within the Sun's fair land,
But down the vale of Tears.

———

Come! Close around me Shades!
That I may give my soul
Into your willing hands—
Ah! Come not quite so fast
I would your faces see
Gaze in your eyes and find
If you be friend or foe—
Why gaze at me grim guests
With eyes so sinister?—
What have I done to you?—
I fear that you are fiends,
That come to mock at me,
And make my end as black
As all my wretched life:—
I know that you are fiends
For I can feel your eyes,
Can feel your groping hands
Upon my dying breast!—
You shall not have my soul!
While there remains one breath
Within this feeble frame
I swear I will defend

It from your greedy grasp!
Stand back! Stand back! I say!
Aha! You cringe and shrink
You are but craven curs
For one, weak, frenzied, man
Can keep you there at bay!
You'd mock at me would you?
And laugh, and jeer, and grin
Because you think me weak?
But see how firm this arm,
How blazing bright this eye!—
Aha! I shall behold
The sun arise again,
Shall see his glowing feet
Upon the mountain-tops,—
Dear Life thou'rt sweet indeed
I will not give thee up,
Nor will I yield my soul:—
Stay!—Stay where you are
This weakness soon will pass
I beg you come not near!
See! Though I am so proud
I'll fall upon my knees,
And beg, and pray, of you
To spare this little soul!
Ah see! How white and pure
And beautiful it is!
And I have kept it so
Throughout my shadowed life:
I've hugged it close and firm
Within my hungry breast,
I've given it my love
(And it were truly much)

I've safely sheltered it
From every breath of sin,
And luring, tempting, winds,
It's been my only joy
And when I've suffered most
I've taken it from out
My troubled, fearsome, breast,
And its white purity
Has lightened all my pain:
Ah! Let me keep my soul!
Why grows the room so dark
I cannot hear or see
Your faces are not there!
But I can feel your hands
Of chilling, numbing, ice
Creep down my shaking frame—
I fear that this is Death!—
I will not, will not die!
I want to see the sun,
I want my tortured Life,
Although I hated it
I love it, love it now!
Remove your icy hands!
They numb my failing, brain,
They strangle at its birth,
Each, feeble, labored, breath—
Give me but time to think!—
Ah God! I fear 'tis o'er:—
It is: I die! I die!

[ASK OF LIFE NOTHING, NOTHING] [28]

Ask of life nothing, nothing.
Ask only to go greyly, grey ways
Ask only to touch grey things
        With grey fingers.

Ask life for numbness only.
Forget there is love in the world
        And kisses
        And a man's arms
        And joy
        And hate.

YOUR HANDS

        I love your hands:
They are big hands, firm hands, gentle hands;
Hair grows on the back near the wrist . . . .
I have seen the nails broken and stained
From hard work.
And yet, when you touch me,
I grow small . . . . and quiet . . . . . .
. . . . And happy . . . .
If I might only grow small enough
To curl up into the hollow of your palm,
Your left palm,
Curl up, lie close and cling,
So that I might know myself always there,
. . . . Even if you forgot.

28. Poem is untitled in typescript.

SURRENDER [(1)] [29]

We ásk for peáce. We, neár the boúnd
Of lífe, are weáry óf the úseless roúnd
In seárch of Trúth. We knów the quést
Is nót for ús, the vísion blést
Is meánt for óther éyes. Uncrówned
We gó, with heáds bent tó the groúnd,
And óld hands seámed, and hárd and brówned;—
Let ús forgét the pást unrést,
　　We ásk for peáce.

Our straínéd eárs are deáf;—no soúnd [30]
May reách us móre; no síght may woúnd
Our wórn-out éyes. Revére our hést;— [31]
While we pass feebly out and west [32]
Untó that lást, that wáiting moúnd,
　　We ask for peace.

SURRENDER [(2)]

　　We ask for peace. We, at the bound
　　Of Life, are weary of the round

29. The original typescript of this version has holograph markings of revisions and stress marks. I have retained stress marks in this edition. A second version of "Surrender" follows, and a third version appears in Grimké's diary entry for 28 October 1909 (see the nonfiction section in this volume).

30. Mark over {ed} of {straínéd} indicates pronunciation of ending rather than stress.

31. Holograph revisions: {We did our best}, {We gave our best}, {We leave no hest}.

32. Holograph revisions: {But Whíle we totter down the west}, {And Whíle we totter down the west}.

In search of Truth. We know the quest
Is not for us, the vision blest
Is meant for other eyes. Uncrowned,
We go, with heads bowed to the ground,
And old hands, gnarled and hard and browned.
Let us forget the past unrest,—
        We ask for peace.

Our strainéd ears are deaf,—no sound
May reach them more; no sight may wound
Our worn-out eyes. We gave our best,
And, while we totter down the West,
Unto that last, that open mound,—
        We ask for peace.

[GIVE ME YOUR EYES (1)] [33]

    Give me your eyes.
I do not ask for lip touch or for hand,
Soft and sweet and fragrant though they be;
No, lift your eyes to mine,
Give me but one last look,
Ere I go forth forever,
E'en though within that moment's unforgettable span, [34]
I shall know all of life and death and heaven and hell.

---

33. I have included three versions of "Give Me Your Eyes" in order to give a sense of Grimké's method of composition and revision. Version 1 is untitled.

34. Holograph revision: {moment's **seismic** span,}.

GIVE ME YOUR EYES [(2)]

Give me your eyes.
I do not ask to touch
The hands of you, the mouth of you,
Soft and sweet and fragrant though they be.
No, lift your eyes to mine;
Give me but one last look
Ere I step forth forever;
E'en though within that moment's crashing space
I shall know all of life and death and heaven and hell.

GIVE ME YOUR EYES [(3)] [35]

Give me your eyes.
I do not ask to touch
The hands of you, the mouth of you,
Soft and sweet and fragrant though they be.
No, lift your eyes to mine;
Give me but one last look
Before I step forth forever;
Even though within that moment's crashing space,
I shall know all of life and death heaven and hell.

35. On the original typescript, the word {Before} in line 7 is emended
in holograph from {Ere}. {Even} in line 8 is similarly emended from {E'en}.
Version 3 is the only signed version of "Give Me Your Eyes" in the Grimké
papers.

[AS WE HAVE SOWED] [36]

I

As we have sowed so shall we also reap;
And it were sweet indeed if blossoms fair
Grow from the seeds to scent the sunlit air,
But oh! How sad if weeds that hide and creep
Grow in their stead to prick and sting our feet.
Too soon we'll meet the Master on our path,
And in His deep sad eyes we'll feel the wrath
Of justice or the thrill of praises sweet.
I do but pray within this humble breast,
That little flowers may blossom on my way,
But yet so pure they change the night to day,
I beg that one more fair than all the rest
So please the Master that with glad surprise
He proudly plucks it, smiling in my eyes.

II

As we have sowed so shall we also reap:—
How sweet if by our path the blossoms fair
Grow from the seeds to scent the sunlit air;
But Oh! How sad if weeds that hide and creep
Grow in their stead to prick and sting our feet.
We know not when the Master passing by
May pause, nor when from out his deep sad eye
May leap the flame of wrath or praises sweet
The sweetest flowers are those not proudly drest,
But little ones that brighten all the way,
They are so pure and white. For me I pray
That one white flower more pure than all the rest
May burst in blossom 'neath the Master's eyes,
That only He may know the sacrifice.

36. These two sonnets are untitled in original typescript.

ROSABEL[37]

I

Leaves, that whisper, whisper ever,
 Listen, listen, pray;
Birds, that twitter, twitter softly,
 Do not say me nay;
Winds, that breathe about, upon her,
 (Since I do not dare)
Whisper, twitter, breathe unto her
 That I find her fair.

II

Rose whose soul unfolds white petaled
 Touch her soul rose-white;
Rose whose thoughts unfold gold petaled
 Blossom in her sight;
Rose whose heart unfolds red petaled
 Quick her slow heart's stir;
Tell her white, gold, red my love is;
 And for her,—for her.

TO MY FATHER
UPON HIS FIFTY-FIFTH
BIRTHDAY[38]

As bright as is this day, dear father, be thy life
Henceforth. This day on which a new-made mother watched[39]
You lying in her arms, your little head against

37. In the holograph dated 25 October (no year), the title {Rosalee} is crossed out and {Rosabel} added.
38. Holograph revision: {**Fifty-third** Birthday}.
39. Holograph revision: {day, **in which my grand mother**}.

Her breast; and as you lay there, tiny wriggling mass,[40]
Her eyes adored you, softly bright with a great hope.[41]
Her trembling lips smiled ever, as she gazed upon
Your form, and at the first long kiss, the great[42]
Sweet World of Motherhood was opened to her eyes,[43]
A World so beautiful and so divine, the breath
Forsook her lips, and God's grand face lit up the room[44]
All dark before, and wrapped the mother and the babe
In haloed glory fair. Ah, gift of Motherhood!
Ah, precious boon to woman, reaping priceless joy
Through weary pain! Ah, emblem of the Love Divine!
The great white spark of Heaven in a woman's life.
Well might you smile above that your babe form, dear
    mother[45]
My father, for upon this day you brought into the world
A noble soul, a man that any mother might be
Proud to own. Smile, mother, in the other lands,
Aye laugh for joy. All that Is good in me, all that
I long to be, are due unto thy great true love,[46]
Thy guiding hand, thy sympathy so generous[47]
And great. What were I, father dear, without thy help?[48]
I turn my eyes away before the figure and
Rejoice; and yet your loving hands have moulded me[49];

40. Holograph revision: {tiny, **helpless**, mass,}.
41. Holograph revision: {a **sweet** hope.}.
42. Holograph revision: {kiss, the **deep**}.
43. Holograph revision: {Motherhood **unfolded to**}.
44. Holograph revision: {God's **great love** lit}.
45. Original typescript {your precious form}, with {precious} erased and
revised in holograph to read {your babe}.
46. Holograph revision: {unto **his watchful** great true}.
47. Holograph revision: {**His** guiding hand, **his** sympathy}.
48. Holograph revision: {without **your** help?}.
49. Holograph revision: {Rejoice; **for 'twas** your}.

No credit, father dear, is due to me; 'twas you
Alone, within my life. This is not all you are
And were to me, —not nearly all. Within the years,
When I was still a child, whose was the eye, that watched[50]
Me night and day? Whose ear was ever ready, kind,[51]
Unto my plaints, and ever ready too, to share my joys?
Whose hand was ever stretched to me, to lead my feet?[52]
Whose voice the last I heard before I closed my eyes[53]
In sleep, and whose the first I heard when I awoke?
It should have been my mother, but it was not so[54];
And, father dear, the sweetest tribute, that my hand[55]
Can find to lay before your feet this day, is this,
That you have been a gentle mother to your child.

THE BLACK CHILD

I saw a little black child
Sitting in a gold circle of sunlight;
And in his little black hand,
He had a little black stick,
And he was beating, beating,
With his little black stick,
The sunlight all about him,
      And laughing, laughing.

And he was so fat,
      There were dimples at his tiny, wriggling toes,

50. Holograph revision: {was **yet** a child, **yours** was}.
51. Holograph revision: {day? **Yours the** ear}.
52. Holograph revision: {**Yours the** hand}.
53. Holograph revision: {**Your** voice}.
54. Holograph revision: Entire line in parentheses.
55. Holograph revision: {**Ah!** father}.

And at his knees,
And at his elbows,
And at his fingers,
And in his cheeks,
    And in his little chin.

And his black hair was plaited
    Into innumerable, little braids,
        All over his little head;
    Very even, very fine, very cunning,
        They were.

And his skin was ebon, beautiful,
With a bloom, a shining gleam upon it.
O! he was all black,
    Save for his tiny white teeth
    And the whites of his eyes,
    And the white cloth about his little middle.

And he sat in the gold circle of sunlight
    Kicking with his little feet,
    And wriggling his little toes,
    And beating, beating
    The sunlight all about him,
    With his little black stick,
        And laughing, laughing.

And the circle of gold slipped tip-toeing away,
    Tiptoeing away from the little black child.
    And a little black hand slid into the shadows,
        Into black shadows,
    And a little black leg,
    And a little black foot,
    And the half of a little black braided head,
    And a little black shoulder,

And a little black beating stick,
And a little black beating hand,
And all that was left,
At the edge of the circle of gold,
Was a little black kicking foot
    And little black wriggling toes
    Wriggling—wriggling—gone!

A little black child
    Sat in the black shadows,
    Kicking with his little feet,
    And wriggling his little toes,
    And beating, beating
    The shadows all about him,
    With his little black stick,
        And laughing, laughing.

AT APRIL

Toss your gay heads,
    Brown girl trees;
Toss your gay lovely heads;
Shake your downy russet curls
All about your brown faces;
Stretch your brown slim bodies;
Stretch your brown slim arms;
Stretch your brown slim toes.
Who knows better than we,
With the dark, dark bodies,
What it means
When April comes alaughing and aweeping
Once again
At our hearts?

EVANESCENCE

You are like a pale purple flower
　　　　In the blue spring dusk . . . . .

You are like a yellow star
Budding and blowing
In an apricot sky . . . . . .

You are like the beauty
Of a voice . . . . . .
Remembered after death . . . . . .

You are like thin white petals
　　　　Falling
　　　　　　And
　　　　　　　　Floating
　　　　　　　　　　Down
Upon the white, stilled hushing
　　　　Of my soul.

[KEEP THIS LILY] [56]

I

Keep this lily that I fold
　　In your hushéd hand;
Though they tell me that you sleep,
　　You will understand.

56. Poem is untitled in typescript.

II

Keep this tear upon your cheek;
And this tear its mate;
They will tell you of the tears
That I weep too late.

III

Keep this smile I give to you,
Born mid shame and pain;
Keep it for I never shall
Smile on earth again.

IV

Keep these kisses on your eyes;
Hoard their memory,
So when I shall kiss them then,
They will ope for me.

TO THE ROSES OVER HIM

Under the white, white stars,
Under the gold, gold moon,
Through the silvery, saffron vapors,
To the roses over him, dancing over
him.

I come under the white, white stars,
I come under the gold, gold moon,
I come through the silvery, saffron vapors,
To the roses over him, dancing over
him.

I kneel, I kiss, one by one, and one by one,
The roses red, red, heart-red, dancing over him;

I, who knew not the touch of his hands, or his arms, or his
　　　mouth,
I, who keep but the one look he gave me, when we met
　　　morn-pure,
Far from the feet of men. Then our eyes lifted, met,
Shocked, clung, long, long——I am well content.

　　　Under the white, white stars,
　　　Under the gold, gold moon,
　　　Through the silvery, saffron vapors,
　　　　　　To the roses over him, dancing over
　　　　　　him.

SWEET, YOU ARE LATE

I
　　　Sweet, you are late:——
The dew-born dusk has fled,
Its purple wings outspread,
Into the wistful west;
Each bird is in its nest,
Except one, lone, shy thrush
Athrob within the hush:——
　　　Sweet, you are late.

II
　　　Sweet, you are late:——
The gate is openéd;
My roses white and red,
You so much love to twine
Within these curls of mine,
Lean o'er the parapet,

Their eyes with tear-drops wet:—
Sweet, you are late.

III

Sweet, you are late:—
The moonlight falls in showers
Upon my turret-towers;—
Afar across the brakes
The nightingale awakes;
And yet,—and yet, quite white
The path slips out of sight:—
Sweet, you are late.

A MONA LISA

1

I should like to creep
Through the long brown grasses
That are your lashes;
I should like to poise
On the very brink
Of the leaf-brown pools
That are your shadowed eyes;
I should like to cleave
Without sound,
Their glimmering waters,
Their unrippled waters,
I should like to sink down
And down
And down . . . . .
And deeply drown.

2

Would I be more than a bubble breaking?
　　Or an ever-widening circle
　　Ceasing at the marge?
Would my white bones
　　Be the only white bones
Wavering back and forth, back and forth
　　In their depths?

THE EYES OF MY REGRET

Always at dusk, the same tearless experience,
The same dragging of feet up the same well-worn path
To the same well-worn rock;
The same crimson or gold dropping away of the sun,
The same tints,—rose, saffron, violet, lavender, grey,
Meeting, mingling, mixing mistily;
Before me the same blue black cedar rising jaggedly to a
　　point;
Over it, the same slow unlidding of twin stars,
Two eyes unfathomable, soul-searing,
Watching, watching—watching me;
The same two eyes that draw me forth, against my will dusk
　　after dusk;
The same two eyes that keep me sitting late into the night,
　　chin on knees,
Keep me there lonely, rigid, tearless, numbly miserable—
　　The eyes of my Regret.

REGRET [(1)]

Stars through my window's poor pane;
    The shriveling husk
Of a yellowing moon on the wane;—
    And the dusk.

Star paths descending to earth
    Through the tear drops wet;
    And the dusk pain again,—the rebirth
    Of regret.

REGRET [(2)]

1

Stars through my dull window pane;
    The shriveling husk
Of a yellowing moon on the wane;
    And the dusk,

2

Star cascades spraying the earth
    Through my tear drops wet;
And the soul-sob of dusk,—the rebirth
    Of Regret.

IN SUNSET LAND

In sunset-land, in sunset-land,
The ruddy trees in splendor stand,
The rainbowed waters fleetly flow,
And dainty breezes whisper low,

Where sleepy flowers of mystery grow.
O realm of dreams and visions grand,
Sweet sunset-land, sweet sunset-land!

In sunset-land, in sunset-land,
Calm Beauty reigns from strand to strand;
And in her gardens by the streams
Where ruby sunlight ever gleams,
She tends her flowers of wondrous dreams.
O give one dream from thy fair hand
To one, who yearns for sunset-land!

TWO FIGURES OF GRIEF AND DESPAIR [57]

I

Last dusk, when down my purpled paths
    The light had flown,
I stole into the cypress grove
    Alone.

II

And sought mid pacings up and down
    Beneath its gloom
To crush the pain that stifled in
    The room.

III

And there sat one whom *I* ne'er knew
    Nor saw before,
Who moaned, and beat her breast, and wept
    Full sore.

57. The words {Two Figures Of} are an emendation in holograph to the typescript.

IV

"Woman," I said, "why do you weep?"
    She raised her head.
"I weep because the one I love
      is dead."

V

And swift I dropped unto my knees
    In sudden woe,
And kissed her lips. "I know," I said,
     "I know."

VI

We clung in silence each to each,
    A little space.
Then soft she breathed, "To-day they hid
     His face."

VII

And great tears fell upon my brow
    And cheeks, and crept
Into my hands, until I thought
     I wept.

VIII

"Woman," I said, "you do not know,—
    But you are blest;
If I might weep as you, I should
     Find rest.

IX

"The one I love has ceased to be
    These many years;
Yet to this time my eyes have known
     No tears."

X

I saw within her eyes, she could
    Not understand;

And so I kissed her brow; and pressed
　　Her hand;
　　　　XI
And went away into the house,
　　Where lights ne'er shone,
Dry-eyed, and drear, and oh! so much
　　Alone.

BROWN GIRL

In the hot gold sunlight,
　　Brown girl, brown girl,
　　　　You smile;
　　And in your great eyes,
　　　　Very gold, very bright,
　　　　　I see little bells,
　　　　Shaking so lazily,
　　　　　　(Oh! small they are) . . . . .
　　　　　　I hear the bells.
. . . .
But at fawn dusk
　　Brown girl, brown girl,
　　　　I see no smile,
　　　　I hear no bells.
　　Your great eyes
　　Are quiet pools;
　　They have been drinking, drinking,
　　　　All the day,
　　The hot gold of sunlight.
　　Your eyes spill sunlight
　　　　Over the dusk.

Close your eyes,
I hear nothing but the beating of my heart.

DUSKED LILIES

My lilies, listless, dim,
There where the shadows are;
My lilies, still and slim,
Each a blurred white star.

———————

In the sun,
Softly to each I moved;
Lightly I lipped and loved
Every one.

———————

I did not know a touch
Could hurt so much;
I did not dream a breath
Meant death.

———————

My lilies, listless, dim,
There where the shadows are;
My lilies, still and slim,
Each a blurred white star.

MY STAR

I

There is a star I love,
Oh! very much;
I see it when the dusk
And day-time touch.

II

It is not very large,
        Or very clear;
But though its light is dim,
        'Tis very dear.

III

It is a friend to me,
        I understand;
Although it never, never speaks,[58]
        Or takes my hand.

IV

Each dusk I sit with it
        A little while;
I do not have to make believe,
        Or have to smile.[59]

V

But just be what I am,[60]
        Until I know,
'Tis time to kiss my hand
        To it,—and go.

---

58. Holograph revision: {it never speaks,}.

59. Holograph revisions of Stanza IV, lines 3 and 4: The third line is crossed out in two separate strokes, and the fourth line has two revisions: {Or have, or smile}, {Believe, or smile.}. There is a final revision written at the side of the stanza with stress marks: {I neéd not máke beliéve/ You seé or smíle}.

60. Holograph revision: {But be just what}.

DUSK[61]

Twin stars through my purpling pane,
    The shriveling husk
Of a yellowing moon on the wane,—
    And the dusk.

DAWN [(1)]

Slim trees, filmy against grey skies;
    Grey mist, grey hush;
And then frail, exquisite, afar,
    A hermit-thrust.

DAWN [(2)]

Grey trees, grey skies, and not a star;
    Grey mist, grey hush;
And then frail, exquisite, afar,
    A hermit-thrush.

AT THE SPRING DAWN

I watched the dawn come,
    Watched the spring dawn come,
And the red sun shouldered his way up
    Through the grey, through the blue,

61. Grimké presented "Dusk" and "Dawn [(1)]" as companion pieces and typed them on the same page. On another typescript, "Dusk" was paired with "The Puppet-Player," which appears later in this section.

Through the lilac mists.
The quiet of it! The goodness of it!
And one bird awoke, sang, whirred
A blur of moving black against the sun,
Sang again—afar off.
And I stretched my arms to the redness of the sun,
Stretched to my finger tips,
And I laughed.
Ah! It is good to be alive, good to love,
At the dawn,
At the spring dawn.

AT MORN

Body of me, soul of me, listless, numb;
Lazily I arise onto an elbow;
Dully I look forth;
Morn again, sun again, colorless sunlight;
Afar over the city, over the deeper white of the river,
Sheetings of white fog,
White, moving, mysterious fog,
Blurring into a pallid sky above.
At hand, two cedars, one green, one browning,
Standing motionless, unyielding, ungracious, militant;
Window-close, the squat, silent body of a Norway pine,
Its millions of straight and hairy fingers pointing aimlessly;
Just beyond, the branches of a tulip-tree,
Cluttered with brown and shriveling cups,
All shining and gaping wetly in the sun.
Nothing more . . . . . .
No bird songs, no silken whirrings of wings,

Nothing but quiet—quiet,—quiet,
Pervasive, ominous, sense-stabbing,
Winter at hand, oh! soul of me, winter at hand.

A TRILOGY

I

Mid the dim, shy, woods
Where the grey light broods,
And the shadows sleep
Like deep-dreaming sheep
'Neath the long, vague, aisles.

———

Not a leaf or needle stirs
On the birches or the firs,
Ev'ry bird, and tree, and bush,
Is enthralled in one, deep, hush
Waiting patient, mile on mile
        For the rapture, for the bliss
        Of the drowsy Dawn's first kiss
When she wakes with sleepy smile.

———

Hark! a little bird awakes
To his mate a twitter makes,
Then from out his slim, brown, throat
Thrilling song begins to float,—
First so low 'tis hard to hear,
Then it mounts without a fear,
Ever higher, ever higher
Soaring, one, long, stream of fire,
Blinding the fair face of Day,
Then it throbbing dies away.

See! A shiver shakes the trees,
Sighing softly wakes the breeze,
Ev'ry bird awakes and sings
Till the forest swings and rings,
And the whole, vague, aisles along
Swoon with an ecstasy of song;
　　　Awake! Awake! 'Tis day!

II

A whimsical, laughing, lazy, breeze
Teasing and pleasing the little green leaves,
And kissing the feet of noon 'neath the trees.

The words are aleap with life and sound
From the tree-tops high to the genial ground:—
The bumble bee with his buzzing song
Is gathering honey the whole day long,—
The mother bird on her swaying nest
Is singing the song she loves the best;
A song to the darlings beneath her breast;
And flitting father is finding food
To fill the beaks of his feathered brood;—
The tall, graves trees are the thinkers that think,
And in weighty thoughts their high heads sink,
The tall, grave trees are the dreamers that dream,
And Oh! for the dreams which in them teem!

So work, and sing and dream, while you may,
For Death may speak at the end of Day.

III

A sleep-seducing stillness broods
Within the wistful, waiting, woods
And Shades, precursors of their queen
The falling flowers of darkness gleam,

And sitting down behind each tree
They weave their wreaths with witchery,
But they are wild, and shy, and free,
And on approaching quickly flee.
The speeding Day purloins the light,
And from afar the voice of Night
Melodious, and full, and deep,
Is coaxing sleep, is coaxing sleep.

———

The stars appear and coyly wink,
And Dian stops to think and think
Her pale, high, brow aglow with light
The woods are still with straining sight—
The woods are still with straining sight—
Behold! She comes, the queen of Night!
A queen indeed in shape and size
With haunting grace, and haunting eyes.
The grass and flowers beneath her feet
Sink into slumber strange and sweet,
She charms to rest by slow degrees
The birds, the leaves, the trees, the breeze:
And then she sits upon her throne
A figure motionless, alone,
Her solemn, radiant, vigil keeping
Never sleeping, never sleeping,—
      So sleep! sleep! sleep!

A WINTER TWILIGHT

A silence slipping around like death,
Yet chased by a whisper, a sigh, a breath;
One group of trees, lean, naked and cold,
Inking their crests 'gainst a sky green-gold;

One path that knows where the corn flowers were;
Lonely, apart, unyielding, one fir;
And over it softly leaning down,
One star that I loved ere the fields went brown.

THE WANT OF YOU

A hint of gold where the moon will be;
Through the flocking clouds just a star or two;
Leaf sounds, soft and wet and hushed,
And oh! the crying want of you.

EL BESO [62]

Twilight—and you,
Quiet—the stars;
Snare of the shine of your teeth,
Your provocative laughter,
The gloom of your hair;
Lure of you, eye and lip;
Yearning, yearning,
Languor, surrender;
        Your mouth,
And madness, madness,
Tremulous, breathless, flaming,
The space of a sigh;
Then awakening—remembrance,
Pain, regret—your sobbing;
And again quiet—the stars,
Twilight—and you.

62. The Grimké papers include an untitled copy of this poem on leather.

ENTREATY

When the year is young, and the heart is young,
And the billing birds sing to each other;
When the blossoms sweet, and the breezes sweet
Are so tenderly kissing each other—
    Then why should I not kiss thee?
    So a kiss, a kiss, my sweet.

When the year is old, and the heart is old,
And the birds never sing to each other;
When the bushes bleak, and the wild winds bleak
Are so frigidly greeting each other—
    Wouldst thou not e'en so greet me?
    So a kiss, a kiss, my sweet.

ANOTHER HEART IS BROKEN [63]

    Another heart is broken,
        Broken, and dead.
Take it up carelessly, jubilantly,
You who were father and mother to it,
Take it up in your twitching hands;
Skippingly, bear it forth to the place,
Where lie the things that are dead, long dead;
Hurl it forth into the quiet blackness,
    Then return.
No more tears, will you know,
No more pain, no more joy,—
Nothing but blankness eternal,
Blankness, and the hollowness of rasping laughter.

63. Typescript untitled; holograph title is addition.

Rejoice!
Another heart is broken,
Broken and dead.

LITTLE GREY DREAMS

Little grey dreams,
I sit at the ocean's edge,
At the grey ocean's lacy edge,
With you in my lap.

I launch you one by one,
And one by one,
Little grey dreams,
Under the grey, grey clouds
Out on the grey, grey sea.

You go sailing away
From my empty lap.
Little grey dreams.
Sailing! Sailing!
Into the black
At the horizon's edge.

I WEEP

——I weep——
Not as the young do noisily,
Not as the aged rustily,
But quietly.
Drop by drop the great tears
Splash upon my hands,

And save you saw them shine,
You would not know
I wept.

BUTTERFLIES

Butterflies, white butterflies, in the sunshine,
Have you seen them? *Really* seen them?
            Lovely things!

Two windows has the little room,
One to the north, the other to the south;
Open, both, for the sun and the air
She needed so. But now . . . .

And from the brow of this hill, here,
To-day, just as before,
The house under its snug hat of a new red roof,
And the wide eye of the south window there,
The wide unlidded eye,
Open to sun and air,
Just as before, just as before.

And, nearer, the north window,
One has to swing around to and pass
To reach the house,
A blind eye, wide, unblinking,
Open, too, just as before.

And through its greyness,
Quite clearly to be seen from here,
The white chest of drawers,
So clearly to be seen, so memory stabbing,
One seems again within that little room,

Sitting on a little chair there,
Facing that white chest of drawers,
Opposite to her who sat her back to the white chest,
Her dark head slanting against her chair's white back
Her dark head heavy,
Her dark head weary.
Nothing but weariness left:
Weariness of hand and foot and knee and back;
Weariness of wide, unquiet eyes glimpsing things unseen,
Weariness of wide, unquiet eyes forgetting you.
Remembering you, forgetting you again;
Weariness of the journey from the weary ring finger
To the wearier middle finger,
Of her mother's wedding ring;
The silence of weariness;
The slow withdrawal of her who sat in that unresponsive
     body,
The young soul whiteness of her unloosening its shell,
And slipping out—and slipping out—and slipping out—

Things to know! Things to know!
I shall not see her, today.
In that little room,
With its windows wide to north and south,
          This I know;
The chair with the white back is empty,
The room is quiet,
          This I know;
Shells, shells, shells everywhere,
Above ground, under ground,
          This I know;
Hers up there, in that little room,
Lying there,

A still thing under a still, white sheet
    And this I know.

Butterflies, white butterflies, in the sunshine,
Have you seen them? *Really* seen them?
    Lovely things!

AT AUTUMN

1

Fall: red leaf, yellow leaf and brown
Falling one by one, and one by one;
Browning fields and browning grass and weeds;
Silence save for a wind disconsolate, grave;
Birds, where are they? Gone, all gone, save one;
Sunsets greenish gold, and shivering darks;
And the one lone robin sobbing through the dusk;
And your love, your love of the spring, where is it?
And my love ah! my love for you, what of it?

2

Spring was it? Only one wee, short spring ago?
Time of the delicate grass, the crimsoning trees;
The exquisite arbutus hiding 'neath the brown;
The chaste anemones, the purpling violets,
The maddening shouts of joyous, mating birds;
The tender, languid twilights, the wooing winds;
The slim slips of maiden moons, the shimmering stars;
And our love, our first love, glorious, yielding;
Our clinging hands, our clinging lips—Ah cease, the Spring
    Is dead!

3

And we stand here under the autumn skies,
Under the twilight stars, under the gold, gold moon,

Big, phlegmatic. Here,—but you have forgot;
And the wind prods the dead leaves to our feet.
Your hand does not seek mine. You smile, the smile
Is not for me. It is for the new life and dreams
Wherein I have no part. You speak, can I hear?
You smile, can smile, and your dead love lies between.
I am a woman, I smile, too, only we women know why.[64]

AUTUMN[65]

As yearns a mother o'er her little one,
Whose baby cheek grows paler ev'ry sun,
And baby eyes grow mystical near Death;
And though she fears each sobbing breath
Will be the last; and though her eyes are dim,
She dresses it (to please some passing whim)
In costly garments beautiful and bright.
But while so gayly drest an angel white
Outstretched her arms to take her little child,
And leaves her, hopeless, desolate, and wild.

—

Just so the trees, when Fall with chilly breath
Steals o'er the country in the form of Death,
Bedeck in wondrous dress their baby leaves;
And though their hearts are wrung, and though it grieves
Them sore yet do they bravely laugh and smile
So that no presage mar their little while:
But as they laugh they see Death's form advance
Unsheathing without sound his cruel lance,

64. Holograph revision: {smile. We women}.
65. Typescript untitled; holograph title is addition.

And ev'ry leaf pierced through mid swift surprise
With deep'ning horror growing in their eyes,[66]
And baby laughter dying on their lips[67]
Forgets to cling and sadly downward slips.

———

Then all the trees o'erwrought with grief and woe
Join their wild wails with all the winds that blow
And writhing, lift their hungry arms on high
Disconsolate, beneath a sullen sky.

AT THE AUTUMN DUSK

I watched the dusk come,
    Watched the autumn dusk come.
And the pale sun sagged down and down listlessly,
    Caught in a mesh of wanly opaled mists,
    Fell into a flat sad sea.
And a bat slipped by silent and dark,
    Returned, flicked my cheek with furtive wing,
Sped on and came no more.
And in the west one star was not,
    Then was,
A sallow star, a somber star.
And through the mists between the star and sea,
The face of one long dead looked out at me
And the eyes called . . . .
O, eyes that call and call,
    Life is not sweet, life is not sweet

66. Holograph revision: {in **its** eyes,}.
67. Holograph revision: {on **its** lips}.

At the dusk,
At the autumn dusk.

PARADOX

When face to face we stand
    And eye to eye,
How far apart we are————————
As far, they say, as God can ever be
From what, they say, is Hell.
    — / / — — / / —
But, when we stand
Fronting the other,
Mile after mile slipping in between,
O, close we are,
As close as is the shadow to the body,
As breath, to life, ...
As kisses are to love.

NAUGHTY NAN

I

Naughty Nan
If you can
Tell me how your frowns and smiles,
Sudden tears, and naive wiles,
Linked into a glittering band
Follow swiftly hand in hand?
Tell me wayward April-born,
Child of smiles and tears forlorn,
Have you ever felt the smart

Of a lacerated heart?
Are you but a sprite of moods?
Heartless, that fore'er deludes
    Tell me naughty Nan?
        II
    Naughty Nan
    If you can
Tell me why you have such eyes
Gleaming when not drooped in sighs
Or when veiled by falling rain?
Haughty oft but never vain
Sometime wistful orbs of brown,
Sometimes blazing in fierce scorn
But eyes that are never free
From some glance of witchery.
Tell me why you have such lips
Tempting me to stolen sips
Tender, drooping, luring, sad,
Laughing, mocking, madly glad,
      Tell me naughty Nan?
        III
    Naughty Nan
    If you can
Tell me why you play with me,
Take my heart so prettily
In your dainty, slender, hands,
Bruise its tender, loving, bands?
Tell me why your eyes are brown
Mock and glitter when I frown?
Flitting, luring, little, sprite
In a garb of moods bedight,
Dancing here, and dancing there,
Changeling strange, but ever fair

You have caught me in your snare,—
Naughty Nan.

CAPRICHOSA[68]

I

Little lady coyly shy
With deep shadows in each eye
Cast by lashes soft and long,
Tender lips just bowed for song,
And I oft have dreamed the bliss
Of the nectar in one kiss
          But 'tis clear
          That I fear
The white anger that can lie
In the depths of her veiled eye,
Little nose so bold and pert,
That I fear me she's a flirt
And her eyes and smile demure
Are intended for a lure,
Cruel, dainty, little lady.

II

Dimples too in cheek and chin
Deep'ning when the smiles begin
Dancing o'er her mystic face;
Tiny hands of fragile grace
Yet for me their mighty sway
May crush out the light of day.
          And her feet
          So discreet

68. In the Grimké papers, this poem is dated 12 December 1901.

Only dare to coyly flirt
From beneath her filmy skirt.
Soft her curls and dusky deep
Hoarding all the shades for sleep,
And in drinking their perfume
I sink down mid lotus-bloom,
Cruel, dainty, little lady.

III

On some days she's shy and sweet
Gentler maid 'twere hard to meet:
Other days a lady grand
Cold and hard to understand
Greets me with a haughty stare—
Seeing naught but empty air;
    If I fume
    At my doom
Bows her dusky head to weep
Till I humbly to her creep
Grovelling in the very dirt—
But she's laughing! Little flirt!
Then, when I am most forlorn,
Wishing I had ne'er been born,
Woos me with alluring eyes,
Cooing words, and monstrous sighs,
But, if my foot one step advances
Lightly, swiftly, from me dances,
Darting at me mocking glances,
Cruel, dainty, little lady.

THE PUPPET-PLAYER [69]

Sometimes it seems as though some puppet-player
    A clenchéd claw cupping a craggy chin,
Sits just beyond the border of our seeing,
    Twitching the strings with slow, sardonic grin.

A TRIOLET

    Molly raised shy eyes to me,
        On an April day;
    Close we stood beneath a tree;
    Molly raised shy eyes to me,
    Shining sweet and wistfully,
    Wet and yet quite gay;
    Molly raised shy eyes to me,
        On an April day.

LULLABY [(1)] [70]

I

Baby mine, the sun's abed;
    Shadows creep;
All the world sings lullaby:—
    Go to sleep.

II

Not a bird within its nest
    Lifts a cheep;

69. On another typescript, "The Puppet-Player" is paired with "Dusk,"
which appears earlier in this section.
70. The typescript has many illegible words in holograph.

Hush! then little, babbling voice;—
　　Go to sleep.
　　　　III
Not a single, frisky lamb
　　Makes a leap;
Hush! then little, feet and hands;—
　　Go to sleep.
　　　　IV
Not a single, baby bud
　　Tries to peep;—
Close, then little, drowsy, eyes;—
　　Go to sleep.
　　　　V
Fear not, round about is love,
　　Great and deep,
Love of God and love of me;—
　　Go to sleep.

LULLABY [(2)] [71]

Moon astarin' troo de trees,
Stars ablinkin' as you sees,
Li'l leaves adreamin' deep,
Shadders comin' creep and creep,
Dey sha'n't tech you don' you cheep.
　　Dere! Dere! Sleep! Sleep!

'Taint a li'l bird awake,
'Taint a nothin', goodness sake!

71. Grimké's rare use of African-American diction in poetry should be compared with her quite successful use of this form in her short story, "Jettisoned," which appears in the fiction section of this volume.

'Cep' dese laffin' eyes so sweet,
De way dey shines, it sho' do beat.
God, I lubs you head to feet.
    Dere! Dere! Sleep! Sleep!

Ain't you quit dis laffin' yet?
Don' you know de sun's done set?
Wan' me kiss dis li'l han'?
Well, well, laf de w'ile you can,
You won' laf w'en you'se a man,
    Dere! Dere! Sleep! Sleep!

YOU

I love your throat, so fragrant, fair,
The little pulses beating there;
Your eye-brows' shy and questioning air;
    I love your shadowed hair.

I love your flame-touched ivory skin;
Your little fingers frail and thin;
Your dimple creeping out and in;
    I love your pointed chin.

I love the way you move, you rise;
Your fluttering gestures, just-caught cries;
I am not sane, I am not wise,
    God! how I love your eyes!

YOUR EYES

Through the downiness of the grey dawn,
    Through its grey gossamer softness—
        Your eyes;

Through the wonder-shine of the one star,
    Beautiful, solitary, in the East—
        Your eyes;

Through the fierceness, the cymbaling of colors,
    Through the whitening glory of the springing sun—
        Your eyes;

Through the chattering of birds, through their songs,
    Delicate, lovely, swaying in the tree-tops,
    Through the softness of little feathered breasts and
    throats
    Through the skitterings of little feet,
    Through the whirrings of silken wings—
        Your eyes;

Through the green quiet, the hot languor of noon,
    Sudden, through its cleft peace—
        Your eyes;

Through the slenderness of maiden trees kissed aflame by
    the mouth of the Spring,
    Through them standing against a slowly goldening
    Western sky,
    Through them standing very still, wondering,
    Wistful, waiting—
        Your eyes;

Through the beautiful Dusk, through the beautiful, blue-
    black hair of the Dusk,
Through her beautiful parted hair—
        Your eyes,
        Kissing mine.

MAY

May, thou lovely month of spring!
As a fairy thou com'st dancing,
Sweetness rests upon thy brow,
Smiles upon thy face are glancing,
Angel hands have thee caressed,
Chirrup birds to thee in bowers,
Heaven thy gentle head hath blest;
Underneath thy quiet breast
Softly sleep thy tender flowers.
Every day thou smilest brightly,
Till thou seest has come thy day,
Then, with longing eyes turned backward,
Sighing low, thou steal'st away.

GREENNESS

Tell me is there anything lovelier,
    Anything more quieting
Than the green of little blades of grass
And the green of little leaves?
      . . .
Is not each leaf a cool green hand,
Is not each blade of grass a mothering green finger,
Hushing the heart that beats and beats and beats?

LONGING

As a white dove, against the deep blue sky,
    Skims swiftly far away on restless wings,

As a blithe barque shakes off the clinging spray
   And to the gallant breeze her ensign flings,
      So longs my soul to fly away to thee.

As lights the panting dove in some far land,
   And at the sunset hour sleeps on her nest,
And as the barque tossed by the blust'ring gale
   At last in port lies on the ocean's breast,
      So longs my soul to rest always with thee.

BLUE CYCLE

There is the blue sky,
And there are the blue flowers,
And there are the blue eyes, wide
On the blue flowers.

  . . . .
Other blue flowers have been,
And other blue eyes,
But the blue skies are the same.

  . . . .
And these blue flowers shall pass,
And these blue eyes,
And the blue skies will remain.

FIDES
(A RONDEAU)

Go from me, go; but ere you go
Fan back the firelight's sombre glow;
Snuff out the lights; draw close the shades;

Then bring me where it flames and fades
The scarlet cypress-flower of woe;

And place it in my fingers, so
That when my eyes quite sightless grow,
I still may clutch its bleeding blades.
                            Go from me, go.

Leave wide the door. Across the snow,
I wish the glare of fire to throw
A pathway for him o'er the glades.
O! when he sees my white-veined braids
And flower,—pray God he then may know.
                            Go from me, go.

THE WAYS O' MEN

'Tis queer, it is, the ways o' men,
Their comin's and their goin's'
For there's the grey road,
        The straight-road
With the grey dust liftin'
        With ev'ry step
And the little roads off-flingin'.
                    . . . .
Maybe it's a bit of a sly field
That crooks a finger to them
And sends them to the turnin';
Or the round firm bosom
        Of a little hill
Acallin' to them, them with their heads
                That heavy;
Or maybe it's the black look
        Given out of the tail of the eye;

Or a white word, wingin';
Maybe it's only the back of a little tot's neck
    In the sunlight;
Or the red lips of a woman
      Parting slow . . . . . .
  . . . Sure there's no tellin'.

       . . . .
One I saw goin' towards a white star
    At the edge of a daffydill sky,
      Its lights kissin' straight into his eyes.
Maybe it's a gold piece
To be taken from another
    In the dark;
Or the neat place between the ribs
Waitin' for the knife
That one comes after carryin' for it.
'Tis few, it is, that goes with the grey road
    The straight road
    All the way,
With the grey dust liftin' at ev'ry step.

      . . . .
'Tis queer, it is, the ways o' men,
With a level look at you, or a crooked
    As they be passin'.
      Pouf!
Sure, 'tis so fast they're goin',
Does it matter about the turnin's?

THE BLACK FINGER

I have just seen a most beautiful thing
    Slim and still
   Against a gold, gold sky,

A straight black cypress,
Sensitive,
Exquisite,
A black finger
Pointing upwards.
Why, beautiful still finger, are you black?
And why are you pointing upwards?

TWO PILGRIMS HAND IN HAND
Sonnet to Mr. and Mrs. John J. Smith Upon Their
Fifty-Fifth Wedding Anniversary

White-haired, calm-faced, two pilgrims, hand in hand,
Have shared the world's swift joys and bitter tears
With patient, tender, hearts for fifty-five long years,
And passed with fearless feet through Life's strange land.
Their little babes beneath their loving gaze
Have grown into serene maturity,
All lovers of sweet grace and purity,
An ever present joy unto their latter days.

———————

What though some hours were filled with anguish drear!
What though the sun was hid behind the clouds!
What though their dearest dreams were wrapped in shrouds!
It only drew their souls to Him more near,
For it was given to them to understand—
To see God's face and sometimes feel His hand.

WHEN YOU WALK

When you walk,
I can think only of a white dryad

Slipping out of a brown tree . . . .
And skipping . . . . . .

TO THE DUNBAR HIGH SCHOOL
(A Sonnet)

And she shall be the friend of youth for aye:
Of quickening youth whose eyes have seen the gleam;
Of youth between whose tears and laughter stream
Bright bows of hope; of youth, audacious, gay,
Who dares to know himself a Caesar, say,
A Shakespeare or a Galahad. The dream
To him is real; and things are as they seem,
For Beauty veils from him the feet of clay.

How holy and how wonderful her trust—
Youth's friend—and, yes, how blest. For down the west
Each day shall go the sun, and time in time
Shall die, the unborn shall again be dust;
But she with youth eternal on her breast,
Immortal, too, shall sit serene, sublime.

WRITTEN FOR THE FIFTIETH ANNIVERSARY CELEBRATION AT DUNBAR HIGH SCHOOL[72]

They knew, those gone, bent backs, the lash's out
On crimsoning and shudd'ring flesh and thirst
And hunger and all weariness, yet durst

72. This poem was published as "Then and Now" in Robert T. Kerlin,
ed., *Negro Poets and Their Poems* (Washington, D.C.: Associated Publishers,
1923).

Nor pause, nor rest; but toil and toil till shut
Of day sent them to fall in noisome hut
Herded e'en in sleep. Tortured, accursed,
These knew this life as death and death at worst
A peace when earth above their bones was put.

. . . . . .

But we, their children, bone of them and blood
Bound by new fetters, tortured still, have seen
A light: We know that soul and mind are free
That sorrow, tears and evil all are good;
We know it matters not what we have been
But this, and always this: What we shall be.

BUT YESTERDAY

A RONDEAU

But yesterday the eglantine
Ran rioting beneath the shine
Of sunny skies: the meadow-lark
Made mad the ways until the dark
Lay down beneath the star-kissed pine.

Within the pools the dappled kine
Drowsed lazily or did recline
Within the shade, devoid of cark—
                    But yesterday.

There were no blood hues in the vine:
No wintry sobbing shook the brine:
Within the woods no eye might mark
The first heart-piercing, flame-tongued spark,

That blazes now. The world was mine
But yesterday.

WHY?

Ah! sweet, why did you come
Unto my humble door?
Why did you knock with cold
Sure hand? You knew that I
Could not withstand,—you knew
That I would let you in,
Would stretch my poor arms wide
In welcome shy but true,
Would kneel before you,—kiss
With humble lips your feet,
Believing you to be
My dream-dove, longed-for, king:
Why did you take my hand
So calmly and assured?
Why did you smile into
My eyes, vain, idle, thoughts?
Why did you whisper in
My ear delicious dreams?
Ah! sweet, my cruel sweet,
Why did you do these things?
My woman-heart was but
A folded bud before
You came, but with you near
Where it might see the sun
Your face, where it might
Feed upon your words, your smiles,
It grew, and bloomed, and glowed,

Because it loved, it loved.
Why did you make it bloom?
Would 'twere a folded bud
Why did you watch it grow
With fierce and jealous eyes?
Why did you drink and drink
Its fragrance to the full?
Why did you tear its leaves
With harsh and treacherous hands?
Why did you trample it
Beneath your brutal feet?
Why did you laugh meanwhile
With loud and scornful glee?
Ah! sweet, my cruel sweet,
Why did you do these things?
Why is it that my one,
Mad, wish is but to die
Where I may see your face
May hear your mocking voice?
Why is it hate for you
Cannot survive within
This breast? Why is it that
I must forgive you all
You did or left undone,
And why? Ah! why must this
Be too my added curse,
That I must love you, sweet,
And love you just the same?

[FUTILITY (1)] [73]

When I was young and innocent
    I used to rise and go
Into the night to pray O God [74]
    To feel some love.

Now I am old and worldly-wise
    And walk where shádows grów
Oh hów I yeárn for hér I wás
    So long ago [75]

FUTILITY [(2)] [76]

I
When I was young and innocent,
    I used to softly steal
Away intó the quiet níght
    And beg to feel.
II
Now I am old and worldly-wise,
    And walk where shadows grow,
O! how I yearn for her I was
    So long ago.

---

73. Untitled holograph.
74. Holograph revision: {Within the night}.
75. There are several holograph revisions at the bottom of the page: {I used to slip into}, {The night}, {When I was young and innocent/ I used to rise an . . . [illegible]/ Into the night quiet}, {To suffer love}, {To suffer love}.
76. Untitled typescript; holograph title is the addition.

FUTILITY [(3)] [77]

I

When I was young and innocent,
    I used to rise and go
Intó the níght and práy O God
    To feel some love [78]

II

Now I am old and worldly-wise,
    And walk where shadows grow,
O! how I yearn for her I was
    So long ago.

OH, MY HEART, FOR THE SPRING!

I

Oh, my heart, for the green,—the first green!
    The shy sheen
Of the wistful sun-beams mid the gray
    Tangled sway
Of the proud, yearning arms giving birth:
    Oh, the mirth!
At the first, of the mad, moving masses
    Of grasses,
With the joy on their lips, in the clean
    Air so keen:
Oh, my heart, for the green,—the first green.

II

Oh, my heart, for the mouth,—the first mouth
    From the South!

---

77. Presents holograph revisions to "Futility [(2)]."
78. Holograph revisions: {To live,—to feel.}, {Great pain to feel.}.

To awake at the break of the day,
    In the gray
And the quiet and hear the first throat,
    The first note,
From the lands far away o'er the swell;
    Drink the smell
Of the jessamine bud and the rose,
    And the glows
Of the graceful fair things,—for uncouth
    Is this drouth:
Oh, my heart, for the mouth,—the first mouth.

TREES[79]

God made them very beautiful, the trees:
He spoke and gnarled of bole or silken sleek
They grew; majestic bowed or very meek;
Huge-bodied, slim; sedate and full of glees.
And He had pleasure deep in all of these.
And to them soft and little tongues to speak
Of Him to us, He gave, wherefore they seek
From dawn to dawn to bring us to our knees.

                . . . .

Yet here amid the wistful sounds of leaves,
A black-hued gruesome something swings and swings,
Laughter it knew and joy in little things
Till man's hate ended all. ——And so man weaves.
And God, how slow, how very slow weaves He—
Was Christ Himself not nailéd to a tree?

79. "Trees" and "Beware When He Awakes [(versions 1–3)]" are two
of Grimké's poems that refer directly to lynching, the prime theme of her
drama and fiction.

FAR AWAY

I

The long blue skies are smiling, sweet
The baby-billows with glad feet
Play gently, softly, on the sand,
Soft breezes from far southern land
Bring sighing love-thoughts in their breast,
And on their wings sweet songs of rest,
The sweeping sea-gulls hither fly
And pause and dart with shrilly cry,
For all the world is gay, my sweet,
And this a wondrous day, my sweet,
          A wondrous blithesome day.
But what care I how fair the day
If thou, dear one, art far away?
For though the sunbeams brightly dance
I cannot see your merry glance,
Nor hold thy hand so shy and pure,
Nor kiss thy tender lips demure.

II

The long grey skies are sobbing, sweet,
The waves no more with guileless feet
Play gently, softly, on the shore
But rush and snarl mid endless roar;
The breezes soft are of the past
And from the North the icy blast
Numbs all our senses with the cold,
And with his voices harsh and bold
Wild deeds of ravage fiercely sings,
And carries grief beneath his wings.
For all the world is sad, my sweet,
And not a thing is glad, my sweet,

And not a thing is glad.
But though the day were ever night
Without a star or sunbeam bright
Its blackness could not match my heart,
For far away from me thou art
Beyond the wailing restless waves,
Beyond the tomb of nameless graves,
And I cannot thy soft eyes see,
That dance and glance so prettily,
Nor hold thy hand so shy and pure,
Nor kiss thy tender lips demure.

A MOOD

A rollicking breeze, and a frollicking breeze,
     Cajoling and chaffing with coquettish glee,
And winding, and climbing, a whimsical road,
The moon-beams shy haunt and the shadows abode,
Ah! a country road with its earth-breathing smells,
Its heart-stirring heights, and its dallying dells,
Where I, either walking or running may go
May laugh with the winds, or may sigh with them low,
For in me a spirit of daring delight
Compels me to wander this rollicking night
     This rushing night, this gushing night,
     Mid shadows soft, or moon-beams bright,
     Past meadows where the bull frogs sing,
     Past woodlands where the shadows cling;
     Past houses dark and hushed in sleep,
     Past grave-yards where the willows weep,
     Past brooks that sing their little lay
     So loud all night, but hushed all day,

O'er rivers silent, black, and grim,
With grasses floating in their brim;
Up mocking, teasing, little, hill;
Past dancing, glancing, little, rills,
And up or down to left or right
The same compelling, wild, delight!
        No thoughts of rest
        Within the breast;
        Beyond the snare
        Of Reason's eyes
        And wise replies
And on! On! On! into the night!

TO JOSEPH LEE

How strange, how passing strange, when we awake
    And lift our faces to the light
To know that you are lying shut away
    Within the night.

How strange, how passing strange, when we lie down
    To sleep, to know that you are quite
Alone beneath the moon, the stars, the little leaves,
    Within the night.

How strange, how passing strange to know—our eyes
    Will gladden at the fine sweet sight
Of you no more, for now your face is hid
    Within the night.

Strange, strange indeed, these things to us appear
    And yet we know they must be right;
And though your body sleeps, your soul has passed
    Beyond the night.

Ah! friend, it must be sweet to slip from out
    The tears, the pain, the losing fight
Below, and rest, just rest eternally
    Beyond the night.

And sweet it must be too, to know the kiss
    Of Peace, of Peace, the pure, the white
And step beside her hand in hand quite close
    Beyond the night.

TENEBRIS[80]

There is a tree, by day,
That, at night,
Has a shadow,
A hand huge and black,
With fingers long and black.
    All through the dark,
Against the white man's house,
    In the little wind,
The black hand plucks and plucks
    At the bricks.
The bricks are the color of blood and very small.
    Is it a black hand,
    Or is it a shadow?

80. "Tenebris" is one of two published and complete Grimké poems that touch on the theme of blacks taking revenge on whites. The other poem is "Beware Lest He Awakes [Beware When He Awakes (3)]." See all three versions of this poem which follow. Compare these also with the poem "Trees."

UNDER THE DAYS

The days fall upon me;
One by one, they fall,
Like leaves . . . .
They are black,
They are grey.
They are white;
They are shot through with gold and fire.
They fall,
They fall
Ceaselessly.
They cover me,
They crush,
They smother.
Who will ever find me
Under the days?

BEWARE WHEN HE AWAKES [(1)] [81]

A man as clean and white
In thoughts and deeds of Right
As you, you noble man
Advancing in the van

81. Versions 1 and 2 of this poem are in holograph in the Grimké
Collection, MSRC. They, as well as the Third, published version, "Beware
Lest He Awakes," reveal Grimké's politically radical concerns regarding
racism, lynching, and the usually disallowed subject of revenge on whites.
In *Life and Writings of the Grimké Family* (N.p.: self-published, 1951),
Anna Julia Cooper records a fragment of a similar poem by Grimké,
"Enceladus": "Beware, Beware, O Land o' Dreams,/ The black giant sleeps,
unquiet yet awhile;/ Anon, he turns to ease his tired side./ Beware, O Land
o' Dreams!"

Of culture and of might
Engrossing all the light,
You woúld not éven dream
Of letting go[82] one beam
To guide a lowly man
Who strúggles ás he cán
To grope his way along
And if he should go wrong
You bray this playful song[83]
To cheer the waiting throng.

———

But though he virtue lack
And though his skin be black
Beware when he awakes!

———

{When called he follows you
With arm as strong and true,
As thoúgh you wére his friend
And fights unto the end,
That you may quietly live
And in return you give
The gifts of earned meéd
Reliéf from év'ry neéd—?
Ah nó with laúgh and jeér
With curse and cruel sneer
You páy him fór his aíd
And oft with sudden raid
You hang him to a tree
If he should not agree
And asks that he be free

82. Holograph records and eliminates: {sending forth}.
83. Holograph: {playful} is almost illegible and replaces another word.

(You burn him if he speaks
Until your country reeks)}[84]
You spurn him with your scorn
You lash him night and morn
If he should whisper "free"
You hang him to a tree
You hounds of deviltry
You burn him if he speak
Until your freelands reek
From gory peaks to peaks
With bloody, bloody sod—
And still there lives a God!

—

But though he virtue lack
And though his skin be black
Beware when he awakes!

BEWARE WHEN HE AWAKES [(2)]

A man as clean and white
In thoughts and deeds of Right
As thou, thou faultless man
Advancing in the van
Of Culture and of Might.
A miser with thy Light
Thou would'st not even dream
Of letting go one beam
To guide a groping man
Who struggles as he can
To tread the path you tread
Up steps of gushing red

84. Lines in braces are crossed out in holograph; parentheses are Grimké's.

And if he should go wrong
Thou brayest loud and long
In accents strident, strong,
Forgetting that perchance
That in thine own advance
The slips were even more
And marked by clots of gore,
Thou art a nobler man
Because thou hast no tan
And he a very brute
Because of nature's soot.
But though he virtue lack
And though his skin be black
Beware when he awakes!

II

When called he follows thee
O'er hill and vale and sea
As though thou wert his friend
And fights unto the end
That thou may'st safely líve
Then surely thou must give
The olive branch and crown
And gifts of just renown?
At least thou must and can
Call him thy brother man?[85]
Ah no! The cruel jeer
The ready curse and sneer
Are all that he may have
A little less than slave,
He's spúrnéd with thy scorn
And bound both night and morn

---

85. Holograph records and eliminates: {Beside his brother man?}.

In chains of living Death
And if with longing breath
He breathes your air so free
Thou hang'st him to a tree
Thou hounds of deviltry
Thou dost burn him if he speak
Until your freelands reek
From gory peak to peak
With bloody, bloody sod—
And still there lives a God.

—

But list! There slowly nears
A day of endless fears
A day of endless tears
Beware when he awakes!

BEWARE LEST HE AWAKES[86]
[BEWARE WHEN HE AWAKES (3)]

A man as clean and white
In thoughts and deeds of right
As you, you faultless man
Advancing in the van
Of culture and of might;
A miser with your light
You would not even dream
Of letting go one beam,
To guide a groping man,
Who struggles as he can

86. Published version of "Beware When He Awakes," from the *Pilot*
(10 May 1902). Grimké cut out this version and put it in her scrapbook,
now in the Grimké collection.

To tread the path you tread,
Up steps of gushing red;
And if he but go wrong
You bellow loud and long,
In accents, strident, strong;—
Forgetting this, perchance,
That in your own advance,
The slips were even more,
And marked by pools[87] of gore;—
You are a nobler man
Because you have no tan,
And he a very brute
Because of nature's soot;
But though he virtue lack,
And though his skin be black,
Beware lest he awakes!
When called he follows you
With arm as strong and true
As though you were his friend,
And fights unto the end,
That you may safely live;
Then surely you must give
The laurel branch and crown,
And gifts of just renown;
At least you must and can
Call him your brother man!

Ah, no! The cruel jeer
The ready curse and sneer
Are all that he may have—
A little less than slave,
He's spurned by your scorn,

87. Holograph revision to published text: {clots}.

And bound, both night and morn,
In chains of living death;
And if with longing breath
He breathes your air so free,
You hang him to a tree,
You hound of deviltry.
You burn him if he speak,
Until your freelands reek
From gory peak to peak,
With bloody, bloody sod,
And still there lives a God.
But mark! there may draw near
A day red-eyed and drear,
A day of endless fear;
Beware, lest he awakes!

DRAMA

❧ ❧ ❧

RACHEL

A Play in Three Acts

CHARACTERS

Mrs Mary Loving, *a widow.*
Rachel Loving, *her daughter.*
Thomas Loving, *her son.*
Jimmy Mason, *a small boy.*
John Strong, *a friend of the family.*
Mrs. Lane, *a caller.*
Ethel Lane, *her daughter.*
Mary,
Nancy,
Edith,
Jenny,
Louise,
Martha, *little friends of Rachel.*

Time: The first decade of the Twentieth Century.

Act I.   October 16th.
Act II.   October 16th, four years later.
Act III. One week later.

Rachel was originally published in Boston by the Cornhill Company in 1920. Reproduced in this volume by courtesy of Harvard University Library, Cambridge, MA. This play is Grimké's only completed drama. Also see her article " 'Rachel' The Play of the Month" in the nonfiction section of this volume.

PLACE: A northern city. The living room in the small apartment of Mrs. Loving.

All of the characters are colored.

ACT I

The scene is a room scrupulously neat and clean and plainly furnished. The walls are painted green, the woodwork, white. In the rear at the left an open doorway leads into a hall. Its bare, green wall and white baseboard are all that can be seen of it. It leads into the other rooms of the flat. In the center of the rear wall of the room is a window. It is shut. The white sash curtains are pushed to right and left as far as they will go. The green shade is rolled up to the top. Through the window can be seen the red bricks of a house wall, and the tops of a couple of trees moving now and then in the wind. Within the window, and just below the sill, is a shelf upon which are a few potted plants. Between the window and the door is a bookcase full of books and above it, hanging on the wall, a simply framed, inexpensive copy of Millet's "The Reapers." There is a run extending from the right center to just below the right upper entrance. It is the vestibule of the flat. Its open doorway faces the left wall. In the right wall near the front is another window. Here the sash curtains are drawn together and the green shade is partly lowered. The window is up from the bottom. Through it street noises can be heard. In front of this window is an open, threaded sewing-machine. Some frail, white fabric is lying upon it. There is a chair in front of the machine and at the machine's left a small table covered with a green cloth. In the rear of the left wall and directly opposite to the entrance to the flat is the doorway leading into the kitchenette, dishes on shelves can be seen behind glass doors.

In the center of the left wall is a fireplace with a grate in it for coals; over this is a wooden mantel painted white. In the center is a small clock. A pair of vases, green and white in coloring, one at each end, complete the ornaments. Over the mantel is a narrow mirror; and over this, hanging on the wall, Burne-Jones' "Golden Stairs," simply framed. Against the front end of the left wall is an upright piano with a stool in front of it. On top is music neatly piled. Hanging over the piano is Raphael's "Sistine Madonna." In the center of the floor is a green rug, and in the center of this, a rectangular dining-room table, the long side facing front. It is covered with a green table-cloth. Three dining-room chairs are at the table, one at either end and one at the rear facing front. Above the table is a chandelier with four gas jets enclosed by glass globes. At the right front center is a rather shabby arm-chair upholstered in green.

Left and right from the spectator's point of view.

Before the sewing-machine, Mrs. Loving is seated. She looks worried. She is sewing swiftly and deftly by hand upon a waist in her lap. It is a white, beautiful thing and she sews upon it delicately. It is about half-past four in the afternoon; and the light is failing. Mrs. Loving pauses in her sewing, rises and lets the window-shade near her go up to the top. She pushes the sash-curtains to either side, the corner of a red brick house wall being thus brought into view. She shivers slightly, then pushes the window down at the bottom and lowers it a trifle from the top. The street noises become less distinct. She takes off her thimble, rubs her hands gently, puts the thimble on again, and looks at the clock on the mantel. She then reseats herself, with her chair as close to the window as possible and begins to sew. Presently a key is heard, and the door opens and shuts noisily. Rachel comes in from the vestibule. In her left arm she carries four or five books strapped together; under her right, a roll of music. Her hat is twisted over her left ear and her hair is falling in tendrils about her face. She brings into the room with her the spirit of abounding life, health, joy, youth. Mrs. Loving pauses, needle in hand, as soon as she hears the turning key and the banging door. There is a smile on her face. For a second, mother and daughter smile at each other. Then Rachel throws her books upon the dining-room table, places the music there also, but with care, and rushing to her mother, gives her a bear hug and a kiss.

RACHEL: Ma dear! dear, old Ma dear!

MRS. LOVING: Look out for the needle, Rachel! The waist! Oh, Rachel!

RACHEL (*On her knees and shaking her finger directly under her mother's nose.*): You old, old fraud! You know you adore being hugged. I've a good mind . . .

MRS. LOVING: Now, Rachel, please! Besides, I know your tricks. You think you can make me forget you are late. What time is it?

RACHEL (*Looking at the clock and expressing surprise*): Jiminy Xmas! (*Whistles*) Why, it's five o'clock!

MRS. LOVING (*Severely*): Well!

RACHEL (*Plaintively*): Now, Ma dear, you're going to be horrid and cross.

MRS. LOVING (*Laughing*): Really, Rachel, that expression is not particularly affecting, when your hat is over your ear, and you look, with your hair over your eyes, exactly like some one's pet poodle. I wonder if you are ever going to grow up and be ladylike.

RACHEL: Oh! Ma dear, I hope not, not for the longest time, two long, long years at least. I just want to be silly and irresponsible, and have you to love and torment, and, of course, Tom, too.

MRS. LOVING (*Smiling down at Rachel*): You'll not make me forget, young lady. Why are you late, Rachel?

RACHEL: Well, Ma dear, I'm your pet poodle, and my hat is over my ear, and I'm late, for the loveliest reason.

MRS. LOVING: Don't be silly, Rachel.

RACHEL: That may sound silly, but it isn't. And please don't "Rachel" me so much. It was honestly one whole hour ago when I opened the front door down stairs. I know it was, because I heard the postman telling some one it was four o'clock. Well, I climbed the first flight, and was just starting up the second, when a little shrill voice said, " 'Lo!" I raised my eyes, and there, half-way up the stairs, sitting in the middle of a step, was just the dearest, cutest, darlingest little brown baby boy you ever saw. " 'Lo! yourself," I said. "What are you doing, and who are you anyway?" "I'm Jimmy; and I'm widing to New York on the choo-choo tars." As he looked entirely too young to be going such a distance by himself, I asked him if I might go too. For a minute or two he considered the question and me very seriously, and then he said, " 'Es," and made room for me on the step beside him. We've been everywhere: New York, Chicago, Boston, London, Paris and Oshkosh. I wish you could have heard him say that last place. I suggested going there just to hear him. Now, Ma dear, is it any wonder I am late? See all the places we have been in just one "teeny, weeny" hour? We would have been traveling yet, but his horrid, little mother came out and called him in. They're in the flat below, the new people. But before he went, Ma dear, he said the "cunningest" thing. He said, "Will you tum out an' p'ay wif me aden in two minutes?" I nearly hugged him to death, and it's a wonder my hat is on my head at all. Hats are such unimportant nuisances anyway!

MRS. LOVING: Unimportant nuisances! What ridiculous

language you do use, Rachel! Well, I'm no prophet, but I see very distinctly what is going to happen. This little brown baby will be living here night and day. You're not happy unless some child is trailing along in your rear.

RACHEL (*Mischievously*): Now, Ma dear, whose a hypocrite? What? I suppose you don't like children! I can tell you one thing, though, it won't be my fault if he isn't here night and day. Oh, I wish he were all mine, every bit of him! Ma dear, do you suppose that "she woman" he calls mother would let him come up here until it is time for him to go to bed? I'm going down there this minute. (*Rises impetuously*).

MRS. LOVING: Rachel, for Heaven's sake! No! I am entirely too busy and tired today without being bothered with a child romping around in here.

RACHEL (*Reluctantly and a trifle petulantly*): Very well, then. (*For several moments she watches her mother, who has begun to sew again. The displeasure vanishes from her face.*) Ma dear!

MRS. LOVING: Well.

RACHEL: Is there anything wrong today?

MRS. LOVING: I'm just tired, chickabiddy, that's all.

RACHEL (*Moves over to the table. Mechanically takes off her hat and coat and carries them out into the entryway of the flat. She returns and goes to the looking glass over the fireplace and tucks in the tendrils of her hair in rather a preoccupied manner. The electric doorbell rings. She returns to the speaking tube in the vestibule. Her voice is heard answering*): Yes!—Yes!—No, I'm not Mrs. Loving. She's here, yes!—What? Oh! come right up! (*Appearing in the doorway.*) Ma dear, it's some man, who is coming for Mrs. Strong's waist.

MRS. LOVING (*Pausing and looking at Rachel*): It is probably her son. She said she would send for it this afternoon.

(*Rachel disappears. A door is heard opening and closing. There is the sound of a man's voice. Rachel ushers in Mr. John Strong.*)

STRONG (*Bowing pleasantly to Mrs. Loving*): Mrs. Loving? (*Mrs. Loving bows, puts down her sewing, rises and goes toward Strong*). My name is Strong. My mother asked me to come by and get her waist this afternoon. She hoped it would be finished.

MRS. LOVING: Yes, Mr. Strong, it is all ready. If you'll sit down a minute, I'll wrap it up for you. (*She goes into hallway leading to other rooms in flat.*)

RACHEL (*Manifestly ill at ease at being left alone with a stranger; attempting, however, to be the polite hostess*): Do sit down, Mr. Strong. (*They both sit.*)

RACHEL (*Nervously after a pause*): It's a very pleasant day, isn't it, Mr. Strong?

STRONG: Yes, very. (*He leans back composedly, his hat on his knee, the faintest expression of amusement in his eyes.*)

RACHEL (*After a pause*): It's quite a climb up to our flat, don't you think?

STRONG: Why, no! It didn't strike me so. I'm not old enough yet to mind stairs.

RACHEL (*Nervously*): Oh! I didn't mean that you are old! Anyone can see you are quite young, that is, of course, not too young, but,—(*Strong laughs quietly*). There! I don't blame you for laughing. I'm always clumsy just like that.

MRS. LOVING (*Calling from the other room*): Rachel, bring me a needle and the sixty cotton, please.

RACHEL: All right, Ma dear! (*Rummages for the cotton in the machine drawer, and upsets several spools upon the floor. To Strong*): You see! I can't even get a spool of cotton without spilling things all over the floor. (*Strong smiles, Rachel picks up the spools and finally gets the cotton and needle.*) Excuse me!

(*Goes out door leading to other rooms. Strong left to himself, looks around casually. The "Golden Stairs" interests him and the "Sistine Madonna."*)

RACHEL (*Reenters, evidently continuing her function of hostess*): We were talking about the climb to our flat, weren't we? You see, when you're poor, you have to live in a top flat. There is always a compensation, though; we have bully—I mean nice air, better light, a lovely view, and nobody "thud-thudding" up and down over our heads night and day. The people below have our "thud-thudding," and it must be something *awful*, especially when Tom and I play "Ivanhoe"✓ and have a tournament up here. We're entirely too old, but we still play. Ma dear rather dreads the climb up three flights, so Tom and I do all the errands. We don't mind climbing the stairs, particularly when we go up two or three at a time,—that is—Tom still does. I can't, Ma dear stopped me. (*Sighs.*) I've got to grow up it seems.

STRONG (*Evidently amused*): It is rather hard being a girl, isn't it?

RACHEL: Oh, no! It's not hard at all. That's the trouble; they won't let me be a girl. I'd love to be.

MRS. LOVING (*Reentering with parcel. She smiles*): My chatterbox, I see, is entertaining you, Mr. Strong. I'm sorry to have kept you waiting, but I forgot, I found, to sew the ruching in the neck. I hope everything is satisfactory. If it isn't, I'll be glad to make any changes.

STRONG (*Who has risen upon her entrance*): Thank you, Mrs. Loving, I'm sure everything is all right. (*He takes the package and bows to her and Rachel. He moves towards the vestibule, Mrs. Loving following him. She passes through the doorway first. Before leaving, Strong turns for a second and looks back quietly at Rachel. He goes out too. Rachel returns to the mirror, looks at her face for a second, and then begins to touch*

*and pat her hair lightly and delicately here and there. Mrs.
Loving returns.*)

RACHEL (*Still at the glass*): He *was* rather nice, wasn't he,
Ma dear?—for a man? (*Laughs.*) I guess my reason's a vain
one,—he let me do all the talking. (*Pauses.*) Strong? Strong?
Ma dear, is his mother the little woman with the sad, black
eyes?

MRS. LOVING (*Resuming her sewing; sitting before the machine*). Yes. I was rather curious, I confess, to see this son of
hers. The whole time I'm fitting her she talks of nothing
else. She worships him. (*Pauses.*) It's rather a sad case, I
believe. She is a widow. Her husband was a doctor and left
her a little money. She came up from the South to educate
this boy. Both of them worked hard and the boy got through
college. Three months he hunted for work that a college man
might expect to get. You see he had the tremendous handicap
of being colored. As the two of them had to live, one day,
without her knowing it, he hired himself out as a waiter. He
has been one now for two years. He is evidently goodness
itself to his mother.

RACHEL (*Slowly and thoughtfully*): Just because he is *colored!*
(*Pauses.*) We sing a song at school, I believe, about "The
land of the free and the home of the brave." What an amusing
nation it is.

MRS. LOVING (*Watching Rachel anxiously*): Come, Rachel,
you haven't time for "amusing nations." Remember, you
haven't practised any this afternoon. And put your books
away; don't leave them on the table. You didn't practise any
this morning either, did you?

RACHEL: No, Ma dear,—didn't wake up in time. (*Goes to
the table and in an abstracted manner puts books on the bookcase;
returns to the table; picks up the roll of sheet music she has brought
home with her; brightens; impulsively.*) Ma dear, just listen to

this lullaby. It's the sweetest thing. I was so "daffy" over it, one of the girls at school lent it to me. (*She rushes to the piano with the music and plays the accompaniment through softly and then sings, still softly and with great expression, Jessie Gaynor's "Slumber Boat"*)—

> Baby's boat's the silver moon;
>   Sailing in the sky,
> Sailing o'er the sea of sleep,
>   While the clouds float by.
>
> Sail, baby, sail,
>   Out upon that sea,
> Only don't forget to sail
>   Back again to me.
>
> Baby's fishing for a dream,
>   Fishing near and far,
> His line a silver moonbeam is,
>   His bait a silver star.
>
> Sail, baby, sail, etc.

Listen, Ma dear, right here. Isn't it lovely? (*Plays and sings very softly and slowly*):

> "Only don't forget to sail
>   Back again to me."

(*Pauses; in hushed tones*) Ma dear, it's so beautiful—it—it hurts.

MRS. LOVING (*Quietly*): Yes, dear, it is pretty.

RACHEL (*For several minutes watches her mother's profile from the piano stool. Her expression is rather wistful*): Ma dear!

MRS. LOVING: Yes, Rachel.

RACHEL: What's the matter?

MRS. LOVING (*Without turning*): Matter! What do you mean?

RACHEL: I don't know. I just *feel* something is not quite right with you.

MRS. LOVING: I'm only tired—that's all.

RACHEL: Perhaps. But—(*Watches her mother a moment or two longer; shakes her head; turns back to the piano. She is thoughtful; looks at her hands in her lap*). Ma dear, wouldn't it be nice if we could keep all the babies in the world—always little babies? Then they'd be always little, and cunning, and lovable; and they could never grow up, then, and—and—be bad. I'm so sorry for mothers, whose little babies—grow up—and—and—are bad.

MRS. LOVING (*Startled; controlling herself, looks at Rachel anxiously, perplexedly. Rachel's eyes are still on her hands. Attempting a light tone*): Come, Rachel, what experience have you had with mothers whose babies have grown up to be bad? You—you talk like an old, old woman.

RACHEL (*Without raising her eyes, quietly*): I *know* I'm not old; but, just the same I know that is true. (*Softly*) And I'm so sorry for the mothers.

MRS. LOVING (*With a forced laugh*): Well, Miss Methuselah, how do you happen to know all this? Mothers whose babies grow up to be bad don't, as a rule, parade their faults before the world.

RACHEL: That's just it—that's *how* you know. They don't talk at all.

MRS. LOVING (*Involuntarily*): Oh! (*Ceases to sew; looks at Rachel sharply; she is plainly worried. There is a long silence. Presently Rachel raises her eyes to Raphael's "Madonna" over the piano. Her expression becomes rapt; then, very softly, her eyes still on the picture, she plays and sings Nevin's "Mighty Lak A Rose"*)—

> Sweetest li'l feller,
>   Ev'rybody knows;
> Dunno what to call him,
>   But he mighty lak' a rose!
> Lookin' at his Mammy

Wid eyes so shiny blue,
Mek' you think that heav'n
    Is comin' clost ter you!

W'en his dar a sleepin'
    In his li'l place
Think I see de angels
    Lookin' thro' de lace:
W'en de dark is fallin',
    W'en de shadders creep,
Den dey comes on tip-toe,
    Ter kiss him in his sleep.

Sweetest li'l feller, etc.

(*With head still raised, after she has finished, she closes her eyes.
Half to herself and slowly*) I think the loveliest thing of all
the lovely things in this world is just (*almost in a whisper*)
being a mother!

MRS. LOVING (*Turns and laughs*): Well, of all the startling
children, Rachel! I am getting to feel, when you're around
as though I'm shut up with dynamite. What next? (*Rachel
rises, goes slowly to her mother, and kneels down beside her.
She does not touch her mother.*) Why so serious, chickabiddy?

RACHEL (*Slowly and quietly*): It is not kind to laugh at
sacred things. When you laughed, it was as though you
laughed—at God!

MRS. LOVING (*Startled*): Rachel!

RACHEL (*Still quietly*): It's true. It was the best in me that
said that—it was God! (*Pauses.*) And, Ma dear, if I believed
that I should grow up and not be a mother, I'd pray to die
now. I've thought about it a lot, Ma dear, and once I
dreamed, and a voice said to me—oh! it was so real—"Rachel,
you are to be a mother to little children." Wasn't that

beautiful? Ever since I have known how Mary felt at the "Annunciation." (*Almost in a whisper*) *God spoke to me through some one, and I believe.* And it has explained so much to me. I know now why I just can't resist any child. I have to love it—it calls me—it—draws me. I want to take care of it, wash it, dress it, live for it. I want the feel of its little warm body against me, its breath on my neck, its hands against my face. (*Pauses thoughtfully for a few moments.*) Ma dear, here's something I don't understand: I love the little black and brown babies best of all. There is something about them that—that—clutches at my heart. Why—why—should they be—oh!—pathetic? I don't understand. It's dim. More than the other babies, I feel that I must protect them. They're in danger, but from what? I don't know. I've tried so hard to understand, but I can't. (*Her face radiant and beautiful.*) Ma dear, I think their white teeth and the clear whites of their big black eyes and their dimples everywhere—are—are (*Breaks off.*) And, Ma dear, because I love them best, I pray God every night to give me, when I grow up, little black and brown babies—to protect and guard. (*Wistfully.*) Now, Ma dear, don't you see why you must never laugh at me again? Dear, dear, Ma dear? (*Buries her head in her mother's lap and sobs.*)

MRS. LOVING (*For a few seconds, sits as though dazed, and then instinctively begins to caress the head in her lap. To herself*) And I suppose my experience is every mother's. Sooner or later—of a sudden she finds her own child a stranger to her. (*To Rachel, very tenderly*) Poor little girl! Poor little chicka-biddy!

RACHEL (*Raising her head*): Why do you say, "Poor little girl," like that? I don't understand. Why, Ma dear, I never saw tears in your eyes before. Is it—is it—because you know the things I do not understand? Oh! it *is* that.

MRS. LOVING (*Simply*): Yes, Rachel, and I cannot save you.

RACHEL: Ma dear, you frighten me. Save me from *what?*

MRS. LOVING: Just life, my little chickabiddy!

RACHEL: Is life so terrible? I had found it mostly beautiful. How can life be terrible, when the world is full of little children?

MRS. LOVING (*Very sadly*): Oh, Rachel! Rachel!

RACHEL: Ma, dear, what have I said?

MRS. LOVING (*Forcing a smile*): Why, the truth, of course, Rachel. Life is not terrible when there are little children— and you—and Tom—and a roof over our heads—and work— and food—and clothes—and sleep at night. (*Pauses.*) Rachel, I am not myself today. I'm tired. Forget what I've said. Come, chickabiddy, wipe your eyes and smile. That's only an imitation smile, but it's better than none. Jump up now, and light the lamp for me, will you? Tom's late, isn't he? I shall want you to go, too, for the rolls and pie for supper.

RACHEL (*Rises rather wearily and goes into the kitchenette. While she is out of the room Mrs. Loving does not move. She sits staring in front of her. The room for some time has been growing dark. Mrs. Loving can just be seen when Rachel reenters with the lamp. She places it on the small table near her mother, adjusts it, so the light falls on her mother's work, and then lowers the window shades at the windows. She still droops. Mrs. Loving, while Rachel is in the room, is industrious. Rachel puts on her hat and coat listlessly. She does not look at the glass.*) Where is the money, Ma dear? I'm ready.

MRS. LOVING: Before you go, Rachel, just give a look at the meat and see if it is cooking all right, will you, dearie?

RACHEL (*Goes out into the kitchenette and presently returns*): It's all right, Ma dear.

MRS. LOVING (*While Rachel is out of the room, she takes her pocket-book out of the machine-drawer, opens it, takes out money and gives it to Rachel upon her return*): A dozen brown rolls, Rachel. Be sure they're brown! And, I guess,—an apple pie. As you and Tom never seem to get enough apple pie, get the largest she has. And here is a quarter. Get some candy—any kind *you* like, Chickabiddy. Let's have a party tonight, I feel extravagant. Why, Rachel! why are you crying?

RACHEL: Nothing, dear Ma dear. I'll be all right when I get in the air. Goodbye! (*Rushes out of the flat. Mrs. Loving sits idle. Presently the outer door of the flat opens and shuts with a bang, and Tom appears. Mrs. Loving begins to work as soon as she hears the banging door.*)

TOM: 'Lo, Ma! Where's Sis,—out? The door's off the latch. (*Kisses his mother and hangs hat in entryway.*)

MRS. LOVING (*Greeting him with the same beautiful smile with which she greeted Rachel*): Rachel just went after the rolls and pie. She'll be back in a few minutes. You're late, Tommy.

TOM: No, Ma—you forget—it's pay day. (*With decided shyness and awkwardness he hands her his wages.*) Here, Ma!

MRS. LOVING (*Proudly counting it*): But, Tommy, this is every bit of it. You'll need some.

TOM: Not yet! (*Constrainedly*) I only wish—. Say, Ma, I hate to see you work so hard. (*Fiercely*) Some day—some day—. (*Breaks off.*)

MRS. LOVING: Son, I'm as proud as though you had given me a million dollars.

TOM (*Emphatically*): I may some day,—you see. (*Abruptly changing the subject*): Gee! Ma, I'm hungry. What's for dinner? Smell's good.

MRS. LOVING: Lamb and dumplings and rice.

TOM: Gee! I'm glad I'm living—and a pie too?

MRS. LOVING: Apple pie, Tommy.

TOM: Say, Ma, don't wake me up. And shall "muzzer's" own little boy set the table?

MRS. LOVING: Thank you, Son.

TOM (*Folds the green cloth, hangs it over the back of the arm-chair, gets white table-cloth from kitchenette and sets the table. The whole time he is whistling blithely a popular air. He lights one of the gas jets over the table*): Ma!

MRS. LOVING: Yes, Son.

TOM: I made "squad" today,—I'm quarterback. Five other fellows tried to make it. We'll all have to buy new hats, now.

MRS. LOVING (*With surprise*): Buy new hats! Why?

TOM (*Makes a ridiculous gesture to show that his head and hers are both swelling*): Honest, Ma, I had to carry my hat in my hand tonight,—couldn't even get it to perch aloft.

MRS. LOVING (*Smiling*): Well, I for one, Son, am not going to say anything to make you more conceited.

TOM: You don't *have* to say anything. Why, Ma, ever since I told you, you can almost look down your own back your head is so high. What? (*Mrs. Loving laughs. The outer door of the flat opens and shuts. Rachel's voice is heard.*)

RACHEL (*Without*): My! that was a "drefful" climb, wasn't it? Ma, I've got something here for you. (*Appears in the doorway carrying packages and leading a little boy by the hand. The little fellow is shy but smiling.*) Hello, Tommy! Here, take these things for me. This is Jimmy. Isn't he a dear? Come, Jimmy. (*Tom carries the packages into the kitchenette. Rachel leads Jimmy to Mrs. Loving.*) Ma dear, this is my brown baby. I'm going to take him right down stairs again. His mother is as sweet as can be, and let me bring him up just to see you. Jimmy, this is Ma dear. (*Mrs. Loving turns expectantly to see the child. Standing before her, he raises his face *to hers with an engaging smile. Suddenly, without word or warning, her body stiffens; her hands grip her sewing convulsively; her eyes stare. She makes no sound.*)

RACHEL (*Frightened*): Ma dear! What is the matter? Tom! Quick! (*Tom reenters and goes to them.*)

MRS. LOVING (*Controlling herself with an effort and breathing hard*): Nothing, dears, nothing. I must be—I am— nervous tonight. (*With a forced smile*) How do-you-do, Jimmy? Now, Rachel—perhaps—don't you think—you had better take him back to his mother? Good-night, Jimmy! (*Eyes the child in a fascinated way the whole time he is in the room. Rachel, very much perturbed, takes the child out.*) Tom, open that window, please! There! That's better! (*Still breathing deeply.*) What a fool I am!

TOM (*Patting his mother awkwardly on the back*): You're all pegged out, that's the trouble—working entirely too hard. Can't you stop for the night and go to bed right after supper?

MRS. LOVING: I'll see, Tommy dear. Now, I must look after the supper.

TOM: Huh! Well, I guess not. How old do you think Rachel and I are anyway? I see; you think we'll break some of this be-au-tiful Hav-i-land china, we bought at the "Five and Ten Cent Store." (*To Rachel who has just reentered wearing a puzzled and worried expression. She is without hat and coat.*) Say, Rachel, do you think you're old enough?

RACHEL: Old enough for what, Tommy?

TOM: To dish up the supper for Ma.

RACHEL (*With attempted sprightliness*): Ma dear thinks nothing can go on in this little flat unless she does it. Let's show her a thing or two. (*They bring in the dinner. Mrs. Loving with trembling hands tries to sew. Tom and Rachel watch her covertly. Presently she gets up.*)

MRS. LOVING: I'll be back in a minute, children. (*Goes out the door that leads to the other rooms of the flat. Tom and Rachel look at each other*).

RACHEL (*In a low voice keeping her eyes on the door*): Why do you suppose she acted so strangely about Jimmy?

TOM: Don't know—nervous, I guess,—worn out. I wish—(*Breaks off*).

RACHEL (*Slowly*): It may be that; but she hasn't been herself this afternoon. I wonder—. Look out! Here she comes!

TOM (*In a whisper*): Liven her up. (*Rachel nods. Mrs. Loving reenters. Both rush to her and lead her to her place at the right end of the table. She smiles and tries to appear cheerful. They sit down, Tom opposite Mrs. Loving and Rachel at the side facing front. Mrs. Loving asks grace. Her voice trembles. She helps the children bountifully, herself sparingly. Every once in a while she stops eating and stares blankly into her plate; then, remembering where she is suddenly, looks around with a start and goes on eating. Tom and Rachel appear not to notice her.*)

TOM: Ma's "some" cook, isn't she?

RACHEL: Is she! Delmonico's isn't in it.

TOM (*Presently*): Say, Rachel, do you remember that Reynolds boy in the fourth year?

RACHEL: Yes. You mean the one who is flat-nosed, freckled, and who squints and sneers?

TOM (*Looking at Rachel admiringly*): The same.

RACHEL (*Vehemently*): I hate him!

MRS. LOVING: Rachel, you do use such violent language. Why hate him?

RACHEL: I do—that's all.

TOM: Ma, if you saw him just once, you'd understand. No one likes him. But, then, what can you expect? His father's in "quod" doing time for something, I don't know just what. One of the fellows says he has a real decent mother, though. She never mentions him in any way, shape or form, he says. Hard on her, isn't it? Bet I'd keep my head shut too;—you'd never get a yap out of me. (*Rachel looks up quickly at her mother; Mrs. Loving stiffens perceptibly, but keeps her eyes on her plate. Rachel catches Tom's eye; silently draws his attention to their mother; and shakes her head warningly at him.*)

TOM (*Continuing hastily and clumsily*): Well, anyway, he called me "Nigger" today. If his face isn't black, his eye is.

RACHEL: Good! Oh! Why did you let the other one go?

TOM (*Grinning*): I knew he said things behind my back; but today he was hopping mad, because I made quarterback. He didn't!

RACHEL: Oh, Tommy! How lovely! Ma dear, did you hear that? (*Chants*) Our Tommy's on the team! Our Tommy's on the team!

TOM (*Trying not to appear pleased*): Ma dear, what did I say about er—er "capital" enlargements?

MRS. LOVING (*Smiling*): You're right, Son.

TOM: I hope you got that "capital," Rachel. How's that for Latin knowledge? Eh?

RACHEL: I don't think much of your knowledge, Tommy dear; but (*continuing to chant*) Our Tommy's on the team! Our Tommy's on the team! Our— (*Breaks off*). I've a good mind to kiss you.

TOM (*Threateningly*): Don't you dare.

RACHEL (*Rising and going toward him*): I will! I will! I will!

TOM (*Rising, too, and dodging her*): No, you don't, young lady. (*A tremendous tussle and scuffle ensues.*)

MRS. LOVING (*Laughing*): For Heaven's sake! children, do stop playing and eat your supper. (*They nod brightly at each other behind her back and return smiling to the table.*)

RACHEL (*Sticking out her tongue at Tom*): I will!

TOM (*Mimicking her*): You won't!

MRS. LOVING: Children! (*They eat for a time in silence.*)

RACHEL: Ma dear, have you noticed Mary Shaw doesn't come here much these days?

MRS. LOVING: Why, that's so, she doesn't. Have you two quarreled?

RACHEL: No, Ma dear. (*Uncomfortably.*) I—think I know the reason—but I don't like to say, unless I'm certain.

TOM: Well, I know. I've seen her lately with those two girls who have just come from the South. Twice she bowed stiffly, and the last time made believe she didn't see me.

RACHEL: Then you think—? Oh! I was afraid it was that.

TOM (*Bitterly*): Yes—we're "niggers"—that's why.

MRS. LOVING (*Slowly and sadly*): Rachel, that's one of the things I can't save you from. I worried considerably about Mary, at first—you do take your friendships so seriously. I knew exactly how it would end. (*Pauses.*) And then I saw that if Mary Shaw didn't teach you the lesson—some one else would. They don't want you, dearies, when you and they grow up. You may have everything in your favor—but they don't *dare* to like you.

RACHEL: I know all that is generally true—but I had hoped that Mary— (*Breaks off*).

TOM: Well, I guess we can still go on living even if people don't speak to us. I'll never bow to *her* again—that's certain.

MRS. LOVING: But, Son, that wouldn't be polite, if she bowed to you first..

TOM: Can't help it. I guess I can be blind, too.

MRS. LOVING (*Wearily*): Well—perhaps you are right—I don't know. It's the way I feel about it too—but—but I wish my son always to be a *gentleman*.

Tom: If being a *gentleman* means not being a *man*—I don't wish to be one.

Rachel: Oh! well, perhaps we're wrong about Mary—I hope we are. (*Sighs.*) Anyway, let's forget it. Tommy guess what I've got. (*Rises, goes out into entryway swiftly, and returns holding up a small bag.*) Ma dear treated. Guess!

Tom: Ma, you're a thoroughbred. Well, let's see—it's—a dozen dill pickles?

Rachel: Oh! stop fooling.

Tom: I'm not. Tripe?

Rachel: Silly!

Tom: Hog's jowl?

Rachel: Ugh! Give it up—quarterback.

Tom: Pig's feet?

Rachel (*In pretended disgust*): Oh! Ma dear—send him from the table. It's CANDY!

Tom: Candy? Funny, I never thought of that! And I was just about to say some nice, delicious chitlings. Candy! Well! Well! (*Rachel disdainfully carries the candy to her mother, returns to her own seat with the bag and helps herself. She ignores Tom.*)

Tom (*In an aggrieved voice*): You see, Ma, how she treats me. (*In affected tones*) I have a good mind, young lady to punish you, er—er corporeally speaking. Tut! Tut! I have a mind to master thee—I mean—you. Methinks that if I should advance upon you, apply, perchance, two or three digits to your glossy locks and extract—aha!—say, a strand—you would no more defy me. (*He starts to rise.*)

Mrs. Loving (*Quickly and sharply*): Rachel! give Tom the candy and stop playing. (*Rachel obeys. They eat in silence. The old depression returns. When the candy is all gone, Rachel pushes her chair back, and is just about to rise, when her mother,*

who is very evidently nerving herself for something, stops her.)
Just a moment, Rachel. (*Pauses, continuing slowly and very
seriously.*) Tom and Rachel! I have been trying to make up
my mind for some time whether a certain thing is my duty
or not. Today—I have decided it is. You are old enough,
now,—and I see you ought to be told. Do you know what
day this is? (*Both Tom and Rachel have been watching their
mother intently.*) It's the sixteenth of October. Does that mean
anything to either of you?

Tom and Rachel (*Wonderingly*): No.

Mrs. Loving (*Looking at both of them thoughtfully, half to
herself*): No—I don't know why it should. (*Slowly*) Ten years
ago—today—your father and your half-brother died.

Tom: I do remember, now, that you told us it was in
October.

Rachel (*With a sigh*): That explains—today.

Mrs. Loving: Yes, Rachel. (*Pauses.*) Do you know—how
they—died?

Tom and Rachel: Why, no.

Mrs. Loving: Did it ever strike you as strange—that
they—died— the same day?

Tom: Well, yes.

Rachel: We often wondered, Tom and I; but—but somehow we never quite dared to ask you. You—-you—always
refused to talk about them, you know, Ma dear.

Mrs. Loving: Did you think—that—perhaps—the reason—I—I—wouldn't talk about them—was—because, because—I was ashamed—of them? (*Tom and Rachel look uncomfortable.*)

Rachel: Well, Ma dear—we—we—did—wonder.

Mrs. Loving (*Questioningly*): And you thought?

Rachel (*Haltingly*): W-e-l-l—

Mrs. Loving (*Sharply*): Yes?

Tom: Oh! come, now, Rachel, you know we haven't bothered about it at all. Why should we? We've been happy.

Mrs. Loving: But when you have thought—you've been ashamed? (*Intensely*) Have you?

Tom: Now, Ma, aren't you making a lot out of nothing?

Mrs. Loving (*Slowly*): No. (*Half to herself*) You evade—both—of you. You *have* been ashamed. And I never dreamed until today you *could* take it this way. How blind—how almost criminally blind, I have been.

Rachel (*Tremulously*): Oh! Ma dear, don't! (*Tom and Rachel watch their mother anxiously and uncomfortably. Mrs. Loving is very evidently nerving herself for something.*)

Mrs. Loving (*Very slowly, with restrained emotion*): Tom—and Rachel!

Tom: Ma!

Rachel: Ma dear! (*A tense, breathless pause*).

Mrs. Loving (*Bracing herself*): They—they—were lynched!!

Tom and Rachel (*In a whisper*): Lynched!

Mrs. Loving (*Slowly, laboring under strong but restrained emotion*): Yes—by Christian people—in a Christian land. We found out afterwards they were all church members in good standing—the best people. (*A silence.*) Your father was a man among men. He was a fanatic. He was a Saint!

Tom (*Breathing with difficulty*): Ma—can you—will you—tell us—about it?

Mrs. Loving: I believe it to be my duty. (*A silence.*) When I married your father I was a widow. My little George was seven years old. From the very beginning he worshiped your father. He followed him around—just like a little dog. All children were like that with him. I myself have never seen anybody like him. "Big" seems to fit him better than any other word. He was big-bodied—big-souled. His loves were big and his hates. You can imagine, then, how the wrongs of the Negro—ate into his soul. (*Pauses.*) He was utterly fearless. (*A silence.*) He edited and owned, for several years, a small negro paper. In it he said a great many daring things. I used to plead with him to be more careful. I was always afraid for him. For a long time, nothing happened— he was too important to the community. And then—one night—ten years ago—a mob made up of the respectable people in the town lynched an innocent black man—and what was worse—they knew him to be innocent. A white man was guilty. I never saw your father so wrought up over anything: he couldn't eat; he couldn't sleep; he brooded night and day over it. And then—realizing fully the great risk he was running, although I begged him not to—and all his friends also—he deliberately and calmly went to work and published a most terrific denunciation of that mob. The old prophets in the Bible were not more terrible than he. A day or two later, he received an anonymous letter, very evidently from an educated man, calling upon him to retract his words in the next issue. If he refused his life was threatened. The next week's issue contained an arraignment as frightful, if not more so, than the previous one. Each word was white-hot, searing. That night, some dozen masked men came to our house.

RACHEL (*Moaning*): Oh, Ma dear! Ma dear!

MRS. LOVING (*Too absorbed to hear*): We were not asleep— your father and I. They broke down the front door and made their way to our bedroom. Your father kissed me—and took up his revolver. It was always loaded. They broke down the door. (*A silence. She continues slowly and quietly*) I tried to shut my eyes—I could not. Four masked men fell—they did not move any more—after a little. (*Pauses.*) Your father was finally overpowered and dragged out. In the hall—my little seventeen-year-old George tried to rescue him. Your father begged him not to interfere. He paid no attention. It ended in their dragging them both out. (*Pauses.*) My little George—was—a man! (*Controls herself with an effort.*) He never made an outcry. His last words to me were: "Ma, I am glad to go with Father." I could only nod to him. (*Pauses.*) While they were dragging them down the steps, I crept into the room where you were. You were both asleep. Rachel, I remember, was smiling. I knelt down by you—and covered my ears with my hands—and waited. I could not pray—I couldn't for a long time—afterwards. (*A silence.*) It was very still when I finally uncovered my ears. The only sounds were the faint rustle of leaves and the "tap-tapping of the twig of a tree" against the window. I hear it still—sometimes in my dreams. *It was the tree—where they were.* (*A silence.*) While I had knelt there waiting—I had made up my mind what to do. I dressed myself and then I woke you both up and dressed you. (*Pauses.*) We set forth. It was a black, still night. Alternately dragging you along and carrying you—I walked five miles to the house of some friends. They took us in, and we remained there until I had seen my dead laid comfortably at rest. They lent me money to come North—I couldn't bring you up—in the South. (*A silence.*) Always remember this: There never lived anywhere—or at any time—any two whiter or more beautiful souls. God gave me one for a husband and one for a son and I am proud. (*Brokenly*) You—must—be—proud—too. (*A long silence. Mrs. Loving bows her head in her hands. Tom controls himself with an effort. Rachel creeps softly to her mother, kneels beside her and lifts the hem of her dress to her lips. She does not dare touch her. She adores her with her eyes.*)

MRS. LOVING (*Presently raising her head and glancing at the clock*): Tom, it's time, now, for you to go to work. Rachel and I will finish up here.

TOM (*Still laboring under great emotion goes out into the entryway and comes back and stands in the doorway with his cap. He twirls it around and around nervously*): I want you to know, Ma, before I go—how—how proud I am. Why, I didn't believe two people could be like that—and live. And then to find out that one—was your own father—and one—your own brother.—It's wonderful! I'm—not much yet, Ma, but— I've—I've just got to be something now. (*Breaks off.*) (*His face becomes distorted with passion and hatred.*) When I think— when I think—of those devils with white skins—living somewhere today—living and happy—I—see—red! I—I—good-bye! (*Rushes out, the door bangs.*)

MRS. LOVING (*Half to herself*): I was afraid—of just that. I wonder—if I did the wise thing—after all.

RACHEL (*With a gesture infinitely tender, puts her arms around her mother*): Yes, Ma dear, you did. And, hereafter, Tom and I share and share alike with you. To think, Ma dear, of ten years of this—all alone. It's wicked! (*A short silence.*)

MRS. LOVING: And, Rachel, about that dear, little boy, Jimmy.

RACHEL: Now, Ma dear, tell me tomorrow. You've stood enough for one day.

MRS. LOVING: No, it's better over and done with—all at once. If I had seen that dear child suddenly any other day than this—I might have borne it better. When he lifted his little face to me—and smiled—for a moment—I thought it was the end—of all things. Rachel, he is the image of my boy—my George!

RACHEL: Ma dear!

MRS. LOVING: And Rachel—it will hurt—to see him again.

RACHEL: I understand, Ma dear. (*A silence. Suddenly*) Ma

dear, I am beginning to see—to understand—so much. (*Slowly and thoughtfully*) Ten years ago, all things being equal, Jimmy might have been—George? Isn't that so?

MRS. LOVING: Why—yes, if I understand you.

RACHEL: I guess that doesn't sound very clear. It's only getting clear to me, little by little. Do you mind my thinking out loud to you?

MRS. LOVING: No, chickabiddy.

RACHEL: If Jimmy went South now—and grew up—he might be—a George?

MRS. LOVING: Yes.

RACHEL: Then, the South is full of tens, hundreds, thousands of little boys, who, one day may be—and some of them with certainty—Georges?

MRS. LOVING: Yes, Rachel.

RACHEL: And the little babies, the dear, little, helpless babies, being born today—now—and those who will be, tomorrow, and all the tomorrows to come—have *that* sooner or later to look forward to? They will laugh and play and sing and be happy and grow up, perhaps, and be ambitious— just for *that*?

MRS. LOVING: Yes, Rachel.

RACHEL: Then, everywhere, everywhere, throughout the South, there are hundreds of dark mothers who live in fear, terrible, suffocating fear, whose rest by night is broken, and whose joy by day in their babies on their hearts is three parts—pain. Oh, I know this is true—for this is the way I should feel, if I were little Jimmy's mother. How horrible! Why—it would be more merciful—to strangle the little things at birth. And so this nation—this white Christian nation— has deliberately set its curse upon the most beautiful—the most holy thing in life—motherhood! Why—it—makes— you doubt—God!

Mrs. Loving: Oh, hush! little girl. Hush!

Rachel (*Suddenly with a great cry*): Why, Ma dear, *you know. You* were a *mother, George's mother*. So, this is what it means. Oh, Ma dear! Ma dear! (*Faints in her mother's arms.*)

ACT II

Time: *October sixteenth, four years later; seven o'clock in the morning.*

Scene: *The same room. There have been very evident improvements made. The room is not so bare; it is cosier. On the shelf, before each window, are potted red geraniums. At the windows are green denim drapery curtains covering fresh white dotted Swiss inner curtains. At each doorway are green denim portieres. On the wall between the kitchenette and the entrance to the outer rooms of the flat, a new picture is hanging, Millet's "The Man With the Hoe." Hanging against the side of the run that faces front is Watts's "Hope." There is another easy-chair at the left front. The table in the center is covered with a white table-cloth. A small asparagus fern is in the middle of this. When the curtain rises there is the clatter of dishes in the kitchenette. Presently Rachel enters with dishes and silver in her hands. She is clad in a bungalow apron. She is noticeably all of four years older. She frowns as she sets the table. There is a set expression about the mouth. A child's voice is heard from the rooms within.*

Jimmy (*Still unseen*): Ma Rachel!

Rachel (*Pauses and smiles*): What is it, Jimmy boy?

Jimmy (*Appearing in rear doorway, half-dressed, breathless, and tremendously excited over something. Rushes toward Rachel*): Three guesses! Three guesses! Ma Rachel!

RACHEL (*Her whole face softening*): Well, let's see—maybe there is a circus in town.

JIMMY: No siree! (*In a sing-song*) You're not right! You're not right!

RACHEL: Well, maybe Ma Loving's going to take you somewhere.

JIMMY: No! (*Vigorously shaking his head*) It's—

RACHEL (*Interrupting quickly*): You said I could have three guesses, honey. I've only had two.

JIMMY: I thought you had three. How many are three?

RACHEL (*Counting on her fingers*): One! Two! Three! I've only had one! two!—See? Perhaps Uncle Tom is going to give you some candy.

JIMMY (*Dancing up and down*): No! No! No! (*Catches his breath*) I leaned over the bath-tub, way over, and got hold of the chain with the button on the end, and dropped it into the little round place in the bottom. And then I runned lots and lots of water in the tub and climbed over and fell in splash! just like a big stone; (*Loudly*) and took a bath all by myself alone.

RACHEL (*Laughing and hugging him*): All by yourself, honey? You ran the water, too, boy, not "runned" it. What I want to know is, where was Ma Loving all this time?

JIMMY: I stole in "creepy-creep" and looked at Ma Loving and she was awful fast asleep. (*Proudly*) Ma Rachel, I'm a "nawful," big boy now, aren't I? I are almost a man, aren't I?

RACHEL: Oh! Boy, I'm getting tired of correcting you— "I am almost a man, am I not?" Jimmy, boy, what will Ma Rachel do, if you grow up? Why, I won't have a little boy any more! Honey, you mustn't grow up, do you hear? You mustn't.

JIMMY: Oh, yes, I must; and you'll have me just the same,

Ma Rachel. I'm going to be a policeman and make lots of money for you and Ma Loving and Uncle Tom, and I'm going to buy you some trains and fire-engines, and little, cunning ponies, and some rabbits, and some great 'normous banks full of money—lots of it. And then, we are going to live in a great, big castle and eat lots of ice cream, all the time, and drink lots and lots of nice pink lemonade.

RACHEL: What a generous Jimmy boy! (*Hugs him.*) Before I give you "morning kiss," I must see how clean my boy is. (*Inspects teeth, ears and neck.*) Jimmy, you're sweet and clean enough to eat. (*Kisses him; he tries to strangle her with hugs.*) Now the hands. Oh! Jimmy, look at those nails! Oh! Jimmy! (*Jimmy wriggles and tries to get his hands away.*) Honey, get my file off of my bureau and go to Ma Loving; she must be awake by this time. Why, honey, what's the matter with your feet?

JIMMY: I don't know. I thought they looked kind of queer, myself. What's the matter with them?

RACHEL (*Laughing*): You have your shoes on the wrong feet.

JIMMY (*Bursts out laughing*): Isn't that most 'normously funny? I'm a case, aren't I—(*pauses thoughtfully*) I mean— am I not, Ma Rachel?

RACHEL: Yes, honey, a great big case of molasses. Come, you must hurry now, and get dressed. You don't want to be late for school, you know.

JIMMY: Ma Rachel! (*Shyly*) I—I have been making something for you all the morning—ever since I waked up. It's awful nice. It's—stoop down, Ma Rachel, please—a great, big (*puts both arms about her neck and gives her a noisy kiss. Rachel kisses him in return, then pushes his head back. For a long moment they look at each other; and, then, laughing joyously, he makes believe he is a horse, and goes prancing out of the room.*

Rachel, with a softer, gentler expression, continues setting the table. Presently, Mrs. Loving, bent and worn-looking, appears in the doorway in the rear. She limps a trifle.)

MRS. LOVING: Good morning, dearie. How's my little girl, this morning? (*Looks around the room.*) Why, where's Tom? I was certain I heard him running the water in the tub, sometime ago. (*Limps into the room.*)

RACHEL (*Laughing*): Tom isn't up yet. Have you seen Jimmy?

MRS. LOVING: Jimmy? No. I didn't know he was awake, even.

RACHEL (*Going to her mother and kissing her*): Well! What do you think of that! I sent the young gentleman to you, a few minutes ago, for help with his nails. He is very much grown up this morning, so I suppose that explains why he didn't come to you. Yesterday, all day, you know, he was a puppy. No one knows what he will be by tomorrow. All of this, Ma dear, is preliminary to telling you that Jimmy boy has stolen a march on you, this morning.

MRS. LOVING: Stolen a march! How?

RACHEL: It appears that he took his bath all by himself and, as a result, he is so conceited, peacocks aren't in it with him.

MRS. LOVING: I heard the water running and thought, of course, it was Tom. Why, the little rascal! I must go and see how he has left things. I was just about to wake him up.

RACHEL: Rheumatism's not much better this morning, Ma dear. (*Confronting her mother*) Tell me the truth, now, did you or did you not try that liniment I bought you yesterday?

MRS. LOVING (*Guiltily*): Well, Rachel, you see—it was this way, I was—I was so tired, last night,—I—I really forgot it.

RACHEL: I thought as much. Shame on you!

MRS. LOVING: As soon as I walk around a bit it will be all right. It always is. It's bad, when I first get up—that's all. I'll be spry enough in a few minutes. (*Limps to the door; pauses*) Rachel, I don't know why the thought should strike me, but how very strangely things turn out. If any one had told me four years ago that Jimmy would be living with us, I should have laughed at him. Then it hurt to see him; now it would hurt not to. (*Softly*) Rachel, sometimes—I wonder— if, perhaps, God—hasn't relented a little—and given me back my boy,—my George.

RACHEL: The whole thing was strange, wasn't it?

MRS. LOVING: Yes, God's ways are strange and often very beautiful; perhaps all would be beautiful—if we only understood.

RACHEL: God's ways are certainly very mysterious. Why, of all the people in this apartment-house, should Jimmy's father and mother be the only two to take the smallpox, and the only two to die. It's queer!

MRS. LOVING: It doesn't seem like two years ago, does it?

RACHEL: Two years, Ma dear! Why it's three the third of January.

MRS. LOVING: Are you sure, Rachel?

RACHEL (*Gently*): I don't believe I could ever forget that, Ma dear.

MRS. LOVING: No, I suppose not. That is one of the differences between youth and old age—youth attaches tremendous importance to dates,—old age does not.

RACHEL (*Quickly*): Ma dear, don't talk like that. You're not old.

MRS. LOVING: Oh! yes, I am, dearie. It's sixty long years since I was born; and I am much older that that, much older.

RACHEL: Please, Ma dear, please!

MRS. LOVING (*Smiling*): Very well, dearie, I won't say it

any more. (*A pause.*) By the way,—how—does Tom strike you, these days?

RACHEL (*Avoiding her mother's eye*): The same old, bantering, cheerful Tom. Why?

MRS. LOVING: I know he's all that, dearie, but it isn't possible for him to be really cheerful. (*Pauses; goes on wistfully*) When you are little, we mothers can kiss away all the trouble, but when you grow up—and go out—into the world—and get hurt—we are helpless. There is nothing we can do.

RACHEL: Don't worry about Tom, Ma dear, he's game. He doesn't show the white feather.

MRS. LOVING: Did you see him, when he came in, last night?

RACHEL: Yes.

MRS. LOVING: Had he had—any luck?

RACHEL: No. (*Firmly*) Ma dear, we may as well face it— it's hopeless, I'm afraid.

MRS. LOVING: I'm afraid—you are right. (*Shakes her head sadly*) Well, I'll go and see how Jimmy has left things and wake up Tom, if he isn't awake yet. It's the waking up in the mornings that's hard. (*Goes limping out rear door. Rachel frowns as she continues going back and forth between the kitchenette and the table. Presently Tom appears in the door at the rear. He watches Rachel several moments before he speaks or enters. Rachel looks grim enough.*)

TOM (*Entering and smiling*): Good-morning, "Merry Sunshine"! Have you, perhaps, been taking a—er—prolonged draught of that very delightful beverage—vinegar? (*Rachel, with a knife in her hand, looks up unsmiling. In pretended fright*) I take it all back, I'm sure. May I request, humbly, that before I press my chaste, morning salute upon your forbidding lips, that you—that you—that you—er—in some way rid yourself of that—er—knife? (*Bows as Rachel puts it down.*)

I thank you. (*He comes to her and tips her head back; gently*) What's the matter with my little Sis?

RACHEL (*Her face softening*): Tommy dear, don't mind me. I'm getting wicked, I guess. At present I feel just like— — like curdled milk. Once upon a time, I used to have quite a nice disposition, didn't I, Tommy?

TOM (*Smiling*): Did you, indeed! I'm not going to flatter you. Well, brace yourself, old lady. Ready, One! Two! Three! Go! (*Kisses her, then puts his hands on either side of her face, and raising it, looks down into it.*) You're a pretty, decent little sister, Sis, that's what T. Loving thinks about it; and he knows a thing or two. (*Abruptly looking around*) Has the paper come yet?

RACHEL: I haven't looked, it must have, though, by this time. (*Tom, hands in his pockets, goes into the vestibule. He whistles. The outer door opens and closes, and presently he saunters back, newspaper in hand. He lounges carelessly in the arm-chair and looks at Rachel.*)

TOM: May T. Loving be of any service to you?

RACHEL: Service! How?

TOM: May he run, say, any errands, set the table, cook the breakfast? Anything?

RACHEL (*Watching the lazy figure*): You look like working.

TOM (*Grinning*): It's at least—polite—to offer.

RACHEL: You can't do anything; I don't trust you to do it right. You may just sit there, and read your paper—and try to behave yourself.

TOM (*In affectedly meek tones*): Thank you, ma'am. (*Opens the paper, but does not read. Jimmy presently enters riding around the table on a cane. Rachel peeps in from the kitchenette and smiles. Tom puts down his paper.*) 'Lo! Big Fellow, what's this?

JIMMY (*Disgustedly*): How can I hear? I'm miles and miles

away yet. (*Prances around and around the room; presently stops near Tom, attempting a gruff voice*) Good-morning!

TOM (*Lowering his paper again*): Bless my stars! Who's this? Well, if it isn't Mr. Mason! How-do-you-do, Mr. Mason? That's a beautiful horse you have there. He limps a trifle in his left, hind, front foot, though.

JIMMY: He doesn't!

TOM: He does!

JIMMY (*Fiercely*): He doesn't!

TOM (*As fiercely*): I say he does!

MRS. LOVING (*Appearing in the doorway in the rear*): For Heaven's sake! What is this? Good-morning, Tommy.

TOM (*Rising and going toward his mother, Jimmy following astride of the cane in his rear*): Good-morning, Ma. (*Kisses her; lays his head on her shoulder and makes believe he is crying; in a high falsetto*) Ma! Jimmy says his horse doesn't limp in his hind, front right leg, and I say he does.

JIMMY (*Throws his cane aside, rolls on the floor and kicks up his heels. He roars with laughter*): I think Uncle Tom is funnier than any clown in the "Kickus."

TOM (*Raising his head and looking down at Jimmy; Rachel stands in the kitchenette doorway*): In the *what*, Jimmy?

JIMMY: In the "kickus," of course.

TOM: "Kickus"! "Kickus"! Oh, Lordy! (*Tom and Rachel shriek with laughter; Mrs. Loving looks amused; Jimmy, very much affronted, gets upon his feet again. Tom leans over and swings Jimmy high in the air.*) Boy, you'll be the death of me yet. Circus, son! Circus!

JIMMY (*From on high, soberly and with injured dignity*): Well, I thinks "Kickus" and circus are very much alike. Please put me down.

RACHEL ((*From the doorway*): We laugh, honey, because we love you so much.

JIMMY (*Somewhat mollified, to Tom*): Is that so, Uncle Tom?

TOM: Surest thing in the world! (*Severely*) Come, get down, young man. Don't you know you'll wear my arms out? Besides, there is something in my lower vest pocket, that's just dying to come to you. Get down, I say.

JIMMY (*Laughing*): How can I get down? (*Wriggles around.*)

TOM: How should I know? Just get down, of course. (*Very suddenly puts Jimmy down on his feet. Jimmy tries to climb up over him.*)

JIMMY: Please sit down, Uncle Tom?

TOM (*In feigned surprise*): Sit down! What for?

JIMMY (*Pummeling him with his little fists, loudly*): Why, you said there was something for me in your pocket.

TOM (*Sitting down*): So I did. How forgetful I am!

JIMMY (*Finding a bright, shiny penny, shrieks*): Oh! Oh! Oh! (*Climbs up and kisses Tom noisily.*)

TOM: Why, Jimmy! You embarrass me. My! My!

JIMMY: What is 'barrass?

TOM: You make me blush.

JIMMY: What's that?

MRS. LOVING: Come, come, children! Rachel has the breakfast on the table. (*Tom sits in Jimmy's place and Jimmy tries to drag him out.*)

TOM: What's the matter, now?

JIMMY: You're in *my* place.

TOM: Well, can't you sit in mine?

JIMMY (*Wistfully*): I wants to sit by my Ma Rachel.

TOM: Well, so do I.

RACHEL: Tom, stop teasing Jimmy. Honey, don't you let him bother you; ask him please prettily.

JIMMY: Please prettily, Uncle Tom.

TOM: Oh! well then. (*Gets up and takes his own place. They sit as they did in Act I, only Jimmy sits between Tom, at the end, and Rachel.*)

JIMMY (*Loudly*): Oh, goody! goody! goody! We've got sau-sa-ges.

MRS. LOVING: Sh!

JIMMY (*Silenced for a few moments; Rachel ties a big napkin around his neck, and prepares his breakfast. He breaks forth again suddenly and excitedly*): Uncle Tom!

TOM: Sir?

JIMMY: I took a bath this morning, all by myself alone, in the bath-tub, and I ranned, no (*Doubtfully*) I runned, I think—the water all in it, and got in it all by myself; and Ma Loving thought it was you; but it was *me*.

TOM (*In feignedly severe tones*): See here, young man, this won't do. Don't you know I'm the only one who is allowed to do that here? It's a perfect waste of water—that's what it is.

JIMMY (*Undaunted*): Oh! no, you're not the only one, 'cause Ma Loving and Ma Rachel and me—alls takes baths every single morning. So, there!

TOM: You 'barrass me. (*Jimmy opens his mouth to ask a question; Tom quickly*) Young gentleman, your mouth is open. Close it, sir; close it.

MRS. LOVING: Tom, you're as big a child exactly as Jimmy.

TOM (*Bowing to right and left*): You compliment me. I thank you, I am sure.

(*They finish in silence.*)

JIMMY (*Sighing with contentment*): I'm through, Ma Rachel.

MRS. LOVING: Jimmy, you're a big boy, now, aren't you? (*Jimmy nods his head vigorously and looks proud.*) I wonder if you're big enough to wash your own hands, this morning?

JIMMY (*Shrilly*): Yes, ma'am.

MRS. LOVING: Well, if they're beautifully clean, I'll give you another penny.

JIMMY (*Excitedly to Rachel*): Please untie my napkin, Ma Rachel! (*Rachel does so.*) "Excoose" me, please.

MRS. LOVING AND RACHEL: Certainly. (*Jimmy climbs down and rushes out at the rear doorway.*)

MRS. LOVING (*Solemnly and slowly; breaking the silence*): Rachel, do you know what day this is?

RACHEL (*Looking at her plate; slowly*): Yes, Ma dear.

MRS. LOVING: Tom.

TOM (*Grimly and slowly*): Yes, Ma.

(*A silence.*)

MRS. LOVING (*Impressively*): We must never—as long—as we live—forget this day.

RACHEL: No, Ma dear.

TOM: No, Ma.

(*Another silence.*)

TOM (*Slowly; as though thinking aloud*): I hear people talk about God's justice—and I wonder. There, are you, Ma. There isn't a sacrifice—that you haven't made. You're still working your fingers to the bone—sewing—just so all of us may keep on living. Rachel is a graduate in Domestic Science; she was high in her class; most of the girls below her in rank have positions in the schools. I'm an electrical engineer—and I've tried steadily for several months—to practice my profession. It seems our educations aren't of much use to us: we aren't allowed to make good—because our skins are dark. (*Pauses.*) And, in the South today, there are white men— (*Controls himself*). They have everything; they're well-dressed, well-fed, well-housed; they're prosperous in business; they're important politically; they're pillars in the church. I know all this is true—I've inquired. Their children (our ages, some of them) are growing up around them; and they are having a square deal handed out to them—college, position, wealth, and best of all, freedom, without galling restrictions, to work out their own salvations. With ability, they may become— anything; and all this will be true of their children's children after them. (*A pause.*) Look at us—and look at them. We are destined to failure—they, to success. Their children shall grow up in hope; ours, in despair. Our hands are clean;— theirs are red with blood—red with the blood of a noble man—and a boy. They're nothing but low, cowardly, bestial murderers. The scum of the earth shall succeed. —God's justice, I suppose.

MRS. LOVING (*Rising and going to Tom; brokenly*): Tom, promise me—one thing.

TOM (*Rises gently*): What is it, Ma?

MRS. LOVING: That—you'll try—not to lose faith—in God. I've been where you are now—and it's black. Tom, we don't understand God's ways. My son, I know, now—He is beautiful. Tom, won't you try to believe, again?

TOM (*Slowly, but not convincingly*): I'll try, Ma.

MRS. LOVING (*Sighs*): Each one, I suppose, has to work out his own salvation. (*After a pause*) Rachel, if you'll get Jimmy ready, I'll take him to school. I've got to go down town shopping for a customer, this morning. (*Rachel rises and goes out the rear doorway; Mrs. Loving, limping very slightly now, follows. She turns and looks back yearningly at Tom, who has seated himself again, and is staring unseeingly at his plate. She goes out. Tom sits without moving until he hears Mrs. Loving's voice within and Rachel's faintly; then he gets the paper, sits in the arm-chair and pretends to read.*)

MRS. LOVING (*From within*): A yard, you say, Rachel? You're sure that will be enough. Oh! you've measured it. Anything else?—What?—Oh! all right. I'll be back by one o'clock, anyway. Good-bye. (*Enters with Jimmy. Both are dressed for the street. Tom looks up brightly at Jimmy.*)

TOM: Hello! Big Fellow, where are you taking *my* mother, I'd like to know? This is a pretty kettle of fish.

JIMMY (*Laughing*): Aren't you funny, Uncle Tom! Why, I'm not taking her anywhere. She's taking me. (*Importantly*) I'm going to school.

TOM: Big Fellow, come here. (*Jimmy comes with a rush.*) Now, where's that penny I gave you? No, I don't want to see it. All right. Did Ma Loving give you another? (*Vigorous noddings of the head from Jimmy.*) I wish you to promise me solemnly—Now, listen! Here, don't wriggle so! not to buy— Listen! too many pints of ice-cream with my penny. Understand?

JIMMY (*Very seriously*): Yes, Uncle Tom, cross my "tummy"! I promise.

TOM: Well, then, you may go. I guess that will be all for the present. (*Jimmy loiters around looking up wistfully into his face*). Well?

JIMMY: Haven't you—aren't you—isn't you—forgetting something?

TOM (*Grabbing at his pockets*): Bless my stars! what now?

JIMMY: If you could kind of lean over this way. (*Tom leans forward.*) No, not that way. (*Tom leans toward the side away from Jimmy.*) No, this way, this way! (*Laughs and pummels him with his little fists.*) This way!

TOM (*Leaning toward Jimmy*): Well, why didn't you say so, at first?

JIMMY (*Puts his arms around Tom's neck and kisses him*): Good-bye, dear old Uncle Tom. (*Tom catches him and hugs him hard.*) I likes to be hugged like that—I can taste—sausa-ges.

TOM: You 'barrass me, son. Here, Ma, take your boy. Now remember all I told you, Jimmy.

JIMMY: I 'members.

MRS. LOVING: God bless you, Tom. Good luck.

JIMMY (*To Tom*): God bless you, Uncle Tom. Good luck!

TOM (*Much affected, but with restraint, rising*): Thank you—Good-bye. (*Mrs. Loving and Jimmy go out through the vestibule. Tom lights a cigarette and tries to read the paper. He soon sinks into a brown study. Presently Rachel enters humming. Tom relights his cigarette; and Rachel proceeds to clear the table. In the midst of this, the bell rings three distinct times.*)

RACHEL and TOM: John!

TOM: I wonder what's up—It's rather early for him.—I'll go. (*Rises leisurely and goes out into the vestibule. The outer door opens and shuts. Men's voices are heard. Tom and John Strong enter. During the ensuing conversation Rachel finishes clearing the table, takes the fern off, puts on the green table-cloth, places a doily carefully in the center, and replaces the fern. She apparently pays no attention to the conversation between her brother and Strong. After she has finished, she goes to the kitchenette. The rattle of dishes can be heard now and then.*)

RACHEL (*Brightly*): Well, stranger, how does it happen you're out so early in the morning?

STRONG: I hadn't seen any of you for a week, and I thought I'd come by, on my way to work, and find out how things are going. There is no need of asking how you are, Rachel. And the mother and the boy?

RACHEL: Ma dear's rheumatism still holds on.—Jimmy's fine.

STRONG: I'm sorry to hear that your mother is not well. There isn't a remedy going that my mother doesn't know about. I'll get her advice and let you know. (*Turning to Tom*) Well, Tom, how goes it? (*Strong and Tom sit.*)

TOM (*Smiling grimly*): There's plenty of "go," but no "git there."

(*There is a pause.*)

STRONG: I was hoping for better news.

TOM: If I remember rightly, not so many years ago, you tried—and failed. Then, a colored man had hardly a ghost of a show;—now he hasn't even the ghost of a ghost. (*Rachel has finished and goes into the kitchenette.*)

STRONG: That's true enough. (*A pause.*) What are you going to do?

TOM (*Slowly*): I'll do this little "going act" of mine the rest of the week; (*pauses*) and then, I'll do anything I can get to do. If necessary, I suppose, I can be a "White-wing."

STRONG: Tom, I came— (*Breaks off; continuing slowly*) Six years ago, I found I was up against a stone wall—your experience, you see, to the letter. I couldn't let my mother starve, so I became a waiter. (*Pauses.*) I studied waiting; I made a science of it, an art. In a comparatively short time, I'm a head-waiter and I'm up against another stonewall. I've reached my limit. I'm thirty-two now, and I'll die a head-waiter. (*A pause.*) College friends, so-called, and acquaintances used to come into the restaurant. One or two at first—attempted to commiserate with me. They didn't do it again. I waited upon them—I did my best. Many of them tipped me. (*Pauses and smiles grimly.*) I can remember my first tip, still. They come in yet; many of them are already powers, not only in this city, but in the country. Some of them make a personal request that I wait upon them. I am an artist, now, in my proper sphere. They tip me well, extremely well—the larger the tip, the more pleased they are with me. Because of me, in their own eyes, they're philanthropists. Amusing, isn't it? I can stand their attitude now. My philosophy—learned hard, is to make the best of everything you can, and go on. At best, life isn't so very long. You're wondering why I'm telling you all this. I wish you to see things exactly as they are. There are many disadvantages and some advantages in being a waiter. My mother can live comfortably; I am able, even, to see that she gets some of the luxuries. Tom, it's this way—I can always get you a job as a waiter; I'll teach you the art. If you care to begin the end of the week—all right. And remember this, as long as I keep my job—this offer holds good.

TOM: I—I— (*Breaks off*) Thank you. (*A pause; then smiling wryly*) I guess it's safe enough to say, you'll see me at the end of the week. John you're— (*Breaking off again. A silence interrupted presently by the sound of much vigorous rapping on the outer door of the flat. Rachel appears and crosses over to the vestibule.*) Hear the racket! My kiddies gently begging for admittance. It's about twenty minutes of nine, isn't it? (*Tom nods.*) I thought so. (*Goes into the entryway; presently reappears with a group of six little girls ranging in age from five to about nine. All are fighting to be closer to her; and all are talking at once. There is one exception: the smallest tot is self-possessed and self-sufficient. She carries a red geranium in her hand and gives it her full attention.*)

LITTLE MARY: It's my turn to get "Morning kiss" first, this morning, Miss Rachel. You kissed Louise first yesterday. You said you'd kiss us "alphabettically." (*Ending in a shriek.*) You promised! (*Rachel kisses Mary, who subsides.*)

LITTLE NANCY (*Imperiously*): Now, me. (*Rachel kisses her, and then amid shrieks, recriminations, pulling of hair, jostling, etc., she kisses the rest. The small tot is still oblivious to everything that is going on.*)

RACHEL (*Laughing*): You children will pull me limb from limb; and then I'll be all dead; and you'll be sorry—see, if you aren't. (*They fall back immediately. Tom and John watch in amused silence. Rachel loses all self-consciousness, and seems to bloom in the children's midst.*) Edith! come here this minute, and let me tie your hair-ribbon again. Nancy, I'm ashamed of you, I saw you trying to pull it off. (*Nancy looks abashed but mischievous.*) Louise, you look as sweet as sweet, this morning; and Jenny, where did you get the pretty, pretty dress?

LITTLE JENNY (*Snuffling, but proud*): My mother made it. (*Pauses with more snuffles.*) My mother says I have a very bad cold. (*There is a brief silence interrupted by the small tot with the geranium.*)

LITTLE MARTHA (*In a sweet, little voice*): I—have—a—pitty—'ittle flower.

RACHEL: Honey, it's beautiful. Don't you want "Morning kiss" too?

LITTLE MARTHA: Yes, I do.

RACHEL: Come, honey. (*Rachel kisses her.*) Are you going to give the pretty flower to Jenny's teacher? (*Vigorous shakings of the head in denial.*) Is it for—mother? (*More shakings of the head.*) Is it for—let's see—Daddy? (*More shakings of the head.*) I give up. To whom are you going to give the pretty flower, honey?

LITTLE MARTHA (*Shyly*): "Oo."

RACHEL: You, darling!

LITTLE MARTHA: Muzzer and I picked it—for "oo." Here 't is. (*Puts her finger in her mouth, and gives it shyly.*)

RACHEL: Well, I'm going to pay you with three big kisses. One! Two! Three!

LITTLE MARTHA: I can count, One! Two! Free! Tan't I? I am going to school soon; and I wants to put the flower in your hair.

RACHEL (*Kneels*): All right, baby. (*Little Martha fumbles and Rachel helps her.*)

LITTLE MARTHA (*Dreamily*): Miss Rachel, the 'ittle flower loves you. It told me so. It said it wanted to lie in your hair. It is going to tell you a pitty 'ittle secret. You listen awful hard—and you'll hear. I wish I were a fairy and had a little wand, I'd turn everything into flowers. Wouldn't that be nice, Miss Rachel?

RACHEL: Lovely, honey!

LITTLE JENNY (*Snuffling loudly*): If I were a fairy and had a wand, I'd turn you, Miss Rachel, into a queen—and then I'd always be near you and see that you were happy.

RACHEL: Honey, how beautiful!

LITTLE LOUISE: I'd make my mother happy—if I were a fairy. She cries all the time. My father can't get anything to do.

LITTLE NANCY: If I were a fairy, I'd turn a boy in my school into a spider. I hate him.

RACHEL: Honey, why?

LITTLE NANCY: I'll tell you sometime—I hate him.

LITTLE EDITH: Where's Jimmy, Miss Rachel?

RACHEL: He went long ago; and chickies, you'll have to clear out, all of you, now, or you'll be late. Shoo! Shoo! (*She drives them out prettily before her. They laugh merrily. They all go into the vestibule.*)

TOM (*Slowly*): Does it ever strike you—how pathetic and tragic a thing—a little colored child is?

STRONG: Yes.

TOM: Today, we colored men and women, everywhere— are up against it. Every year, we are having a harder time of it. In the South, they make it as impossible as they can for us to get an education. We're hemmed in on all sides. Our one safeguard—the ballot—in most states, is taken away already, or is being taken away. Economically, in a few lines, we have a slight show—but at what a cost! In the North, they make a pretence of liberality: they give us the ballot and a good education, and then—snuff us out. Each year, the problem just to live, gets more difficult to solve. How about these children—if we're fools enough to have any? (*Rachel reenters. Her face is drawn and pale. She returns to the kitchenette.*)

STRONG (*Slowly, with emphasis*): That part—is damnable! (*A silence.*)

TOM (*Suddenly looking at the clock*): It's later than I thought. I'll have to be pulling out of here now, if you don't mind. (*Raising his voice*) Rachel! (*Rachel still drawn and pale, appears in the doorway of the kitchenette. She is without her apron.*) I've got to go now, Sis. I leave John in your hands.

STRONG: I've got to go, myself, in a few minutes.

TOM: Nonsense, man! Sit still. I'll begin to think, in a minute, you're afraid of the ladies.

STRONG: I am.

TOM: What! And not ashamed to acknowledge it?

STRONG: No.

TOM: You're lots wiser than I dreamed. So long! (*Gets hat out in the entry-way and returns; smiles wryly.*) "Morituri Salutamus." (*They nod at him—Rachel wistfully. He goes out. There is the sound of an opening and closing door. Rachel sits down. A rather uncomfortable silence, on the part of Rachel, ensues. Strong is imperturbable.*)

RACHEL (*Nervously*): John!

STRONG: Well?

RACHEL: I—I listened.

STRONG: Listened! To what?

RACHEL: To you and Tom.

STRONG: Well,—what of it?

RACHEL: I didn't think it was quite fair not to tell you. It—it seemed, well, like eavesdropping.

STRONG: Don't worry about it. Nonsense!

RACHEL: I'm glad—I want to thank you for what you did for Tom. He needs you, and will need you. You'll help him?

STRONG (*Thoughtfully*): Rachel, each one—has his own little battles. I'll do what I can. After all, an outsider doesn't help much.

RACHEL: But friendship—just friendship—helps.

STRONG: Yes. (*A silence.*) Rachel, do you hear anything encouraging from the schools? Any hope for you yet?

RACHEL: No, nor ever will be. I know that now. There's no more chance for me than there is for Tom,—or than there was for you—or for any of us with dark skins. It's lucky for me that I love to keep house, and cook, and sew. I'll never get anything else. Ma dear's sewing, the little work Tom has been able to get, and the little sewing I sometimes get to do—keep us from the poor-house. We live. According to your philosophy, I suppose, make the best of it—it might be worse.

STRONG (*Quietly*): You don't want to get morbid over these things, you know.

RACHEL (*Scornfully*): That's it. If you see things as they are, you're either pessimistic or morbid.

STRONG: In the long run, do you believe, that attitude of mind—will be—beneficial to you? I'm ten years older than you. I tried your way. I know. Mine is the only sane one. (*Goes over to her slowly; deliberately puts his hands on her hair, and tips her head back. He looks down into her face quietly without saying anything.*)

RACHEL (*Nervous and startled*): Why, John, don't! (*He pays no attention, but continues to look down into her face.*)

STRONG (*Half to himself*): Perhaps—if you had—a little more fun in your life, your point of view would be—more normal. I'll arrange it so I can take you to some theatre, one night, this week.

RACHEL (*Irritably*): You talk as though I were a—a jelly-fish. You'll take me, how do you know *I'll* go?

STRONG: You will.

RACHEL (*Sarcastically*): Indeed! (*Strong makes no reply.*) I wonder if you know how—how—maddening you are. Why, you talk as though my will counts for nothing. It's as if you're trying to master me. I think a domineering man is detestable.

STRONG (*Softly*): If he's, perhaps, *the* man?

RACHEL (*Hurriedly, as though she had not heard*): Besides, some of these theatres put you off by yourself as though you had leprosy. I'm not going.

STRONG (*Smiling at her*): You know I wouldn't ask you to go, under those circumstances. (*A silence.*) Well, I must be going now. (*He takes her hand, and looks at it reverently. Rachel, at first resists; but he refuses to let go. When she finds it useless, she ceases to resist. He turns his head and smiles down into her face.*) Rachel, I am coming back to see you, this evening.

RACHEL: I'm sure *we'll* all be very glad to see you.

STRONG (*Looking at her calmly*): I said—*you*. (*Very deliberately, he turns her hand palm upwards, leans over and kisses it; then he puts it back into her lap. He touches her cheek lightly.*) Good-bye—little Rachel. (*Turns in the vestibule door and looks back, smiling.*) Until tonight. (*He goes out. Rachel sits for some time without moving. She is lost in a beautiful day-dream. Presently she sighs happily, and after looking furtively around the room, lifts the palm John has kissed to her lips. She laughs shyly and jumping up, begins to hum. She opens the window at the rear of the room and then commences to thread the sewing-machine. She hums happily the whole time. A light rapping is heard at the outer door. Rachel listens. It stops, and begins again. There is something insistent, and yet hopeless in the sound. Rachel looking puzzled, goes out into the vestibule. . . . The door closes. Rachel, a black woman, poorly dressed, and a little ugly, black*

*child come in. There is the stoniness of despair in the woman's
face. The child is thin, nervous, suspicious, frightened.*)

MRS. LANE (*In a sharp, but toneless voice*): May I sit down?
I'm tired.

RACHEL (*Puzzled, but gracious; draws up a chair for her*):
Why, certainly.

MRS. LANE: No, you don't know me—never even heard
of me—nor I of you. I was looking at the vacant flat on this
floor—and saw your name—on your door,—"Loving!" It's a
strange name to come across—in this world.—I thought,
perhaps, you might give me some information. (*The child
hides behind her mother and looks around at Rachel in a frightened
way.*)

RACHEL (*Smiling at the woman and child in a kindly manner*):
I'll be glad to tell you anything, I am able Mrs.—

MRS. LANE: Lane. What I want to know is, how do they
treat the colored children in the school I noticed around the
corner? (*The child clutches at her mother's dress.*)

RACHEL (*Perplexed*): Very well—I'm sure.

MRS. LANE (*Bluntly*): What reason have you for being
sure?

RACHEL: Why, the little boy I've adopted goes there; and
he's very happy. All the children in this apartment-house go
there too; and I know they're happy.

MRS. LANE: Do you know how many colored children
there are in the school?

RACHEL: Why, I should guess around thirty.

MRS. LANE: I see. (*Pauses.*) What color is this little
adopted boy of yours?

RACHEL (*Gently*): Why—he's brown.

MRS. LANE: Any black children there?

RACHEL (*Nervously*): Why—yes.

MRS. LANE: Do you mind if I send Ethel over by the piano to sit?

RACHEL: N—no, certainly not. (*Places a chair by the piano and goes to the little girl holding out her hand. She smiles beautifully. The child gets farther behind her mother.*)

MRS. LANE: She won't go to you—she's afraid of everybody now but her father and me. Come Ethel. (*Mrs. Lane takes the little girl by the hand and leads her to the chair. In a gentler voice*) Sit down, Ethel. (*Ethel obeys. When her mother starts back again toward Rachel, she holds out her hands pitifully. She makes no sound.*) I'm not going to leave you, Ethel. I'll be right over here. You can see me. (*The look of agony on the child's face, as her mother leaves her, makes Rachel shudder.*) Do you mind if we sit over here by the sewing-machine? Thank you. (*They move their chairs.*)

RACHEL (*Looking at the little, pitiful figure watching its mother almost unblinkingly*): Does Ethel like apples, Mrs. Lane?

MRS. LANE: Yes.

RACHEL: Do you mind if I give her one?

MRS. LANE: No. Thank you, very much.

RACHEL (*Goes into the kitchenette and returns with a fringed napkin, a plate, and a big, red apple, cut into quarters. She goes to the little girl, who cowers away from her; very gently.*) Here, dear, little girl, is a beautiful apple for you. (*The gentle tones have no appeal for the trembling child before her.*)

MRS. LANE (*Coming forward*): I'm sorry, but I'm afraid she won't take it from you. Ethel, the kind lady has given you an apple. Thank her nicely. Here! I'll spread the napkin for you, and put the plate in your lap. Thank the lady like a good little girl.

ETHEL (*Very low*): Thank you. (*They return to their seats. Ethel with difficulty holds the plate in her lap. During the rest *of the interview between Rachel and her mother, she divides her attention between the apple on the plate and her mother's face. She makes no attempt to eat the apple, but holds the plate in her lap with a care that is painful to watch. Often, too, she looks over her shoulder fearfully. The conversation between Rachel and her mother is carried on in low tones.*)

MRS. LANE: I've got to move—it's *Ethel.*

RACHEL: What is the matter with that child? It's—it's heartbreaking to see her.

MRS. LANE: I understand how you feel,—I don't feel anything, myself, any more. (*A pause.*) My husband and I are poor, and we're ugly and we're black. Ethel looks like her father more than she does like me. We live in 55th Street—near the railroad. It's a poor neighborhood, but the rent's cheap. My husband is a porter in a store; and, to help out, I'm a caretaker. (*Pauses.*) I don't know why I'm telling you all this. We had a nice little house—and the three of us were happy. Now we've got to move.

RACHEL: Move! Why?

MRS. LANE: It's Ethel. I put her in school this September. She stayed two weeks. (*Pointing to Ethel*) That's the result.

RACHEL (*In horror*): You mean—that just two weeks—in school—did that?

MRS. LANE: Yes. Ethel never had a sick day in her life— before. (*A brief pause.*) I took her to the doctor at the end of the two weeks. He says she's a nervous wreck.

RACHEL: But what could they have done to her?

MRS. LANE (*Laughs grimly and mirthlessly*): I'll tell you what they did the first day. Ethel is naturally sensitive and backward. She's not assertive. The teacher saw that, and, after I had left, told her to sit in a seat in the rear of the class. She was alone there—in a corner. The children, immediately feeling there was something wrong with Ethel because of the teacher's attitude, turned and stared at her. When the teacher's back was turned they whispered about her, pointed their fingers at her and tittered. The teacher divided the class into two parts, divisions, I believe, they are called. She forgot all about Ethel, of course, until the last minute, and then, looking back, said sharply: "That little girl there may join this division," meaning the group of pupils standing around her. Ethel naturally moved slowly. The teacher called her sulky and told her to lose a part of her recess. When Ethel came up—the children drew away from her in every direction. She was left standing alone. The teacher then proceeded to give a lesson about kindness to animals. Funny, isn't it, *kindness to animals?* The children forgot Ethel in the excitement of talking about their pets. Presently, the teacher turned to Ethel and said disagreeably: "Have you a pet?" Ethel said, "Yes," very low. "Come, speak up, you sulky child, what is it?" Ethel said: "A blind puppy." They all laughed, the teacher and all. Strange, isn't it, but Ethel loves that puppy. She spoke up: "It's mean to laugh at a little blind puppy. I'm glad he's blind." This remark brought forth more laughter. "Why are you glad," the teacher asked curiously. Ethel refused to say. (*Pauses.*) When I asked her why, do you know what she told me? "If he saw me, he might not love me any more." (*A pause.*) Did I tell you that Ethel is only seven years old?

RACHEL (*Drawing her breath sharply*): Oh! I didn't believe any one could be as cruel as that—to a little child.

MRS. LANE: It isn't very pleasant, is it? When the teacher found out that Ethel wouldn't answer, she said severely: "Take your seat!" At recess, all the children went out. Ethel could hear them playing and laughing and shrieking. Even the teacher went too. She was made to sit there all alone—in that big room—because God made her ugly—and black.

(*Pauses.*) When the recess was half over the teacher came back. "You may go now," she said coldly. Ethel didn't stir. "Did you hear me?" "Yes'm." "Why don't you obey?" "I don't want to go out, please." "You don't, don't you, you stubborn child! Go immediately!" Ethel went. She stood by the school steps. No one spoke to her. The children near her moved away in every direction. They stopped playing, many of them, and watched her. They stared as only children can stare. Some began whispering about her. Presently one child came up and ran her hand roughly over Ethel's face. She looked at her hand and Ethel's face and ran screaming back to the others, "It won't come off! See!" Other children followed the first child's example. Then one boy spoke up loudly: "I know what she is, she's a nigger!" Many took up the cry. God or the devil interfered—the bell rang. The children filed in. One boy boldly called her "Nigger!" before the teacher. She said, "That isn't nice,"—but she smiled at the boy. Things went on about the same for the rest of the day. At the end of school, Ethel put on her hat and coat—the teacher made her hang them at a distance from the other pupils' wraps; and started for home. Quite a crowd escorted her. They called her "Nigger!" all the way. I *made* Ethel go the next day. I complained to the authorities. They treated me lightly. I was determined not to let them force my child out of school. At the end of two weeks—I had to take her out.

RACHEL (*Brokenly*): Why,—I never—in all my life—heard anything—so—pitiful.

MRS. LANE: Did you ever go to school here?

RACHEL: Yes. I was made to feel my color—but I never had an experience like that.

MRS. LANE: How many years ago were you in the graded schools?

RACHEL: Oh!—around ten.

MRS. LANE (*Laughs grimly*): Ten years! Every year things are getting worse. Last year wasn't as bad as this. (*Pauses.*) So they treat the children all right in this school?

RACHEL: Yes! Yes! I know that.

MRS. LANE: I can't afford to take this flat here, but I'll take it. I'm going to have Ethel educated. Although, when you think of it,—it's all rather useless—this education! What are our children going to do with it, when they get it? We strive and save and sacrifice to educate them—and the whole time—down underneath, we know—they'll have no chance.

RACHEL (*Sadly*): Yes, that's true, all right.—God seems to have forgotten us.

MRS. LANE: God! It's all a lie about God. I know.—This fall I sent Ethel to a white Sunday-school near us. She received the same treatment there she did in the day school. Her being there, nearly broke up the school. At the end, the superintendent called her to him and asked her if she didn't know of some nice colored Sunday-school. He told her she must feel out of place, and uncomfortable there. That's your Church of God!

RACHEL: Oh! how unspeakably brutal. (*Controls herself with an effort; after a pause*) Have you any other children?

MRS. LANE (*Dryly*): Hardly! If I had another—I'd kill it. It's kinder. (*Rising presently*) Well, I must go, now. Thank you, for your information—and for listening. (*Suddenly*) You aren't married, are you?

RACHEL: No.

MRS. LANE: Don't marry—that's my advice. Come, Ethel. (*Ethel gets up and puts down the things in her lap, carefully upon her chair. She goes in a hurried, timid way to her mother and clutches her hand.*) Say good-bye to the lady.

ETHEL (*Faintly*): Good-bye.

RACHEL (*Kneeling by the little girl—a beautiful smile on her face*): Dear little girl, won't you let me kiss you good-bye? I love little girls. (*The child hides behind her mother; continuing brokenly*) Oh!—no child—ever did—that to me—before!

MRS LANE (*In a gentler voice*): Perhaps, when we move in here, the first of the month, things may be better. Thank you, again. Good-morning! You don't belie your name. (*All three go into the vestibule. The outside door opens and closes. Rachel as though dazed and stricken returns. She sits in a chair, leans forward, and clasping her hands loosely between her knees, stares at the chair with the apple on it where Ethel Lane has sat. She does not move for some time. Then she gets up and goes to the window in the rear center and sits there. She breathes in the air deeply and then goes to the sewing-machine and begins to sew on something she is making. Presently her feet slow down on the pedals; she stops; and begins brooding again. After a short pause, she gets up and begins to pace up and down slowly, mechanically, her head bent forward. The sharp ringing of the electric bells breaks in upon this. Rachel starts and goes slowly into the vestibule. She is heard speaking dully through the tube.*)

RACHEL: Yes!—All right! Bring it up! (*Present she returns with a long flower box. She opens it listlessly at the table. Within are six, beautiful crimson rosebuds with long stems. Rachel looks at the name on the card. She sinks down slowly on her knees and leans her head against the table. She sighs wearily*) Oh! John! John!——What are we to do?—I'm—I'm—afraid! Everywhere—it is the same thing. My mother! My little brother! Little, black, crushed Ethel! (*In a whisper*) Oh! God! You who I have been taught to believe are so good, so beautiful how could—You permit—these—things? (*Pauses, raises her head and sees the rosebuds. Her face softens and grows beautiful, very sweetly.*) Dear little rosebuds—you—make me think— of sleeping, curled up, happy babies. Dear beautiful, little rosebuds! (*Pauses; goes on thoughtfully to the rosebuds*) When— I look—at you—I believe—God is beautiful. He who can make a little exquisite thing like this, and this can't be cruel. Oh! He can't mean me—to give up—love—and the hope of little children. (*There is the sound of a small hand knocking at the outer door. Rachel smiles.*) My Jimmy! It must be twelve o'clock. (*Rises.*) I didn't dream it was so late. (*Starts for the vestibule.*) Oh! the world can't be so bad. I don't believe it. I won't. I *must* forget that little girl. My little Jimmy is happy—and today John—sent me beautiful rosebuds. Oh, there are lovely things, yet. (*Goes into the vestibule. A child's eager cry is heard; and Rachel carrying Jimmy in her arms comes in. He has both arms about her neck and is hugging her. With him in her arms, she sits down in the armchair at the right front.*)

RACHEL: Well, honey, how was school today?

JIMMY (*Sobering a trifle*): All right, Ma Rachel. (*Suddenly sees the roses*) Oh! look at the pretty flowers. Why, Ma Rachel, you forgot to put them in water. They'll die.

RACHEL: Well, so they will. Hop down this minute, and I'll put them in right away. (*Gathers up box and flowers and goes into the kitchenette. Jimmy climbs back into the chair. He looks thoughtful and serious. Rachel comes back with the buds in a tall, glass vase. She puts the fern on top of the piano, and places the vase in the centre of the table.*) There, honey, that's better, isn't it? Aren't they lovely?

JIMMY: Yes, that's lots better. Now they won't die, will they? Rosebuds are just like little "chilyun," aren't they, Ma Rachel? If you are good to them, they'll grow up into lovely roses, won't they? And if you hurt them, they'll die. Ma Rachel do you think all peoples are kind to little rosebuds?

RACHEL (*Watching Jimmy shortly*): Why, of course. Who

could hurt little children? Who would have the heart to do such a thing?

JIMMY: If you hurt them, it would be lots kinder, wouldn't it, to kill them all at once, and not a little bit and a little bit?

RACHEL (*Sharply*): Why, honey boy, why are you talking like this?

JIMMY: Ma Rachel, what is a "Nigger"?

(*Rachel recoils as though she had been struck.*)

RACHEL: Honey boy, why—why do you ask that?

JIMMY: Some big boys called me that when I came out of school just now. They said: "Look at the little nigger!" And they laughed. One of them runned, no ranned, after me and threw stones; and they all kept calling "Nigger! Nigger! Nigger!" One stone struck me hard in the back, and it hurt awful bad; but I didn't cry, Ma Rachel. I wouldn't let them make me cry. The stone hurts me there, Ma Rachel; but what they called me hurts and hurts here. What is a "Nigger," Ma Rachel?

RACHEL (*Controlling herself with a tremendous effort. At last she sweeps down upon him and hugs and kisses him*): Why, honey boy, those boys didn't mean anything. Silly, little, honey boy! They're rough, that's all. How *could* they mean anything?

JIMMY: You're only saying that, Ma Rachel, so I won't be hurt. I know. It wouldn't ache here like it does—if they didn't mean something.

RACHEL (*Abruptly*): Where's Mary, honey?

JIMMY: She's in her flat. She came in just after I did.

RACHEL: Well, honey, I'm going to give you two big cookies and two to take to Mary; and you may stay in there and play with her, till I get your lunch ready. Won't that be jolly?

JIMMY (*Brightening a little*): Why, you never give me but

one at a time. You'll give me two?—One? Two? (*Rachel gets the cookies and brings them to him. Jimmy climbs down from the chair.*) Shoo! now, little honey boy. See how many laughs you can make for me, before I come after you. Hear? Have a good time, now. (*Jimmy starts for the door quickly; but he begins to slow down. His face gets long and serious again. Rachel watches him.*)

RACHEL (*Jumping at him*): Shoo! Shoo! Get out of here quickly, little chicken. (*She follows him out. The outer door opens and shuts. Presently she returns. She looks old and worn and grey; calmly. Pauses.*) First, it's little, black Ethel—and then's it's Jimmy. Tomorrow, it will be some other little child. The blight—sooner or later—strikes all. My little Jimmy, only seven years old poisoned! (*Through the open window comes the laughter of little children at play. Rachel, shuddering, covers her ears.*) And once I said, centuries ago, it must have been: "How can life be so terrible, when there are little children in the world?" Terrible! Terrible! (*In a whisper, slowly*) That's the reason it *is* so terrible. (*The laughter reaches her again; this time she listens.*) And, suddenly, some day, from out of the black, the blight shall descend, and shall still forever—the laughter on those little lips, and in those little hearts. (*Pauses thoughtfully.*) And the loveliest thing—almost, that ever happened to me, that beautiful voice, in my dream, those beautiful words: "Rachel, you are to be the mother to little children." (*Pauses, then slowly and with dawning surprise.*) Why, God, you were making a mock of me; you were laughing at me. I didn't believe God could laugh at our sufferings, but He can. We are accursed, accursed! We have nothing, absolutely nothing. (*Strong's rosebuds attract her attention. She goes over to them, puts her hand out as if to touch them, and then shakes her head, very sweetly*) No, little rosebuds, I may not touch you. Dear, little, baby rosebuds—I am accursed. (*Gradually her whole form stiffens, she breathes deeply; at last slowly.*) You God!—You terrible, laughing God! Listen! I swear—and may my soul be damned to all eternity, if I do break this oath—I swear—that no child of mine shall ever lie upon my breast, for I will not have it rise up, in the terrible days that are to be—and call me cursed. (*A pause, very wistfully; questioningly.*) Never to know the loveliest thing in all the world—the feel of a little head, the touch of little hands, and beautiful utter dependence—of a little child? (*With sudden frenzy*) You can laugh, oh God! Well, so can I. (*Bursts into terrible, racking laughter*) But I can be kinder than You. (*Fiercely she snatches the rosebuds from the vase, grasps them roughly, tears each head from the stem, and grinds it under her feet. The vase goes over with a crash; the water drips unheeded over the table-cloth and floor.*) If I kill, You Mighty God, I kill at once—I do not torture. (*Falls face downward on the floor. The laughter of the children shrills loudly through the window.*)

ACT III

TIME: *Seven o'clock in the evening, one week later.*

PLACE: *The same room. There is a coal fire in the grate. The curtains are drawn. A lighted oil lamp with a dark green porcelain shade is in the center of the table. Mrs. Loving and Tom are sitting by the table, Mrs. Loving sewing, Tom reading. There is the sound of much laughter and the shrill screaming of a child from the bedrooms. Presently Jimmy clad in a flannelet sleeping suit, covering all of him but his head and hands, chases a pillow, which has come flying through the doorway at the rear. He struggles with it, finally gets it in his arms, and rushes as fast as he can through the doorway again. Rachel jumps at him with a cry. He drops the pillow and shrieks. There is a tussle for possession of it, and they disappear. The noise grows louder and merrier. Tom puts down his paper and grins. He looks at his mother.*

TOM: Well, who's the giddy one in this family now?

MRS. LOVING (*Shaking her head in a troubled manner*): I don't like it. It worries me. Rachel—(*Breaks off*).

TOM: Have you found out, yet—

MRS. LOVING (*Turning and looking toward the rear doorway, quickly interrupting him*): Sh! (*Rachel, laughing, her hair tumbling over her shoulders, comes rushing into the room. Jimmy is in close pursuit. He tries to catch her, but she dodges him. They are both breathless.*)

MRS. LOVING (*Deprecatingly*): Really, Rachel, Jimmy will be so excited he won't be able to sleep. It's after his bedtime, now. Don't you think you had better stop?

RACHEL: All right, Ma dear. Come on, Jimmy; let's play "Old Folks" and sit by the fire. (*She begins to push the big armchair over to the fire. Tom jumps up, moves her aside, and pushes it himself. Jimmy renders assistance.*)

TOM: Thanks, Big Fellow, you are "sure some" strong. I'll remember you when these people around here come for me to move pianos and such things around. Shake! (*They shake hands.*)

JIMMY (*Proudly*): I am awful strong, am I not?

TOM: You "sure" are a Hercules. (*Hurriedly, as Jimmy's mouth and eyes open wide.*) And see here! don't ask me tonight who that was. I'll tell you the first thing tomorrow morning. Hear? (*Returns to his chair and paper.*)

RACHEL (*Sitting down*): Come on, honey boy, and sit in my lap.

JIMMY (*Doubtfully*): I thought we were going to play "Old Folks."

RACHEL: We are.

JIMMY: Do old folks sit in each other's laps?

RACHEL: Old folks do anything. Come on.

JIMMY (*Hesitatingly climbs into her lap, but presently snuggles down and sighs audibly from sheer content; Rachel starts to bind up her hair*): Ma Rachel, don't please! I like your hair like that. You're—you're pretty. I like to feel of it; and it smells like—like—oh!—like a barn.

RACHEL: My! how complimentary! I like that. Like a barn, indeed!

JIMMY: What's "complimentary"?

RACHEL: Oh! saying nice things about me. (*Pinching his cheek and laughing*) That my hair is like a barn, for instance.

JIMMY (*Stoutly*): Well, that is "complimentary." It smells like hay—like the hay in the barn you took me to, one day, last summer. 'Member?

RACHEL: Yes honey.

JIMMY (*After a brief pause*): Ma Rachel!

RACHEL: Well?

JIMMY: Tell me a story, please. It's "story-time," now, isn't it?

RACHEL: Well, let's see. (*They both look into the fire for a space; beginning softly*) Once upon a time, there were two, dear, little boys, and they were all alone in the world. They lived with a cruel, old man and woman, who made them work hard, very hard—all day, and beat them when they did not move fast enough, and always, every night, before they went to bed. They slept in an attic on a rickety, narrow bed, that went screech! screech! whenever they moved. And, in summer, they nearly died with the heat up there, and in winter, with the cold. One wintry night, when they were both weeping very bitterly after a particularly hard beating, they suddenly heard a pleasant voice saying: "Why are you crying, little boys?" They looked up, and there, in the moonlight, by their bed, was the dearest, little old lady. She was dressed all in gray, from the peak of her little pointed hat to her little, buckled shoes. She held a black cane much taller than her little self. Her hair fell about her ears in tiny, grey corkscrew curls, and they bobbed about as she moved. Her eyes were black and bright—as bright as—well, as that lovely, white light there. No, there! and her cheeks were as red as the apple I gave you yesterday. Do you remember?

JIMMY (*Dreamily*): Yes.

RACHEL: "Why are you crying, little boys?" she asked again, in a lovely, low, little voice. "Because we are tired and sore and hungry and cold; and we are all alone in the world; and we don't know how to laugh any more. We should so like to laugh again." "Why, that's easy," she said, "it's just like this." And she laughed a little, joyous, musical laugh. "Try!" she commanded. They tried, but their laughing boxes were very rusty, and they made horrid sounds. "Well," she said, "I advise you to pack up, and go away, as soon as you can, to the Land of Laughter. You'll soon learn there, I can tell you." "Is there such a land?" they asked doubtfully. "To be sure there is," she answered the least bit sharply. "We never heard of it," they said. "Well, I'm sure there must be plenty of things you never heard about," she said just the "leastest" bit more sharply. "In a moment you'll be telling me flowers don't talk together, and the birds." "We never heard of such a thing," they said in surprise, their eyes like saucers. "There!" she said, bobbing her little curls. "What did I tell you? You have much to learn." "How do you get to the Land of Laughter?" they asked. "You go out of the eastern gate of the town, just as the sun is rising; and you take the highway there, and follow it; and if you go with it long enough, it will bring you to the very gates of the Land of Laughter. It's a long, long way from here; and it will take you many days." The words had scarcely left her mouth, when, lo! the little lady disappeared, and where she had stood was the white square of moonlight—nothing else. And without more ado these two little boys put their arms around each other and fell fast asleep. And in the grey, just before daybreak, they awoke and dressed; and, putting on their ragged caps and mittens, for it was a wintry day, they stole out of the house and made for the eastern gate. And just as they reached it, and passed through, the whole east leapt into fire. All day they walked, and many days thereafter, and kindly people, by the way, took them in and gave them food and drink and sometimes a bed at night. Often they slept by the roadside, but they didn't mind that for the climate was delightful—not too hot, and not too cold. They soon threw away their ragged little mittens. They walked for many days, and there was no Land of Laughter. Once they met an old man, richly dressed, with shining jewels on his fingers, and he stopped them and asked: "Where are you going so fast, little boys?" "We are going to the Land of Laughter," they said together gravely. "That," said the old man, "is a very foolish thing to do. Come with me, and I will take you to the Land of Riches. I will cover you with garments of beauty, and give you jewels and a castle to live in and servants and horses and many things besides." And they said to him: "No, we wish to learn how to laugh again; we have forgotten how, and we are going to the Land of Laughter." "You will regret not going with me. See, if you don't," he said; and he left them in quite a huff. And they walked again, many days, and again they met an old man. He was tall and imposing-

looking and very dignified. And he said: "Where are you
going so fast, little boys?" "We are going to the Land of
Laughter," they said together very seriously. "What!" he
said, "that is an extremely foolish thing to do. Come with
me, and I will give you power. I will make you great men:
generals, kings, emperors. Whatever you desire to accomplish
will be permitted you." And they smiled politely: "Thank
you very much, but we have forgotten how to laugh, and we
are going there to learn how." He looked upon them haugh-
tily, without speaking, and disappeared. And they walked
and walked more days; and they met another old man. And
he was clad in rags, and his face was thin, and his eyes were
unhappy. And he whispered to them: "Where are you going
so fast, little boys?" "We are going to the Land of Laughter,"
they answered, without a smile. "Laughter! Laughter! that is
useless. Come with me and I will show you the beauty of life
through sacrifice, suffering for others. That is the only life.
I come from the Land of Sacrifice." And they thanked him
kindly, but said: "We have suffered long enough. We have
forgotten how to laugh. We would learn again." And they
went on; and he looked after them very wistfully. They
walked more days, and at last they came to the Land of
Laughter. And how do you suppose they knew this? Because
they could hear, over the wall, the sound of joyous laughter,—
the laughter of men, women, and children. And one sat
guarding the gate, and they went to her. "We have come a
long, long distance; and we would enter the Land of Laughter." "Let me see you smile, first," she said gently. "I sit at
the gate; and no one who does not know how to smile may
enter the Land of Laughter." And they tried to smile, but
could not. "Go away and practice," she said kindly, "and
come back tomorrow." And they went away, and practiced
all night how to smile; and in the morning they returned,

and the gentle lady at the gate said: "Dear little boys, have
you learned how to smile?" And they said: "We have tried.
How is this?" "Better," she said, "much better. Practice some
more, and come back tomorrow." And they went away
obediently and practiced. And they came the third day. And
she said: "Now try again." And tears of delight came into
her lovely eyes. "Those were very beautiful smiles," she said.
"Now, you may enter." And she unlocked the gate, and kissed
them both, and they entered the Land—the beautiful Land
of Laughter. Never had they seen such blue skies, such green
trees and grass; never had they heard such birds songs. And
people, men, women and children, laughing softly, came to
meet them, and took them in, and made them at home; and
soon, very soon, they learned to sleep. And they grew up
here, and married, and had laughing, happy children. And
sometimes they thought of the Land of Riches, and said: "Ah!
well!" and sometimes of the Land of Power, and sighed a
little; and sometimes of the Land of Sacrifice—and their eyes
were wistful. But they soon forgot, and laughed again. And
they grew old, laughing. And then when they died—a laugh
was on their lips. Thus are things in the beautiful Land of
Laughter. (*There is a long pause.*)

JIMMY: I like that story, Ma Rachel. It's nice to laugh,
isn't it? Is there such a land?

RACHEL (*Softly*): What do you think, honey?

JIMMY: I thinks it would be awful nice if there was. Don't
you?

RACHEL (*Wistfully*): If there only were! If there only were!

JIMMY: Ma Rachel.

RACHEL: Well?

JIMMY: It makes you think—kind of—doesn't it—of sunshine medicine?

RACHEL: Yes, honey,—but it isn't medicine there. It's

always there—just like—well—like our air here. It's *always*
sunshine there.

JIMMY: Always sunshine? Never any dark?

RACHEL: No, honey.

JIMMY: You'd—never—be—afraid there, then, would you?
Never afraid of nothing?

RACHEL: No, honey.

JIMMY (*With a big sigh*): Oh!—Oh! I *wisht* it was here—
not there. (*Puts his hand up to Rachel's face; suddenly sits up
and looks at her.*) Why, Ma Rachel dear, you're crying. Your
face is all wet. Why! Don't cry! Don't cry!

RACHEL (*Gently*): Do you remember that I told you the
lady at the gate had tears of joy in her eyes, when the two,
dear, little boys smiled that beautiful smile?

JIMMY: Yes.

RACHEL: Well, these are tears of joy, honey, that's all—
tears of joy.

JIMMY: It must be awful queer to have tears of joy, 'cause
you're happy. I never did. (*With a sigh.*) But, if you say they
are, dear Ma Rachel, they must be. You knows everything,
don't you?

RACHEL (*Sadly*): Some things, honey, some things. (*A
silence.*)

JIMMY (*Sighing happily*): This is the beautiful-est night I
ever knew. If you would do just one more thing, it would
be lots more beautiful. Will you, Ma Rachel?

RACHEL: Well, what, honey?

JIMMY: Will you sing—at the piano, I mean, it's lots
prettier that way—the little song you used to rock me to sleep
by? You know, the one about the "Slumber Boat"?

RACHEL: Oh! honey, not tonight. You're too tired. It's
bedtime now.

JIMMY (*Patting her face with his little hand; wheedlingly*): Please! Ma Rachel, please! pretty please!

RACHEL: Well, honey boy, this once, then. Tonight, you shall have the little song—I used to sing you to sleep by (*half to herself*) perhaps, for the last time.

JIMMY: Why, Ma Rachel, why the last time?

RACHEL (*Shaking her head sadly, goes to the piano; in a whisper*): The last time. (*She twists up her hair into a knot at the back of her head and looks at the keys for a few moments; then she plays the accompaniment of the "Slumber Boat" through softly, and, after a moment, sings. Her voice is full of pent-up longing, and heart-break, and hopelessness. She ends in a little sob, but attempts to cover it by singing, lightly and daintily, the chorus of "The Owl and the Moon." . . . Then softly and with infinite tenderness, almost against her will, she plays and sings again the refrain of the "Slumber Boat"*):

> "Sail, baby, sail
> Out from that sea,
> Only don't forget to sail
> Back again to me."

(*Presently she rises and goes to Jimmy, who is lolling back happily in the big chair. During the singing, Tom and Mrs. Loving apparently do not listen; when she sobs, however, Tom's hand on his paper tightens; Mrs. Loving's needle poises for a moment in mid-air. Neither looks at Rachel. Jimmy evidently has not noticed the sob.*)

RACHEL (*Kneeling by Jimmy*): Well, honey, how did you like it?

JIMMY (*Proceeding to pull down her hair from the twist*): It was lovely, Ma Rachel. (*Yawns audibly.*) Now, Ma Rachel, I'm just beautifully sleepy. (*Dreamily*) I think that p'r'aps I'll go to the Land of Laughter tonight in my dreams. I'll go in the "Slumber Boat" and come back in the morning and tell you all about it. Shall I?

RACHEL: Yes, honey. (*Whispers*)
> "Only don't forget to sail
> Back again to me."

TOM (*Suddenly*): Rachel! (*Rachel starts slightly.*) I nearly forgot. John is coming here tonight to see how you are. He told me to tell you so.

RACHEL (*Stiffens perceptibly, then in different tones*): Very well. Thank you. (*Suddenly with a little cry she puts her arms around Jimmy*) Jimmy! honey! don't go tonight. Don't go without Ma Rachel. Wait for me, honey. I do so wish to go, too, to the Land of Laughter. Think of it, Jimmy; nothing but birds always singing, and flowers always blooming, and skies always blue—and people, all of them, always laughing, laughing. You'll wait for Ma Rachel, won't you, honey?

JIMMY: Is there really and truly, Ma Rachel, a Land of Laughter?

RACHEL: Oh! Jimmy, let's hope so; let's pray so.

JIMMY (*Frowns*): I've been thinking— (*Pauses*). You have to smile at the gate, don't you, to get in?

RACHEL: Yes, honey.

JIMMY: Well, I guess I couldn't smile if my Ma Rachel wasn't somewhere close to me. So I couldn't get in after all, could I? Tonight, I'll go somewhere else, and tell you all about it. And then, some day, we'll go together, won't we?

RACHEL (*Sadly*): Yes, honey, some day—some day. (*A short silence.*) Well, this isn't going to "sleepy-sleep," is it? Go, now, and say good-night to Ma Loving and Uncle Tom.

JIMMY (*Gets down obediently, and goes first to Mrs. Loving. She leans over, and he puts his little arms around her neck. They kiss; very sweetly*): Sweet dreams! God keep you all the night!

Mrs. Loving: The sweetest of sweet dreams to you, dear little boy! Good-night! (*Rachel watches, unwatched, the scene. Her eyes are full of yearning.*)

Jimmy (*Going to Tom, who makes believe he does not see him*): Uncle Tom!

Tom (*Jumps as though tremendously startled; Jimmy laughs*): My! how you frightened me. You'll put my gizzard out of commission, if you do that often. Well, sir, what can I do for you?

Jimmy: I came to say good-night.

Tom (*Gathering Jimmy up in his arms and kissing him; gently and with emotion*): Good-night, dear little Big Fellow! Good-night!

Jimmy: Sweet dreams! God keep you all the night! (*Goes sedately to Rachel, and holds out his little hand*). I'm ready, Ma Rachel. (*Yawns*) I'm so nice and sleepy.

Rachel (*With Jimmy's hand in hers, she hesitates a moment, and then approaches Tom slowly. For a short time she stands looking down at him; suddenly leaning over him*): Why, Tom, what a pretty tie! Is it new?

Tom: Well, no, not exactly. I've had it about a month. It is rather a beauty, isn't it?

Rachel: Why, I never remember seeing it.

Tom (*Laughing*): I guess not. I saw to that.

Rachel: Stingy!

Tom: Well, I am—where my ties are concerned. I've had experience.

Rachel (*Tentatively*): Tom!

Tom: Well?

Rachel (*Nervously and wistfully*): Are you—will you—I mean, won't you be home this evening?

Tom: You've got a long memory, Sis. I've that engagement, you know. Why?

RACHEL (*Slowly*): I forgot; so you have.

TOM: Why?

RACHEL (*Hastily*): Oh! nothing—nothing. Come on, Jimmy boy, you can hardly keep those little peepers open, can you? Come on, honey. (*Rachel and Jimmy go out the rear doorway. There is a silence.*)

MRS. LOVING (*Slowly, as though thinking aloud*): I try to make out what could have happened; but it's no use—I can't. Those four days, she lay in bed hardly moving, scarcely speaking. Only her eyes seemed alive. I never saw such a wide, tragic look in my life. It was as though her soul had been mortally wounded. But how? how? What could have happened?

TOM (*Quietly*): I don't know. She generally tells me everything; but she avoids me now. If we are alone in a room—she gets out. I don't know what it means.

MRS. LOVING: She will hardly let Jimmy out of her sight. While he's at school, she's nervous and excited. She seems always to be listening, but for what? When he returns, she nearly devours him. And she always asks him in a frightened sort of way, her face as pale and tense as can be: "Well, honey boy, how was school today?" And he always answers, "Fine, Ma Rachel, fine! I learned—"; and then he goes on to tell her everything that has happened. And when he has finished, she says in an uneasy sort of way: "Is—is that all?" And when he says "Yes," she relaxes and becomes limp. After a little while she becomes feverishly happy. She plays with Jimmy and the children more than ever she did—and she played a good deal, as you know. They're here, or she's with them. Yesterday, I said in remonstrance, when she came in, her face pale and haggard and black hollows under her eyes: "Rachel, remember you're just out of a sick-bed. You're not well enough to go on like this." "I know," was all she would say, "but I've got to. I can't help myself. This part of their little lives must be happy—it just must be." (*Pauses.*) The last couple of nights, Jimmy has awakened and cried most pitifully. She wouldn't let me go to him; said I had enough trouble, and she could quiet him. She never will let me know why he cries; but she stays with him, and soothes him until, at last, he falls asleep again. Every time she has come out like a rag; and her face is like a dead woman's. Strange isn't it, this is the first time we have ever been able to talk it over? Tom, what could have happened?

TOM: I don't know, Ma, but I feel, as you do; something terrible and sudden has hurt her soul; and, poor little thing, she's trying bravely to readjust herself to life again. (*Pauses, looks at his watch and then rises, and goes to her. He pats her back awkwardly.*) Well, Ma, I'm going now. Don't worry too much. Youth, you know, gets over things finally. It takes them hard, that's all——. At least, that's what the older heads tell us. (*Gets his hat and stands in the vestibule doorway.*) Ma, you know, I begin with John tomorrow. (*With emotion*) I don't believe we'll ever forget John. Good-night! (*Exit. Mrs. Loving continues to sew. Rachel, her hair arranged, reenters through the rear doorway. She is humming.*)

RACHEL: He's sleeping like a top. Aren't little children, Ma dear, the sweetest things, when they're all helpless and asleep? One little hand is under his cheek; and he's smiling. (*Stops suddenly, biting her lips. A pause*) Where's Tom?

MRS. LOVING: He went out a few minutes ago.

RACHEL (*Sitting in Tom's chair and picking up his paper. She is exceedingly nervous. She looks the paper over rapidly; presently trying to make her tone casual*): Ma,—you—you— aren't going anywhere tonight, are you?

MRS. LOVING: I've got to go out for a short time about half-past eight. Mrs. Jordan, you know. I'll not be gone very long, though. Why?

RACHEL: Oh! nothing particular. I just thought it would be cosy if we could sit here together the rest of the evening. Can't you—can't you go tomorrow?

MRS. LOVING: Why, I don't see how I can. I've made the engagement. It's about a new reception gown; and she's exceedingly exacting, as you know. I can't afford to lose her.

RACHEL: No, I suppose not. All right, Ma dear. (*Presently, paper in hand, she laughs, but not quite naturally.*) Look! Ma dear! How is that for fashion, anyway? Isn't it the "limit"? (*Rises and shows her mother a picture in the paper. As she is in the act, the bell rings. With a startled cry.*) Oh! (*Drops the paper, and grips her mother's hand.*)

MRS. LOVING (*Anxiously*): Rachel, your nerves are right on edge; and your hand feels like fire. I'll have to see a doctor about you; and that's all there is to it.

RACHEL (*Laughing nervously, and moving toward the vestibule*): Nonsense, Ma dear! Just because I let out a whoop now and then, and have nice warm hands? (*Goes out, is heard talking through the tube*) Yes! (*Her voice emitting tremendous relief.*) Oh! bring it right up! (*Appearing in the doorway*) Ma dear, did you buy anything at Goddard's today?

MRS. LOVING: Yes; and I've been wondering why they were so late in delivering it. I bought it early this morning. (*Rachel goes out again. A door opens and shuts. She reappears with a bundle.*)

MRS. LOVING: Put it on my bed, Rachel, please. (*Exit Rachel rear doorway; presently returns empty-handed; sits down again at the table with the paper between herself and mother; sinks in a deep revery. Suddenly there is the sound of many loud knocks made by numerous small fists. Rachel drops the paper, and comes to a sitting posture, tense again. Her mother looks at her, but says nothing. Almost immediately Rachel relaxes.*)

RACHEL: My kiddies! They're late, this evening. (*Goes out into the vestibule. A door opens and shuts. There is the shrill, excited sound of childish voices. Rachel comes in surrounded by the children, all trying to say something to her at once. Rachel puts her finger on her lip and points toward the doorway in the rear. They all quiet down. She sits on the floor in the front of the stage, and the children all cluster around her. Their conversation takes place in a half-whisper. As they enter they nod brightly at Mrs. Loving, who smiles in return.*) Why so late, kiddies? It's long past "sleepy-time."

LITTLE NANCY: We've been playing "Hide and Seek," and having the mostest fun. We promised, all of us, that if we could play until half-past seven tonight we wouldn't make any fuss about going to bed at seven o'clock the rest of the week. It's awful hard to go. I *hate* to go to bed!

LITTLE MARY, LOUISE AND EDITH: So do I! So do I! So do I!

LITTLE MARTHA: I don't. I love bed. My bed, after my muzzer tucks me all in, is like a nice warm bag. I just stick my nose out. When I lifts my head up I can see the light from the dining-room come in the door. I can hear my muzzer and fazzer talking nice and low; and then, before I know it, I'm fast asleep, and I dream pretty things, and in about a minute it's morning again. I love my little bed, and I love to dream.

LITTLE MARY (*Aggressively*): Well, I guess I love to dream too. I wish I could dream, though, without going to bed.

LITTLE NANCY: When I grow up, I'm never going to bed at night! (*Darkly*) You see.

LITTLE LOUISE: "Grown-ups" just love to poke their heads out of windows and cry, "Child'run, it's time for bed now;

and you'd better hurry, too, I can tell you." They "sure" are queer, for sometimes when I wake up, it must be about twelve o'clock, I can hear by big sister giggling and talking to some silly man. If it's good for me to go to bed early—I should think—

RACHEL (*Interrupting suddenly*): Why, where is my little Jenny? Excuse me, Louise dear.

LITTLE MARTHA: Her cold is awful bad. She coughs like this (*giving a distressing imitation*) and snuffles all the time. She can't talk out loud, and she can't go to sleep. Muzzer says she's fev'rish—I thinks that's what she says. Jenny says she knows she could go to sleep, if you would come and sit with her a little while.

RACHEL: I certainly will. I'll go when you do, honey.

LITTLE MARTHA (*Softly stroking Rachel's arm*): You're the very nicest "grown-up", (*loyally*) except my muzzer, of course, I ever knew. You knows all about little chil'run and you can be one, although you're all grown up. I think you would make a lovely muzzer. (*To the rest of the children*) Don't you?

ALL (*In excited whispers*): Yes, I do.

RACHEL (*Winces, then says gently*): Come, kiddies, you must go now, or your mothers will blame me for keeping you. (*Rises, as do the rest. Little Martha puts her hand into Rachel's.*) Ma dear, I'm going down to sit a little while with Jenny. I'll be back before you go, though. Come, kiddies, say good-night to my mother.

ALL (*Gravely*): Good-night! Sweet dreams! God keep you all the night.

MRS. LOVING: Good-night dears! Sweet dreams, all!

(*Exeunt Rachel and the children. Mrs. Loving continues to sew. The bell presently rings three distinct times. In a few moments, Mrs. Loving gets up and goes out into the vestibule. A door opens and closes. Mrs. Loving and John Strong come in. He is a trifle pale but his imperturbable self. Mrs. Loving, somewhat nervous, takes her seat and resumes her sewing. She motions Strong to a chair. He returns to the vestibule, leaves his hat, returns, and sits down.*)

STRONG: Well, how is everything?

MRS. LOVING: Oh! about the same, I guess. Tom's out. John, we'll never forget you—and your kindness.

STRONG: That was nothing. And Rachel?

MRS. LOVING: She'll be back presently. She went to sit with a sick child for a little while.

STRONG: And how is she?

MRS. LOVING: She's not herself yet, but I think she is better.

STRONG (*After a short pause*): Well, what *did* happen—exactly?

MRS. LOVING: That's just what I don't know.

STRONG: When you came home—you couldn't get in—was that it?

MRS. LOVING: Yes. (*Pauses.*) It was just a week ago today. I was down town all the morning. It was about one o'clock when I got back. I had forgotten my key. I rapped on the door and then called. There was no answer. A window was open, and I could feel the air under the door, and I could hear it as the draught sucked it through. There was no other sound. Presently I made such a noise the people began to come out into the hall. Jimmy was in one of the flats playing with a little girl named Mary. He told me he had left Rachel here a short time before. She had given him four cookies, two for him and two for Mary, and had told him he could play with her until she came to tell him his lunch was ready. I saw he was getting frightened, so I got the little girl and her mother to keep him in their flat. Then, as no man was

at home, I sent out for help. Three men broke the door
down. (*Pauses.*) We found Rachel unconscious, lying on her
face. For a few minutes I thought she was dead. (*Pauses.*) A
vase had fallen over on the table and the water had dripped
through the cloth and onto the floor. There had been flowers
in it. When I left, there were no flowers here. What she
could have done to them, I can't say. The long stems were
lying everywhere, and the flowers had been ground into the
floor. I could tell that they must have been roses from the
stems. After we had put her to bed and called the doctor,
and she had finally regained consciousness, I very naturally
asked her what had happened. All she would say was, "Ma
dear, I'm too—tired—please." For four days she lay in bed
scarcely moving, speaking only when spoken to. That first
day, when Jimmy came in to see her, she shrank away from
him. We had to take him out, and comfort him as best we
could. We kept him away, almost by force, until she got up.
And, then, she was utterly miserable when he was out of her
sight. What happened, I don't know. She avoids Tom, and
she won't tell me. (*Pauses.*) Tom and I both believe her soul
has been hurt. The trouble isn't with her body. You'll find
her highly nervous. Sometimes she is very much depressed;
again she is feverishly gay—almost reckless. What do you
think about it, John?

STRONG (*Who has listened quietly*): Had anybody been here,
do you know?

MRS. LOVING: No, I don't. I don't like to ask Rachel; and
I can't ask the neighbors.

STRONG: No, of course not. (*Pauses.*) You say there were
some flowers?

MRS. LOVING: Yes.

STRONG: And the flowers were ground into the carpet?

MRS. LOVING: Yes.

STRONG: Did you happen to notice the box? They must have come in a box, don't you think?

MRS. LOVING: Yes, there was a box in the kitchenette. It was from "Marcy's." I saw no card.

STRONG (*Slowly*): It is rather strange. (*A long silence, during which the outer door opens and shuts. Rachel is heard singing. She stops abruptly. In a second or two she appears in the door. There is an air of suppressed excitement about her.*)

RACHEL: Hello! John. (*Strong rises, nods at her, and brings forward for her the big arm-chair near the fire.*) I thought that was your hat in the hall. It's brand new, I know—but it looks—"Johnlike." How are you? Ma! Jenny went to sleep like a little lamb. I don't like her breathing, though. (*Looks from one to the other; flippantly*) Who's dead? (*Nods her thanks to Strong for the chair and sits down.*)

MRS. LOVING: Dead, Rachel?

RACHEL: Yes. The atmosphere here is so funereal,—it's positively "crapey."

STRONG: I don't know why it should be—I was just asking how you are.

RACHEL: Heavens! Does the mere inquiry into my health precipitate such an atmosphere? Your two faces were as long, as long—(*Breaks off*). Kind sir, let me assure you, I am in the very best of health. And how are you, John?

STRONG: Oh! I'm always well. (*Sits down.*)

MRS. LOVING: Rachel, I'll have to get ready to go now. John, don't hurry. I'll be back shortly, probably in three-quarters of an hour—maybe less.

RACHEL: And maybe more, if I remember Mrs. Jordan. However, Ma dear, I'll do the best I can—while you are away. I'll try to be a credit to your training. (*Mrs. Loving smiles and goes out the rear doorway.*) Now, let's see—in the books of etiquette, I believe, the properly reared young lady, always asks the young gentleman caller—you're young enough, aren't you, to be classed still as a "young gentleman caller"? (*No answer.*) Well, anyway, she always asks the young gentle-man caller sweetly something about the weather. (*Primly*) This has been an exceedingly beautiful day, hasn't it, Mr. Strong? (*No answer from Strong, who, with his head resting against the back of the chair, and his knees crossed is watching her in an amused, quizzical manner.*) Well, really, every properly brought up young gentleman, I'm sure, ought to know, that it's exceedingly rude not to answer a civil question.

STRONG (*Lazily*): Tell me what to answer, Rachel.

RACHEL: Say, "Yes, very"; and look interested and pleased when you say it.

STRONG (*With a half-smile*): Yes, very.

RACHEL: Well, I certainly wouldn't characterize that as a particularly animated remark. Besides, when you look at me through half-closed lids like that—and kind of smile—what are you thinking? (*No answer*) John Strong, are you deaf or—just plain stupid?

STRONG: Plain stupid, I guess.

RACHEL (*In wheedling tones*): What were you thinking, John?

STRONG (*Slowly*): I was thinking—(*Breaks off*)

RACHEL (*Irritably*): Well?

STRONG: I've changed my mind.

RACHEL: You're not going to tell me?

STRONG: No.

(*Mrs. Loving dressed for the street comes in.*)

MRS. LOVING: Goodbye, children. Rachel, don't quarrel so much with John. Let me see—if I have my key. (*Feels in her bag*) Yes, I have it. I'll be back shortly. Goodbye. (*Strong and Rachel rise. He bows.*)

RACHEL: Good-bye, Ma dear. Hurry back as soon as you can, won't you? (*Exit Mrs. Loving through the vestibule. Strong leans back again in his chair, and watches Rachel through half-closed eyes. Rachel sits in her chair nervously.*)

STRONG: Do you mind, if I smoke?

RACHEL: You know I don't.

STRONG: I am trying to behave like—Reginald—"the properly reared young gentleman caller." (*Lights a cigar; goes over to the fire, and throws his match away. Rachel goes into the kitchenette, and brings him a saucer for his ashes. She places it on the table near him*). Thank you. (*They both sit again, Strong very evidently enjoying his cigar and Rachel.*) Now this is what I call cosy.

RACHEL: Cosy! Why?

STRONG: A nice warm room—shut in—curtains drawn—a cheerful fire crackling at my back—a lamp, not an electric or gas one, but one of your plain, old-fashioned kerosene ones—

RACHEL (*Interrupting*): Ma dear would like to catch you, I am sure, talking about *her* lamp like that. "Old-fashioned! plain!"—You have nerve.

STRONG (*Continuing as though he had not been interrupted*): A comfortable chair—a good cigar—and not very far away, a little lady who is looking charming, so near, that if I reached over, I could touch her. You there—and I here.—It's living.

RACHEL: Well! of all things! A compliment—and from *you!* How did it slip out, pray? (*No answer.*) I suppose that you realize that a conversation between two persons is absolutely impossible, if one has to do her share all alone. Soon my ingenuity for introducing interesting subjects will be exhausted; and then will follow what, I believe, the story books call, "an uncomfortable silence."

STRONG (*Slowly*): Silence—between friends—isn't such a bad thing.

RACHEL: Thanks awfully. (*Leans back; cups her cheek in her*

*hand, and makes no pretense at further conversation. The old
look of introspection returns to her eyes. She does not move.*)

STRONG (*Quietly*): Rachel! (*Rachel starts perceptibly*) You
must remember I'm here. I don't like looking into your
soul—when you forget you're not alone.

RACHEL: I hadn't forgotten.

STRONG: Wouldn't it be easier for you, little girl, if you
could tell—some one?

RACHEL: No. (*A silence.*)

STRONG: Rachel,—you're fond of flowers,—aren't you?

RACHEL: Yes.

STRONG: Rosebuds—red rosebuds—particularly?

RACHEL (*Nervously*): Yes.

STRONG: Did you—dislike—the giver?

RACHEL (*More nervously; bracing herself*): No, of course
not.

STRONG: Rachel,—why—why—did you—kill the roses—
then?

RACHEL (*Twisting her hands*): Oh, John! I'm so sorry, Ma
dear told you that. She didn't know, you sent them.

STRONG: So I gathered. (*Pauses and then leans forward;
quietly.*) Rachel, little girl, why—did you kill them?

RACHEL (*Breathing quickly*): Don't you believe—it—a—
a—kindness—sometimes—to kill?

STRONG (*After a pause*): You—considered—it—a—kindness—to kill them?

RACHEL: Yes. (*Another pause.*)

STRONG: Do you mean—just—the roses?

RACHEL (*Breathing more quickly*): John!—Oh! must I say?

STRONG: Yes, little Rachel.

RACHEL (*In a whisper*): No. (*There is a long pause. Rachel
leans back limply, and closes her eyes. Presently Strong rises, and
moves his chair very close to hers. She does not stir. He puts his
cigar on the saucer.*)

STRONG (*Leaning forward; very gently*): Little girl, little girl, can't you tell me why?

RACHEL (*Wearily*): I can't.—It hurts—too much—to talk about it yet,—please.

STRONG (*Takes her hand; looks at it a few minutes and then at her quietly*): You—don't—care, then? (*She winces*) Rachel!— Look at me, little girl! (*As if against her will, she looks at him. Her eyes are fearful, hunted. She tries to look away, to draw away her hand; but he holds her gaze and her hand steadily.*) Do you?

RACHEL (*Almost sobbing*): John! John! don't ask me. You are drawing my very soul out of my body with your eyes. You must not talk this way. You mustn't look—John, don't! (*Tries to shield her eyes.*)

STRONG (*Quietly takes both of her hands, and kisses the backs and the palms slowly. A look of horror creeps into her face. He deliberately raises his eyes and looks at her mouth. She recoils as though she expected him to strike her. He resumes slowly*) If— you—do—care, and I know now—that you do—nothing else, *nothing* should count.

RACHEL (*Wrenching herself from his grasp and rising. She covers her ears; she breathes rapidly*): No! No! No!—You *must* stop. (*Laughs nervously; continues feverishly*) I'm not behaving very well as a hostess, am I? Let's see. What shall I do? I'll play you something, John. How will that do? Or I'll sing to you. You used to like to hear me sing; you said my voice, I remember, was sympathetic, didn't you? (*Moves quickly to the piano.*) I'll sing you a pretty little song. I think it's beautiful. You've never heard it, I know. I've never sung it to you before. It's Nevin's "At Twilight." (*Pauses, looks down, before she begins, then turns toward him and says quietly and sweetly*) Sometimes—in the coming years—I want—you to remember—I sang you this little song.—Will you?—I think it will make it easier for me—when I—when I— (*Breaks off and*

*begins the first chords. Strong goes slowly to the piano. He leans
there watching intently. Rachel sings*):

> "The roses of yester-year
>   Were all of the white and red;
> It fills my heart with silent fear
>   To find all their beauty fled.
>
> The roses of white are sere,
>   All faded the roses red,
> And one who loves me is not here
> And one that I love is dead."

(*A long pause. Then Strong goes to her and lifts her from the
piano-stool. He puts one arm around her very tenderly and pushes
her head back so he can look into her eyes. She shuts them, but is
passive.*)

STRONG (*Gently*): Little girl, little girl, don't you know
that suggestions—suggestions—like those you are sending
yourself constantly—are wicked things? You, who are so
gentle, so loving, so warm—(*Breaks off and crushes her to
him. He kisses her many times. She does not resist, but in the
midst of his caresses she breaks suddenly into convulsive laughter.
He tries to hush the terrible sound with his mouth; then brokenly*)
Little girl—don't laugh—like that.

RACHEL (*Interrupted throughout by her laughter*): I have
to.—God is laughing.—We're his puppets.—He pulls the
wires,—and we're so funny to Him.—I'm laughing too—
because I can hear—my little children—weeping. They come
to me generally while I'm asleep,—but I can hear them
now.—They've begged me—do you understand?—begged
me—not to bring them here;—and I've promised them—not
to.—I've promised. I can't stand the sound of their crying.—
I have to laugh—Oh! John! laugh!—laugh too!—I can't
drown their weeping.

(*Strong picks her up bodily and carries her to the armchair.*)

STRONG (*Harshly*): Now, stop that!

RACHEL (*In sheer surprise*): W-h-a-t?

STRONG (*Still harshly*): Stop that!—You've lost your self-control.—Find yourself again!

(*He leaves her and goes over to the fireplace, and stands looking down into it for some little time. Rachel, little by little, becomes calmer. Strong returns and sits beside her again. She doesn't move. He smooths her hair back gently, and kisses her forehead—and then, slowly, her mouth. She does not resist; simply sits there, with shut eyes, inert, limp.*)

STRONG: Rachel!—(*Pauses*). There is a little flat on 43rd Street. It faces south and overlooks a little park. Do you remember it?—it's on the top floor?—Once I remember your saying—you liked it. That was over a year ago. That same day—I rented it. I've never lived there. No one knows about it—not even my mother. It's completely furnished now—and waiting—do you know for whom? Every single thing in it, I've bought myself—even to the pins on the little bird's-eye maple dresser. It has been the happiest year I have ever known. I furnished it—one room at a time. It's the prettiest, the most homelike little flat I've ever seen. (*Very low*) Everything there—breathes love. Do you know for whom it is waiting? On the sitting-room floor is a beautiful, Turkish rug—red, and blue and gold. It's soft—and rich—and do you know for whose little feet it is waiting? There are delicate curtains at the windows and a bookcase full of friendly, eager, little books.—Do you know for whom they are waiting? There are comfortable leather chairs, just the right size, and a beautiful piano—that I leave open—sometimes, and lovely pictures of Madonnas. Do you know for whom they are waiting? There is an open fireplace with logs of wood, all carefully piled on gleaming andirons—and waiting. There is a bellows and a pair of shining tongs—waiting. And in the kitchenette painted blue and white, and smelling sweet with paint is everything: bright pots and pans and kettles, and blue and white enamel-ware, and all kinds of knives and forks and spoons—and on the door—a roller-towel. Little girl, do you know for whom they are all waiting? And somewhere—there's a big, strong man—with broad shoulders. And he's willing and anxious to do anything—everything, and he's waiting very patiently. Little girl, is it to be—yes or no?

RACHEL: (*During Strong's speech life has come flooding back to her. Her eyes are shining; her face, eager. For a moment she is beautifully happy.*) Oh! you're too good to me and mine, John. I—didn't dream any one—could be—so good. (*Leans forward and puts his big hand against her cheek and kisses it shyly.*)

STRONG (*Quietly*): Is it—yes—or no, little girl?

RACHEL (*Feverishly, gripping his hands*): Oh, yes! yes! yes! and take me quickly, John. Take me before I can think any more. You mustn't let me think, John. And you'll be good to me, won't you? Every second of every minute, of every hour, of every day, you'll have me in your thoughts, won't you? And you'll be with me every minute that you can? And, John, John!—you'll keep away the weeping of my little children. You won't let me hear it, will you? You'll make me forget everything everything—won't you?—Life is so short, John. (*Shivers and then fearfully and slowly*) And eternity so—long. (*Feverishly again*) And, John, after I am dead—promise me, promise me you'll love me more. (*Shivers again.*) I'll need love then. Oh! I'll need it. (*Suddenly there comes to their ears the sound of a child's weeping. It is monotonous, hopeless, terribly afraid. Rachel recoils.*) Oh! John!—Listen!—It's my boy, again.—I—John—I'll be back in a little while. (*Goes

*swiftly to the door in the rear, pauses and looks back. The weeping
continues. Her eyes are tragic. Slowly she kisses her hand to him
and disappears. John stands where she has left him looking down.
The weeping stops. Presently Rachel appears in the doorway. She
is haggard, and grey. She does not enter the room. She speaks as
one dead might speak—tonelessly, slowly.)*

RACHEL: Do you wish to know why Jimmy is crying?

STRONG: Yes.

RACHEL: I am twenty-two—and I'm old; you're thirty-
two—and you're old; Tom's twenty-three—and he is old. Ma
dear's sixty—and she said once she is much older than that.
She is. We are all blighted; we are all accursed—all of us—,
everywhere, we whose skins are dark—our lives blasted by
the white man's prejudice. *(Pauses)* And my little Jimmy—
seven years old, that's all—is blighted too. In a year or two,
at best, he will be made old by suffering. *(Pauses.)* One week
ago, today, some white boys, older and larger than my little
Jimmy, as he was leaving the school—called him "Nigger"!
They chased him through the streets calling him, "Nigger!
Nigger! Nigger!" One boy threw stones at him. There is still
a bruise on his little back where one struck him. That will
get well; but they bruised his soul—and that—will never—
get well. He asked me what "Nigger" meant. I made light
of the whole thing, laughed it off. He went to his little
playmates, and very naturally asked them. The oldest of them
is nine!—and they knew, poor little things—and they told
him. *(Pauses.)* For the last couple of nights he has been
dreaming—about these boys. And he always awakes—in the
dark—afraid—afraid—of the now—and the future—I have
seen that look of deadly fear—in the eyes—of other little
children. I know what it is myself—I was twelve—when
some big boys chased me and called me names—I never left
the house afterwards—without being afraid. I was afraid, in

the streets—in the school—in the church, everywhere, always, afraid of being hurt. And I—was not—afraid in vain. (*The weeping begins again.*) He's only a baby—and he's blighted. (*To Jimmy*) Honey, I'm right here. I'm coming in just a minute. Don't cry. (*To Strong*) If it nearly kills me to hear my Jimmy's crying, do you think I could stand it, when my own child, flesh of my flesh, blood of my blood—learned the same reason for weeping? Do you? (*Pauses.*) Ever since I fell here—a week ago—I am afraid—to go—to sleep, for every time I do—my children come—and beg me—weeping—not to—bring them here—to suffer. Tonight, they came—when I was awake. (*Pauses.*) I have promised them again, now— by Jimmy's bed. (*In a whisper*) I have damned—my soul to all eternity—if I do. (*To Jimmy*) Honey, don't! I'm coming. (*To Strong*) And John,—dear John—you see—it can never be—all the beautiful, beautiful things—you have—told me about. (*Wistfully*) No—they— can never be—now. (*Strong comes toward her*) No,—John dear,—you—must not—touch me—any more. (*Pauses.*) Dear, this—is—"Good-bye."

STRONG (*Quietly*): It's not fair—to you, Rachel, to take you—at your word—tonight. You're sick; you've brooded so long, so continuously,—you've lost—your perspective. Don't answer, yet. Think it over for another week and I'll come back.

RACHEL (*Wearily*): No,—I can't think—any more.

STRONG: You realize—fully—you're sending me—for always?

RACHEL: Yes.

STRONG: And you care?

RACHEL: Yes.

STRONG: It's settled, then for all time—"Good-bye!"

RACHEL (*After a pause*): Yes.

STRONG (*Stands looking at her steadily a long time, and then*

moves to the door and turns, facing her; with infinite tenderness):
Good-bye, dear, little Rachel—God bless you.

RACHEL: Good-bye, John! (*Strong goes out. A door opens
and shuts. There is finality in the sound. The weeping continues.
Suddenly; with a great cry*) John! John! (*Runs out into the
vestibule. She presently returns. She is calm again. Slowly*) No!
No! John. Not for us. (*A pause; with infinite yearning*) Oh!
John,—if it only—if it only—(*Breaks off, controls herself.
Slowly again; thoughtfully*) No—No sunshine—no laughter—
always, always—darkness. That is it. Even our little flat—
(*In a whisper*) John's and mine—the little flat—that calls,
calls us—through darkness. It shall wait—and wait—in vain—
in darkness. Oh, John! (*Pauses.*) And my little children! my
little children! (*The weeping ceases; pauses.*) I shall never—
see—you—now. Your little, brown, beautiful bodies—I shall
never see.—Your dimples—everywhere—your laughter—your
tears—the beautiful, lovely feel of you here. (*Puts her hands
against her heart.*) Never—never—to be. (*A pause, fiercely*)
But you are somewhere—and wherever you are you are mine!
You are mine! All of you! Every bit of you! Even God can't
take you away. (*A pause; very sweetly; pathetically*) Little
children!—My little children!—No more need you come to
me—weeping—weeping. You may be happy now—you are
safe. Little weeping, voices, hush! hush! (*The weeping begins
again. To Jimmy, her whole soul in her voice*) Jimmy! My little
Jimmy! Honey! I'm coming.—Ma Rachel loves you so. (*Sobs
and goes blindly, unsteadily to the rear doorway; she leans her
head there one second against the door; and then stumbles through
and disappears. The light in the lamp flickers and goes out. . . .
It is black. The terrible, heart-breaking weeping continues.*)

THE END

FICTION

෴ ෴ ෴

BLACK IS,
AS BLACK DOES

A Dream

It came to me one, dark, rainy, morning. I was half awake and half asleep. The wind was blowing drearily, and I listened to the swish of the rain on the glass, and the dripping from the eaves and as I lay listening, I thought many things and my thoughts grew hazier and hazier and I fell into deep slumber.

———————

Then, methought, a great feeling of peace come upon me, and that all my cares were falling from me and rolling away—away into infinity. So I lay with my eyes closed and this great feeling of peace increased and my heart was glad within me. Then some one touched me lightly on the shoulder and eyes, and my heart gave a great bound, for I was not prepared for the loveliness of the scene, that now burst on my sight. All around stretched a wide, green, grassy, plain. Each little blade of grass sang in the gentle wind, and here and there massive trees spread their branches, and the leaves sang, and the birds, and a river that passed through the meadow sparkled and sang as it sped on its way. And listening, I heard no discord, for all the voices flowed into each other, and mingled, and swelled and made one, grand, sweet, song. I longed to sing too, and lifted up my voice, but no song

Text taken from two holograph copies in the Angelina Weld Grimké Collection, MSRC, box 38-11, folder 179. One of the copies is subtitled "A Dream." Otherwise the two versions do not vary substantially from each other. The story was published in the *Colored American Magazine* 1 (Aug. 1900): 160.

came so that I wondered. And a voice at my side, answered, "Thou art not one of us yet." And the voice was sweeter than the babbling brook, tenderer than the voice of a mother to her erring child, lower than the beating of the surf on the shore. Then I turned to see whence the voice came, and as I looked I fell weeping on my face.

For there stood before me a figure clad in white, and as she moved she seemed like a snowy cloud, that sails over the sky in summer-time, and a soft light shone above, around, behind, illuminating her, but it was not for this that I fell weeping. I had looked upon the face, and the truth that shone forth from the mild eyes, the sweetness that smiled around the mouth, and all the pity, the mercy, the kindness expressed in that divine countenance revealed to me how wicked I was and had been. But she took me by the hand, bidding me arise, and kissing me on the brow. And between my sobs I asked, "Where am I?" and the low voice answered, "This is Heaven," and I said, "Who art thou?" and she answered "One of the lovers of God." And as she spoke that name, the heavens brightened, the grass sang sweeter, and the leaves and the birds and the silvery river, and looking up I saw that she was no longer by my side, but was moving over the plain, and turning she beckoned to me. And I followed.

Thus we passed silently over the velvety grass, over hill and dale, by laughing brooks, and swift flowing rivers, and often turning she smiled upon me, but on and on we went. Now and then other bright spirits passed us, all smiling kindly upon me as they went their way, and some came and kissed my forehead and said they were glad to see me, and I was happy, *so* happy.

Then, methought, we came to a city, but ah! so unlike our cities, no hurrying this way and that, no deafening roar of passing wagons, no shrieking hucksters, no loud talking, no anxious, worried faces. All was peace. And as we passed up the noiseless streets, many spirits clad in spotless white and gleaming with that ineffable light passed, and all smiled and greeted me tenderly as they went their shining way.

Then we came to a great hall, and the doors thereby were three and opened wide, and I saw many people going in the first door, but they were not clad in snowy white and I could see no light illumining their bodies, and I asked, "Pray tell me, who are these?" And the spirit said, "These are those, like you, who have just come from earth." And as she spoke, I saw some passing forth from the second door, clad in white but I saw no light and I said, perplexed, "Pray who are these and why does no light illumine them?" She answered, "These are they, whom Our Father has blessed of those, who have just come from earth, and they will have the light, when they have been with us a long time, and when they have done some service that has particularly gratified Our Father." She had scarcely ceased speaking, when I saw several ragged ones, with looks down-cast coming out of the third door, and I asked, "Pray who are these?" And as she answered her voice trembled and gazing at her, I saw a tear glide down her cheek and she answered, simply, "The Lost." And, groaning within in me, I said, "Pray what is this place?" And solemnly she said, "This is where God weeds out the wicked from the good." And as she ceased speaking, she glided to the first door and beckoned me.

And we came within a hall, large and gloomy, and we passed down to one end and looking up, I saw a great, dazzling light, that was all, for I fell prostrate on the floor overcome. I had looked upon God!! And as I lay I heard his voice, now low and tender beyond expression, now stern and mighty like the roll of thunder. When I took courage, I gazed around, but I dared not look upon that face again.

I saw a vast multitude of those lately come from Earth, waiting to stand before the bar of judgement, and I saw those who had been tried passing out of the doors, looking at my companion I saw that she was gazing on God and his brightness shown upon her face, and I was dazzled and looked down. When I glanced again upon the throng of the lately dead, I saw one pass to the bar, and I saw him fall with a loud cry for mercy, and I heard him weeping, and confessing all his sins, excusing himself in nothing, and I saw that his skin was black, looking closer I saw that he was lame, torn, and bleeding, and he was quite unrecognizable for most of his features were———— ——— ———— — — – ———— gone.[1] And I saw him waving his poor stumps of arms, begging for mercy. By these tokens I knew, that he came from my country and that he was one of an oppressed race, for in America alas! it makes a difference whether a man's skin be black or white. Nothing was said, but I perceived that he had been foully murdered.

And I heard God's voice speaking to him and I was lost in its sweetness and it seemed to me I was floating down a stream of loveliness, and I was so happy, and when he ceased, I thought I had gently come to some bank and all was peace and rest. And I saw the man pass from the bar and that he was clad in pure white. Beautiful spirits came and tended his wounds and lo! he stood forth glorified and I saw a dim light shining around him and I looked at my companion and she smiled and then I understood.

And behold another stood before the judgement seat. I did not hear him beg for mercy, but I heard him telling all the good he had done, and I heard a sound as of distant mutterings of thunder and I felt the angry flashings above the judgement

1. These dashes occur at the end of the page in holograph.

seat. And I saw the man waiting calmly in his own conceit. And I heard the muffled thunder of God's voice asking, "And didst thou treat all my children justly?" And I heard the man say, "Yea, yea, O Lord" and I heard God again, "Whether their skin was black or white?" And, the man answered, "Yea, yea, Lord" and laughed.

Then I heard the thunder of God's voice saying, "I know thee, who thou art; it wast thou, who didst murder yon man, one of my faithful servants, it wast thou, who didst hate and torture him, and who trampled upon and crushed him, but inasmuch as thou didst this wrong unto him, thou didst it unto me. Begone!" And I saw him who was condemned stagger from the bar, and that his hands were covered with blood, and his clothes, and that he left behind him his foot-prints tracked in blood, and I looked at him more closely and I saw that his skin was white but that his soul was black. For it makes a difference in Heaven whether a man's *soul* be black or white!

And I beheld the man with the black skin creep up to the judgement seat and sob brokenly, "Forgive, oh forgive my brother for he knew not what he did." And I felt my heart beating and trembling against my side and I awoke. The wind was moaning drearily, the rain was still sobbing against the glass and I lay there and wept.

BLACKNESS

I stepped from the warm and wettest blackness I ever remember into the chilling blackness of the cellar.

"Reed," his voice just above a whisper said almost in my ear, "if you will wait here just where you are a moment."

His voice, yes. Low as it was I recognized it beyond a single doubt and that in spite of the fact that in it there was a difference, a difference subtle, indefinable, true; but one that somehow I knew without at all knowing why was permanent. All the vague uneasiness and anxiety I had been feeling ever since the receipt, that morning, of his strange letter with its very definite instructions to me, all the half-formed, nebulous strange premonitions that had been laying dark ghostlike fingers upon me, all the unanalyzable sensations I had just been undergoing because of the mystery and the singularity of his entrance into his home, crystallized suddenly with my acknowledgment of the change in his voice into a dread certainty, no longer of an impending trouble but of a present and very terrible trouble for us both.

I did not hear him close the cellar door and I did not hear him lock it although I knew he was doing both. The swishing, rushing pounding of the windless rain without, tropical in the verticalness of its down pour and its intensity, became slowly deadened; and the hazy, grayish oblong of the open

Text is taken from holograph in the Angelina Weld Grimké Collection, MSRC, box 38-11, folder 180. Also see Grimké's letter to the *Atlantic Monthly* (in the nonfiction section of this volume), regarding the plot of "Blackness."

doorway gradually disappeared. Of these things I was aware. And then, over the place where it had been, flowed the chill blackness that was all about us.

For several seconds the stillness of that oppressive gloom within was unbroken. I moved uneasily; and, then, though I had not heard him, he was again at my side and his low voice in my ear.

"To the right, now." His hand found my elbow and I yielded myself to its guidance.

"Ten steps—straight ahead." I counted. At the end of them we paused.

"We are at the foot, here, of the cellar stairs." It was his voice, low as ever, at my ear. "They are very narrow, so if you don't mind, please give me your umbrella and take off your raincoat as quietly as possible and give it to me also. The walls between these houses seem to be made of cardboard; even mute the sound of the rain outside to help us. We must take no chances. There are nine steps. I am going ahead and will wait for you in the hall."

After a few gropings on my part the umbrella changed hands. There was a some rattlings and cracklings of my raincoat, true, as I divested myself of it but I thought I had succeeded fairly well in being quiet until I noticed that the coat once in his possession no longer seemed to exist.

After a second I asked in a whisper, "Are you still there?"

"Yes."

"Where are the stairs?"

"Lift your foot."

I did so, and discovered the first step.

"Nine, you say?"

"Yes, and do be careful. You had better go up one step at a time."

"All right," I whispered back.

Just where he left me I do not know for there was absolutely no sound.

I waited for a little, listening; and then essayed the first step. I had made no noise. I paused, and felt about to right and left. There was no handrail but a wall at either side rewarded my touch as step by step I went up helped by the walls, the sound of my feet deadened by my rubbers. A certain pleasure came to me at each success.

"Nine," I counted just under my breath. There were no more steps.

"Yes," he said, close to me again, "you managed that very well indeed."

I had been so intent on what I was doing that this voice as though from no where fairly startled me. I brought up with such a jerk that his head again at my elbow must have been very much aware of it for he said:

"Steady! Sorry, I didn't mean to [do] that. To the left, now." Slowly and silently we advanced his hand guiding me as before. We had gone four or five steps in this way when ahead of us and some distance above the level of our heads I noticed a sort of dimmed brightness. I looked again and then I knew it was the opaque glass of the fan light over the front door. It shone dimly yellow due, I suppose, to the street light at the corner. I had my bearings, at last, for once in the front hall and of my own initiative, this time, I turned towards where the front stairs must be.

"You know, I see, where you are now."

"Yes," I answered.

The steps were broad enough for us to go up abreast.

"You had better keep your right hand on the banisters," He warned. I obeyed as usual. Slowly tread by tread we went up his hand at my left elbow all the way.

At the top we paused an instant and then turned towards the right. My hand still followed the balustrade until it ended abruptly in the wall. Only a few steps more and we would be, I knew, in front of his study door.

As I had expected he came soon to a pause.

"Wait there," he commanded, "until I open the door."

I listened but silence was unbroken and then quite suddenly ahead of me appeared three dim yellow oblongs. I knew immediately what they were. They were his three study windows over which the yellow shades had been closely drawn.

I stepped forward into the room and though there was no sound again to prove it I knew he was closing the door behind us.

"Sorry," he said, "I shall not be able to make any light." His hand at my elbow was leading me once more. "Here is your chair. Sorry, too, I'll not be able to give you a little air but I may not open a window. Sit down. I'll put your umbrella in the bathroom. Give me your hat too." I obeyed.

"How do you manage it?" I whispered.

"What?"

"This absolute noiselessness."

"Sneakers" he answered laconically, "and then I've had five days at it."

"Five days!" I exclaimed as softly as I could.

"Yes."

"You've been back here—like this—five days?"

"Yes."

"And you have just sent for me?"

He did not answer for so long that I began to wonder.

"I"—he began and then broke off. "Well, yes," he said abruptly and then turned away without another word. I could see him, now, though dimly, he was moving quietly as ever, towards his bedroom door. Through it I could just make out the deeper moving darkness of him disappear.

I did not lean back as I waited for him. I looked about me curiously, little by little the well-remembered room began to take on form, dimly, mysteriously. In the center I could just make out what must be his desk; that deeper black all along the walls was where his book cases were. That white there must be the marble of the mantle over the fireplace and that huge blur of white above my head in the corner must be the bust of Wendell Phillips.

He had bought this house originally as a business venture, having the intention of remodeling it into two flats. But as months passed and as he had never had enough capital at any one time to begin operations, the house became finally a very white and heavy elephant on his hands. He might have rented it had he been willing to put in the many and necessary repairs of which it stood greatly in need, but to these he had always quite obstinately, as I considered, refused to do until such time, as he said as he should be able to carry out his plans for remodeling. It had ended in his furnishing two rooms on the second floor for himself one, the study, in which I now sat, and the other, the bedroom just adjoining. He had been living here, quite alone, for a little over a year.

"What could all of this mean?" I asked myself.

Ten years we had known each other, ever since, in fact, our Law School days. Certainly we had been friends for five of them—those five during which we had been struggling up together as law partners. But what did I actually know of him before those ten years? I was forced to acknowledge—nothing. Vaguely I seemed to recollect that he had come from the South—no more than that. I smiled a trifle grimly to myself. No one, surely, could accuse him of being a talker.

There had always been about him an impenetrable reserve and a reticence, aloof we called him, odd, a trifle eccentric. And yet there was not one of us but trusted him implicitly and believed in him. Honest he had always been and that to a fault. Generous, too, I could not, as I sat there, recall a single act of his that had shown him petty or mean. Maybe embittered. But then, were we not all of us as colored men, even though living in a northern city, more or less that? Certainly we had cause enough to be. Rather radical, perhaps, and unconventional.

What could all of this mean? No light upon it yet, certainly.

Did he have any enemies? As far as I knew, no. And, then, as in a flash, I remembered the man I had seen the first time I had been here to-night and because of whom I had passed by as though I had had no intention of entering, the man so motionless, leaning against the tree, screened almost but not quite by its trunk.

Why had he been there? Had my instant suspicions been correct? *Was he watching* this house? And if so, why?

I shivered a little.

What could all of this mean? No light, yet.

And then a question that had been persisting for some little time in the back of my mind refused longer to be denied. It was a question that had puzzled me about him, more or less, ever since I had known him. Might the answer to it shed the light?

Why was it he hated women so? No particular woman, but women, all women? One did not hate as he did without a cause. Was this the way?

A little chill of presentiment began to trace itself up and down my back.

And then, suddenly, I made out the deeper moving black that I knew to be silently returning.

Noiselessly, as ever, he drew his chair close to me and opposite and sat down. Dimly I could make out he was leaning back and for the first time, that evening, I did the same. Minute after minute slowly dragged by and still he did not speak or even move, as far as I could see.

Outside an automobile passed slowly and I noticed the rain was falling less heavily. And, then, just as I had begun to feel I could not bear much more of this silence, he spoke:

"It was too bad, Reed, to have to bring you out a night like this.

"I hope, you know," I said, "that it is perfectly all right."

"Yes," he answered, "I do." After a moment he added. "It was to-night, you see, or not at all."

"You mean—?" I began but ended there.

He made no reply although I knew he must have understood my unfinished question.

"You are the only one, Reed," he went on breaking another little silence, "I cared—at all—to send for."

"I appreciate that," I answered with some little difficulty, there was that in his tone that some how hurt.

He made no response to this, either, although I could make out he moved a trifle. Again a well nigh unbearable black quiet lengthened itself out between us before he spoke— once more—. This time, though, his voice was as low as ever, his words came abruptly, as if he had gritted his teeth and was making a plunge.

"I have been South."

"On business?" I was merely trying to help him.

"Yes and no." He waited a second. "I have been home."

I had never dreamed that one could speak of "home" with such bitterness as his.

The silence grew again between us. He was not finding it

the easiest thing to break through a life time of reserve and reticence.

"Sickness? Your family?" I suggested.

"No. —I have no one—living." I had suspected as much. I waited and as abruptly as before, he again spoke:

"I was needed. —I had to go."

"Well, I hope your trip was quite successful?" I could think of nothing else to say.

"Quite so." And again that terrible bitterness was again in his voice.

"She sent for me," The words came with the same abrupt rush as before.

"She," I said to myself and again I felt that chill.

"The telegram," suggested as calmly as I could, "Your last day at the office?"

"Telegram! What telegram?" The surprise in his voice was genuine enough.

"Why, yes. Don't you remember? Just as you were leaving?"

"Oh, that. I had quite forgotten. No."

"Long distance?" I queried.

"No."

"Letter?"

"No."

Just why I kept on persisting in this way, I'd not quite know. It may have been the strangeness of his tone.

"You received no telegram, no long distance, no letter of any description?" I made no attempt to conceal my astonishment.

"No."

"But," I began, "this is absurd." And then another thought struck me, "Some one brought you a message, then?"

"No."

"My god!," I cried out, "Are you crazy or am I?"

"Sh!" he said, "be careful."

He removed his hand but both of us leaned forward, tensely, listening. Time passed but here were no alarming sounds from any side. We could hear only the steady monotonous drumming of the rain drops, dripping from the eaves onto the porch below. The shower was about over. We both leaned back relieved.

"I am perfectly aware this doesn't sound possible but it's quite true: I *knew* she needed me. I had known it for several days and—I went."

"But you *couldn't* have known."

"Yes. —It was that way between us." Then as I made no immediate response. "Oh, well!" and the tone was a trifle irritable, "I can't explain any more than that. You believe— or you don't—that's all."

"I'm trying," I said humbly.

"Well don't strain yourself, Reed," There was a humorous grimness in his voice. "You never were blessed, you know, with over much imagination."

"No," I said still humbly.

Again blackness flowed about us; and during it my anger began to rise and the more I thought of all this he had been telling me implied the angrier I became.

"I might I have guessed," I burst forth with finally.

"Guessed what?"

"That a woman-hater, a confirmed one, would be the easiest of them all to get a strangle hold on."

"Just exactly," his voice very stiff and cold, "just exactly what do you mean by that little speech?"

" 'She' you said, didn't you? 'She'?"

"Yes."

"A woman, I presume, then?"

"Yes, a woman." His voice was ice cold now but I simply refused to stop.

"That you believe you are in love with or believe you are, I suppose."

"You may leave off that last part, yes."

"Well, then," But I found I could not go on.

"Well, then? Go on!" His tone was smooth but freezing.

I made no answer.

"Well?"

"I beg your pardon," I said at length. "It's none of my business after all."

"That was the best way out," he answered.

I was beginning to feel very uncomfortable and my relief was great, indeed, when I noticed, at his next words that all the coldness and stiffness had disappeared from his voice.

"It may [be] a relief to you to know," he said, "she was married."

"Married! To—To—you?"

"No, to some one else." He paused. "The reason? Well, perhaps the less said about this the better." And then he added, "I no longer judge her."

A long silence ensued, each of us busy, I suppose, with his own thoughts. I know I was. So I had been right. Without knowing all I was certain of that much.

"Reed," he said suddenly. "I wish you to have my law books all of them, those that are here and those at the office."

"What?" I almost stammered. He repeated the statement.

"But you can't mean me to understand all that—that seems to imply?"

"Yes."

"That you're breaking up, going away, giving up law?"

"Yes."

"That you're going—for—for—good?"

"Yes."

"But man," I said, "we've just begun to make good and we all believe you have a brilliant future ahead of you?"

"That's kind of all of you."

"Kind, nothing. It's the truth."

"I'm sorry."

"And then, what about me?"

"I know. That's bothered me a good deal. I'm—I'm— Well, I'm not just leaving you in the lurch. There's just nothing else to be done,—now."

"Damn these women?" luckily I had not raised my voice this time.

"Careful," he said. There was an iciness again in his voice.

"I beg your pardon again, but I suppose you are getting ready to make some kind of mess of your life. Run off with her or something."

"No, Reed."

"What?"

"I am going away quite alone."

"She isn't to be with you?"

"No—she will never be with me any more then at this minute."

"Do you mean she is here in this house—somewhere?"

"No, Reed, I shall never see her again."

"Well, then, what you are about to do strikes me as more foolish than ever."

"I'm sorry."

"You're quite sure you've thought this out carefully?"

"Oh yes," he spoke a little wearily.

"And you *must* go?"

"I have no choice in the matter."

"What do you mean?"

"You have forgotten the man, I see, Reed."

"Man! What man?"

"The man who was watching the house the first time you were here to-night. If it had not been for the heaviness of the shower he would have been there the second time. He is probably there now. He has been there off and on for the last three days and nights."

"Does he know you are here?"

"No. He thinks he is waiting for me to return."

"Who is this man?"

"He is from the far and sunny south, Reed."

"Well?"

"He is one of their very redoubtable gun shoe men."

"A detective?"

"Quite so."

"Really, you must be joking but what a ghastly sense of humour you have."

"I am not joking." There was no doubting his seriousness.

"But how do you know he is a detective?"

"I know the man. He is from my home."

I leaned back. My brain felt stupefied, paralyzed.

And again black silence flowed about us.

"Where are you going?" I asked presently.

"I don't know—exactly."

"Surely not South again."

"Well, hardly."

I waited a moment. "You don't wish me to know, I take it."

"No, not quite that. It will be some where out of the country. I am quite honest when I say I don't know. It will all depend on—circumstances. But even if I did know I should not tell you. It will be much better for you to be able to say quite truthfully, if you are questioned, that you do not know."

"Well, perhaps you are right," I said.

"I know I am. And, now, Reed, one of my reasons for sending for you to-night is to give you power of attorney for me so that you may settle up everything for me. I hope I'm not asking too much."

"Certainly not."

"Thank you for that. Anything of mine you want I wish you to have. You understand me?"

"Yes, but—" I began but he cut me off.

"Sell the rest. You have the bank book, haven't you, that I left with you in the Langston?"[1]

"Yes."

"Well deposit whatever there is for me. I may find a way to get it some time. And if I don't, well, it doesn't matter. Now, this house, here, do you want it?"

"No," I said.

"I don't know as I blame you much. first and last it has been rather a joke on me, hasn't it?"

"Wait," I said, "it wasn't that, you're being too generous—."

"Well, what's the use in going into all that" he broke hurriedly. "Do what you choose with the shack: Keep it, sell it, rent it, I leave it entirely to you." He paused a moment. "And, Reed,"

"Yes."

"Don't judge me too soon."

"I'm not. Am I not your friend?"

"I believe," he spoke slowly and with an unwanted emotion

---

1. Word unclear in holograph.

in his voice, "I believe that was the very finest thing that was ever said to me. I am so glad it was you who said it. I shall never forget."

"Don't," I said. My throat began to hurt in a way I had not remembered in years and I was glad for once for the darkness.

"Reed," he went on after a little and even now I can scarcely bear to remember the sadness of his voice. "Reed, I am a breaker of the law, an outcast with a price upon my head and from to-night a wanderer over the face of the earth."

"Well," I said, "I hope you know I believe in you."

It was some little time before he spoke again and when he did it was almost brokenly:

"If—you—could—only—know—what you are doing for me."

And silence once more fell upon us.

"I am going to do," he was speaking once more, "I am going to do a thing I never remember doing before and, after to-night, I shall never do again. I am going to talk about myself and I am going to do it for several reasons. One is that in going off in this way, you will understand I am not really unreliable a man who is deliberately failing to meet his obligations."

"If that is your main reason," I said, "it won't be necessary."

"I said there were others," he answered quietly. "You are going to hear of the whole thing and in all likelihood it will be a distorted, garbled account. It strikes me that the only fair thing for me to do is to tell you the truth about it." After a second or so he went on again. "And, then, I am human enough to wish my only friend to see—well my point of view throughout." He paused. "Do not misunderstand me! I am not asking for sympathy. I have no regrets for what I have

done, no not one. And if I had it to do over again I should
not hesitate one second. In the most lawless part of a country
that is itself steadily growing lawless, I have broken a man-
made law, but if there is a God, and He is just, and He is
understanding, I shall not be afraid, at any time, because of
the one act of mine, to stand before Him and look Him in
the eyes."

I was too moved to speak and the black quiet remained
unbroken for some time.

"After I left you that day two weeks ago, I caught a train
for Washington and from there for two nights and a day I
rode in the pig pen."

"Pig pen!"

"Yes. Some I believe, perhaps for the sake of euphony call
it the "Jim-Crow" car; but as vile as is the sound of that
name it is not as vile as the thing itself. When I left the
South ten years ago I swore never to ride on one again, well,
it [is] so Fate pulls the little strings."

Outside suddenly there came to our ears a sound as of
myriad tappings. I sat forward alert and tense. But it was
only the first rain drops, another shower had commenced.
When he spoke again the noise without was so great I could
not hear what he said. He moved his chair so we [were] side
by side almost in a vis-a-vis.

"I was saying" he repeated, "that I never remember you
mentioning the fact you had been South."

"No, Washington is the nearest I have been."

"Then you know nothing of the 'Jim-Crow' car from actual
experience?"

"No."

"Good thing. May you never. And yet," he went on half
musingly as if to himself, "and yet, will you believe it, there

is a beauty still left in the South—that even the polluting touch of the white man can never spoil."

"Beauty! In the South?"

"Yes, Reed, beauty in The South."

"It must be nature, then, you're meaning."

"I am. They may never spoil, try as they may, the beauty of the days and of the nights, those of the dawns, and of the dusks. Each has a loveliness, all its own, you know here, so much more genial are they, so much more exquisite, so much softer. Nor can they spoil the beauty of the bird songs, nor of the flower-blooms, nor the beauty of the wave-like, wave flung changing green on green of the little bulls and of the mountains; nor can they spoil the beauty, either, of their peace to tired eyes made weary with long waiting."

"Why," I exclaimed softly though, "you are a poet."

"Oh no, hardly that."

"You are," I reiterated. "But are you not forgetting?"

"Forgetting?"

"Yes, one more at least of the beautiful things there."

"What?"

"Why, the trees?"

I was certain, at that, I heard him draw in his breath sharply and suddenly. I strained my eyes. I could not see that he moved.

"You do not think them beautiful?" I persisted.

"Once," he said finally.

"But not, now?"

"No." And I knew from the tone, I was to ask no more. Later I was to understand; and since that night no tree has been or ever will be quite the same to me again.

"But I was telling you," he said, "of my two nights and my one day of travel in the pig pen. It was half of the baggage car and next to the engine. The filth of it was quite unspeakable. I doubt whether it had ever been cleaned since it was built. Into it we were herded, men, women and children. At one time, a hundred of us, at least, were crowded into that little space, squeezed into the seats and into the aisles, body wedged in against body. For sixty odd miles, maybe more, I stood, for I could not bear to see a frail, little black woman standing there with a heavy sleeping child in her arms. I do not believe I could have moved much even if I had tried. If you remember, the weather at that time was far from cool. Can you imagine, then, something of the heat those hot bodies generated, in addition, jammed in close up against each other? And also something of those body odors they exhaled? Do not misunderstand me, I can not help it— can I?—because I was born with a certain fastidiousness in that line and I am not blaming, either, my poor black brothers and sisters kept in a deliberate ignorance of all such needs by the white man. To what purpose, God alone knows."

"Possibly," I suggested, "that is another evidence of his long sighted policy. In case of an epidemic, for instance."

"Exactly. Let me in all fairness say this, though. Some of the cleanest people I have known have been colored. And," he added, "some of the dirtiest have been white and all of them not among the so-called lower classes. You do not misunderstand me, then?"

"Of course, not."

"Well, if you know anything about it at all you know that the car next to the engine gets most of the motion. To other discomforts was added that of a constant pitching, jerking, and rocking; then there was the cinders and soot—the windows had to be left open. And the flies. Well! I never remember so many or such aggressive ones and at night the mosquitoes took their places." He paused a second. "During that day and two nights I was unable to sleep, to wash, or to shave. Unless one is used to being a sardine one cannot sleep very well under the circumstances. And there was no place to wash, I mean that literally, or to shave. There was one toilet, true, and that was for all of us—so outrageously disgusting, well, Faugh! the very thought of it now makes me sick."

"God!" I said, "what a state of affairs. And eat, did you eat at all?"

"I might have eaten in the diner, but I didn't."

"But why?"

"Why? Because I was unwilling to go in there to eat after everybody with a white skin had eaten."

"That was the condition?"

"Yes. If in addition I had been willing to take what was left—and I wasn't. Starving was rather preferable, I thought, to those conditions."

"Right! But did you have nothing at all?"

"Yes. I was able to buy fruit and chocolate at some of the stations and the little black woman was kind enough to share her sandwiches with me. If it had not been for the tonics of one kind and another though I believe I might have died of thirst."

"There was no water?"

"Yes, plenty of that, but paper cups, I suppose, are rather advanced for colored people. So there was one tumbler. Do I need to describe it?"

"But," I cried, "the things you are telling me are frightful."

"And, Reed," he went on slowly, "cent for cent, dollar for dollar each of us in that car had paid exactly as much as the white man riding in comfort in the other coaches—think of it!—I have described to you what are called equal accommodations in the sight of the law."

"But this," I said, "can not go on indefinitely, it simply can't."

"No. I agree with you it cannot—and it will not."

"I have told you all this so you can understand something of what I was feeling when I stepped off the train, in the middle of the night, at my hometown, town, no, village better. Almost as soon as I alighted upon the wooden platform the train pulled out and was gone. I was far up the platform and in order to reach my road had to walk, I knew the length of it. I looked about me. Even in the dark I knew everything was just as I had left it ten years ago. About mid way was the dark outline of what I was certain was the crude wooden station. The door was open, and the lamplight within poured out in a wide yellow band. In it at the edge, I judged of the platform, a man was standing, holding a lantern in which glowed a white light. He was just about to turn back into the station when I suppose the sound of my feet arrested him. He paused, half-faced me and waited. He was the stationmaster, in all likelihood, and caught myself wondering if he was the same man as at the time I left. Something about the contour of him made me believe so. I had never liked the man. I had suffered at his hands from a boy many petty persecutions and insults there is no need of going into here. In my heart there awoke suddenly a hatred and a dull unreasoning rage towards this man. I do remember wondering at it but all I can tell you, now, is it was so. He was standing, this man, in the lamp light in such a position that I had to pass between the station and him and directly across the yellow path. The recognition on both sides was instant and mutual and it seemed to me for one second or so before he recovered himself that there was more than mere surprise in his face.

" 'Well, howdy, Colonel, howdy!' " He said in a voice that he tried to make sound jovial.

" 'How do you do,' I said shortly.

" 'Well! Well!' He went on. 'So you came back did you?'

" 'Yes.'

" 'Goin to make us a little visit or are you back for good?'

" 'I do not expect to stay long,' I said shortly.

" 'That's too bad, now' and the grin I remembered so well was in his voice, 'that's not fair to us, is it? Why, you'll be a sight to sore eyes. That's what you will be,' and he chuckled a little.

"I found it easier to say nothing.

" 'Le's see, now, you been gone roun ten yeahs, ain't you?'

" 'Yes, ten years exactly.'

" 'Well, Well! Think of that now. Reckon mebbe you's goin' to fine a few li'l changes here.'

"It was not so much what he said as the way he said it that gave me my first feeling of alarm.

" 'Changes?' I asked and I was pleased to notice no difference in my voice.

" 'Whah? You didn' reckon, did you, you could go way and come back and fine nuffin changed, did you? Ten yeahs an' all?'

" 'Is that what you meant?'

" 'Mebbe! Mebbe!'

" 'And maybe not,' I was controlling myself with an effort.

" 'My! Ain't he the little guesser, now. Mebbe not, he says.' And he chuckled again.

" 'Colonel, you're comin', that's what, you're comin'.' This time he bared the yellow fangs, I remembered so well in a broad grin. I turned my eyes away and knew that the best thing for me to do was to leave and that immediately.

" 'Thank you' and I was showing more feeling than I wished, 'Thank you for this very kindly meant bit of information of yours. Good-night.' And I left him.

"I had walked to the end of the platform and jumped down into my road, when I noticed for the first time he was slowly following me. The platform runs north and south and my road east and west. Once in the road I struck off briskly towards the west for I knew I had a good mile or so to go. I did not seem to notice but out of the tail of my eye, I saw him come to the end of the platform and stop, the lantern was still swaying from his hand, He had no, intention, it seemed of following me further.

"I had gone only a few steps when he called.

" 'Say, Colonel.'

"I paused and looked back.

" 'Well?'

" 'Lis'n,' he said, 'I ain't sayin much but I's tellin' you that you's goin' to fine when yo' gets there, one of the bigges an pleasantes' little ole surprises you's lible ever to git.' He paused a second. 'It's theah now, its been theah several days. Why,' he exploded, 'it's jus' like it fix all itself up spressly for you.'

" 'Is that all?' I asked curtly.

" 'No, just one thing more what you in such a doggoned hurry for? When yo' gits it,' he said, 'my complimen's.— Unnerstan'?'

" 'I do,' I said grimly and started on again.

"With that he burst forth into peal after peal of hideous laughter. I walked on faster than ever. After he had got his breath, he called once more.

" 'Say, Colonel, don' forget, now, ma complimen's.' And again he began to laugh.

"There came a time, however, where the air was clean from all sound of him."

It was very still in that black room for a space. Outside the worst of another shower was over.

"Reed," he said, "it was one of those beautiful nights about which I have told you. There was no wind, no moon, no clouds. The skies were crowded with stars large white ones and little white ones. It was such a relief to be at last alone amid all this goodness of quiet and beauty and cleanness that I refused to think at all for a while just to absorb it, drink it all in, as it were, if you understand."

"Yes," I answered.

"Presently I began to wonder, as I walked along, my eyes on the stars, whether perhaps somewhere in one of those white worlds another just as I might not be walking along under other stars because to him out of the silence a will had called. Who knows? And suddenly the whole thing, the voice, the woman, I, myself, what I was to find, what I might need to do seemed utterly unimportant, insignificant and God very far off and unreal. On I went. The only sounds I heard were little leaf ones, the noise made by a cracking twig or of a dry leaf rustling under some stealthy, tiny woodland foot. On either side of me tall black trees, nothing more, line on line, row on row, deep on deep. Trees, Reed."

He paused and I shuddered involuntarily and quite unaccountably.

"And, then, little by little, all the thoughts and fears I had been refusing steadily to entertain came back, not singly but together." He paused. "I need not, I think tell you what they were." Again there was a little silence. "It was soon after this that I began passing on either side the little homes I remem-

bered so well, they which had once been my own included.
All were unlighted and very still. And hers? I looked ahead.
It was I knew just beyond that little stretch of woods on the
right. What I had expected I do not know exactly but when
I looked up and saw the house there I had my first distinct
feeling of relief. It was as quiet and dark as the others but
that was as it should be. I began to climb the path with the
hazy idea of sitting on the steps to wait until daylight. That
could not be very far off and it seemed unnecessary to wake
any one up. I had come to the foot of the steps when I re-[2]

. . . . . .

"I leaned far over and examined the floor. I discovered a
spot, another. Step by step I followed them they led me out
the door down the hall to the front door and down the steps.
There I lost them.

"I came back to the steps, set the lamp there and sat down.
A most horrible nausea was upon me. How long I leaned
forward there, I have no way of knowing, When I lifted my
head it was still dark, all about me, and the lamp was burning
at my side. I blew it out. There was nothing to be done
before daylight. I sat and waited. Was this the 'little surprise?'
And was it all? Wasn't it possible that those two might have
escaped and were some where in hiding? What were his last
words—that man's—'an when you gits it—my complimen's.'
Had I got it? Why had he laughed so? And then quite
suddenly a well-nigh ungovernable feeling of rage urged up
in me. I got it under control finally, there was no need for
that—not yet."

There was nothing to be heard within the black room for
several minutes. And outside, even, it was very quiet for the

2. One page of the holograph is missing here. I presume originally this
portion described the protagonist's discovery of the destroyed house, as in
"Goldie."

least dripping of the last rain drops had ceased—another shower was over.

"Reed," his voice went on quietly "would you believe it, that night continued to be as genial, as gracious, as beautiful, and yes, as peaceful as ever. And as I sat there, presently, a little breeze woke up, gentle, it was, and full of balm—as[3] it too, Reed could be. And then I began to hear what I came to call 'the two voices and the duet.' Somewhere—from over there it came—where the blackness was—of the trees."

And with the blackness of that room I shuddered involuntarily again.

But he was speaking once more.

" 'Creak! Creak! Creak!' That was the voice that was a little higher.

" 'Creak! Creak! Creak!' And that was the voice that was a little lower.

" 'Creak! Creak! Creak!' And that was the two together. Stillness would follow and then it would begin all over again—and end. And I noticed the stillness always came when the breeze was still and the voices—it blew. What was it? Where was it?

" 'Creak! Creak! Creak!,' First voice.

" 'Creak! Creak! Creak!,' Second voice.

" 'Creak! Creak! Creak!,' the duet.

" 'Silence!'

"All of me came to concentrate in these four things. And then somehow I must have fallen asleep for when I opened my eyes and looked about me it was day again."

He paused a second. "Reed, I wish I could tell you of the breath taking, poignant beauty and wistfulness of it all, the pale twilight everywhere, the freshness, the softness of the

3. Holograph: {and}.

greens—the deep blue and purple shadows, the frailest gossamers of mist softly iridescent. The wonder of the bird songs here there and everywhere and with every bird well hidden, well I can't, I sat there drawing it in.[4] And then the breeze blew.

" 'Creak! Creak! Creak!' First voice.

" 'Creak! Creak! Creak!' Second voice.

" 'Creak! Creak! Creak!' The duet.

" 'Silence!'

"And I looked towards that glory and freshness and wonder of what was the trees—but saw nothing to explain my voices.

"I got up. I was stiff and sore all over and had to walk up and down the little path several times to limber up.

" 'Creak! Creak! Creak!'

" 'Creak! Creak! Creak!'

" 'Creak! Creak! Creak!'

" 'Silence.'

"I paused and turned in the direction of the sounds. And, then, I knew, quite suddenly, what it was I was to do. I began to walk towards the trees; and as I went, although the morning was warm, a coldness was upon me. All about my heart the blood felt frozen. My feet felt heavy. I lifted them with difficulty.

" 'Creak! Creak! Creak!' Nearer it was, now, and louder and then, again came the silence. The branches grew low and I could see nothing—yet. For a moment it seemed impossible to go on—I had to grit my teeth to do so. Each foot seemed made of lead.—I went on—and—I reached the—trees.

" 'Creak! Creak! Creak!' very near now it was. A numbness was creeping on me, and a horror. And then not far away

---

4. Holograph: punctuation and word order are difficult to determine here.

shyly, softly, a little bird sung and it was the loveliest song, I think, I have ever heard. I closed my eyes for a few seconds and held onto the trees for support.

" 'Creak Creak Creak.' Only a short distance farther, I knew, and I had it to do. I moved the branches aside, they resisted, but I went on.

" 'Creak Creak Creak!' Nothing yet to be seen. Dully I went on.

" 'Creak! Creak! Creak!' And I knew that between me and *it* whatever it was, was only now this thin screen of delicate and beautiful and [?] green leaves. I put up my hands to them and then I noticed an inch worm making his awkward, energetic and seemingly important journey along the leaves and the twigs. I watched him a long time, and just beyond were the creaking and the stillness.

"I closed my eyes and pulled the branches aside.

" 'Creak! Creak! Creak!'

Nothing between, now, but my closed eyelids

"I stepped forward; I opened my eyes—and I saw."

His deep and shuddering breathing was the only sound to be heard for some time. At last that quieted down.

"It was—those two?" I asked, and my voice was strange in my ears.

"Yes. Each with a rope around the neck—strung up—onto the same limb—that made the creaking—. Their faces swollen, distorted, unrecognizable—awful!—and naked—both of them."

He paused, drew in another shuddering breath. I leaned forward. It was he striking one knee with a clenched fist. For the first time his words came brokenly in little gasps.

"Her beautiful golden body—swaying there—ripped open—"

I cried out at this but he did not pause.

"Ripped open—I say—and under her poor little swaying golden feet—her child—unborn—beautiful—tiny hands and feet perfect—one little hand reached up—as though—appealing—the little head—blotted out—crushed—its little brains"—

"Stop!" I cried out. "Oh Stop!" And before I knew it was on my feet. I could not keep still. Up and down I went luckily there was nothing for me to lash against and the rug deadened my steps. At last I was able to sit down.

"Go on," I said and my voice was strange to me.

"A good many hours afterward I made my way to the home of a cousin of hers. He lived in a little house by himself.

"It must have [been] around noon for he answered my knocking.

"When he saw who it was his face suddenly became bloodless—seemed to shrivel up; and when he spoke finally his lips trembled.

" 'I did not know you were here. When did you come? You are ill. Come in.'

"I did not move.

" 'Tell me,' I said, 'Who did it?' And I vomited.

"Fear was in his eyes now. He never bared his lips.

" 'You know then?' He said in a half whisper.

" 'Yes.—Who did it?'

"He seemed unable to answer. I stepped forward and struck him none to gently I am afraid.

" 'Tell me,' I commanded. Still he could not speak.

" 'Was it the station-master?'

"This seemed to fill him with a frenzy of fear.

" 'For God's sake,' he said, 'can't you be quiet?'

" 'Was it?' I repeated.

" 'Yes,' he finally said weakly.

"Why?" I asked.

"He struck him."

"Who struck whom?"

" 'Her husband struck the—the—him,' he ended.

" 'The station-master?'

" 'Yes.'

" 'Why?'

" 'He found him—trying to make love—to her.' Something in my face must have warned him for he cried out quickly, 'Wait! Wait! I don't mean what you think—She was defending herself.'

" 'That's better,' I said, 'Well?'

" 'He—he beat him up—pretty—well.'

" 'Thank God,' I said. 'There was one man here, anyway.'

"He had the grace to flush a little and look away.

" 'Go on,' I commanded.

"Well, he—"

" 'The station-master?' I cut in.

" 'Yes. He came back that night—late.'

" 'Alone?'

" 'No.'

" 'That's all,' I said and turned on my heel.

" 'Aren't you coming in?' he faltered.

" 'No. I haven't time.—By the way—what have you—any of you done?'

" 'About this?'

" 'Yes.'

" 'Why-why,' he stammered, 'there—there isn't anything—I know of—can be done. There's no law—'

" 'Don't you suppose I know that?' I looked him squarely in the eyes and again he dropped his. I turned away once more.

" 'Where are you going?' He was hardly able to get out the question.

" 'A little matter of importance, which must be attended to, before I leave.'

" 'You are coming back?'

" 'No.'

" 'Good-bye,' he called, quaveringly.

" 'Don't amuse me,' I said.

"I paused long enough to look at him. He turned without another word and seemed to slink back into the house."

Black silence fell again within the room. Outside another shower was beginning. Then he spoke again.

"I waited for him. I waited a long time. I had picked my place—a little patch of woods. It seemed fitting we should meet—where trees were.

"It was early dusk when he came along. He was chewing a straw and was coming as though he had not a care in the world.

"When he was almost upon me, I stepped out of the bushes.

" 'Good evening,' I said.

"He went a horrible tallowy color and his little eyes became ratlike.

" 'Good evening,' I repeated.

" 'Why, howdy, Colonel!—Howdy!' But his grin was sickly and I caught him furtively looking back over his shoulder.

" 'Well, now,' he said, 'I wasn't specktin for to see [you] so soon again.'

" 'Don't mention it,' I replied, 'just *my* little surprise, as it were, for you.'

"For one instant I saw his restless little eyes grow wide and fixed and his nostrils dilated. He stood very still.

" 'Come, now,' I said, 'You weren't expecting to hog all the little surprises that ever were—were you?'

" 'He ran a finger around between his neck and collar. I saw him swallow. His little eyes were busy again watching looking. Here there everywhere they were.

" 'You don't seem exactly overjoyed to see me,' I said again.

" 'Mebbe,' he said and his voice came husky and low, 'mebbe you're a little too modest.'

" 'Well,' I answered, 'We'll let it go at that.'

"He shot a single venomous look in my direction and looked away.

"Neither of us spoke for several seconds and then he said:

" 'Well-I'll be going, I guess.'

" 'Try another.'

" 'What do you mean?'

" 'Another guess!'

" 'I—I—don't think—I—I get you?'

" 'Just this that—*that you're not going!* Get me, now?'

"He gave me another passing evil glance.

" 'You see,' I went on, 'your little surprise to me, came, as you might say in—installments.—Well, I have planned—the same for you. Tit for tat, you know.'

"For a second again the same stillness was upon him.

"With that, I stepped up to him suddenly and with the palm of either hand struck him full and hard on either cheek.

"I stopped back and waited abit.

" 'My compliments!' I said.

"At first he seemed numbed, dazed. His cheeks turned a purplish red and he put a hand up gingerly and felt them. And then what do you suppose he did? He said: 'Don't do that! Don't do that! That hurts!' And his voice was peevish, actually peevish. I laughed aloud, I couldn't help [it], it was so unexpectedly funny.

"Quick as a flash he took advantage of my lapse, and twisted on a heel and ran. Luckily I was quicker than he and I caught him.

"Panting from the exercise both of us stood facing each other for several minutes.

" 'I warn you,' I said finally, 'not to try that again.'

"He made no response, merely stood there breathing heavily.

"Minute after minute passed and at last he said:

" 'This is—oh—this is—all very interesting but I must really be going.'

" 'Must you? Were you thinking, perhaps, of getting together—another of your little lynching bees?'

"I saw then I had hit the mark.

" 'Let me tell you,' I said, 'that you've led—your last, little lynching bee—your very last.'

"Then it was, I suppose, fear turn him suddenly insane. His mottled face became twisted and distorted his eyes glassy and fixed and his mouth slavering. With his ten talons raised and bent crooked he made for my face. Over and over he kept saying:

" 'You let me go! You let me go! You let me go!'

"I struck his hands down, just in time, there was something of a struggle and then my hands met around his throat."

He paused.

"I kept them there until there was no more need.—It was dark, by that time and I left him there hidden away among— the trees.

"You can imagine the rest," he went on after a little. "I made my way to the station. I had not long to wait for the northern train. Surprise was expressed naturally when the station-master did not turn up. No one, however, suspected me. The trains were few and far between and it was not unusual for him to leave between times. He had no business, of course, being late in returning, etc. Well, I got back here safely. But the station-master[5] must have talked for how otherwise explain the presence of this man waiting outside of the house here?

"One thing more. If there were any law in the South that protected a colored man or gave him any redress, I should have had no excuse for what I have done. But there is no law. And what I did, I believe was the only thing to do."

"To have done less would have been to be less than a man," I said.

"Those words and the knowledge of your friendship will mean all—to me," he said simply.

I found difficulty again in swallowing.

"Have you money enough?" I asked presently.

"Yes. Plenty—enough. I luckily drew—all I had out of the other bank just before leaving."

"And food, what have you had to eat?"

"I had a considerable lot of canned goods laid in. I have not starved."

"There is nothing, I can do?"

"Do! Do! I don't believe you realize what you have done for me."

"Well," he said suddenly and he got to his feet. "This I believe is finished. That last shower has been over some little time. We must leave during the next."

"The power of attorney?" I asked.

5. Holograph: Grimké debated between the words {man} and {station-master} here. Also, since the station-master is killed Grimké does not account for the spread of information about the murder within the plot.

"Oh, yes," and noiselessly he went over to his desk.

He was again at my side.

"Here," he said. I put it carefully away in my breast pocket.

"I will get ready, now, and bring you your things," and without a sound he had gone.

For a long time it seemed to me I sat there waiting. A great loneliness and desolateness was upon me.

And then came, again, the sound of the first heavy rain drops. And with that sound—I found him again beside me.

"Are you ready?" he asked.

"Yes."

I got to my feet.

"I'll carry your umbrella and rain coat," he said, "if you don't mind."

"But your own baggage!" I asked surprised.

He laughed a trifle. "I'll not be needing much of that, I'm thinking. I have a small hand bag here."

I could say nothing. The aching in my throat was well-nigh intolerable.

We made a slow noiseless journey down to the cellar but this time we went to the rear door not the front. We halted here and put on our things. I did not hear the door open but the rain was spattering in my face. We raised our umbrellas and stepped out into the dark yard. He shut and locked the door behind him and picked up his bag. Side by side under the down pour we went to the gate that led into the alley. Silently he opened this. I held his bag. We went through into the alley. He shut the gate and I handed him his bag.

Even above the sound of the petty rain I heard him draw in his breath. He held out his hand and mine gripped it. I am not ashamed to say my eyes were wet. Neither of us said a word and then abruptly he turned away and went down the alley. I had not moved. He would have to pass I knew under the gas light at the corner. He came to it, passed through and was lost in the blackness beyond. I have reason, to believe, he escaped. But I have never heard from him or seen him since.

THE CLOSING DOOR

I was fifteen at the time, diffident and old far beyond my years from much knocking about from pillar to post, a yellow, scrawny, unbeautiful girl, when the big heart of Agnes Milton took pity upon me, loved me and brought me home to live with her in her tiny, sun-filled flat. We were only distantly related, very distantly, in fact, on my dead father's side. You can see then there was no binding blood-tie between us, that she [was] absolutely under no obligations to do what she did. I have wondered time and again how many women would have opened their hearts and their homes, as Agnes Milton did, to a forlorn, unattractive, homeless girl-woman. That one fine, free, generous act of hers alone shows the wonder-quality of her soul.

Just one little word to explain me. After my father had taken one last cup too many and they had carried him, for the last time, out of the house into which he had been carried so often, my mother, being compelled to work again, returned to the rich family with whom she had been a maid before her marriage. She regarded me as seriously I suppose as she did anything in this world; but as it was impossible to have me with her, I was passed along from one of her relatives to another. When one tired of me, on I went to the next. Well, I can say this for each and all of them, they certainly believed

Text is taken from typescript in the Angelina Weld Grimké Collection, MSRC, box 38-11, folder 186. The story was published serially in *Birth Control Review*, special number (Sept. 1919): 10–14; 3 (Oct. 1919).

in teaching me how to work! Judging by the number of homes in which I lived until I was fifteen, my mother was rich in-deed in one possession—an abundance of relatives.

And then came Agnes Milton.

Have you ever, I wonder, known a happy person? I mean a really happy one? He is as rare as a white blackbird in this sombre-faced world of ours. I have known two and only two. They were Agnes Milton and her husband Jim. And their happiness did not last. Jim was a brown, good-natured giant with a slow, most attractive smile and gleaming teeth. He spoke always in a deep sad drawl and you would have thought him the most unhappy person imaginable until you glimpsed his black eyes fairly twinkling under their half-closed lids. He made money—what is called "easy money," by playing ragtime for dances. He was one of a troupe that are called "social entertainers." As far as Jim was concerned, it would have slipped away in just as easy a manner, if it hadn't been for Agnes. For she, in spite of all her seeming carefree joyousness was a thrifty soul. As long as Jim could have good food and plenty of it, now and then the theatre, a concert or a dance, and his gold-tipped cigarettes, he didn't care what became of his money.

"Oh, Ag!"

If I close my eyes I can hear his slow sad voice as clearly as though these ten long years had not passed by. I can hear the click of the patent lock as he closed the flat door. I can hear the bang of his hat as he hung it on the rack. I can get the whiff of his cigarette.

"Oh, Ag!"

"That you, Jim?" I can see Agnes' happy eyes and hear her eager, soft voice.

And then a pause, that sad voice:

"No, Ag!"

I can hear her delighted little chuckle. She very seldom laughed outright.

"Where are you, anyway?" It was the plaintive voice again. "Here!"

And then he'd make believe he couldn't find her and go hunting her all over that tiny flat, searching for her in every room he knew she was not. And he'd stumble over things in pretended excitement and haste and grunt and swear all in that inimitable slow way of his. And she'd stand there, her eyes shining and every once in a while giving that dear little chuckle of hers.

Finally he'd appear in the door panting and disheveled and would look at her in pretended intense surprise for a second, and then he'd say in an aggrieved voice:

" 'S not fair, Agnes! 'S not fair!"

She wouldn't say a word, just stand there smiling at him. After a little, slowly, he'd begin to smile too.

That smile of theirs was one of the most beautiful things I have ever seen and each meeting it was the same. Their joy and love seemed to gush up and bubble over through their lips and eyes.

Presently he'd say:

"Catch!" She'd hold up her little white apron by the corners and he'd put his hand in his pocket and bring out sometimes a big, sometimes a little wad of greenbacks and toss it to her and she'd catch it, too, I can tell you. And her eyes would beam and dance at him over it. Oh! she didn't love the money for itself but him for trusting her with it.

For fear you may not understand I must tell you no more generous soul ever lived than Agnes Milton. Look at what she did for me. And she was always giving a nickel or a dime to some child, flowers or fruit to a sick woman, money to tide over a friend. No beggar was ever turned away, empty, from her flat. But she managed, somehow, to increase her little horde in the bank against that possible rainy day.

Well, to return. At this juncture, Jim would say oh! so sadly his eyes fairly twinkling:

"Please, ma'm, do I get paid today too?"

And then she'd screw up her mouth and twist her head to the side and look at him and say in a most judicial manner:

"Well, now, I really can't say as to that. It strikes me you'll have to find that out for yourself."

Oh! they didn't mind me. He would reach her, it seemed, in one stride and would pick her up bodily, apron, money and all. After a space, she'd disentangle herself and say sternly, shaking the while her little forefinger before his delighted eyes:

"Jim Milton, you've overdrawn your wages again."

And then he'd look oh! so contrite and so upset and so shocked at being caught in such a gigantic piece of attempted fraud.

"No?" he'd say. If you only could have heard the mournful drawl of him.

"No? Now, is that so? I'm really at heart an honest, hardworking man. I'll have to pay it back."

He did. I can vouch for it.

Sometimes after this, he'd swing her up onto his shoulder and they'd go dashing and prancing and shrieking and laughing all over the little flat. I know the neighbors thought them mad. I can hardly blame them. Once after I had seen scared faces appearing at various windows, at times like these, I used to rush around and shut the windows down tight. Two happy children, that's what they were. Then—younger even than I.

There was just the merest suspicion of a cloud over their

happiness, these days, they had been married five years and
had no children.

It was the mother heart of Agnes that had yearned over
me, had pity upon me, loved me and brought me to live in
the only home I have ever known. I have cared for people.
I care for Jim; but Agnes Milton is the only person I have
ever really loved. I love her still. And before it was too late,
I used to pray that in some way I might change places with
her and go into that darkness where though still living, one
forgets sun and moon and stars and flowers and winds—and
love itself, and existence means dark, foul-smelling cages,
hollow clanging doors, hollow monotonous days. But a month
ago when Jim and I went to see her, she had changed—she
had receded even from us. She seemed—how can I express
it—blank, empty, a grey automation, a mere shell. No soul
looked out at us through her vacant eyes.

We did not utter a word during our long journey homeward. Jim had unlocked the door before I spoke.

"Jim," I said, "they may still have the poor hush of her
cooped up there but her soul, thank God, at least, for that!
is free at last."

And Jim, I cannot tell of his face, said never a word but
turned away and went heavily down the stairs. And I, I went
into Agnes Milton's flat and closed the door. You would
never have dreamed it was the same place. For a long time I
stood amid all the brightness and mockery of her sun-
drenched rooms. And I prayed. Night and day I have prayed
since the same prayer—that God if he knows any pity at all
may soon, soon, release the poor spent body of hers.

I wish I might show you Agnes Milton of those far off
happy days. She wasn't tall and she wasn't short: she wasn't
stout and she wasn't thin. Her back was straight and her head
high. She was rather graceful, I thought. In coloring she was

Spanish or Italian. Her hair was not very long but it was soft and silky and black. Her features were not too sharp, her eyes clear and dark, a warm leaf brown in fact. Her mouth was really beautiful. This doesn't give her I find. It was the shining beauty and gayety of her soul that lighted up her whole body and somehow made her her, and she was generally smiling or chuckling. Her eyes almost closed when she did so and there were the most delightful crinkles all about them. Under her left eye there was a small scar, a reminder of some childhood escapade, that became, when she smiled, the most adorable of dimples.

One day, I remember, we were standing at the window in the bright sunlight. Some excitement in the street below had drawn us. I turned to her—the reason has gone from me now—and called out suddenly:

"Agnes Milton!"

"Heavens! What is it!"

"Why, you're wrinkling!"

"Wrinkling! Where?" And she began inspecting the smooth freshness of her housedress.

"No, your face," I exclaimed. "Honest! Stand still there in that light. Now! Just look at them all around your eyes."

She chuckled.

"How you ever expect me to see them I don't know without a glass or something!"

And her face crinkled up into a smile.

"There! That's it!—That's how you get them."

"How?"

"Smiling too much."

"Oh, no! Lucy, child, that's impossible."

"How do you mean impossible! You didn't get them that way? Just wait till I get a glass."

"No, don't." And she stopped me with a detaining hand.

"I'm not doubting you. What I mean is—it's absolutely impossible to smile too much."

I felt my eyes stretching with surprise.

"You mean," I said, "You don't mind being wrinkled? You, a woman?"

She shook her head at me many times, smiling and chuckling softly the while.

"Not the very littlest, tiniest bit—not this much," and she showed me just the fairest tip of her pink tongue between her white teeth. She smiled, then, and there was the dimple.

"And you only twenty-five?" I exclaimed.

She didn't answer for a moment and when she did she spoke quietly:

"Lucy, child, we've all got to wrinkle sometime, somehow, if we live long enough. I'd much rather know mine were smile ones than frown ones." She waited a second and then looked at me with her beautiful clear eyes and added, "Wouldn't you?"

For reply I leaned forward and kissed them. I loved them from that time on.

Here is another memory of her—perhaps the loveliest of them all and yet, as you will see, tinged with the first sadness. It came near the end of our happy days. It was a May dusk. I had been sewing all the afternoon and was as close to the window as I could get to catch the last of the failing light. I was trying to thread a needle—had been trying for several minutes, in fact, and was just in the very act of succeeding when two soft hands were clapped over my eyes.

"Oh, Agnes!" I said none too pleasantly. It was provoking. "There! You've made me lose my needle."

"Bother your old needle, cross patch!" She said close to my ear. She still held her hands over my eyes.

I waited a moment or so.

"Well," I said, "What's the idea?"

"Please don't be cross," came the soft voice still close to my ear.

"I'm not."

At that she chuckled.

"Well!" I said.

"I'm trying to tell you something. Sh! not so loud."

"Well, go ahead, then: and why must I sh!"

"Because you must."

I waited.

"Well!" I said a third time, but in a whisper to humor her. We were alone in the flat, there was no reason I could see for this tremendous secrecy.

"I'm waiting for you to be sweet to me."

"I am. But why I should have to lose my needle and my temper and be blinded and sweet just to hear something—is beyond me."

"Because I don't wish you to see me while I say it."

Her soft lips were kissing my ear.

"Well, I'm very sweet now. What is it?"

There was another little pause and during it her fingers over my eyes trembled a little. She was breathing quicker too.

"Agnes Milton, what *is* it?"

"Wait, I'm just trying to think of *how* to tell you. Are you sure you're very sweet?"

"Sure."

I loved the feel of her hands and sat very still.

"Lucy!"

"Yes."

"What do you think would be the loveliest, loveliest thing for you to know was—was—there—close—just under your heart?"

But I waited for no more. I took her hands from my eyes

and turned to look at her. The beauty of her face made me catch my breath.

At last I said:

"You mean"—I didn't need to finish.

"Yes, Yes. And I'm so happy, happy, happy! and so is Jim."

"Agnes, Oh my dear, and so am I!" And I kissed her two dear eyes.

"But why mustn't I whoop. I've simply got to," I added.

"No! No! No! Oh, sh!" And for the very first time I saw fear in her eyes.

"Agnes," I said, "what is it?"

"I'm—I'm just a little afraid, I believe."

"Afraid!" I had cried out in surprise.

"Sh! Lucy!—Yes."

"But of what?" I spoke in a half whisper too. "You mean you're afraid you may die?"

"Oh, no, not that."

"What then?"

"Lucy," her answer came slowly a little abstractedly. "there's—such—a thing—as being—*too* happy,—*too* happy."

"Nonsense," I answered.

But she only shook her head at me slowly many times and her great wistful eyes came to mine and seemed to cling to them. It made my heart fairly ache and I turned my head away so that she couldn't see her fears were affecting me. And then quite suddenly I felt a disagreeable little chill run up and down my back.

"Lucy," she said after a little.

"Yes," I was looking out of the window and not at her.

"Do you remember Kipling's 'Without Benefit of Clergy'?" I did and I said so. Agnes had Kipling bound in ten beautiful volumes. She loved him. At first that had been enough for me and then I had come to love him for himself. I had read all of those ten volumes through from cover to cover, poetry and all.

"You haven't forgotten Ameera, then?"

"No." She was thoughtful a moment and then went on:

"Poor Ameera!" She knew what it was to be too happy. "Do you remember what she said once to Holden?"

Again I felt that queer little shiver.

"She said many things, as I remember her, Agnes. Which?"

"This was after Tota's death."

"Well!"

"They were on the roof—she and Holden—under the night."

Here eyes suddenly widened and darkened and then she went on:

"She turned to Holden and said: 'We must make no protestations of delight but go softly underneath the stars, lest God find us out.' " She paused. "Do you remember?"

"Yes," I answered; but I couldn't look at her.

"Well," she spoke slowly and quietly, "I have a feeling here, Lucy." And she placed her left hand against her heart, "Here, that Jim and you and I must go softly—very softly— underneath the stars."

Again I felt that unpleasant chill up and down my back.

She stood just where she was for a little space, her hand still against her heart and her eyes wide, dark and unseeing, fixed straight ahead of her. Then suddenly and without a sound she turned and went towards the door and opened it.

I started to follow her; but she put up her hand.

"No, Lucy, please.—I wish to be alone—for a little."

And with that she went out and shut the door very slowly, quite noiselessly behind her. The closing was so slow, so silent that I could not tell just when it shut. I found myself trembling violently. A sudden and inexplicable terror filled me as that door closed behind her.

We were to become accustomed to it, Jim and I, as much as it was possible to do so, in those terrible days that were to follow. We were to become used to entering a room in search of Agnes, only to find it empty and the door opposite closing, closing, almost imperceptibly noiselessly—and, yes, at last irrevocably between us. And each time it happened the terror was as fresh upon me as at the very first.

The days that immediately followed I cannot say were really unhappy ones. More to humor Agnes at first than anything else "we went softly." But as time passed even we became infected. Literally and figuratively we began to go "softly under the stars." We came to feel that each of us moved ever with a finger to his lips. There came to be also a sort of expectancy upon us, a listening, a waiting. Even the neighbors noticed the difference. Jim still played his ragtime and sang but softly; we laughed and joked but quietly. We got so we even washed the dishes and pots and pans quietly. Sometimes Jim and I forgot, but as certainly as we did there was Agnes in the door, dark-eyed, a little pale and her, "Oh! Jim!—Oh! Lucy! Sh!"

I haven't spoken of this before because it wasn't necessary. Agnes had a brother called Bob. He was her favorite of all her brothers and sisters. He was younger than she, five years, I think, a handsome, harum-scarum, happy-go-lucky, restless, reckless daredevil, but sweet-tempered and good hearted and lovable with all. I don't believe he knew what fear was. His home was in Mississippi, a small town there. It was the family home, in fact. Agnes had lived there, herself until she was seventeen or eighteen. He had visited us two or three times and you can imagine the pandemonium that reigned at such times, for he had come during our happy days. Well, he was very fond of Agnes and, as irresponsible as he seemed, one thing he never failed to do and that was to write her a letter every single week. Each Tuesday morning, just like clock-work, the very first mail there was his letter. Other mornings Agnes was not so particular but Tuesday mornings she always went herself to the mailbox in the hall.

It was a Tuesday morning about four months, maybe, after my first experience with the closing door. The bell rang three times, the postman's signal when he had left a letter, Agnes came to her feet, her eyes sparkling:

"My letter from Bob," she said and made for the door.

She came back slowly, I noticed, and her face was a little pale and worried. She had an opened and an unopened letter in her hand.

"Well, what does Bob say?" I asked.

"This—this isn't from Bob," she said slowly. "It's only a bill."

"Well, go ahead and open his letter," I said.

"There—there wasn't any, Lucy."

"What!" I exclaimed. I was surprised.

"No. I don't know what it means."

"It will come probably in the second mail," I said. "It has sometimes."

"Yes," she said, I thought rather listlessly.

It didn't come in the second mail nor in the third.

"Agnes," I said, "There's some good explanation. It's not like Bob to fail you."

"No."

"He's busy or got a girl maybe."

She was a little jealous of him and I hoped this last would rouse her but it didn't.

"Yes, maybe that's it," she said without any life.

"Well, I hope you're not going to let this interfere with your walk," I said.

"I had thought"—she began but I cut her off.

"You promised Jim you'd go out every single day," I reminded her.

"All right Agnes Milton's conscience," she said smiling a little. "I'll go, then."

She hadn't been gone fifteen minutes when the electric bell began shrilling continuously throughout the flat.

Somehow I knew it meant trouble. My mind immediately flew to Agnes. It took me a second or so to get myself together and then I went to the tube.

"Well," I called. My voice sounded strange and high.

A boy's voice answered.

"Lady here named Mrs. James Milton?"

"Yes." I managed to say.

"Telegram fo' youse."

It wasn't Agnes, after all. I drew a deep breath. Nothing else seemed to matter for a minute.

"Say!" the voice called up from below. "Wot's de mattah wid you'se¹ up dere?"

"Bring it up." I said at last. "Third floor, front."

I opened the door and waited.

The boy was taking his time and whistling as he came.

"Here!" I called out as he reached our floor.

It was inside his cap and he had to take it off to give it to me.

I saw him eyeing me rather curiously.

"You Mrs. Milton?" he asked.

---

1. Spelling of {youse} and {you'se} not consistent in typescript.

"No, but this is her flat. I'll sign for it. She's out. Where do I sign? There? Have you a pencil?"

With the door shut behind me again, I began to think out what I had better do. Jim was not to be home until late that night. Within five minutes I had decided. I tore open the yellow envelope and read the message.

It ran: "Bob died suddenly. Under no circumstances come. Father."

The rest of that day was a nightmare to me. I concealed the telegram in my waist. Agnes came home finally and was so alarmed at my appearance, I pleaded a frightful sick headache and went to bed. When Jim came home late that night Agnes was asleep. I caught him in the hall and gave him the telegram. She had to be told, we decided, because a letter from Mississippi might come at any time. He broke it to her the next morning. We were all hard hit, but Agnes from that time on was a changed woman.

Day after day dragged by and the letter of explanation did not come. It was strange to say the least.

The Sunday afternoon following we were all sitting, after dinner, in the littler parlor. None of us had been saying much.

Suddenly Agnes said:

"Jim!"

"Yes!"

"Wasn't it strange that Father never said how or when Bob died?"

"Would have made the telegram too long and expensive, perhaps," Jim replied.

We were all thinking, in the pause, that followed, the same thing, I dare say.

Agnes' father was not poor and it did seem he might have done that much.

"And why, do you suppose I was not to come under any circumstances?"

"And why don't they write?"

Just then the bell rang and there was no chance for a reply. Jim got up in his leisurely way and went to the tube.

Agnes and I both listened—a little tensely, I remember.

"Yes!" we heard Jim say and then with spaces in between:

"Joe?—Joe who?—I think you must have made a mistake—can't say that I do know anyone called Joe—What?—Milton—Yes, that's my name!—What?—Oh! Brooks.—Joe Brooks?—

"Jim! Jim! It's my brother Joe."

"Look here! Are you Agnes' brother, Joe?" Jim called quietly at him. "Great Jehosaphet! Man! Come up! What a mess I've made of this."

For the first time I saw Jim move quickly. Within a second he was out of the flat and running down the stairs. Agnes followed to the stairs head and waited there. I went back into the little parlor for I had followed her into the hall, and sat down and waited.

They all came in presently. Joe was older than Agnes but looked very much like her. He was thin, his face really haggard and his hair quite grey. I found out afterward that he was in his early twenties but he appeared much older. He was smiling but it did not reach his eyes. They were strange aloof eyes. They rested on you and yet seemed to see something beyond. You felt as though they had looked upon something that could never be forgotten. When he was not smiling his face was grim, the chin firm and set. He was a man of very few words I found.

Agnes and Jim were both talking at once and he answered them now and then in monosyllables. Agnes introduced us. He shook hands, I thought in rather a perfunctory way without saying anything, and we all sat down.

We steered clear quite deliberately from the thought uppermost in all our minds. We spoke of his journey, when he left Mississippi, the length of time it had taken him to come and the weather. Suddenly Agnes jumped up:

"Joe, aren't you famished?"

"Well, I wouldn't mind a little something, Agnes," he answered, and then he added:

"I'm not as starved as I was traveling in the South; but I have kind of a hollow feeling."

"What do you mean?" she asked.

"Jim-Crow cars," he answered laconically.

"I'd forgotten," she said. "I've been away so long."

He made no reply.

"Aren't conditions any better at all?" she asked after a little.

"No, I can't say as they are."

None of us said anything. She stood there a minute or so, pulling away at the full on her apron. She stopped suddenly, drew a long breath, and said:

"I wish you all could move away, Joe,[2] and come North."

For one second before he lowered his eyes I saw a strange gleam in them. He seemed to be examining his shoes carefully from all angles. His jaw looked grimmer than ever and I saw a flickering of the muscles in his cheeks.

"That would be nice," he said at last and then added, "but we can't, Agnes. I love my coffee strong, please."

"Joe," she said, going to the door. "I'm sorry, I was forgetting."

I rose up at that.

"Agnes, let me go. You stay here."

She hesitated, but Joe spoke up.

"No, Agnes, you go. I know your cooking."

2. Typescript: {Jim,}.

You could have heard a pin drop for a minute. Jim looked queer and so did Agnes for a second and then she tried to laugh it off.

"Don't mind Joe. He doesn't mean anything. He always was like that."

And then she left us.

Well, I was hurt. Joe made no attempt to apologize or anything. He even seemed to have forgotten me. Jim looked at me and smiled his nice smile but I was really hurt. I came to understand, however, later. Presently Joe said:

"About Agnes! We hadn't been told anything!"

"Didn't she write about it?"

"No."

"Wanted to surprise you, I guess."

"How long?" Joe asked after a little.

"Before?"

"Yes."

"Four months, I should say."

"That complicates matters some."

I got up to leave. I was so evidently in the way.

Joe looked up quietly and said:

"Oh! don't go! It isn't necessary."

I sat down again.

"No, Lucy, stay." Jim added. "What do you mean 'complicates'?"

Joe examined his shoes for several moments and then looked up suddenly.

"Just where is Agnes?"

"In the kitchen, I guess"; Jim looked a trifle surprised.

"Where is that?"

"The other end of the flat near the door."

"She can't possibly hear anything, then?"

"No."

"Well, then listen, Jim, and you, what's your name? Lucy? Well Lucy, then. Listen carefully, you two, to every single word I am going to say." He frowned a few moments at his shoes and then went on: "Bob went out fishing in the woods near his shack; spent the night there; slept in wet clothes and it had been raining all day—; came home; contracted double pneumonia and died in two days time—Have you that?"

We both nodded. But that didn't satisfy him. He made us each repeat what he had said.

"Now," he said, "That's the story we are to tell Agnes."

Jim had his mouth open to ask something, when Agnes came in. She had very evidently not heard anything, however, for there was a little color in her face and it was just a little happy again.

"I've been thinking about you, Joe," said she, "What on earth are you getting so grey for?"

"Grey!" he exclaimed. "Am I grey?" There was no doubt about it. His surprise was genuine.

"Didn't you know it?" She chuckled a little. It was the first time in days.

"No, I didn't."

She made him get up, at that, and drew him to the oval glass over the mantel.

"Don't you ever look at yourself, Joe?"

"Not much, that's the truth." I could see his face in the mirror from where I sat. His eyes widened a trifle, I saw, and then he turned away abruptly and sat down again. He made no comment. Agnes broke the rather awkward little silence that followed.

"Joe!"

"Yes!"

"You haven't been sick or anything, have you?"

"No, why?"

"You seem so much thinner. When I last saw you you were almost stout."

"That's some years ago, Agnes."

"Yes, but one ought to get stouter not thinner with age."

Again I caught that strange gleam in his eyes before he lowered them. For a moment he sat perfectly still without answering.

"You can put it down to hard work, if you like, Agnes. Isn't that my coffee I smell boiling over?"

"Yes, I believe it is. I just ran in to tell you it'll[3] be ready for you in about ten minutes."

She went out hastily but took time to pull the portiere across the door. I thought it strange at the time and looked at Jim. He didn't seem to notice it, however, but he waited, I saw, until he had heard Agnes' heel taps going into the kitchen.

"Now," he said, "what do you mean when you say that is the story we are to tell Agnes."

"Just that."

"You mean"—he paused, "that it isn't true?"

"No, it isn't true."

"Bob didn't die that way?"

"No."

I felt my-self stiffening in my chair and my two hands gripping the two arms of my chair tightly. I looked at Jim. I sensed the same tensioning in him. There was a long pause. Joe was examining his shoes again. The flickering in his cheeks I saw was more noticeable.

Finally Jim brought out just one word:

"How?"

3. Typescript: {I'll}.

"There was a little trouble," he began and then paused so long Jim said:

"You mean he was—injured in some way?"

Joe looked up suddenly at Jim, at that, and then down again. But his expression even in that fleeting glance set me to trembling all over. Jim, I saw, had been affected too. He sat stiffly bent forward. He had been in the act of raising his cigarette to his lips and his arm seemed as though frozen in mid-air.

"Yes," he said, "injured." But the way in which he said injured made me tremble all the more.

Again there was a pause and again Jim broke it with his one word:

"How?"

"You don't read the papers, I see." Joe said.

"Yes, I read them."

"It was in all the papers."

"I missed it, then."

"Yes."

It was quiet again for a little.

"Have you ever lived in the South?" Joe asked.

"No."

"Nice civilized place, the South." Joe said.

And again I found myself trembling violently. I had to fight with might and main to keep my teeth from chattering. And yet it was not what he had said but his tone again.

"I haven't so heard it described," Jim said after a little.

"No?—you didn't know, I suppose, that there is an unwritten law in the South that when a colored and a white person meet on the sidewalk, the colored person must get off into the street until the white one passes?"

"No, I hadn't heard of it."

"Well, it's so. That was the little trouble."

"You mean—"

"Bob refused to get off the sidewalk."

"Well?"

"The white man pushed him off. Bob knocked him down. The white man attempted to teach the 'damned nigger' a lesson." Again he paused.

"Well?"

"The lesson didn't end properly. Bob all but killed him."

It was so still in that room that although Jim was sitting across the room I could hear his watch ticking distinctly in his vest pocket. I had been holding my breath and when I was forced to expel it the sound was so loud they both turned quickly towards me, startled for the second.

"That would have been Bob." It was Jim speaking.

"Yes."

"I suppose it didn't end there?"

"No."

"Go, on Joe." Even Jim's voice sounded strained and strange.

And Joe went on. He never raised his voice, never lowered it. Throughout, his tone was entirely colorless. And yet as though it had been seared into my very soul I remember, word for word everything he said.

"An orderly mob, in an orderly manner, on a Sunday morning—I am quoting the newspapers—broke into the jail, took him out, slung him up to the limb of a tree, riddled his body with bullets, saturated it with coal oil, lighted a fire underneath him, gouged out his eyes with red hot irons, burnt him to a crisp and then sold souvenirs of him, ears, fingers, toes. His teeth brought five dollars each." He ceased for a moment.

"He is still hanging on that tree.—We are not allowed to have even what is left."

There was a roaring in my ears. I seemed to be a long way off. I was sinking into a horrible black vortex that seemed to be sucking me down. I opened my eyes and saw Jim dimly. His nostrils seemed to be two black inch holes. His face was taut, every line set. I saw him draw a great deep breath. The blackness sucked me down still deeper. And then suddenly I found myself on my feet struggling against that hideous darkness and I heard my own voice as from a great distance calling out over and over again, "Oh, my God! Oh, my God! Oh, my God!"

They both came running to me, but I should have fainted for the first and only time in my life but that I heard suddenly above those strange noises in my ears a little choking, strangling sound. It revived me instantly. I broke from them and tried to get to the door.

"Agnes! Agnes!" I called out.

But they were before me. Jim tore the portiere aside. They caught her just as she was falling.

She lay unconscious for hours. When she did come to, she found all three of us about her bed. Her bewildered eyes went from Jim's face to mine and then to Joe's. They paused there; she frowned a little. And then we saw the whole thing slowly come back to her. She groaned and closed her eyes. Joe started to leave the room but she opened her eyes quickly and indicated he was not to go. He came back. Again she closed her eyes.

And then she began to grow restless.

"Agnes!" I asked, "Is there anything you want?"

"No," she said, "No."

Presently she opened her eyes again. They were very bright. She looked at each of us in turn a second time.

Then she said:

"I've had to live all this time to find out."

"Find out what, Agnes?" It was Jim's voice.

"Why I'm here—why I'm here."

"Yes, of course." Jim spoke oh so gently, humoring her. His hand was smoothing away the damp little curls about her forehead.

"It's no use your making believe you understand, you don't." It was the first time I had ever heard her speak even irritably to Jim. She moved her head away from his hand.

His eyes were a little hurt and took his hand away.

"No." His voice was as gentle as ever. "I don't understand, then."

There was a pause and then she said abruptly:

"I'm an instrument."

No one answered her.

"That's all—an instrument."

We merely watched her.

"One of the many."

And then Jim in his kindly blundering way made his second mistake.

"Yes, Agnes," he said, "Yes."

But at that, she took even me by surprise. She sat up in bed suddenly, her eyes wild and starey, and before we could stop her began beating her breasts.

"Agnes," I said, "Don't! Don't!"

"I shall," she said in a strange high voice.

Well, we let her alone. It would have meant a struggle.

And then amid little sobby breaths, beating her breasts the while she began to cry out: "Yes!—I!—I!—An instrument!—another one of the many! a colored woman—doomed!—cursed!—put here!—willing or unwilling! for what?—to bring children here—men children—for the sport—the lust—of possible orderly mobs—who go about things—in an orderly manner—on Sunday mornings!"

"Agnes," I cried out. "Agnes! Your child will be born in the North. He need never go South."

She had listened to me at any rate.

"Yes," she said, "In the North. In the North—And have there been no lynchings in the North?"

I was silenced.

"The North permits it too," she said. "The North is silent as well as the South."

And then as she sat there her eyes became less wild but more terrible. They became the eyes of a seeress. When she spoke again she spoke loudly, clearly, slowly:

"There is a time coming—and soon—when no colored man—no colored woman—no colored child, born or unborn—will be safe—in this country."

"Oh Agnes," I cried again, "Sh! sh!"

She turned her terrible eyes upon me.

"There is no more need for silence—in this house. God has found us out."

"Oh Agnes," the tears were frankly running down my cheeks. "We must believe that God is very pitiful. We must. He will find a way."

She waited a moment and said simply:

"Will He?"

"Yes, Agnes! Yes!"

"I will believe you, then. I will give Him one more chance. Then, if He is not pitiful, then if He is not pitiful"— But she did not finish. She fell back upon her pillows. She had fainted again.

Agnes did not die, nor did her child. She had kept her body clean and healthy. She was up and around again, but an Agnes that never smiled, never chuckled any more. She was a grey, pathetic shadow of herself. She who had loved joy so much cared more, it seemed, for solitude than anything else in the world. That was why, when Jim or I went looking for her we found so often only the empty room and that imperceptibly closing, slowly closing opposite door.

Joe went back to Mississippi and not one of us, ever again, mentioned Bob's name.

And Jim, poor Jim! I wish I could tell you of how beautiful he was those days. How he never complained, never was irritable, but was always so gentle, so full of understanding, that at times, I had to go out of the room for fear he might see my tears.

Only once I saw him when he thought himself alone. I had not known he was in his little den and entered it suddenly. I had made no sound, luckily, and he had not heard me. He was sitting leaning far forward, his head between his hands. I stood there five minutes at least, but not once did I see him stir. I silently stole out and left him.

It was a fortunate thing that Agnes had already done most of her sewing for the little expected stranger, for after Joe's visit, she never touched a thing.

"Agnes!" I said, one day, not without fear and trepidation it is true. "Isn't there something I can do?"

"Do?" she repeated rather vaguely.

"Yes. Some sewing?"

"Oh! sewing," she said. "No, I think not, Lucy."

"You've—You've finished?" I persisted.

"No."

"Then"—I began.

"I hardly think we shall need any of them." And then she added:

"I hope not."

"Agnes!" I cried out.

But she seemed to have forgotten me.

Well, time passed, it always does. And on a Sunday morning early Agnes' child was born. He was a beautiful, very grave baby with her great dark eyes.

As soon as they would let me, I went to her.

She was lying very still and straight, in the quiet, darkened room, her head turned on the pillow towards the wall. Her eyes were closed.

"Agnes!" I said in the barest whisper. "Are you asleep?"

"No." she said. And turned her head towards me and opened her eyes. I looked into a ravaged face. Agnes Milton had been down into Hell and back again.

Neither of us spoke for some time and then she said:

"Is he dead?"

"Your child?"

"Yes."

"I should say not, he's a perfect darling and so good."

No smile came into her face. It remained as expressionless as before. She paled a trifle more, I thought, if such a thing was possible.

"I'm sorry," she said finally.

"Agnes!" I spoke sharply. I couldn't help it.

But she closed her eyes and made no response.

I sat a long time looking at her. She must have felt my gaze for she slowly lifted her lids and looked at me.

"Well," she said, "what is it, Lucy?"

"Haven't you seen your child, Agnes?"

"No."

"Don't you wish to see it?"

"No."

Again it was wrung out of me.

"Agnes, Agnes, don't tell me you don't love it."

For the first and only time a spasm of pain went over her poor pinched face.

"Ah!" she said, "That's it." And she closed her eyes and her face was as expressionless as ever.

I felt as though my heart was breaking.

Again she opened her eyes.

"Tell me, Lucy," she began.

"What, Agnes?"

"Is he—healthy?"

"Yes."

"Quite strong?"

"Yes."

"You think he will live, then?"

"Yes, Agnes."

She closed her eyes once more. It was very still within the room.

Again she opened her eyes. There was a strange expression in them now.

"Lucy!"

"Yes."

"You were wrong."

"Wrong, Agnes?"

"Yes."

"How?"

"You thought your God was pitiful."

"Agnes, but I do believe it."

After a long silence she said very slowly:

"He—is—not."

This time, when she closed her eyes, she turned her head slowly upon the pillow to the wall. I was dismissed.

And again Agnes did not die. Time passed and again she was up and about the flat. There was a strange, stony stillness upon her, now, I did not like, though. If we only could have understood, Jim and I, what it meant. Her love for solitude, now, had become a passion. And Jim and I knew more and more that empty room and that silently slowly closing door.

She would have very little to do with her child. For some reason, I saw, she was afraid of it. I was its mother. I did for it, cared for it, loved it.

Twice only during these days I saw that stony stillness of hers broken.

The first time was one night. The baby was fast asleep. And she had stolen into look at him, when she thought no one would know. I never wish to see such a tortured, hungry face again.

I was in the kitchen, the second time, when I heard strange sounds coming from my room. I rushed to it and there was Agnes, kneeling at the foot of the little crib, her head upon the spread. Great, terrible racking sobs were tearing her. The baby was lying there, all eyes, and beginning to whimper a little.

"Agnes! Oh, my dear! What is it?" The tears were streaming down my cheeks.

"Take him away! Take him away!" she gasped. "He's been cooing, and smiling and holding out his little arms to me. I can't stand it! I can't stand it."

I took him away. That was the only time I ever saw Agnes Milton weep.

The baby slept in my room, Agnes would not have him in hers. He was a restless little sleeper and I had to get up several times during the night to see that he was properly covered.

He was a noisy little sleeper as well. Many a night I have

lain awake listening to the sound of his breathing. It is a lovely sound, a beautiful one—the breathing of a little baby in the dark.

This night, I remember, I had been up once and covered him over and had fallen off to sleep for the second time, when, for I had heard absolutely no sound, I awoke suddenly. There was upon me an overwhelming utterly paralyzing feeling not of fear but of horror. I thought, at first, I must have been having a nightmare, but strangely instead of diminishing the longer I lay awake, the more it seemed to increase.

It was a moonlight night and the light came in through the open window in a broad white steady stream.

A coldness seemed to settle all about my heart. What was the matter with me? I made a tremendous effort and sat up. Everything seemed peaceful and quiet enough.

The moonlight cut the room in two. It was dark where I was and dark beyond where the baby was.

One brass knob at the foot of the bed shone brilliantly, I remember, in that bright stream and the door that led into the hall stood out fully revealed. I looked at that door and then my heart suddenly seemed to stop beating! I grew deathly cold. The door was closing slowly, imperceptibly silently. Things were whirling around. I shut my eyes. When I opened them again the door was no longer moving: it had closed.

What had Agnes Milton wanted in my room? And the more I asked myself that question the deeper grew the horror.

And then slowly, by degrees, I began to realize there was something wrong within that room, something terribly wrong. But what was it?

I tried to get out of bed; but I seemed unable to move. I strained my eyes, but I could see nothing—only that bright knob, that stream of light, that closed white door.

I listened. It was quiet, very quiet, too quiet. But why too quiet? And then as though there had been a blinding flash of lightning I knew—the breathing wasn't there.

Agnes Milton had taken a pillow off of my bed and smothered her child.

One last word, Jim received word this morning. The door has finished closing for the last time—Agnes Milton is no more. God, I think, may be pitiful, after all.

GOLDIE

He had never thought of the night, before, as so sharply black and white; but then, he had never walked before, three long miles, after midnight, over a country road. A short distance only, after leaving the railroad station, the road plunged into the woods and stayed there most of the way. Even in the day, he remembered, although he had not traveled over it for five years, it had not been the easiest to journey over. Now, in the almost palpable darkness, the going was hard, indeed; and he was compelled to proceed, it almost seemed to him, one careful step after another careful step.

Singular fancies may come to one, at such times: and, as he plodded forward, one came, quite unceremoniously, quite unsolicited, to him and fastened its tentacles upon him. Perhaps it was born of the darkness and the utter windlessness with the resulting great stillness; perhaps—but who knows from what fancies spring? At any rate, it seemed to him, the woods, on either side of him, were really not woods at all but an ocean that had flowed down in a great rolling black wave of flood to the very lips of the road itself and paused there as though suddenly arrested and held poised in some strange and sinister spell. Of course, all of this came, he told himself over and over, from having such a cursed imagina-

Text is taken from typescript in the Angelina Weld Grimké Collection, MSRC, box 38-11, folder 187. A revised version of "Blackness," "Goldie" was published in the *Birth Control Review* 4 (Nov.–Dec. 1920). Also see Grimké's letter to the *Atlantic Monthly* (in the nonfiction section of this volume), regarding the plot of "Goldie."

tion; but whether he would or not, the fancy persisted and the growing feeling with it, that he, Victor Forrest, went in actual danger, for at any second the spell might snap and with that snapping, this boundless, deep upon deep of horrible, waiting sea, would move, rush, hurl itself heavily and swiftly together from the two sides, thus engulfing, grinding, crushing, blotting out all in its path, not excluding what he now knew to be that most insignificant of insignificant pigmies, Victor Forrest.

But there were bright spots, here and there in the going— he found himself calling them white islands of safety. These occurred where the woods receded at some little distance from the road.

"It's as though," he thought aloud, "they drew back here in order to get a good deep breath before plunging forward again. Well, all I hope is, the spell holds O.K. beyond."

He always paused, a moment or so, on one of these islands to drive out expulsively the dank, black oppressiveness of the air he had been breathing and to fill his lungs anew with God's night air, that, here, at least, was sweet and untroubled. Here, too, his eyes were free again and he could see the dimmed white blur of road for a space each way; and, above, the stars, millions upon millions of them, each one hardly brilliant, stabbing its way whitely through the black heavens. And if the island were large enough there was a glimpse, scarcely more, of a very pallid, slightly crumpled moon sliding furtively down the west.—Yes, sharply black and sharply white, that was it, but mostly it was black.

And as he went, his mind busy enough with many thoughts, many memories, subconsciously always the aforementioned [1] fancy persisted, clung to him; and he was never entirely able

1. Holograph revision: {malign}.

to throw off the feeling of his very probably and imminent
danger in the midst of this arrested wood-ocean.

—Of course, he thought, it was downright foolishness, his
expecting Goldie, or rather Cy, to meet him. He hadn't
written or telegraphed.—Instinct he guessed, must have warned
him that wouldn't be safe; but, confound it all! This was the
devil of a road.—Gosh! What a lot of noise a man's feet
could make—couldn't they?—All alone like this—Well, Goldie and Cy would feel a lot worse over the whole business
than he did.—After all it was only once in a lifetime, wasn't
it?—Hoofing it was good for him, anyway.—No doubt about
his having grown soft.—He'd be as lame as the dickens
tomorrow.—Well, Goldie would enjoy that—liked nothing
better than fussing over a fellow.—If (But he very resolutely
turned away from that if.)

—In one way, it didn't seem like five years and yet, in
another, it seemed longer—since he'd been over this road
last. It had been the sunshiniest and the saddest May morning
he ever remembered.—He'd been going in the opposite
direction, then; and that little sister of his, Goldie, had been
sitting very straight beside him, the two lines held rigidly in
her two little gold paws and her little gold face stiff with
repressed emotion. He felt a twinge, yet, as he remembered
her face and the way the great tears would well up and run
over down her cheeks at intervals.—Proud little thing!—
She had disdained even to notice them and treated them as a
matter with which she had no concern.—No, she hadn't
wanted him to go.—Good, little Goldie!—Well, she never
knew, how close, how very close he had been to putting his
hand out and telling her to turn back—he'd changed his mind
and wasn't going after all.—

He drew a sharp breath.—He hadn't put out his hand.

—And at the station, her face there below him, as he

looked down at her through the open window of the train.—
The unwavering way her eyes had held his—and the look in
them, he hadn't understood them, or didn't now, for that
matter.

"Don't," he had said, "Don't Goldie!"

"I must. Vic, I must.—I don't know—Don't you understand I may never see you again?"

"Rot!" he had said. "Am I not going to send for you?"

—And then she had tried to smile and that had been worse
than her eyes.

"You think so, now, Vic,—but will you?"

"Of course."

"Vic!"

"Yes."

"Remember, whatever it is—it's all right. *It's all right.*—
I mean it.—See! I couldn't smile—could I?—If I didn't?"

And then, when it had seemed as if he couldn't stand any
more—he had leaned over, even to pick up his bag to get
off, give it all up—the train had started and it was too late.
The last he had seen of her, she had been standing there,
very straight, her arms at her sides and her little gold paws
two little tight fists.—And her eyes!—And her twisted smile!—
God! that was about enough of that.—He was going to her,
now, wasn't he?

—Had he been wrong to go?—Had he?—Somehow, now,
it seemed that way.—And yet, at the time, he had felt he was
right.—He still did for that matter.—His chance, that's what
it had meant.—Oughtn't he to have had it?—Certainly a
colored man couldn't do the things that counted in the
South.—To live here, just to *live* here, he had to swallow his
self-respect.—Well, he had tried, honestly, too, for Goldie's
sake, to swallow his.—The trouble was he couldn't keep it
swallowed—it nauseated him.—The thing for him to have

done, he saw that now, was to have risked everything and taken Goldie with him.—He shouldn't have waited, as he had from year to year, to send for her.—It would have meant hard sledding, but they could have managed somehow.—Of course, it wouldn't have been the home she had had with her Uncle Ray and her Aunt Millie, still.—Well, there wasn't any use in crying over spilt milk. One thing was certain, never mind how much you might wish to, you couldn't recall the past.—

—Two years ago—(Gosh!) but time flew!—When her letter had come telling him she had married Cy Harper.— Queer thing, this life!—Darned queer thing!—Why he had been in the very midst of debating whether or not he could afford to send for her—had almost decided he could.—Well, sisters, even the very best of them, it turned out, weren't above marrying and going off and leaving you high and dry—just like this.—Oh! of course, Cy was a good enough fellow, clean, steady going, true, and all the rest of it;—no one could deny that—still, confound it all! how could Goldie prefer a fathead like Cy to him.—Hm!—peeved yet, it seemed!—Well, he'd acknowledge it—he was peeved all right.

Involuntarily he began to slow up.

—Good! since he was acknowledging things—why not get along and acknowledge the rest.—Might just as well have this out with himself here and now.—Peeved first, then, what?

He came to an abrupt stop in the midst of the black silence of the arrested wood-ocean.

—There was one thing, it appeared, a dark road could do for you—it could make it possible for you to see yourself quite plainly—almost too plainly.—Peeved first, then what?— No blinking now, the truth.—He'd evaded himself very cleverly—hadn't he?—up until tonight?—No use any more.—

Well, what was he waiting for?—Out with it.—Peeved first; go ahead, now.—Louder!—*Relief!*—Honest, at last.—Relief! Think of it, he had felt relief when he had learned he wasn't to be bothered, after all, with little, loyal, big-hearted Goldie.—*Bothered!*—And he had prided himself upon being rather a decent, upright, respectable fellow.—Why, if he had heard this about anybody else, he wouldn't have been able to find language strong enough to describe him.—A rotter, that's what he was, and a cad.

"And Goldie would have sacrificed herself for you any time, and gladly, and you know it."

To his surprise he found himself speaking aloud.

—Why once, when the kid had been only eight years old and he had been taken with a cramp while in swimming, she had jumped in too!—Goldie, who couldn't swim a single stroke!—Her screams had done it and they were saved. He could see his mother's face yet, quizzical, a little puzzled, a little worried.

"But what on earth, Goldie, possessed you to jump in too?" she had asked. "Didn't you *know* you couldn't save him?"

"Yes, I know it."

"Then, why?"

"I don't know. It just seemed that if Vic had to drown, why I had to drown with him.—Just couldn't live *afterwards*, Momsey. If I lived *then* and he drowned."

"Goldie! Goldie!—If Vic fell out of a tree, would you have to fall out too?"

"Proberbly." Goldie had never been able to master "probably," but it fascinated her.

"Well, for Heavens' sake. Vic, do be careful of yourself hereafter. You see how it is," his mother had said.

And Goldie had answered—how serious, how quaint, how true her little face had been.—

"Yes, that's how it is, isn't it?" Another trick of hers,

ending so often what she had to say with a question.—And he hadn't wished to be bothered with her!—

He groaned and started again.

—Well, he'd try to even up things a little, now.—He'd show her (there was a lump in his throat) if he could.—

For the first time Victor Forrest began to understand the possibilities of tragedy that may lie in those three little words, "If I can."

—Perhaps Goldie had understood and married Cy so that he needn't bother any more about having to have her with him. He hoped, as he had never hoped, for anything before that this hadn't been her reason. She was quite equal to marrying, he knew, for such a motive—and so game, too, you'd never dream it was a sacrifice she was making. He'd rather believe, even, that it had been just to get the little home all her own.—When Goldie was only a little thing and you asked her want she wanted most in all the world when she grew up, she had always answered:

"Why, a little home—all my own—a cunning one—and young things in it and about it."

And if you asked her to explain, she had said:

"Don't you *know?*—not *really?*"

And, then, if you had suggested children, she had answered:

"Of course, all my own; and kittens and puppies and little fluffy chickens and ducks and little birds in my trees, who will make little nests and little songs there because they will know that the trees near the little home all my own are the very nicest ever and ever."—

—Once, she must have been around fifteen, then—how well he remembered that once—he had said:

"Look here, Goldie, isn't this an awful lot you're asking God to put over for you?"

Only teasing, he had been—but Goldie's face!

"Oh! Vic, am I?—Do you *really* think that?"

And then, before he could reply in little, eager, humble rushes:

"I hadn't thought of it—*that* way—before.—Maybe you're right.—If—if—I gave up something, perhaps—the ducks—or the chickens—or the—birds—or the kittens—or the puppies?"

Then very slowly:

"Or-the-children?—Oh!—but I couldn't!—Not any of them.—Don't you think, perhaps,—just perhaps, Vic,—if—if—I'm—good—always—from now on—that—that—maybe—maybe—sometime, Vic, sometime—I—I—might?—Oh! don't you?"—

He shut his mouth hard.

—Well, she had had the little home all her own. Cy had made a little clearing, she had written, just beyond the great live oak. Did he remember it? And did he remember, too, how much Cy loved the trees?—

—No, he hadn't forgotten that live oak—not the way he had played in it—and carved his initials all over it; and he hadn't forgotten Cy and the trees, either.—Silly way, Cy had had, even after he grew up, of mooning among them.

"Talk to me—they do—sometimes.—Tell me big, quiet things, nice things."

—Gosh! after *his* experience, *this* night among them. *Love* 'em!—Hm!—Damned, waiting, greedy things!—Cy could have them and welcome.—

—It had been last year Goldie had written about the clearing with the little home all her own in the very "prezact" middle of it.—They had had to wait a whole year after they were married before they could move in—not finished or something—he'd forgotten the reason.—How had the rest of

that letter gone?—Goldie's letters were easy to remember—
had, somehow, a sort of burrlike quality about them. He had
it, now, something like this:

She wished she could tell him how cunning the little home
all her own was, but there was really no cunning word
cunning enough to describe it.—Why even the very trees
came right down to the very edges of the clearing on all four
sides just to look at it.—If he could only *see* how proudly
they stood there and nodded their entire approval one to the
other!—

Four rooms, the little home, all her own, had.—Four!—
And a little porch in the front and a "littler" one in the back,
and a hall that had really the most absurd way of trying to
get out both the front and rear doors at the same time. Would
he believe it, they had to keep both the doors shut tight in
order to hold that ridiculous hall in? Had he ever, in all his
life, heard of such a thing? And just off of this little hall, at
the right of the front door, was their bedroom, and back of
this, at the end of this same very silly hall was their dining-
room and opposite, across the hall again—she hoped he saw
how this hall simply refused to be ignored—again—opposite
was the kitchen.—He was, then, to step back into the hall
once more, but *this* time he was to pretend very hard not to
see it. There was no telling, it's vanity was so great, if you
paid too much attention to it, what it might do. Why, the
unbearable little thing might rise up, break down the front
and back doors and escape; and then where'd they be, she'd
like to know, without any little hall at all?—He was to step,
then, quite nonchalantly—if he knew what that was, back
into the hall and come forwards but this time he was to look
at the room at the left of the front door; and *there*, if he
pleased, he would see something really to repay him for his

trouble, for here he would behold her sitting room and parlor both in one. And if he couldn't believe how perfectly adorable this little room could be and was, why she was right there to tell him all about it.—Every single bit of the little home all her own was built just as she had wished and furnished just as she had hoped. And, well, to sum it all up, it wasn't safe, if you had any kind of heart trouble at all, to stand in the road in front of the little home all her own, because it had such a way of calling you that before you knew it, you were running to it and running fast. She could vouch for the absolute truth of this statement.

And she had a puppy, yellow all over, all but his little heart—she dared him even to suggest such a thing!—with a funny wrinkled forehead and a most impudent grin. And he insisted upon eating up all the uneatable things they possessed, including Cy's best straw hat and her own Sunday-go-to-meeting slippers; And she had a kitten, a grey one; and the busiest things he did were to eat and sleep. Sometimes he condescended to play with his tail and to keep the puppy in his place. He had a way of looking at you out of blue, very young, very innocent eyes that you knew perfectly well were not a bit young nor yet a bit innocent. And she had the darlingest, downiest, little chickens and ducks and a canary bird, that Emma Elizabeth lent her sometimes when she went away to work, and the canary had been made of two golden songs. And outside of the little home all her own—in the closest trees, the birds were, lots of them, and they had nested there.—If, of a morning, he could only hear them singing!—As if they knew—and did it on purpose—just as she had wished.—How happy it had all sounded—and yet—and yet—once or twice—he had had the feeling that something wasn't quite right.

—He hoped it didn't mean she wasn't caring for Cy.—
He would rather believe it was because there hadn't been
children.—The latter could be remedied—from little hints
he had been gathering lately, he rather thought it was already
being remedied; but if she didn't *care* for Cy, there wasn't
much to be done about that.—Well, he was going to her, at
last.—She couldn't fool him—couldn't Goldie—; and if that
fathead, Cy, couldn't take care of her, now. Just let somebody
start somebody start something.—

—That break ahead there, in the darkness, ought to be
just about where the settlement was.—No one need ever tell
him again it was only three miles from the station—he guessed
he knew better.—More like ten or twenty.—The settlement,
all right.—Thought he hadn't been mistaken.—So far, then,
so good.

The road, here, became the main street of the little colored
settlement. Three or four smaller ones cut it at right angles
and, then, ran off into the darkness. The houses, for the most
part, sat back, not very far apart; and, as the shamed moon
had entirely disappeared, all he could make out of them was
their silent, black little masses. His quick eyes and his ears
were busy. No sound broke the stillness. He drew a deep
breath of relief. As nearly as he could make out everything
was as it should be.

He did not pause until he was about midway of the
settlement. Here he set his bag down, sat on it and looked at
the illuminated hands of his watch. It was half past two. In
the woods he had found it almost cold, but, in this spot, the
air was warm and close. He pulled out his handkerchief,
took off his hat, mopped his face, head and neck, finally the
sweatband of his hat.

—Queer!—but he wouldn't have believed that the mere
sight of all this, after five years, could make him feel this

way. There was something to this home idea, after all.—
Didn't feel,[2] hardly, as though he had ever been away.—

Suddenly he wondered if old man Tom Jackson had fixed
that gate of his yet. Curiosity got the better of him. He arose,
went over and looked. Sure enough the gate swung outward
on a broken hinge. Forrest grinned.

"Don't believe over much here, in change, do they?—That
gate was that way ever since I can remember.—Bet every
window is shut tight too. 'Turrible; the night air always used
to be.—Wonder if my people will ever get over these things."

He came back and sat down again. He was facing a house
that his eyes had returned to more than any other.

"Looks just the same.—Wonder who lives there, now.—
Suppose some one does.—Looks like it.—Mother sure had
courage—more than I would have had—to give up a good
job in the North, teaching school to come down here and
marry a poor doctor in a colored settlement. I give it to
her.—Game!—Goldie's just like her—she'd have done it
too."

—How long had it been since his father had died?—
Nine—ten—why, it was ten years and eight since his mother—.
They'd both been born there—he and Goldie.—That was that
story his mother had used to tell about him when he had first
been brought in to see her?—He had been six at the time.

"Mother," he had asked, "is her gold?"

"What, Son?"

"I say, is her gold?"

"Oh! I see," his mother had said and smiled, he was sure,
that very nice understanding smile of hers. "Why, she *is*
gold, isn't she?"

"Yes, all of her. What's hers name?"

2. Holograph revision: {seem}.

"She hasn't any, yet, Son."

"He aint got no name?—Too bad!—I give her one. Hers name's Goldie, 'cause."

"All right, Son, Goldie it shall be." And Goldie it had always been.—

—No, you couldn't call Goldie pretty exactly.—Something about her, though, mighty attractive.—Different looking!—that was it.—Like herself.—She had never lost that beautiful even gold color of hers.—Even her hair was "goldeny" and her long eye-lashes. Nice eyes, Goldie had, big and brown with flecks of gold in them—set in a little wistful, pointed face.—

He came to his feet suddenly and picked up his bag. He moved swiftly, now, but not so swiftly as not to notice things still as he went.

"Why, hello!" he exclaimed and paused a second or so before going on again. "What's happened to Uncle Ray's house?—Something's not the same.—Seems larger, some-how.—Wonder what it is?—Maybe a porch.—So they do change here a little.—That there ought to be Aunt Phoebe's house.—But she must be dead—though I don't remember Goldie's saying so.—Why, she'd be way over ninety.—Used to be afraid of the dark or something and never slept without a dime light.—Gosh! if there isn't the light—just the same as ever.—And way over ninety.—Whew!—Wonder how it feels to be that old.—Bet I wouldn't like it.—Gee! what's that?"

Victor Forrest stopped short and listened. The sound was muffled but continuous, it seemed to come from the closed faintly lighted pane of Aunt Phoebe's room. It was a sound, it struck him, remarkably like the keening he had heard in an Irish play. It died out slowly and though he waited it did not begin again.

"Probably dreaming or something and woke herself up," and he started on once more.

He soon left the settlement behind and, continuing along the same road found himself, (he hoped for the last time) in the midst of the arrested wood-ocean.

But the sound of that keening, although he had explained it quite satisfactorily to himself had left him disturbed. Thoughts, conjectures, fears that he had refused, until now, quite resolutely to entertain no longer would be denied. They were rooted in Goldie's two last letters, the cause of his hurried trip South.

"Of course, there's no *real* danger.—I'm foolish, even, to entertain such a thought.—Women get like that sometimes—nervous and overwrought.—And if it is with her as I suspect and hope—why the whole matter's explained.—Why it had really sounded *frightened!*—and parts of it were—hm!—almost incoherent.—The whole thing's too ridiculous however, to believe.—Well, when she sees me we'll have a good big laugh over it all.—Just the same, I'm glad I came.—Rather funny—somehow—thinking of Goldie—with a kid—in her arms.—Nice, though.—"

—Lafe Coleman!—Lafe Coleman!—He seemed to remember dimly a stringy, long white man with stringy colorless hair, quite disagreeably underclean; eyes a pale grey and fishlike.—He associated a sort of toothless grin with that face.—No, that wasn't it, either,—Ah! that was it!—He had it clearly, now.—The grin was all right but it displayed the dark and rotting remains of tooth stumps.—

He made a grimace of strong disgust and loathing.

—And—this—this—*thing* had been annoying Goldie, had been in fact, for years.—She hadn't told anybody, it seems, because she had been able to take care of herself.—But since she had married and been living away, from the settlement—

it had been easier for him, and much more difficult for her. He wasn't to worry, though, for the man was stupid and so far she'd always been able to outwit,—What she feared was Cy. It was true Cy was amiability itself—but—well—she had seen him angry once.—Ought she to tell him?—She didn't believe Cy would kill the creature—not outright—but it would be pretty close to it.—The feeling between the races was running higher than it used to.—There had been a very terrible lynching in the next county only last year.—She hadn't spoken of it before—for there didn't seem any use going into it.—As he had never mentioned it, she supposed it had never gotten into the papers. Nothing, of course, had been done about it, nothing ever was. Everybody knew who were in the mob.—Even he would be surprised at some of the names.—The brother of the lynched man, quite naturally, had tried to bring some of the leaders to justice; and he, too, had paid with his life. Then the mob, not satisfied, had threatened, terrorized, cowed all the colored people in the locality.—He was to remember that when you were under the heel it wasn't the most difficult of matters to be terrorized and cowed. There was absolutely no law, as he knew, to protect a colored man.—That was one of the reasons she had hesitated to tell Cy, for not only Cy and she might be made to pay for what Cy might do, but the little settlement as well. Now, keeping all this in mind, ought she to tell Cy?

And the letter had ended:

"I'm a little nervous, Vic, and frightened and not quite sure of my judgment. Whatever you advise me to do, I am sure will be right."

—On the very heels of this had come the "special" mailed by Goldie in another town.—She hadn't dared, it seemed, to post it in Hopewood.—It had contained just twelve words, but they had brought him South on the next train.

"Cy knows," it had said, "and O! Vic, if you love me, come, come, come!"

Way down, inside of him, in the very depths, a dull cold rage began to glow, but he banked it down again, carefully, very carefully, as he had been able to do, so far, each time before that the thoughts of Lafe Coleman and little Goldie's helplessness had threatened anew to stir it.

—That there ought to be the great live oak—and beyond should be the clearing, in the very "prezact" middle of which should be the little home all Goldie's own.—

For some inexplicable reason his feet suddenly began to show a strange reluctance to go forward.

"Damned silly ass!"[3] he said to himself. "There wasn't a thing wrong with the settlement. That ought to be a good enough sign for anybody with a grain of sense."

And then, quite suddenly, he remembered the keening.

He did not turn back to pause, still his feet showed no tendency to hasten. Of necessity, however, it was only a matter of time before he reached the live oak. He came to a halt beside it, ears and every sense keenly on the alert. Save for the stabbing, white stars above the clearing, there was nothing else in all the world, it seemed, but himself and the heavy black silence.

Once more he advanced but, this time, by an act of sheer will. He paused, set his jaw and faced the clearing. In the very centre was a dark small mass, it must be the little home. The breath he had drawn in sharply, while turning, he emitted in a deep sigh. His knees felt strangely weak.—What he had expected to see exactly, he hardly knew. He was almost afraid of the reaction going on inside of him. The relief, the

---

3. Typescript shows that Grimké debated replacing {"Damned silly ass!"} with {"Fool!"}.

blessed relief at merely finding it there, the little house all
her own!

It made him feel suddenly very young and joyous and the
world, bad as it was, a pretty decent old place after all.
Danger!—of course, there was no danger.—How could he
have been so absurd?—Just wait until he had teased Goldie a
plenty about this. He started to laugh aloud but caught himself
in time.

—No use awaking them.—He'd steal up and sit on the
porch, there'd probably be a chair there or something, and
wait until dawn.—They shouldn't be allowed to sleep one
single second after that.—And then he'd bang on their window, and call out quite casually:

"O, Goldie Harper, this is a nice way—isn't it?—to treat
a fellow; not even to leave the latch string out for him?"

He could hear Goldie's little squeal now.

And then he'd say to Cy:

"Hello, you big fathead, you!—what do you mean, any-
how, by making a perfectly good brother-in-law hoof it the
whole way here, like this?"

He had reached the steps by this time and he began softly
to mount them. It was very dark on the little porch and he
wished he dared to light a match, but he mustn't risk anything
that might spoil the little surprise he was planning. He
transferred his bag from his right to his left hand, the better
to feel his way. With his fingers outstretched in front of him
he took a cautious step forward and stumbled over something.

"Clumsy chump!" he exclaimed below his breath, "that
will about finish your little surprise I am thinking." He stood
stockstill for several seconds, but there was no sound.

"Some sleepers," he commented.

He leaned over to find out what it was he had stumbled
against and discovered that it was a broken chair lying on its

side. Slowly he came to a standing posture. He was not as happy for some reason. He stood there, very quiet, for several moments. Then his hand stretched out before, he started forward again. This time, after only a couple of steps, his hand came in contact with the housefront. He was feeling his way along, cautiously still, when all of a sudden his fingers encountered nothing but air. Surprised, he paused. He thought, at first, he had come to the end of the porch. He put out a carefully exploring foot only to find firm boards beneath. A second time he experimented with the same result. And then, as suddenly, he felt the housefront once more beneath his fingers. Gradually it came to him where he must be. He was standing before the door and it was open, wide open!

He could not have moved if he had wished. He made no sound and none broke the blackness all about.

It was sometime afterwards when he put his bag down upon the porch, took a box of matches out of his pocket, lit one and held it up. His hand was trembling, but he managed, before it burned his fingers and he blew it out automatically, to see four things—two open doors to right and left, a lamp in a bracket just beyond the door at the left and a dirty mud-trodden floor.

The minutes went by and then, it seemed to him, somebody else called out:

"Goldie! Cy!" This was followed by silence only.

Again the voice tried, a little louder this time:

"Goldie! Cy!"—There was no response.

———————

This other person who seemed, somehow, to have entered into his body, moved forward, struck another match, lit the lamp and took it down out of the bracket. Nothing seemed to make very much difference to this stranger. He moved his body stiffly; his eyes felt large and dry. He passed through the open door at the left and what he saw there did not surprise him in the least. In some dim way, only he knew that it affected him.

There was not, in this room, one single whole piece of furniture. Chairs, tables, a sofa, a whatnot, all had been smashed, broken, torn apart; the stuffing of the upholstery, completely ripped out; and the entirety thrown, scattered, here, there and everywhere. The piano lay on one side, its other staved in.—Something, it reminded him of—something to do with a grin—the black notes like the rotting stumps of teeth. Oh! yes, Lafe Coleman!—that was it. The thought aroused no particular emotion in him. Only, again he knew it affected him in some far off way.

Every picture on the walls had been wrenched down and the moulding with it, the pictures, themselves, defaced and torn, and the glass splintered and crushed under foot. Knick-knacks, vases, a china clock, all lay smashed and broken. Even the rug upon the floor had not escaped, but had been ripped up, torn into shreds and fouled by many dirty feet. The frail white curtains and window shades had gone down too in this human whirlwind; not a pane of glass was whole. The white woodwork and the white walls were soiled and smeared. Over and over the splay-fingered imprint of one dirty hand repeated itself on the walls. A wanton boot had kicked through the plastering in places.

This someone else went out of the door, down the hall, into the little kitchen and dining-room. In each room he found precisely the same conditions prevailing.

There was one left, he remembered, so he turned back into the hall, went along it to the open door and entered in.—What was the matter, here, with the air?—He raised the lamp higher above his head. He saw the same confusion as elsewhere. A brass bed was overturned and all things else shattered and topsy-turvy. There was something dark at the foot of the bed. He moved nearer, and understood why the air was not pleasant. The dark object was a little dead dog, a yellow one, with a wrinkled forehead. His teeth were bared in a snarl. A kick in the belly had done for him. He leaned over; the little leg was quite stiff. Less dimly, this time, he knew that this affected him.

He straightened up. When he had entered the room there had been something he had noticed for him to do. But, what was it? This stranger's memory was not all that it should be.—Oh! yes, he knew, now. The bed. He was to right the bed. With some difficulty he cleared a space for the lamp and set it down carefully. He raised the bed. Nothing but the mattress and the rumpled and twisted bed clothing. He didn't know exactly just what this person was expecting to find.

He was sitting on the steps, the extinguished lamp at his side. It was dawn. Everything was veiled over with grey. As the day came on a breeze followed softly after, and with the breeze there came to him there on the steps a creaking, two creakings!—Some where there to the right, they were, among the trees. The grey world became a shining green one. Why were the birds singing like that, he wondered.—It didn't take the day long to get here—did it?—once it started. A second time his eyes went to the woods at the right. He was able to see, now. Nothing there, as far as he could make out. His eyes dropped from the trees to the ground and he beheld what looked to him like a trampled path. It began, there at the trees: it approached the house: it passed over a circular bed of little pansies. It ended at the steps. Again his eyes traversed the path, but this time from the steps to the trees.

Quite automatically he arose and followed the path. Quite

automatically he drew the branches aside and saw what he saw. Underneath those two terribly mutilated swinging bodies, lay a tiny unborn child, its head crushed in by a deliberate heel.

Something went very wrong in his head. He dropped the branches, turned and sat down. A spider, in the sunshine, was reweaving the web some one had just destroyed while passing through the grass. He sat slouched far forward watching the spider for hours. He wished the birds wouldn't sing so.—Somebody had said something once about them. He wished, too, he could remember who it was.

About midday, the children of the colored settlement, playing in the road looked up and saw a man approaching. There was something about him that frightened them, the little ones in particular, for they ran screaming to their mothers. The larger ones drew back as unobtrusively as possible into their own yards. The man came on with a high head and an unhurried gait. His should have been a young face, but it was not. Out of its set sternness looked his eyes, and they were very terrible eyes indeed. Mothers with children hanging to them from behind and peering around, came to their doors. The man was passing through the settlement, now. A woman, startled, recognized him and called the news out shrilly to her man eating his dinner within. He came out, went down to the road rather reluctantly. The news spread. Other men from other houses followed the first man's example. They stood about him, quite a crowd of them. The stranger of necessity, came to a pause. There were no greetings on either side. He eyed them over, this crowd, coolly, appraisingly, contemptuously. They eyed him, in turn, but surreptitiously. They were plainly very uncomfortable. Wiping their hands on aprons, women joined the crowd. A larger child or two dared the outskirts. No one would meet his eye.

Suddenly a man was speaking. His voice came sharply, jerkily. He was telling a story. Another took it up and another.

One added a detail here; one a detail there. Heated arguments arose over insignificant particulars; angry words were passed. Then came too noisy explanations, excuses, speeches in extenuation of their own actions, pleas, attempted exoneration of themselves. The strange man said never a word. He listened to each and to all. His contemptuous eyes made each writhe in turn. They had finished. There was nothing more, that they could see to be said. They waited, eyes on the ground, for him to speak.

But what he said was:

"Where is Uncle Ray?"

Uncle Ray, it seemed was away—had been for two weeks. His Aunt Millie with him. No one had written to him for his address was not known.

The strange man made no comment.

"Where is Lafe Coleman?" he asked.

No one there knew where he was to be found—not one. They regretted the fact, they were sorry, but they couldn't say. They spoke with lowered eyes, shifting their bodies uneasily from foot to foot.

Watching their faces he saw their eyes suddenly lift, as if with one accord and focus upon something behind him and to his right. He turned his head. In the brilliant sunshine, a very old, very bent form leaning heavily on a cane was coming down the path from the house in whose window he had seen the dimmed light. It was Aunt Phoebe.

He left the crowd abruptly and went to meet her. When

she was quite sure he was coming she paused where she was, bent over double, her two hands, one over the other, on the knob of her cane, and waited for him. No words, either, between these two. He looked down at her and she bent back her head, tremulous from age, and looked up at him.

The wrinkles were many and deep-bitten in Aunt Phoebe's dark skin. A border of white wool fringed the bright bandana tied tightly around her head. There were grey hairs in her chin; two blue rings encircled the irises of her dim eyes. But all her ugliness could not hide the big heart of her, kind yet, and brave, after ninety years on earth.

And as he stood gazing down at her, quite suddenly he remembered what Goldie had once said about those circled eyes.

"Kings and Queens may have *their* crowns and welcome. What's there to *them?*—But the kind Aunt Phoebe wears— that different. She earned hers, Vic, earned them through many years and long of sorrow, and heartbreak and bitter, bitter tears. She bears with her the unforgetting heart.—And though they could take husband and children and sell them South, though she lost them in the body—Never a word of them, since—she keeps them always in her heart.—I knew, Vic, I know—and God who is good and God who is just touched her eyes, both of them and gave her blue crowns, beautiful ones, a crown for each. Don't you *see* she is of God's Elect?"

For a long time Victor Forrest stood looking down into those crowned eyes. No one disturbed these two in the sun drenched little yard. They, in the road, drew closer together and watched silently.

And then he spoke:

"You are to tell me, Aunt Phoebe—aren't you?—where I am to find Lafe Coleman?"

Aunt Phoebe did not hesitate a second. "Yes," she said and told him.

The crowd in the road moved uneasily, but no one spoke.

And, then, Victor Forrest did a thing he had never done before, he leaned over swiftly and kissed the wrinkled parchment cheek of Aunt Phoebe.

"Goldie loved you," he said and straightened up, turned on his heel without another word and went down the path to the road. Those there made no attempt to speak. They drew closer together and made way for him. He looked neither to the right nor to the left. He passed them without a glance. He went with a steady, purposeful gait and a high head. All watched him for they knew they were never to see him alive again. The woods swallowed Victor Forrest. A low keening was to be heard. Aunt Phoebe had turned and was going more feebly, more slowly than ever towards her house.

Those that know whereof they speak say that when Lafe Coleman was found he was not a pleasant object to see. There was no bullet in him—nothing like that. It was the marks upon his neck and the horror of his blackened face.

And Victor Forrest died, as the other two had died, upon another tree.

There is a country road upon either side of which grow trees even to its very edges. Each tree has been chosen and transplanted here for a reason and the reason is that at some time each has borne upon its boughs a creaking victim. Hundreds of these trees, there are, thousands of them. They form a forest—"Creaking Forrest" it is called. And over this road many pass, very, very many. And they go jauntily, joyously here—even at night. They do not go as Victor Forrest went,—they do not sense the things that Victor Forrest sensed.

If their souls were not deaf, there would be many things for them to hear in "Creaking Forest." At night the trees become an ocean dark and sinister, for it is made up of all the evil in all the hearts of all the mobs that have done to death their creaking victims. It is an ocean arrested at the very edges of the road by a strange spell. But this spell may snap at any second and with that snapping this sea of evil will move, rush, hurl itself heavily and swiftly together from the two sides of the road, engulfing, grinding, crushing, blotting out all in its way.

THE DRUDGE

Jane Flynn was forty-five years old. She was about medium height, perhaps a trifle below and had a short waisted full lumpy figure. For economy's sake she always wore a black dress which was clean and dry. When standing she had the round shoulders and flat-backed appearance and the unkempt appearance of the working woman. She wore Congress shoes too large for her and being flat-footed, moved her body forward, when walking, with uneven awkward jerks from the tops. Her face was broad, heavy and sallow. Her muddy brown greying hair which was thin and short, was parted in the middle and tightly drawn back on either side and twisted in a small pin at the back of her neck. Through this were stuck two more wire hair pins both ends of which were always visible. Her eyes were wide slate-colored and glissless. Her nose was short and fleshy, her mouth, small and thin-lipped. The upper lip had a number of deep perpendicular wrinkles caused by the fact that she had lost four front teeth

Text is taken from holograph in the Angelina Weld Grimké Collection, MSRC, box 38-11, folder 188. Grimké debated using four possible titles for this story: "Inevitable," "The Drudge," "The Drab," and "Drab Dippler." The collection at the Moorland-Spingarn Research Center entitles the story "The Inevitables." I have chosen the title "The Drudge" because it most nearly describes the main character. This story is quite evidently incomplete as well as contradictory (in one place we are told the wife endured oppression twenty years and in another place we are told this oppression lasted only a few years). The story has been included in spite of its incompleteness because it is Grimké's strongest fictional statement opposing the abusive violence of husbands against wives.

and had never had them replaced. As she was constantly pushing her tongue through this gap her upper lip had a pulsating movement. Her large hands were discolored and deformed from constant work. The backs were mottled and the palms callous and pale in color. Every line of her was [a] lump. She was absolutely and utterly negative from her dead hair to her misshapen shoes.

Life had meant to her just two things—work and sleep. Not that she had thought the matter out: but if you had told her this she would have looked at you with her dull wide eyes and answered, "yes," with a colorless wrinkled look and then have forgotten you immediately. Nothing was of any importance to her.

She was a poor farmer's daughter. Even when she was a little thing, she had been found work by a shrill-voiced, flat-bosomed, querulous mother. The first thing heard in the morning and the last at night had been that shrewish voice. In appearance and character, Jane and her father were alike. They were generally silent. When they spoke it was in answer and then in monosyllables. Until she was eighteen they had both been lashed on by that tongue. Not that they ever complained or replied.

Whatever came they took dully as a matter of course. That year he had fallen sick. When the doctor broke the news that he could not live to him,[1] his thin lips had [?] into a grin. He looked grinning at his wife and then turned his face to the wall. They found him dead the next morning but the grin was still on his lips.

That same year she had married. There had worked on the farm helping her father at the busy seasons a man from the city by the name of Bill Flynn. He was twenty years older

1. Several words in holograph illegible.

than she, a hairy man with a bold, black, eye, that told a woman audaciously that he understood her and could conquer her. His shoulders were broad but he carried them forward but he was badly knock-kneed. He never straightened his knees when he walked.

It was a curious love-making. After her father's death, whenever he knew she was working alone, he would sneak in to her and talk. He was a good bragger and she was a good listener—that is she never interrupted or cared to say anything herself. She never stopped working the whole time, and seldom raised her eyes. When he left her she would look at his back as he swaggered to the door with a dull glow back of her eyes.

"Come again," she would vouchsafe in her emotionless voice. When he turned to look back at her from the door way, her eyes were lowered.

"Sure, Mike," he said.

One day without any preface whatever had asked her leeringly, "Marry me, Jan?"

She never paled nor blushed. Without hesitation she had answered. "All right."

He looked at her curiously, "When?"

"Oh! any time."

"Now?"

"All right."

"Do you mean it?"

"Yes." She was washing dishes. She finished and put them away, washed out the dish towels, hung them on the line in the yard, washed out the pan and sink, and washed her hands and face with the yellow soap and dried them on a clean spot on the roller-towel. She took off her apron, went to the back hall and came back with her shabby black hat and coat on.

"I'm ready," she said.

"That way?" he jeered.

"I ain't got nothing else to wear," [she said,] fastening her black cotton gloves.

"Awright comes on then."

So they were married.

When they came back to the house he asked, "What you going to do?"

"Tell Ma."

"Yes, I guess you'd might's well, I got a room in the city."

Her mother was in the kitchen by the window peeling potatoes. She looked up crossly. "Who told you you could go out?"

"No one."

"Didn't I tell you to wash out the front window curtain?"

"Yes."

"Why didn't you do it?"

No answer.

"Where you been anyway?"

"Out."

"Out! Who you talking too? Yer needn't think 'caus your pa's dead I'm dead, too. I'll 'out' you. Now you tell me quick where you been?"

"To the minister's."

"Minister's! What for?"

"To get married."

For once Mrs. Hall was speechless. Her mouth fell open, her upper false teeth dropped, her face grew livid and her eyes seemed to criss-cross. Her knife slipped and cut her thumb. Jane stood motionless watching with dull face and eyes the blood dropping onto the potatoes. Mechanically her mother swept her teeth back in place, putting the hurt thumb into her mouth, went to the sink. She pumped the water with her uninjured hand and washed her thumb. At the same time, she dashed the water on her face and went to the roller. She did not wipe her face and the water dripped from it. She kept dabbing the blood from her thumb onto the roller and turning the towel around. "What did you say, again?" She asked in a strangled voice.

"I went to the minister's and got married," Jane said again in the same uninterested expressionless way.

"Who'd you marry?"

"Bill Flynn."

"Bill Flynn! Bill Flynn!" Her mother shrilled and went off into cackle after cackle of hysterical laughter.

There was nothing in Jane's inert figure to indicate she even heard her mother. She raised her dull eyes and looked through the kitchen window to where she could see Bill leaning against the barn hands in his pockets nervously chewing tobacco.

"You fool!" her mother hissed finally. "What do you mean by marrying that good for nothing? Don't [you] know he drinks and fools with women? Say, don't you."

"Yes."

"Well, what do you mean then?"

"Nothin."

"What are [you] goin' to do?"

"I dunno."

"You dunno! You dunno! Do you expect to stay here?"

"I dunno!"

Her mother came across the room to her, her eyes bright with anger.

"Shut up that 'I dunno'," she said and forgetful [of] her bleeding hand, she raised it and slapped Jane strongly on the cheek. Jane merely stepped backward out of her mother's

reach and wiped the blood off her face on her soiled pocket
handkerchief. The side of her face grew blood red.[2] She
raised her eyes and again watched Bill through the window.

"Who're you looking at?" her mother asked turning quickly.

"Well, if it ain't Mr. Flynn." She said mockingly.

She threw up the window.

"Say, Mr. Flynn, yer wife's asking for you. Come on in."
She called jocosely.

Bill approached warily and stood in the kitchen door.

Jane stood with her weight on one foot looking at her
cotton gloves.

Mrs. Hall went across the kitchen to him in a mincing
way. The black bold eyes of the man watcher her alertly.

"I congratulate you, Mr. Flynn, you've drawn a woman
if I do say so. I've jus' ben congratulatin' her. You sure to
do make a fine lookin' couple. Ain't I got a han'some daughter?
You certainly wanter be careful none of yer men friends sees
her. I suppose you're calcalatin to live on here."

"Well, I dunno, ma."

"Ma!" shrilled the woman her eyes blazing. "One fool's
enough to be a 'ma' to." Then losing control of herself she
shrieked:

"Get out here, both of you. Get out, I say. And may God
curse you both and your children after yer and their children
and their children's children until all of yer are dead. Don't
either one of yer pie-faced fools ever put foot in this house
again. Get out, I say."

Bill shrivelled up and shrunk out to the back door. Jane
started towards the back stairs.

"Where you goin'?" her mother screamed.

---

2. Holograph: {blood red} is crossed out and replaced by an illegible
word.

"To pack my things."

"You ain't got no things. I'll give you what you got on yer back as a wedding present. When the folks in town says to you 'Where'd you get that beautiful trooso you got on?' You can say 'Why this is my Ma's wedding present.' Ha! Ha! Get, both of you. Get, I say."

As they started down the back steps Jane said "Goodbye, Ma."

"I ain't yer ma. Don't you dare to call me that ever no more," and she disappeared in the house to reappear almost immediately. She stood in one stocking foot. There was a great hole at the toe. She held the shoe in her hand and threw it. It struck Bill in the small of his back.

"That's my weddin' present to you, son-in-law."

A shower of rice followed the shoe.

"You can't say, now that you ain't had a sure enough wedding." She burst again in shrill harsh laughter and went into the house banging the door behind her.

They took the open trolley-car to the city, a distance of about twenty miles. Bill made several attempts to make his bride talk but as she answered only in monosyllables, he got tired, left her, and went back to the rear seat to smoke. She was occupied the whole way in holding her hat on her head, and keeping her skirt from billowing out around her. It was dark when they arrived in the city. The car went through the slum part first. Once when the car stopped she heard Bill call,

"Say, Jan, get off here."

She climbed over two women and took the two long steps to the ground unassisted.

He stood on the sidewalk, his hat on the back of his head and the moist stump of cigar in the corner of his mouth.

"Come on," he mumbled through the other corner.

He went first. She followed.

Hat on the back of his head still, shoulders round, hands in pockets, knees bent, he shuffled forward. Once in a while he took one hand out to salute some passing acquaintance, sometimes he winked at a woman who returned his stare brazenly and watched her knowingly out of the corner of his eye. At such times he swaggered and spat onto the side-walk. She followed her hands folded in front of her over her stomach, a white line showing between the end of her short coat sleeve and her cotton gloves. Most of the time her eyes were on the pavement. Now and then she raised them blankly to the back of his coat and dropped them again. She walked inertly.

Although the place reeked of heat, grease, dirt, stale cooking, men, women, and hundreds of children, there was nothing to indicate that she noticed [or] saw them. Now and then a racing child hurled itself before her. She stopped until the child moved out of her way and went on again. The strike and the clamor did not seem to pierce through her indifference.

They went up one block, crossed the street, went down another, and then turned at right angles up a third. Before one of the houses he paused. On the steps six men and a woman were sitting. Three or four knew Bill.

There were cries of "Well, see who's here." "Oh you Bill. Where'd you pipe the skirt." One half drunk started to say in cracked, maudlin voice, "Oh tell me pretty maiden are there any more at home like you?"

Bill pushed his hat farther back on his head. Slapped one jocosely here and pushed another there. Whenever he laughed it was though something exploded inside of his mouth. This sound was followed by a long prolonged "Haw! Haw!" which might be heard easily for a distance. He laughed now and told them to "quit their kiddin' and move out of the way."

They left space for the two to climb the steps to the door. The front stairs were on a line with the door and one man and the woman watched them till they were out of sight. Then they turned *and grinned* at each other. The others had forgotten them immediately.

Bill's room was on the top floor at the front. There was a very dim gas flame flickering in the hall. Bill tried the door, found it locked, hunted through various pockets for the key and finally found it. He unlocked the door took a match out of his vest pocket, scratched it on his thigh and hunted around until he found the lamp. He lit it. It was very dirty the chimney was badly smoked. He threw up the one window. The room was stifling and unpleasant otherwise. At the left of the door-way filling up the entire space was a rickety iron bed. It was made up but was not clean. When the door swung open it hit the right hand wall. Against this wall an inch out of the reach of the door was a dingy wooden chair, next to this was a small table upon which was the lamp beyond, with one side to her and the other against the front wall was a yellow pine bureau on these were a dirty broken basin and pitcher. There was nothing else in the room.

Jane stood in the doorway her dull eyes watched Bill.

He looked at her nervously and rather furtively. And he said

"Come in, come in, Mrs. Flynn. Welcome home. T'ain't much but it's something. You're kinder hungry now ain't yer?"

"No, not very."

"Well, I am. You spread up that there table. You'll find cups and plates and things in that lowest bureau drawer. I'll just step out and get something around the corner and be right back. So, long. Give us a kiss, Mrs. Flynn." He screwed up his face after that kiss and went out banging the door.

Jane took off her gloves put then one in each coat-pocket, took off her hat and stuck the one hair-pin back carefully into the [?], took off her coat and then looking around found several nails on the back of the door. Some of Bill's clothes were hanging there. One nail was vacant and she carefully hung up her things.

She set the table and then sat down in the only chair and holding her hands limply in her lap, waited. In about an hour's time the light began to sputter and grow dim. She blew it out, opened the door and sat down again. There was plenty of noise within and without the house, but she probably did not notice it. At twelve o'clock or thereabouts she shut the door, lay down on the bed and went to sleep. At two Bill came home and he was drunk. Two things of importance happened. He told her he had married her to make her support him and he solemnized the occasion by beating her thoroughly.

So their married life began.

For two weeks after this he was busy—but busy getting her places to do scrubbing and cleaning. He succeeded in [providing] [3] five after that he stopped. He slept all day waited for her to come home from work at night, took the money she had made and went out not to be seen again until the next morning. Jane, however, never gave him all she earned. She lied to him, each night, kept some and put it carefully away.

---

3. Holograph illegible.

Sometimes before he went out to [?] his hand in he beat her. She never resisted or seemed to expect other treatment.

For twenty years this kind of life went on for these two. She became stout and more negative if possible in appearance. He became a shaking, blear-eyed, purple faced ugly-tempered old man. Three children were born to them. Two prematurely. They all died.

During this time only one incident of any moment occurred. It happened two years after they were married. They were living at the time in two rooms. The back, was the bedroom, the front was the kitchen, dining and sitting rooms.

It was a Friday night. She had been at home about an hour and was doing the family wash by the dim light of a lamp. She had already finished some of the things and had hung them up on a line that was stretched across the room. Bill, not entirely sober, had not yet gone out. He was lounging in a chair eyeing her back which was forwards to him with evident disform. It was an ugly misshapen back. As she leaned over the tub he saw her ponderous feet in their new over shoes. Never in all these years had Jane ever volunteered any remark. She answered, nothing more. Now, as he watched her he heard her speak.

She said in her emotionless voice,

"I want that you should leave these women alone."

Bill gasped. His jaw dropped.

"Ha?" he managed to ask.

"I want that you should leave these women alone."

"What women?" He demanded thickly and in an ugly tone. No answer.

"Did you hear me?" he snarled. "What women?"

No answer but the rubbing of the clothes and the thumping of the soap.

He went over to her unsteadily, and raised one hairy dirty fist.

He swore at her vilely and called her unspeakable names. At last she said,

"I want that you should leave those women alone."

He gave her the answer of the fighter who knows himself cornered. With all his power he struck her in the mouth. That was the time she lost the four teeth. Then he beat her as he had never beaten her before. She took it unresistingly as ever.

When he was utterly worn out he reeled across to the chair and sat down breathing heavily. He rested his elbows on his knees and his head in his hand.

Suddenly for no distinct reason he raised his eyes. He had not heard Jane but she had left the washing and was standing over him. Fascinated he watched. She did not move. Her body was as listless as was her face and eyes as expressionless. She strangely stopped and looked at him. For one long minute without moving she stared. Then she turned and went into the bed-room. As soon as the door had closed, fearfully with eyes on the door he tip-toed after his hat, felt for it without looking, put it on, and went out of the door leading to the hall. He closed it so there was no sound.

He did not come back for a week. He stood there before the closed door. His whole body was apologetic. He knocked timidly.

To her

"Come in":

He opened the door cautiously. She was cooking her supper. She looked up and saw who it was then went on about her work.

"Say, Jan. I'm sorry. Can't I come back?"

"Yes," She said from the stove with her back to him.

He came up and awkwardly put his arm around [her].

"Ain't you going to kiss me?"

She did not respond to nor retreat from the arm.

She was stirring something in a pan.

She made no answer.

He gave her a quick kiss on the cheek and took his arm away. He breathed with relief. She set two places and they ate. He never beat her again and he never asked for money. She gave some to him just the same every night. Whenever he looked at her now fear was at the bottom of his eyes.

One night in the twenty-first year after their marriage, a short time after he had gone out they brought him back.

"He was took with some kind of a fit. Here's the doctor." One of the men said huskily.

She put Bill to bed. He was breathing stertorously, the left side of his face sagged and the right side of his body was lifeless. It was a stroke of apoplexy. For seven years he was bed-ridden, a hopeless paralytic and almost an idiot.

At the end of this time Jane was forty-five and Bill seventy-five.

JETTISONED

Miss Lucy turned westward, at the corner, into the block where the home of her little room was, a sordid enough, narrow little street in the white ungracious glare of the sun, but beautiful, now, its darkness veiled over and about with the lavender and greys of a late fall twilight. It was noticeably quiet, nothing moved it seemed, the entire length, so quiet that the delicate intricate very black tracery of the naked tree tops lay, at the horizon, like still fingers, against the deepest of deep gold that slipped above imperceptibly, without a whisper of its going into the palest of pale lemon overhead. But was Miss Lucy concerned with all this wistful loveliness? She was not. Even if her mind had not been so fully pre-occupied, I regret to say, this beauty would have gone, unobserved, unfelt by her. No, she was concerned wholly and solely with just one thing, or to be more accurate two,— her feet.

Miss Lucy was no longer a young woman and by no stretch of the imagination could she or her feet be described as small; but she was certain, this evening, that never, at any time, under any circumstances, had anyone ever possessed feet as painful, as enormous, as heavy as hers. She was submerged in, dominated by these ponderous things that she seemed barely able to raise and move one in front of the other.

All day long she had been standing at the "white folks' " ironing board, eight solid hours with a short time out for

Text taken from typescript in the Angelina Weld Grimké Collection, MSRC, box 38-11, folder 189–91.

lunch. There had been sheets and pillow cases and table-cloths and napkins and shirts and towels and annoyingly delicate silk underwear and more sheets and towels and shirts until she had become convinced the entire wash of the whole world had, somehow or other, found its way into her basket. And at the end of the day the hard-lipped, hard-eyed, hard-lined Mrs. Jester with a hard smile had paid her the munificent sum of one dollar and fifty cents! To save her car fare and to buy little Mary Lou something she liked, she therefore had forced her tired old body and her swelling, aching feet to carry her home over a long mile on hard torturing concrete pavement.

When, at last, she felt under her hand the cold of the rickety iron railing that guarded the three stone steps leading up to the front door, she paused and emitted a sound that was partly a sigh and partly a groan. She had just heaved herself, with the aid of the swaying support, onto the lowest step, when she was startled by a whining monotonous voice behind her. Where had the man come from? As far as she had been aware, there had been nothing to suggest his approach.

"Lady, Ah ain't had nuffin tah eat foh two days. No, ma'm. An' Ah's hungry an' tiahed. Ennyt'ing yo' cud gib me—nebbah mine how li'l. Ah sho wud 'prechiate. Yas'm. Ah ain't et nuffin for two days, lady; an' Ah's so hollow inside me—mah derned stummick—beg pahdon, lady!—but hit's jes disaway—mah stummick seems tah be kine ob rollin' roun' an' roun' inside ob me—Ah's dat hollow. lady, Ah ain't et nuffin—an'—"

"Well, foh de Lawd's sake, cayn' yo' stop a-tall? Dah's one t'ing—sartin sho—dat tongue ob yoahs ain't tiahed."

"No. ma'm Lady—Ah—"

Miss Lucy turned slowly and squarely about on the bottom

step and with her near-sighted eyes peered down at the man. At the corner of the alley, two doors away, the lamp-lighter had just briskly, with the aid of his ladder brought into being a dim white glow; and she made out a dark, stooping figure, coat collar turned up closely about the neck, cap pulled far down over the face at a decidedly rakish angle, elbows bent forward and hands thrust deep into trouser pockets. She tried to see the man's eyes but though she was not able to clearly, of one thing she was satisfied, they were not quiet a single second for she could make out the constant moving, flickering and glittering of the whites. The mouth, however, was not hidden and an ugly one it was, very large, the upper teeth protruding so far forward they seemed almost horizontal. As it was an utter impossibility to draw his lips together over this formidable ledge, the lower jaw hung heavily loose.

"Lady—"

"Doan yo' go foh tah stahrt dat all obah again, now."

"No, ma'm. Ef yo' only knew, lady, how mah feet huhrts me. Ah jes' been awalkin' and awalkin' foh two days. Ah ain't sot down nowhahs a-tall. Ah loss all mah money, an' Ah's been lookin' for work ebrywhah. An' mah feets huhrts me. Mmh!"

A tiny spring of sympathy bubbled up and over in Miss Lucy's heart.

"Is dat so? Yo' poor fellah! Yas, Ah kin unnastan' too."

"No, ma'm. De pain dat Ah is suff'rin' at de presen' time am 'scrushiatin'. Yas ma'm. An' ef yo' cud jes lemme hab a li'l somepin. An ain't axin' yo' foh much—"

Miss Lucy chuckled.

"Ah guess yo' ain't axin' me foh much. Whah yo' specks Ah's gwinetah git hit."

"No ma'm, but—"

Miss Lucy fumbled in her old black bag for her old black

pocket book. The man stepped forward eagerly. She could not see his eyes but the dark closeness of him exuded slyness and greed.

"Now, looky hyah, ef yo' wants somepin, doan yo' come no closah dan yo' is. An' wot is mo', yo' go right on back whah you wuz befoh.—Now, dat's bettah."

"Lady—"

"Oh hesh up, cayn' yo'? Ah ain't got no mo' dan a dime. Will dat do?"

"Yas'm. Ob cose, now, ef yo' cud kinedah open up yo' heahrt, ef de Lawd cud mek yo' see yo' oughtah gib me mebbe a quahrtah. La—"

"Yo' teks de dime er nuffin." There was no mistaking the sharpness of that tone.

"Yas'm."

Miss Lucy dropped the coin into the grasping outstretched dark hand.

"An' go 'long now. Ah ain't gibbin' hit tah yo' nohow— Ah's gibbin' hit tah yo' feet."

"Ma'm?"

"Yo' hyahed me. Clean out, Ah says. Ah knows yo' lyin' tah me."

"Lady, Ah swahs Ah ain't. May de good Lawd strike me daid, ef Ah ain't tayin' ob yo' de truf."

"Huh!—dat so?—Well yo' bettah be movin' on pretty fas' jes ahbout hyah, foh Ah gets de pleeceman to come an' tek away de corpse dat de good Lawd gwinetah drap roun' hyah presen'ly."

The word police was enough and, before a second seemed to have fairly begun, the slinking figure had vanished around the corner of the alley. Miss Lucy chuckled again.

"Yo' ole fool, yo'. Ah reckon dey ain't nuffin' ebbah gwinetah tech yo' no sense. Mahry Lou she is gwinetah 'joy dis a-one on pooh me. Glad Ah got somepin, ennyhows, foh tah mek huh laff."

She mounted lumberingly the two remaining steps and presently was opening the door. A most delicious fragrance assailed her nostrils—the odor of freshly boiling coffee.

"Whopee!" She blew her breath out expulsively as she closed the door behind her.

From the darkness, at the rear, a voice high, piercing, but somehow unaccountably muffled, accosted her.

"Dat you, Miss Lucy?"

"Uh-huh! wot's lef' ob me. Huh! Huh!' Yo' mekkin' coffee, Miss Robinson? Sho do smell good."

A whistling stuttering yellow fanlight of gas, bluish near the jet, dimly lit the gloomy narrowness of the hall. The worn, uncarpeted floor and the dingy bare stairs, seemingly cut off short by the deep blackness above, could be seen indistinctly. Near the front door, a mirror cracked and crookedly hung was ornamented with age-dulled brass hooks upon two of which hung a couple of limp and dejected-looking men's felt hats. Beside this, nailed against the wall, was a wire frame which held loosely and indifferently what was evidently the whiteness of three letters.

"No, dat ain't me mekkin' coffee. Yo' mought know who 'tis. Hit's dat Mahry Lou. Ef yo' axes me, dat chile sho do drink too much ob datah stuff.—Say, Miss Lucy, Ah gottah pot ob tea, dough, on de back ob de stove; an' Ah kin shove hit to de fron' an' het yo' up a nice cup in no time. Wot yo' say?"

"No, t'anks, jes de same. Not dis ebenin'. Ah reckon Mahry Lou got mah name in dat coffee pot upstahs.—

"Ah know yo' ain't nebbah hyah ob ma tekkin' tea wen Ah kin git coffee. Hun! Hun!—Wot de mattah wid yo'? Yo' soun's hoahrse er somepin. Gottah cole?"

"No, hit's ma face. Ah got de mis'ry in hit. Ah'll be dah in jes a momen'. Ah's hettin' mase'f up some watah. Mahry Lou done len' me huh hot watah bag. Ma face done swell up so Ah looks lak Ah had a wash basin or somepin' in hit."

As the hall boasted no such luxury as a chair, Miss Lucy proceeded to lower her none too slender frame onto the lowest steps. Age and weariness, however, proved too much and before she realized what had happened, she had arrived at her destination with a thud that jarred both herself and the house and with the sound of considerable cracking and creaking of wood.

"Foh Gawd's sake, wot dat, Miss Lucy? Wotcha doin'?"

"Huh! Huh! Jes' tryin' tah—sot down, honey. Ah—kine—ah—er—slip down quickern Ah looked foh, Ah reckon."

"Reely, Miss Lucy, yo' oughtah—. Ah tought for a secon' de house wuz ah fallin' down. You know de stahs cayn' stan' much ob dat foolishness. Yo' oughtah be moah keerful.—Yo' reckon!" The wadded shrill voice was plainly trembling and querulous.

Miss Lucy lost none of her good humor.

"Sohry.—Ah did'n' mean foh tah do hit. But, ef you's 'speckin' ob me tah wait hyah foh you, Ah sho hez gottah res' dese achin' bones an' feet ob mine—. An' dey ain't no two ways ahbout dat," she answered mildly.

Miss Robinson was still too much irritated, evidently, to make any response to this, for a prolonged silence followed.

Miss Lucy did not seem unduly concerned, for she prepared to make herself thoroughly at ease. She stretched out one foot, inspected it and then the other, rested each heel carefully on the hall floor, thus tilting up the offending members pleasantly in the air. Presently she attempted to wriggle her toes, an effort which brought forth a smothered groan and an exclamation which sounded very much like

"Ma Gawd!" She placed her bag on the stairs beside her, pulled off her black felt hat, which had decidedly the appearance of a child's sailor only, instead of a bow at the side, it was decorated by a very ancient battered black flower of some description. She deposited the hat by her bag, bent her elbows, put them on the most convenient tread behind her and leaned back. She drew in a long breath and expelled it audibly. Even hard steps can be exceedingly comfortable, it seems.

Whatever Miss Lucy might have been once, she could no longer lay any claims to beauty. At least, however, she was not injurious to the eyes. Her rather thin hair, parted in the middle, was brushed flatly down on either side of her face and ended, when you saw the back of her head, in a little button of a knot. But the hair itself was lovely, not a yellowish tint in it, but literally, really literally the white white of snow, new-fallen. In texture, it was the quality of a little newborn lamb's. Her nose was strong, though inclined to flatness, the nostrils large, full, almost circular in shape. The mouth was wide, the lips generously but evenly full. One of her few peculiarities was a habit of biting the under part of the upper lip. In color, she was of a light brown, the skin somewhat parchmentlike but strangely free from wrinkles: with the exception of two deep horizontal ones in her forehead, two deeper vertical ones at either side of her nose, where it joined the brow, and two deeper ones still from the corners of each nostril to the ends of her mouth, none other was noticeable. Her chin was medium in size but firm. Her eyes, I have not described, for I have been almost afraid to try, I am certain I cannot do them justice. They were round, large, not deeply set under her scanty but very dark eye-brows; of either a deep brown color or of a black and softly luminous. They were wide eyes with considerable of the white showing all around the iris. But the expression is the difficulty. In them you saw an abundance of good nature, a heart much, much too large for her large body and some little shrewdness but not enough to be a burden. The amazing thing about them, however, I wonder if I can make you see. Close your own a minute; remember, if you can, those of a little child. Can you recollect, in them, that wide look of utter confidence, utter belief in you and in the utter goodness of the whole world? Well, Miss Lucy, sixty-odd years old, having had certainly her full share of suffering and hardships, owning as home a little hall bedroom on a third floor front, knowing six days out of the seven—what it means to return to that room with tired body and aching feet, possessing the great privilege of earning one dollar and fifty cents a day—kept in her eyes, in spite of all, beautiful and undimmed, this look of a little child.

She had not been waiting long, when, from the shadows behind her down the hall, came the scuffing sound made by shoes that are too big to be lifted, by their wearer, from the floor, and Miss Robinson, after noisily rounding the newel-post, faced her. Very tall, very thin, was this lady, garbed in a faded print dress that was too tight where it should have been loose and too short where it should have been long. As a result, an exceedingly unattractive length of wrinkled stocking and what appeared to be old Oxfords without lacings were revealed; also two bony, long yellow arms ending in two bony, long yellow hands and, to put it mildly, a shoulder girdle a little too decidedly prominent. Her hair, taffyish in hue, and not of the so-called best quality was twisted into round protuberances all over her long narrow head. Her nose was very thin and far from short as was also her bloodless mouth. The right cheek, the normal one, was flat, sallow with a slight hollow in the center. The other, as completely covered as possible by the hot water bottle, did lead one to wonder if her own idea of a wash basin was so far fetched after all. Her eyes were small, dark, darting and so expressive of an insatiable curiosity that they gave the impression of picking, pecking and boring into the watched one's soul. Miss Robinson was unmarried, of uncertain years, highly respectable, as she did not hesitate to tell you upon the slightest provocation and what she did not know of the affairs of her lodgers and of the neighbors in the block was virtually unknowable.

"Lawd, Miss Robinson, yo' sho hab gottah face on yo', ain't you'?"

"Ain't hit so!" answered the high thickened voice. "Dey's jes' one t'ing wohrryin' me, now, dough. Ah hopes hit gits tah go bah Sunday. As Ah allus says, ef dey's one t'ing Ah hates tah miss, hit's ma church. Yas, indeedy."

"Aw, Ah reckon hit'll sho be gone ba dat time. Mebbe Ah kin do somepin. Kin Ah?"

"No, t'anks, not dat Ah knows ob, now. Hit's easin' off, sense hit done swole up lak dis.—Yo' ain't lookin' so pert yo'se'f."

"Huh! Huh! Ah knows hit's de truf. Ah seems tah be nuffin 'tall, dis ebenin', but jes' feet.—Dat's all."

"Dah, now, Miss Lucy, ez Ah allus says, Ah wish de Lawd cud he'p me tah laff t'ings off de way yo' duz." Then in the same breath, "Dah's a lettah foh yo'."

"A lettah!—yo' *sho?*"

"Uhhuh!"

"Whah f'om?"

"New Yohk, hit say.—Dat's whah yo' da'hter is, hain't hit?—Specks hit's f'om huh."

It was only a little oh! that Miss Lucy emitted, but if you had heard it, you would not have forgotten it in a hurry. She bent forward with an eagerness, a tenseness that was pathetic. She gnawed nervously at her upper lip.

Miss Robinson shuffled her way slowly over to the letter rack, adjusted the bag to her swollen cheek carefully, holding it with her left hand and bent forward. There was a deliberation about her that would have been maddening to any one but the good-natured Miss Lucy.

"Mr. Joseph Martin!—Dat ain't hit. Mr. Paul Brown! Nor dis." Here she turned one piercing eye on Miss Lucy.

"Nice fellah, ain't he?"

"Who?"

"Mr. Brown."

"Seems tah be."

"Kine ob tekkin' ah shine, ain't he? tah Mahry Lou?"

"Es he?" The old eyes in all probability were entirely too innocent. "Cayn' say dat Ah blames him much, ef he es."

No satisfaction to be gained evidently in this direction. Miss Robinson turned back to the rack.

"Miss Lucy Golden!"

But it seemed that the letter had to be felt with care by the long bony fingers and inspected atom by atom by the pecking eyes, before it could be turned over to the shaking old hand.

"Feels lak a t'ick one.—Well, Ah declah!—Ef yo'—wall, law's—yo'—w'y—ef yo' doan look jes' lak somebuddy done lit a great big light inside ob yo'."

"Ah reckon somebuddy has. Ah's been lookin' foh dis lettah foh—foh th'ee weeks—an'—an' hyah hit is." She smiled down wonderingly at the smallness and whiteness of it between her dark clumsy hands. And when she raised her soft old eyes presently half slyly to Miss Robinson's hard ones there was all the child's joy and rapture in them at the coming to pass of a very beautiful, much desired but hardly to be expected thing.

"Wants dat Ah shud read hit to yo'? Ma eyes ain't swole up yet." Miss Robinson discharged two or three sharp rasping sounds which she intended for laughter, but the eyes and the thick voice were very disagreeably inquisitive the while. Luckily the old woman was too engrossed in her happiness to notice.

"No t'anks.—Reckon hit enuff jes' at fus'—lak—tah—hole hit—disaway." She dropped her head a little shamefacedly. "Mahry Lou'll read hit tah me, aftah a wile.—She allus duz."

"Ah hopes dey's good news in hit." She still had to put out this last tentative feeler.

"Uhuh! So duz Ah."

Miss Robinson lowered her baffled eyes but not for long. She was off on a new scent.

"Seems lak ebrybody gittin' mail tah-day.—Mahry Lou too."

The old eyes were alert enough now.

"She gottah lettah?"

"Uhuh!"

In the pause that followed neither took her eyes off the other's.

"Ah reckon yo' notice, mebbe, whah hit f'om?"

The old woman really had no intention of making her question a barbed one, but Miss Robinson's sharp eyes grew sharper as they bored their way suspiciously into Miss Lucy's.

"Wall, lemme see," she began cautiously, "seems tah me, now, Ah did notice—not dat Ah genully duz, yo' unnastan',— but somehow ma eyes jes' kin' ob fell on dis widout ma intendin'—Now, whah wuz dat f'om?—Seems lak down in Vaginny somewhah."

"Hit wuz?" Miss Lucy made no attempt to conceal her eagerness.

"Uhuh, dat de way hit strike me, now.—Ain't she f'om down dah somewhah?"

"Uhuh!"

"She gottah stepfaddah er somepin dah still, ain't she?"

Miss Lucy nodded without lowering her watchful eyes.

"Reckon, den, hit from him."

"Mos' lakly."

One pair of unblinking eyes still held the other. Miss Lucy waited.

"She took de lettah, w'en Ah call huh unconsarned lak an' ran long back upstahs."

Still Miss Lucy waited.

"Ah wuz doin' somepin down hyah in de hall, at de time, mah face uz huhrtin' me so bad Ah doan jes' 'membah now wot hit wuz.—Ah wuzn' lis'n' yo' unnastan'. Ez Ah allus says ef yo's gwine tah run a house right yo' cayn' do nuffin lak dat. No sah."

She broke off tantalizingly. Miss Lucy never moved.

" 'Twon' so long aftah dat Ah hyahed huh."

"Hyahed huh?"

"Uhhuh."

"Wot she doin'?"

"Singin'."

Miss Lucy expelled her breath audibly. She smiled.

"Yo's gibbin' me good news, Miss Robinson."

And then the frown that had puckered her forehead reappeared again.

"Mahry Lou, she ain't been hyah all day, habs she?"

"Wall, yas, foh de mos' paht. She wen' out jes ahbout noon, *so she say,* tah get huhse'f some lunch."

"Wot yo' mean bah 'wot she say'?"

"Wot Ah mean? Wall, Ah t'inks she meks bleeb a lottah times she gwinetah get somepin tah eat, w'en she ain't. She's jes' dat proud, Miss Lucy, an' yo' knows hit, she ain't gwinetah 'knowledge she cayn' git huhse'f much. No sah."

"But—," Miss Lucy began. Miss Robinson, however, cut her short.

"Ah'll tay yo' w'y ah feels so sho. De uddah day, Ah wen' out, mebbe 'bout fifteen minutes aftah she did. An' what yo' spose Ah seen huh?" She paused dramatically. "She didn' see me."

"Whah?"

"Down dah at de cohrnah, at Tony's newsstand looking at magazines er somepin."

"Dat doan mean nuffin! She cud git huhse'f somepin tah eat an' do dat too. Ah doan see ennyt'ing in dat."

"Yo' doan? Wall, Ah'd only wen' down tah de mail box an' come right long back again, when mos' befoh Ah'd close de doo' she wuz smack behine me comin' in.—Dat lunch room she goes tah, leas' two blocks away an' yo' habs tah wait.—No sah, dey ain't ennyt'ing gwinetah mek me bleeb she got huhse'f some lunch in dat li'l bit of time. An' stoppin' in Tony's too! 'Sides she—she ain't got none ob de look ob a pusson dats had a good meal. She jes' ez peaked and weeny lookin' w'en she come back ez w'en she go' out. Wot yo' spose she say, dough?"

"Wot?"

" 'Ah sho did hab one good feed dis noon, Miss Robinson.' "

"Dah now?"

"Ain't Ah tayin' yo'? She ain't got none ob de signs ob eatin'. As Ah allus says, yo' cayn' fool me, Ah kin tay w'en a pusson's had a good meal. Dey habs a—wall—a satisfy way—wid dem. An' she sho didn' look datahway." Miss Robinson was enjoying herself to the full now. "An' annuddah t'ing—dat chile drinks too much coffee. W'en she goes out an' comes back in—dat's de fus' t'ing yo' kin smell; an' ef she doan go out, yo' kin smell hit mos' enny ole time. She's libbin' 'pon coffee an' moughty li'l' else, dat's wot Ah t'inks." Miss Robinson readjusted the bag to her face. "An' annuddah t'ing—how she gwinetah git much, tay me dat?"

"Wot yo' mean?"

"She ain't been wukkin' foh a monf, habs she?"

"No."

"Well, den, Ez Ah says f'om de fus', ef she hadn' been a li'l fool, she'd a had a job yit, an' a good one. Sposin' de boss did up an' say, "Niggah!" or somepin. Wot ob hit? Wot foh she gottah gib him a whole lottah sass? Sass doan git yo' nowhah's, less'n hit's out. Names cayn' kill yo'. As Ah allus says, dey's t'ings in dis worl' yo' gottah be deef tah. Ef hit huhrts yo', doan heyah hit.—Yessah.—Dat's right—yo' knows hit."

Miss Lucy looked meditatively for a minute or two at little Mary Lou's hot water bag lying so closely against Miss Robinson's inflated cheek. Whatever was the result of her thinking, she restrained herself and left her thoughts unspoken. At last she said:

"Foh yo' an' me, Miss Robinson, dat is all right. Reckon we wud swallaw mos' ennyt'ing tah keep a job; but Mahry Lou, she ain't lak us. Somehow she's mek outah diffren' kine ob goods, entiahly from usses.—She's proud-lak, jes ez yo' say, an'—an' all-strung up—an' wall, yo' doan haftah hit huh hahrd tah huht huh—she's dat sensitive-lak.—Wealls hastah ack de way we's made, doan yo' reckon?—An' de Lawd dat mek huh lak she am, ah 'specks—unnastan's huh, jes de same as He unnastan's usses."

The old voice was kind and gentle but Miss Robinson felt in some manner rebuked. She did not enjoy this and replied acidly.

"Wall, Ah hopes she gits a job soon er dey wuz money in dat lettah tahday. Ah duz that."

"Yo' soun's moughty consarned 'bout hit?" For the first time the tone was a little sharp.

"Tah morrow's de fus' ob de monf, ain't hit?"

"Yo' mean—yo' mean—she owes you—?" Miss Lucy's voice trailed off.

"No, Ah doan mean she owes me nuffin yit. An' ef she cayn' pay me tahmorrah, Ah ain't a-tuhrnin' ob huh intah de street. As Ah allus says, Ah wudden' do dat to a cat. But— Ah hastah lib, Miss Lucy, yo' knows dat. Ah rents dis house an' hit cost me right smahrt tah run hit, an', ob c'ose, Ah cudden' keep huh on monf aftah monf wid out nuffin."

"Dat's so, but how yo' know she cayn' pay yo' tahmorrah— less'n' dat lettah—?" she broke off.

"Ah go long wid yo', Miss Lucy.—How Ah know ma face all swell up? Hits ez plain ez dat ezackly."

A hard little light came into Miss Lucy's eyes.

"Wall," she said slowly, "de chile ain't no kin tah me an' Ah nebbah seed huh befoh she come hyah—but she's close— pow'ful close tah me, now, yassah.—An' ez long ez Ah got ma senses 'bout me, an' kin wuk—an' mobe ahbout—Ah ain't gwinetah let nuffin happen tah huh—an' dat's flat."

"Doan misunnastan' me, now Miss Lucy." The tone was ingratiating, a little anxious. "Yo' hyahed me say Ah wudden tuhrn huh out tah-morrah, now, didn' yo'? Ah wudden. Ez Ah allus says—"

Miss Lucy broke in relentlessly. "Ah unnastan's awright.— Wall, wot ebbah else yo' kin say 'bout huh yo' habs tah gib de pooh li'l kid dis—dat she sho habs been tryin' hahrd enuff tah get huhse'f somepin tah do."

"Ah'll say she habs. Dah, now, Ah come pretty nigh

fahgittin' tah tay yo' 'bout de gal dat come hyah aftah huh, jes a li'l befoh yo' come in."

"A gal?"

"Uhhuh!—Says dey sen' huh roun' f'om dat manicurin' an' hahr-dressin' place."

"Wot she wan'?"

"Tole me tah tay Mahry Lou dat ef she gwinetah tek dat co'se, she bettah begin tah-morrah."

"She see Mahry Lou?"

"No. Say she cudden wait.—Tole me to tay huh."

"Did yo'?"

"Uh huh."

"Wot she say?"

"Mahry Lou?—Nuffin—jes 'awright'."

"Dat all she say? How she look?"

"How yo' mean look?"

"Wall, wuz she happy lak—or—?"

Look jes de same ez allus ez—fah ez Ah cud mek out. But, Lawsee, yo' ain't 'speckin' tah tay wot Mahry Lou's t'inkin' f'om de way she looks an' acts, is yo'?"

"Wall, Ah kin tay yo' wot *Ah's* t'inkin'. *Ah's* t'inkin' somehow, she got good news in dat lettah."

"Ah hopes yo' right, Miss Lucy, Ah sho duz."

With the aid of the bannisters, the old woman pulled herself painfully to her feet.

"Ooo!—Great day in de mawnin!—Ah sho is stiff. Ooo. Ah bettah be gittin' along up foh de chile t'inks somepin's happen' tah me.—Hopes yo' face'll be bettah by tah-morrow.—Ef yo' needs me—jes gib me a call."

"All right, Ah will. T'anks."

"G'night!"

"G'night!"

Miss Robinson scuffed her noisy way back to her dark regions, at the rear and Miss Lucy, with the dearness of her letter in her left hand, her bag under her arm, her hat perched at a precarious angle on her head (as the easiest means of carrying it) and aided by the rail gripped firmly under her right hand, began her slow, laborious climb into the blackness ahead. There was no light in the hall above her, but she groped her way along with sure, accustomed feet and finally after what seemed to her an interminable time, commenced the ascent of the second and last flight that ended at the floor where home and Mary Lou were. And all that long wearisome journey, the letter in her hand sent the most delightful of glows up her old arm to her old heart. Midway of the stairs, she looked up and came to a pause. The hallway for some reason, up here, was almost bright, a most unusual occurrence. She listened, but except for her own heavy breathing, she could hear nothing. "Whopee!" Miss Lucy called, after she had been able to get her breath, and waited.

There was a sound, then, of a door quickly thrown open and of the lightest of light feet running. With the opening door, the hall above became almost bright. A dark, diminutive head peered down over the railing.

"That you, Miss Lucy?"

It was a small voice just as almost everything about Mary Lou was small and it was huskily soft with an added quality almost impossible to define—but somehow, as you listened to it, it seemed to put forth tiny fingers and get inside of your heart against the very strings themselves. And lastly, it held an unforgettable breathless little catch that was simply adorable. The old face looking up was beaming. It was a second or so before Miss Lucy could answer. Climbing always left her out of breath. Between quite audible wheezes she brought out:

" 'Tain't—nobuddy else!—Huh! Huh!"

"Oh! hello, hello, then!"

" 'Lo!—yo'se'f."

"You're awful late to-night. Why?"

"Gassin'—downstahs—wid Miss Robinson—'bout huh face."

"I *was* getting excited."

"Wall—dey ain't—no cause—foh 'citement—.Hyah—Ah is."

"Miss Lucy!" The soft voice was reproachful.

"Huh?—Wot's de mattah—honey?"

"I believe—.Yes, you *did*." There was accusation now in the tone.

"Done—wot?"

"You've been and gone and walked your poor tired old self home again to-night."

"Yo' mus'—be seein' t'ings—honey."

"Seeing things or not, I know *that*."

"How yo'—know, now?—Come on!"

There was a sudden vivid flash of small teeth and a decidedly impish expression on the little face.

"Easy as lapping up milk to a cat. It's this way: when you make one whole step in half a minute—you rode; when you make one whole step in a minute—you walked."

She waggled triumphantly the darkness of her little head at Miss Lucy.

The old woman stopped stockstill and seemed to be addressing the stairs in front of her.

"Hain't hit—jus' wunnaful—the smahrtness—ob some folks?—Hain't hit?"

"Grr!" said Mary Lou.

"Wot's—dat?"

"That is my very bestest growl; and it's to warn you to

watch your step. I'm a dangerous person, I'll have you to
know—and not to be trifled with. Grrr!"

"Ah—bleebs—she's serious."

"Serious! That's mild to what I am."

"Huh! Huh!" Miss Lucy laughed. "Ah reckon—Ah kin—
tay yo'—somepin—ta mek yo'—mo' seriousah—dan yo' is."

"I know it's outrageous. What is it?"

"Lis'n—Ah walk' home—jes' ez yo' say—tah sabe—ma
cah fahre.—An', chile,—jes', now—a man—comes 'long—
out de doo'—hyah—an' wot—yo' 'spose—ah done?"

"I'm prepared for the worst."

"Ah give him—Huh! Huh!—a dime!—Kin yo' beat hit?"

"Miss Lucy! Miss Lucy! you are incorrigible. What possessed you to do that?"

"Wot's dat—yo' say?—in—wot? Ef hit means—ez bad—
ez hit soun's—Ah' specks—Ah's donefoh."

"But what did you do it for, Miss Lucy?"

"Oh—wall—he say—he's feets—is bad—an' befoh Ah's
knowin' hit—Ah's—shellin'—out—de dime."

"Feet bad. H'm! Of course. It's as easy to understand as
can be.—You're all in—and your feet are more all in than
you are.—You're a terrible responsibility to a young thing
like me, Miss Lucy. No wonder my mind feels as though it
is giving away at times. What can I *do* to make you ride.—
will you tell me?—I've never seen you come upstairs as slow
as this before. For a little, I'd come down and carry you up!"

"Huh! Huh!" Miss Lucy laughed.

"Well, what's so funny about that?"

"Somehow—Ah ain't recollec'—ebbah—hyahin' befoh—
ob a skeetah—cahrryin'—an—elefan'—upstahs—on he back."

"Well, if you dare, just dare, to try walking home once
more, you'll not only *hear* about it but *know* about it as well."

By this time, puffing and wheezing, Miss Lucy had arrived

at the second step from the top and stopped. Mary Lou was waiting for her. All of a sudden she clapped her small hands and broke into a soft little husky gurgle of a laugh.

"Wot's—de mattah?" Miss Lucy was still out of breath.

"O, you *do* look funny! you *do!* I hope you didn't come through the street with your hat like that. Here, give it to me," the little imperious voice insisted. "Put your bag down, so I can help you off with your coat.—Oh, Miss Lucy! You've a letter. Is it *the* letter? Is it?"

The old woman, one broad smile, nodded her head slowly and in her eyes was the same child-like look of wonder and joy as before.

The little figure again clapped its little hands as best it could with the hat in them.

"O! O! Lovely! I'm *so* glad! I'll hold it for you and as soon as we get this old coat off, I'll give it right straight back. There!—Now I'll run ahead and put your things on your bed." She had not taken but a few steps, however, when she stopped abruptly, turned quickly and shook a tiny forefinger at Miss Lucy. "Now, listen, you're not to go in your room first. Understand? I've something to show you in mine."

"Huh! Huh!" Miss Lucy laughed. "Ah kin guess wot hit is?"

"What?"

Miss Lucy sniffed. "Coffee."

"Is that so. That's all *you* know about it. That isn't the half."

"W'y dey's a light in ma room!—Wot's dat foh?—An' de doo' settin' wide open!"

"You want to know entirely too much. Wait."

"So dat's how come de hall up hyah so bright dis ebenin'. Ah jes' cudden' mek hit out."

Miss Lucy, the letter still held closely in her hand moved

slowly and painfully forward down the hall. By the time she had arrived at Mary Lou's door, the owner of the light quick feet had already deposited the old woman's belongings on her bed, very carefully too, and was waiting, a little nervously, just inside her own door. As the room was fairly bright she could be quite clearly seen. She was perhaps five feet in height, certainly no more and wore a maroon colored jersey dress set off by a white immaculate little collar and white immaculate little cuffs. About the low waist line was a thin patent leather belt. If it had been a little brighter you could have seen that her black silk stockings showed evidence of many darnings and that her small black pumps, though cleaned and polished, had been patched in several places.

Her color was an even deep olive, almost a brown. Her eyebrows were level, very black and had the effect of being penciled. Her small head from the low forehead to the slender nape of neck was a mass of little delightful jet black curls. All the features were delicate, the slender nose "tip-tilted at the end," the firm small mouth, pale pink in color rather than red, and the firm small pointed chin. The only thing large about her was her eyes. They were immense and intensely black. They were eyes that could be anything—soft or eager; kind or merry, gentle or impish; but although Mary Lou was perhaps only twenty years of age, they had a trick of veiling themselves and keeping their own secrets. As she stood waiting you could see that she was thin rather than slender and very pale.

Miss Lucy still breathing somewhat heavily, hesitated a moment at the door and looked around.

"W'y—w'y—wot foh yo' room so bahr, Mahry Lou?" she asked at length in startled surprise.

The big eyes opened wider still in simulated innocence.

"Bare, Miss Lucy, bare!"

"Dot's wot ah sed. Whah's de nice crispy cuhrtin dat go 'at yo' side windah dah?—An' whah yo' baidspread and sham dat mek yo' baid look so nice? An' de li'l brown rug dat b'longs at de side ob yo' baid foh yo' tah step out on? An' yo' big rockin' chahr.—An'—an'—wot's dis? Yas hit is so—dat's ma ole rickety chahr. Wot hit doin' in hyah? Wot on earf yo' been up tah, Mahry Lou? Ef dis is wot yo' brung me in hyah tah show me, Ah doan t'inks much ob hit."

Under the reproving old eyes, Mary Lou was anything but at ease. If possible the sensitive, delicate face went a little paler; and it seemed as though there was a shadow of fear in the great soft eyes. But she answered gaily enough and taking the old woman by her free hand dragged her into the room.

"Oh *that*, that's not it. You're almost as bad as old 'Long-Nose' downstairs." Here, now, look!—what do you see?"

"Ah see an oil stobe an' a pot ob coffee abilin' hits head off."

"What else?"

"A sass pan, looks-lak, wid a cobah on hit."

Little Mary Lou leaned over and slipped off the lid. All of her seemed to sparkle—her great eyes, her little teeth, her shining jet curls, her whole small body, in fact.

"Now, what do you see?"

Miss Lucy peered down earnestly.

"Looks lak—yes, hit duz—Is dose yams, honey?"

Mary Lou nodded her little head so vigorously up and down you wondered it did not come off.

"Two of them. I bought them just for 'usses' for dinner tonight. Now, look here." She had opened a paper bag and displayed two big crusty Vienna rolls. "Don't they look good? Don't they? And there's butter—oh, not much—you needn't scold—but really and truly butter, in the ice box." She made a grand and supercilious gesture towards the window. Suddenly her whole face crinkled up and she broke into her delicious husky gurgle. "Don't the coffee smell good? And aren't we two going to have the grandest, wonderfullest time? Aren't we?—Miss Lucy, don't—don't cry!—I—I dare you!" Her own eyes, though, were suspiciously bright.

"Well, Ah declah! Ah declah!" the old woman said rather weakly. "You've 'bout tok wot li'l' bref Ah got lef'.—Chile, yo' oughtn' tah hab done hit. Yo' knows yo' cayn' 'fohrd hit."

"And that's all *you* know about it. Afford it, indeed. The very idea!"

"Looky hyah, Mahry Lou, dat lettah dat come foh yo' tah day? Did dat mek t'ings all right foh yo' again?"

Mary Lou nodded again vigorously. Strangely enough, however, she did not lift her eyes to Miss Lucy's.

"So Long-Nose told you. I knew she would."

"Mahry Lou!—O, dat's good, honey, Dat's good. Dat sho is a big 'lief tah me to know dat—No, Ah ain't gwinetah cry, but—wall—seems lak all dis kine ob struck me ob a heap.— Nobuddy nebbah done nuffin lak dis foh me befoh—not dat Ah kin 'membah. So yo' jes natchully gottah forgibe de ole woman ef she fill up foh a momen'. Hit sho am true dat hit nebbah rain but hit poa'ahs—ain't hit?—Dey's yo' lettah an' ma lettah—an'—an' now dis. Ah's, wall—Ah's jes' tickled clean mos' tah deaf, honey,—But Ah ain't gwinetah cry."

She turned her poor working old face away.

"Of course you're not," said little Mary Lou briskly. "For one thing there isn't time. Now, first we're going to fix up your feet all nice and comfy; and then we are going to eat and eat and eat; and then when we simply can't eat any more, I'm going to read your letter to you. Oh what a perfectly scrumptious ending. Go on, now, and get ready. Bring your bowl and a towel back with you. I've simply 'oodles of nice hot water."

Miss Lucy, as Mary Lou was only too glad to see when she glanced up, was herself again. She had started obediently towards her room—when with a sharp exclamation she came to an abrupt halt.

"Well, sah, Ah mus' be losin' ma mine. Ah mus' be. How on earf, come Ah tah fahgit da?"

Mary Lou looked a trifle startled.

"What's the matter, Miss Lucy?"

"Mattah! mattah 'nuff! Run, chile, run jes ez fas' ez ebbah yo' kin an' bring me a passel you'll fine in ma bag all wrap up in brown papah. Doan yo' nebbah git ole lak me, honey. De t'ings yo' oughtah 'membah, jes ez sho ez yo' bawn, slips away widout yo' knownin' hit."

"All right, I won't. Back in a jiffy."

She was as good as her word.

"Now, open hit," Miss Lucy commanded.

"Oh! oh! oh! Aren't they cunning? Little sausages, I love them, Are we, are we to have them tonight too?"

" 'Tain't foh nuffin else."

"It's too perfect, just too perfect to be true."

Although Mary Lou was demonstrative about some things she was not very much so in expressing her affection; Miss Lucy, however, felt fully repaid by the gratitude and the love she saw shining very clearly and steadily for her in the big dark eyes.

"Run along, you old dear. I'll put these on right away. The coffee and yams are all ready and, by the time your feet are fixed, these'll be done too."

But for some reason, Mary Lou did not put them on right away. She stood listening, the pan in one hand and the package of sausages in the other. The slow feet crossed the hall and entered their own little room. Mary Lou held her breath; she seemed to be all eyes. She turned one little ear towards the open door and the silence grew and grew. At last there came a voice, a terrible voice, one she had never heard before.

"*Mahry Lou!*"

"Yes." She tried to make her own sound natural and easy "*Come hyah!*"

"Just as soon, Miss Lucy, as I put these sausages on."

The putting on must have taken considerable time, but at last, she stood just without the door. It was a very terrifying Miss Lucy she saw.

"Miss Lucy, please, won't you please smile? Won't you?"

There was something suddenly timid, piteous about the little face.

"Dis is no smilin' mattah. Come in hyah."

Mary Lou obeyed. She advanced to the bottom of the old iron bed and gripped the foot tightly in her two little hands.

"Now, wot dis mean?"

"What does what mean?"

"Mahry Lou, Ah'm not foolin' wid yo'. —Youah cuhrtain dah at mah windah, youah baid spread hyah on ma bed, youah sham hyah on ma pillah, youah rug hyah on ma floo', youah good rockin' chahr obah dah, an' youah pitchah nail' up on ma wall dah! Wot's hit all mean?"

"Why—why—I thought it would look—look pretty," the little voice faltered.

"Pretty! co'se hit look pretty! But wot hit mean?"

"Miss Lucy, please.—I never thought you'd, you'd feel this way about it. I'll, I'll take them back. I'll—"

"Answah me!" Miss Lucy interrupted.

"Why—why—"

"Duz hit mean yo' gwine away?—Duz hit?"

The small face blanched suddenly. The knuckles showed

white from the sudden clutch of the little hands on the rail; but she answered quietly enough:

"Going away! Where on earth would I be going?"

"Did yo' step-daddy—write an' tay yo' tah come along home?"

A dry little smile flickered for a second about the taut little mouth.

"No, he didn't."

"Youah not gwine nowhahs, den?"

"Be reasonable, Miss Lucy. Where could I go?"

"God knows," the old woman said and moving slowly over to Mary Lou, tilted her face up with a trembling hand.

"Look at me, Mahry Lou."

Mary Lou's great eyes went straight enough to hers; but there was a tenseness in them, a wariness, even, if the nearsighted old eyes above could but have seen clearly.

"Doan lie to me, now. Dat lettah, wuz hit a nice one, jes' ez yo' say?"

"Oh, very nice."

"Duz hit mean—all ob dis—yo' ain't gwinetah tah need dem no mo', cos yo' gwinetah git yose'f new t'ings? Duz hit?"

A look of genuine relief swept over the small face; a trifle of color stole back into it. She answered eagerly, too eagerly. But Miss Lucy, at best, was not very acute.

"Yes, yes, that's just it. I'm not going to need them any more—any of them. Won't it be great to start all over again with everything new? brand new?—And—and these things here aren't so—so terribly worn out,—are they? And—and—instead of selling them—I—I'd much rather have you have them."

"Chile, yo' had me mos' night skeered tah deef. Ef yo' keps on, yo' sho will hab me cryin' an' no mistake.—Hit looks lubbly! jes' lubbly!—An' yo' pitchah dah, whah Ah kin allus see hit.—Ah didn' know yo' hab one.—Jes' de spit an' image ob yo' too.——Wants dem! C'ose Ah wants dem."

"The picture was my mother's, Miss Lucy."

"Was hit now."

"After she died last year I got it back, I guess maybe you'd call it stealing. My step-father doesn't know I have it."

"An' yo' gibbin' hit tah *me?* tah *me?*"

Mary Lou nodded her head jerkily. A pale little smile just brushed her lips. She winked her eyes violently and then turning abruptly, without a word, fled from the room.

For quite a while Miss Lucy stood looking at the lovely pictured face of Mary Lou; and if she wiped something from her old cheek, there was no one there to see. As she gazed she saw that the face in the photograph was somehow a much happier one than the one she knew. It was fuller, rounder; and then suddenly that soft contour of cheek smote at her heart, for strangely it brought back to her sharply, vividly the face of the real Mary Lou. Quite clearly she could remember little shadows and hollows about the sensitive and delicately moulded face—about eye socket and temple and nose and cheek and mouth. And for the first time it came home to her, how very thin had grown the laughing little face.

"Ah sho mus' be a hahrtless ole woman tah need a pitchah tah show me dis. Eben Miss Robinson cud see hit. Wall, ef dat chile been a-stahrvin' ob huhse'f, glory be, she ain't gwinetah—tah need foh tah do hit no mo'. Dose days am obah, praise de Lawd."

Sighing a little she turned to a shelf against the wall, opposite Mary Lou's picture. On it there were three things, a blatantly ticking alarm clock, at one end, and at the other, a sort of oriental figure, a slit in his huge protuberant stomach.

This was Miss Lucy's bank. In the centre of the shelf was another photograph, a framed one. It was of a little boy, possibly a year old, almost entirely naked. He was leaning forward each chubby hand clutching a chubby foot. His head was thrown back and on his face was a smile, the sunniest and most infectious imaginable. This was Miss Lucy's little grandson. He was five years old now; and she had never seen him. As she stood before him, her precious letter still in her hand, a smile answered the little boy's and there dawned again in her eyes that lovely child's expression. She leaned forward suddenly and kissed the little foot.

"Miss Lu—cy!" The calling voice was gay again.

For some time from across the hall there had come stealing into the room the most delicious fragrance of frying sausage. Miss Lucy sniffed, now, appreciatively.

"Comin'—jes' a momen'—lemme drap mah quahtah in man bank, an' Ah'll be wid yo'."

The money fell through the slot with a pleasant clinking. She lifted her bank, and you could see how proud its heaviness made her. Soon, however, the letter tucked carefully into her arm pit, and carrying bowl and towel, as commanded, she was back in Mary Lou's room.

Then began for these two a memorable evening. After Miss Lucy's feet had been made "all nice and comfy," as Mary Lou had promised, they sat down to eat. And such a supper. Never before has sausage been done to such a perfect, such a delicate turn, or yams been so richly golden and luscious or rolls been so divinely crisp and so filling or coffee so beautifully golden a brown or so "scrumptiously" delicious. They ate and they ate and they ate just as Mary Lou had predicted.

"I simply can't eat any more, can you?" finally inquired Mary Lou's joyous voice. "Feel!"

"Ah declah ef yo' ain't jes' ez tight ez a—li'l 'ole drum. Huh! Huh! Ah cayn' tawk, coz ef yo' is a li'l one, wot you 'specks Ah is?"

"We'll rest a few minutes and then clean up and then, then, then—the letter."

"Now," said Mary Lou, when dishes and pans had been washed and everything set to rights again, "you're to sit by the stove here and lean back so.—All set?—Good!—I'll get down here by your feet.—The letter, Miss Lucy, dear. Drat the old gas. Wish it would learn to stop cussing for once and give more light."

She tore open the envelope and leaned back against Miss Lucy's old knees. Suddenly she twisted round and patted them gently.

"You're trembling, and they're trembling like I don't know what, you poor old dear."

"Huh! Huh! Ah is a silly ole fool, ain't Ah?"

"You are not. Here goes."

She leaned back once more and began to read:

> 20 Cliff Road,
> Nongaset, L. I.,
> Nov. 23, 1924.

" 'Dear Ma,

I meant to have written long before this but you have no idea how busy I've been moving and everything into our new house. It is lovely if I do say so, as shouldn't. On the first floor there's a duck of a living room, a sun parlor, just off of it, a dining-room and, of course, a kitchen. On the second floor, is Fred's and my room—, Buster's and a couple of guest chambers. What do you think? We've had the attic finished off into the nicest of quarters for our maids; Molla our Swedish girl, and a perfect jewel, is up there and is crazy about it. The neighborhood is grand and the neighbors, two or three of them, have called already and seem tremendously impressed by us. Isn't it a scream? Fred and I nearly die laughing when we wonder what on earth they would do, if they dreamed for one second what we are. Buster is fine—all over the whooping cough and, with the diet I'm giving him, is really getting a little fat again.

Now, Ma, about your coming up here. First of all, don't get angry or hurt at what I'm going to say, will you? Fred and I have talked this over lots and we're anxious to have you make the visit; but you can see under the circumstances we simply have got to be careful. We have to watch our step every second of the time. Now, for all our sakes, I know you won't mind my asking you to do this for us. You've never failed me, you're the best mother ever and a dear into the bargain, so I'm sure this won't be much of a sacrifice to you. It's this:—we think the best way for you to come to us is as my old Mammy. I've already prepared the way for your visit, told one of the neighbors in fact, that I'm from the South and have the dearest old Mammy who's so devoted to me, she wants to come up and see Buster and take care of him for a while. We'd love to give you a guest room but you can see for yourself that wouldn't do for a minute, would cause a whole lot of talk and maybe give away the whole shooting match. So we've decided to fix up the room next to Molla's for you. You'll cotton to her at once, I know; and, as I said before, the attic rooms really are attractive. We'll give you, as good a time as we're able, you know that. So do come, Ma. By the way, we've decided that for you to be in character, that you will have to wear some kind of uniform— a cap and other fixings, you know. Buster, of course, mustn't dream for a moment, you're his grandmother. A child can simply ruin things for you—they're so innocent and honest and say just what they think and to *anybody*. I know he'll love you, though. He asks me every morning now, "Wen's yo' ole Mammy tummin?" Isn't that cute?

Now, let us know exactly when to expect you. Fred will

meet you with the new car—some car too, let me tell you. We don't think his meeting you will arouse any suspicions. Do you? I'm crazy to see you again.

Lots of love,
Kit.

P. S. Don't bother about the
   uniform—I'll attend to that.
         K.' "

When Mary Lou had finished her great black eyes were fairly blazing; and her two little hands were two clenched little fists. It was she who was trembling now.

"I hate her! I hate her!" she said in a fierce repressed voice. "I don't care whether she's your daughter or not, that's a *cruel* letter. *Cruel!*" She hadn't the heart to look around. "Of course you're not going. I wouldn't have believed anyone could have done a thing like that to a mother—but to a mother like you." Her little nostrils inflated suddenly, the muscles about her mouth and chin tightened. "I hoped to goodness, I never see her or that I'm near enough to know who she is."

She glanced around timidly, then. Miss Lucy was leaning back inertly. Every line of the old body sagged. The knees had fallen weakly apart and her two worn old hands, palms uppermost, lay limply open on each one. The lines of the face were heavy. The eyes had a dazed expression but in them, too, was the look of the dog, that hurt inexplicably by the loved hand, still believes, still trusts.

At last she said slowly:

"Ah ain't so fas', Ah reckon, ez Ah ustah be 'bout tekkin' t'ings in.—Wot she mean, Mahry Lou?"

Mary Lou knelt up, her voice was scarcely more than a whisper but tense with anger. She did not realize it but, in her excitement, she was beating the lifeless, heavy knees before her with her little fists.

"She means, your daughter, that she is asking you to come to her as her mammy, *her mammy*, Miss Lucy; and wear a uniform, a cap and apron; and be a servant in her house; and take care of her son; and sleep in an attic; and never, never, never let that dear little Buster know you're his grandmother, because she's a miserable, selfish, skulking old coward.— *Damn her!* O!" she wailed, "I've hurt you. I'm sorry. Please! Please! But you would make me tell you."

"Yes, dat's wattah t'ought she sed.—Wall, now, yo' come, tah t'ink ob hit, dey wahn't much else—was dey?—foh huh tah say?"

"Wasn't much else! *Wasn't!* O, Miss Lucy!"

"Ef dey's gwinetah pass foh w'ite an'—an' Ah's gwine up dah—dats de onlies' way, ain't it?" She paused and then went on slowly. "A servant in huh house!—Wall, dats all Ah's allus been, ain't hit?—fus' to dis w'ite pusson an' dat w'ite pusson?—'Twon' be so hahrd, Ah reckon, ef yo' ain't knowed nuffin else. Ah guess Ah kin stan' hit in ma da'hter's house.— An' ez for a uniform—clo'se cayn' huhrt you none.—no, cayn' huhrt yo'."

"They *can*. They *can*."

"No, not if yo' doan let 'em, dey cayn'. 'Sides Ah ain't gittin' no youngah, Mahry Lou, yo' knows dat. An' Ah's been sabin' ma money for dis, a right smahrt time now. Ah's got hit all. Ebry penny Ah'll need; an'—an'—Ah jes natchully gottah see dat li'l' gran'son ob mine. Ah *gottah*. Seems somehow lak Ah cudden die, widout dat. So—Ah guess Ah's gottah go.—Ah ain't gwinetah stay long—ef Ah jes has a couple ob weeks wid 'im, jes dose, Ah'll be satisfy.—Yo' pays foh wot yo' teks, honey—an'—an'—Ah ain't mindin' de payin'.—Wall, de ebenin's obah, Ah reckon."

"Yes and it's spoiled, spoiled!"

The old woman gathered herself together slowly and pain-fully got to her feet. "No, not spiled, Mahry Lou, not spiled.—Dey's been yo' dis ebenin'—an' dey's gwinetah be ma li'l' granchile.—How come yo' kin call dat spiled? —Ah gottah mek early time again tah-morrah, so Ah guess Ah bettah be tuhrn'in in, now.—We's had a large ebenin'—large—an' Ah's nebbah gwinetah fahgit hit an' yo'. —G'night!"

"Good-night, Miss Lucy—dear."

As the old woman was just on the point of closing her door, a little voice just outside called softly:

"Miss Lucy!"

"O!—yo' kine ob gib me a stahrt, chile. Ah wuzn' 'speckin' foh tah see yo' again."

"I'm sorry, but would you—" The soft voice broke off.

"Wud Ah wot, Mahry Lou?"

"Would you—would you mind, making believe"—

"Wot yo' wan', chile?"

Then all in a hurry it came:

"Would—you mind, very much, just for once, making believe you are my mother and—and—"

"Mahry Lou!"

"And—and kissing me good-night?"

"Mine! Mine! Come hyah!"

The old arms went around the little figure that came to them in a little rush and they held it close. This was an entirely new Mary Lou that clung tightly, frankly, almost with abandon, to her. Even Miss Lucy ordinarily dull about such things saw, when the little thing loosed its hold suddenly and stood looking at her intently, unblinkingly for a second, how very bright the great eyes were, how pale the small face and remembered how hot had been the little mouth.

At length Mary Lou said:

"Thank you! Thank you, Miss Lucy. You've been sweet to me, sweet as ever my own mother could have been.—And next to her—I love you best—in all the world.—Good-night."

She was gone, then—without a backward look. Her door, even, had closed behind her, before the astonished Miss Lucy could open her mouth to say anything.

"Wall, Ah nebbah!" she brought forth at last and stood staring for several minutes at the door. Finally she went and shut her own. She paused, however, with her hand on the knob.

"Dat sutenly am quahr. Wan't a bit lak huh. Nebbah knowed huh do nuffin lak dat befoh." The heavy frown on her forehead cleared suddenly. "Ob cos—dat's hit—. Huh li'l hahrt gottah feelin' sohry foh me—an' she t'ought dis mek me feel bettah. Bress huh!"

With that she dismissed the matter from her mind.

"Now, lemme see," she said speaking aloud, "Ah gottah t'ink wot Ah's gwinetah tek wid me. Yas, ma black dress, de silk one, jes about ez good ez new. Ma Sunday coat ain't so good, mebbe, but hit'll do. Hit gottah.—Uh huh!—Good t'ing Ah bought doze shoes, w'en Ah did, dey's jes' de t'ing. Dat bein' so. Ah kin 'fohd tah buy dat li'l' black hat, Ah's been lookin' at—wid de wi'lets on hit. Hit's a real stylish li'l' trick; ah t'inks foh five dollahs. Ah's got glubs an' hangshefs an' unnaclose. Dah's one t'ing Ah's proud ob."

Here she moved awkwardly over to a wooden box under the shelf, opened it, sat on the side of her bed that sagged under her weight with a screeching protest and began fingering these luxuries of hers with delight. All of them were very simple, very old-fashioned and made out of strong white cotton. But to her they were wonderful.

"Ah wudden be shame foh ennybody tah see dese. No indeedy."

At the bottom of the box she unearthed a little Indian suit

about large enough to fit a small boy of five, a toy automobile, and an illustrated fairy book. Her old eyes shone as she touched these caressingly before stowing them carefully away again.

"Ah hopes he loves dem—Ah mos' knows he will."

"Now, lemme see," she continued aloud presently, "wot Ah gwinetah do 'bout a bag. Ah knows right now, Ah cayn' 'fohd tah—buy me one.—Ob co'se—de berry t'ing—Mahry Lou's got one. She ain't gwinetah nedd it, de Lawd be praise'—.Seems lak Ah didn't feel at fus', as dough Ah cud stan' hit, w'en Ah t'ought she gwine away.—Ah bettah jes run obah an' ask huh now."

A few moments later she was rapping on Mary Lou's door.

"Mahry Lou!" she called in a low voice. "Mahry Lou!" and again after a pause. "Mahry Lou!" But there was no response.

She stood back and looked up at the glass transom above the door. It was dark.

"Dat's funny. Ah ain't nebbah 'membah huh sleepin' wid-out a li'l' light buhrnin' befoh. Mebbe's she's lis'en tah me at las'. Ah's tole huh of'en nuff dat hit dang'rous tah sleep wid huh gas tuhrned low an' huh windah open.—She sho' kin git huhse'f undress' an' in bead an' sleep—quickern—ennyone Ah ebbah hyah tell ob.—Huh! Huh!"—She laughed to herself. "Yo'd t'ink f'om de great huhry Ah's in Ah's leebin' tah-morrah on de fus' train, widout fail. Dey's plenty ob time to see 'bout dat bag."

Back in her room again, she began slowly to undress and fifteen minutes, perhaps later, enveloped in a large flannel night-gown, her scant hair rolled up in four knots, two in the front and two in the back, she reached up and turned off her gas.

"Feels kinds cole tah-night. Ah 'specks ah oughtah open

ma windah a li'l', dough." The shade shot up noisily. "De windah's rattlin' lak dey's a win' come up." She lowered the upper sash about an inch and raised the lower the same distance. Even so the wind came rushing in and struck her with almost a blow. "Ooo!—dat's cole. Hope hit ain't gwine-tah rain tah-morrah. Hit's so hahrd tah git tah Miss Preston w'en hit duz.—No, dey ain't no clouds—nuffin but stahrs ebbywhah." Again the wind came and struck cold against her bare feet and ankles. "Oo! Lemme git in baid quick. Hit sho is cole.—Ah's glad Mahry Lou ain't got huh gas buhrnin' tah-night."

Shivering she crept into the noisily protesting bed and lay down flat on her back. She was too excited to fall asleep immediately.

"Dah, now," her thoughts ran, "Ah clean fahgit 'bout dem trains.[1] Ah wondah who ah kin git tah fine out 'bout dem for me."

As if by magic a man's face appeared before her, a dark face, with its lazy, amused, half-closed eyes, leaf brown in color, quizzical eyes, the left, larger and the left eye-brow curiously higher than the other;—and its mouth, large, not beautiful, but sensitive, wide generally with laughter showing to their full two even, strong, very white rows of teeth that were really beautiful.

"Paul Brown, ob co'se, de berry one." For a moment or so she thought of him. "Nice kid, ebrybuddy laks 'im. Kine of crazy, mebbe, but allus good-nature'-lak an' ez for jokin'—at hit all de time. Nuffin, Ah 'specks, he ain't gwinetah see somepin funny in—eben he own fun'ral. Mos' ebryt'ing tickels 'im. Ah declah Ah laks tah see 'im double up an' hyah

---

1. Holograph incomplete revision: {Ah clean wen' away f'om me 'bout dem trains.}

dat Hah! Ha! ob his'n.—Habs a hahrd time too, Ah reckon,
tah mek bofe ends meet, so he kin finish datah medical co'se
he's tekkin. Kine tah ebrybody, do ennyt'ing too, for enny-
buddy. Ah knows dey ain't ennyone dat's craziah but jes de
same yo' knows somehow yo' kin depen' on 'im." She smiled
to herself. "Yassah, ah ain't 'jectin' none of he do lak Mahry
Lou. Dat's one t'ing he ain't hidin' f'om me needah an' Ah
hopes dat somepin comes of hit."

She chuckled aloud, moved more comfortably down in the
bed and her thoughts returned to their old channel.

"Ah doan know but p'raps, hit de bes' t'ing aftah all, ma
gwine updah eza—eza mammy.—Jes' lis'n tah dat win',
now.—Ah kin be wid Bustah—dataway—all de time. Yassah,
Ah kin wek him up evry mawnin' an' wash he li'l face an'
comb he pretty hahr, and gib him he breakfas'. An' Ah kin
play wid him, and tek him he lunch, an' see dat he gits he
nap, an' wek him up agin, an' put on he li'l cute t'ings, an'
tek him out tah walk, and bring him back home an' gib him
he bafe, an' he suppah an' tuck him all up good at night.—
Yassah, hit's gwinetah be fine.—No, now, I comes tah t'ink
ob hit, Ah wudden hab hit no uddah ways, nohow."

With that she turned on her right side and drew the
covering closely about her head. It was not long before she
was snoring heavily. And she had a dream, a delightful one
except for the one fact she was wearing a blue dress of some
kind, a white cap and a big white apron. But she and little
Buster were together, nothing could spoil that. And the
loveliest thing about the dream to her was the feel of that
little hand in hers. They seemed to be walking slowly about
a small brown pond. His face was turned up to hers and he
was talking and laughing just as in the picture. She could
hear him as plainly as could be and then suddenly, strangely,

his childish treble seemed to change into a man's deep tones calling her. Hubbub and darkness followed and she had lost him. Slowly she came back to consciousness. Vaguely she realized the hubbub was a constant low knocking somewhere. Then a voice, a man's voice low and insistent seemed to be calling her name over and over again.

"Miss Lucy!—Miss Lucy!—Miss Lucy!"

"Huh!"

"This is Brown."

"Brown?"

"Yes, Paul Brown."

"Paul Brown?" She was still stupid with sleep.

"Yes, you know, the medical student in the back room on this floor."

"Oh, yes, Mr. Brown.—Yo' ezn' sick, ez yo'?"

"No.—But—well, really there isn't time to break this to you nicely.—The fact is I'm terribly afraid something has happened to Mary Lou."

She was fully awake now. It seemed to her that with one bound, she was outside her room standing in the dim hall, illuminated only by the light that was streaming out of Mr. Brown's open door at the rear. The need for slippers or a wrap never once entered her head. Her teeth were inclined to chatter but not entirely from cold as she peered up into Paul Brown's face, a changed face, this, stern, unsmiling and somehow older.

"Mistah Brown, Ah didn' hyah yo' right, did Ah? didn' [yo'] say, Mahry Lou?"

"Yes."

"But wot *kin* yo' mean?" She wrinkled her nose. "An' wot—wot dis Ah smells?"

"It's gas, Miss Lucy." The voice was sharp, abrupt. "I

came in a minute or so ago and smelt it, smelt it strong. I
sniffed at your door and it wasn't here and then I went to
Mary Lou's—"

"An' hit wuz dah?"

"Yes."

Paul Brown beside she moved over to Mary Lou's door.
Her bare feet hit the floor with a dry sound.

"Ah's tole dat chile, an' tole dat chile," the old voice
trembled, "somepin lak dis boun' tah happen, ef she 'sist on
leabin hah light buhrnin' an huh window open. Ah—" she
broke off suddenly. Her jaw dropped, and the fear she had
been fighting seemed to congeal and tighten about her old
heart. She had remembered. Breathing heavily, she gripped
the man's arm.

"Ah's wrong. Ah's wrong!"

"What do you mean?"

" 'Tain't ez Ah says—a-tall."

"Well?"

"Huh light—hit cudden hab blown out ez Ah says."

"Why not?"

"Ah wuz out hyah—aftah Ah lef' huh foh de night.—Ah
seen.—Dey wahn't no light hyah tall—tah blow out. Mistah
Brown, Mistah Brown, Ah's—Ah's skeered!"

"Steady, now, Miss Lucy. Steady!"

"Yas, Ah knows. Ah—Ah'll try."

"Are you listening to me?"

"Uh huh!"

"There isn't a bit of good of knocking or calling. Try the
door."

"W'y—w'y—Mistah Brown, hit's—hit's lock'. She—she
doan nebbah lock hit."

He made no comment, merely nodded; but he was watching
her keenly. Even in the dimness he could feel as well as see

the horror slowly mounting in the old eyes. She made no outcry, but her hands went in an aimless way up to her throat. She leaned weakly against the wall. Over and over, just above a whisper, she was saying:

"Ma Gawd! Ma Gawd! Ma—"

"Now, see here, Miss Lucy." His voice was almost hard. He shook her roughly by the arm. "Do you want to be of any use or don't you? Speak up."

"W'y, w'y, ob c'ose."

"You've simply got to get a grip on yourself then. Everything may depend on just that. *You must not give up.* Are you listening to me?"

"Uhuh."

"I don't think things are as bad as you imagine. The gas doesn't smell strong enough to me to have been on very long."

"Bress yo; ef yo's only right."

"That's better, now. I knew you'd be a good sport."

"Reckon Ah kin Stick, now, t'anks tah yo'. Wot we—wot we gwinetah do?"

"The key to your room door! Have you one? Good. Is it in the door? Does it unlock this one? Fine. No, stay here, I'll get it."

He was back in a flash, on a knee and working at the lock.

"I may be able to push her key out with this.—If I can I'll get in without any difficulty. If I can't—well, there'll be nothing then—for it but to break the door down. I don't want to do that—I'm hoping we can keep this just among ourselves."

Only a few seconds after he had finished speaking there was the sound of something falling with a tinkling sound.

"Not dat? De key."

"Yes." He straightened up and unlocked the door.

"This is where you come in, Miss Lucy. No, not in here, I mean, this is what you're to do." He gave her a sharp glance. "You all right again? Good. I've opened the window there in the hall and all those in my room. Go back and open yours—top and bottom—open it wide. Get me?—Fine. Put your feet into something first and wrap yourself up good and warm or we'll have you on our hands next.—Leave your door just as it is, light your gas and wheel your bed right in between the window and the door. Luckily there's a good stiff breeze tonight. What she is going to need more than anything else is air—lots of it.—Plenty of covering on your bed, so she'll be warm—Fine.—I'll bring her to you.—That's it—I knew you were a good old scout, Miss Lucy."

The old woman turned away and entered her room. His coolness, the crispness of his orders had filled her with courage and an unaccountable confidence in him and in herself. She obeyed him to the letter. She was just wheeling her bed between the door and window, when he appeared on the threshold. Try as she could, though, she was unable to repress a slight whimpering sound at what she saw. He was carrying the small limp white clad figure, one arm under her knees and the other under her shoulders. The bare thin little arms and legs, the tiny helpless feet dangled inertly. The small head with its soft silken curls had fallen backward and swung lifelessly from side to side; the mouth was twisted and open, the beautiful great eyes were open too, staring and dull. The smell of gas was very strong in the room.

Very gently he put her down on the bed and they covered her over.

"Gee!" he said, "she doesn't weigh a thing.—Poor little kid!"

The chin and lower lip of the old woman began to tremble; a tear or two fell on the bed clothes.

"Mr. Brown! Mr. Brown!—Look at huh—huh poo' li'l face. Oh, she ain't gwine, ez she?"

"Going! I should say not. She'll be all right in a short time now.—In a day or two she won't even know that it happened. It's just as I thought—the gas can't have been on very long. Good thing I came home just when I did."

"But look at huh! Look at huh! An' de way she breavin'. Is yo' sho? Isn' day enny mo' we kin do?"

"I'll agree she isn't the pleasantest sight at present and her breathing is rather awful—but the important thing is—she is breathing. She's getting what she needs most—air. Have you any aromatics of ammonia?—Never mind, I have. I'll bring you some. Got a hot water bag? Good. Get it for me. Luckily I possess a mother who insisted on giving me one, too. The water is hot in the faucet to-night.—See! She's already looking better."

He was back shortly with the two bags and the medicine.

"You'll know best where to put these, and when she's conscious, give her this."

"Wot on erf's dat?" asked Miss Lucy as he was pulling an object entirely unknown to her out of his coat pocket.

"What? This do you mean?—Did it frighten you? Only a flashlight. It's been a good friend to all of us this night. I'm going now to open up her windows. I've already turned off the gas."

He stood looking down at Mary Lou for several moments upon his return.

"Looks a bit more normal, doesn't she? Breathing's much easier too. The smell of gas isn't so strong either—it's going. Fortunately Miss Robinson is good and dead to the world. I wouldn't have her snooping around here for worlds.—I'll tell you how we'd better fix this up. If any one says "gas" in the morning, I'll explain I was studying late and fell asleep—

everybody knows I'm liable to do that fool thing any old time—the wind was strong—don't we run in luck?—and blew my light out. I woke up just in time, found the house full of gas and so on. How's that? All right? Good. I'm going now, I see she's almost out of it and it's just as well if she doesn't see me to-night. If you need me for anything, though, don't hesitate—knock on my door. I'll be ready. Good-night."

"Mistah Brown, yo' doan look lak no angel but yo' sho has been one dis night.—Ah—"

"Forget it, Miss Lucy."

"Well, ef yo' won' lis'n."

"I won't."

"G-night, den."

He smiled at her, and was gone. It was a big relief to see his white teeth again.

And altogether scarcely more than fifteen minutes had elapsed since the time he had been knocking on Miss Lucy's door to wake her up!

The old woman sat down by the bed; the wind and the room were cold and she drew her old woolen wrapper close up around her neck. The little face on the pillow had lost all of its dark agonized look; the eyes were closed naturally, now; and the breathing was almost regular again. Presently the lids fluttered, the eyes opened. Their gaze was wide and blank, it roved around until it settled upon Miss Lucy. Slowly it came to a focus. A little frown appeared and she closed her eyes. In a moment they were open once more. Intelligence was there and questioning.

"Miss Lucy!" The voice was little more than a whisper.

"Yas, honey."

"It is you, then?"

"Uh huh!"

There was a pause during which her eyes moved around a second time; she turned her head a trifle to see more clearly.

"Where am I?"

"In my room, honey."

The lids dropped again. She was plainly thinking.

"How did I get here?" she asked presently.

"Mistah Paul Brown brung yo', honey."

The eyelids flickered at this; she turned her head away.

"Mahry Lou, raise yo' head up a li'l, so.—Ah'll he'p yo'. He say foh yo' to tek this."

She did not demur, but swallowed the draught obediently. For a long time afterwards she lay with shut eyes, so long Miss Lucy hoped she had fallen asleep. The next minute, quite unexpectedly, they opened wide, beseechingly.

"You can't go to bed, can you? It's a shame.—I do mess things up for everybody, don't I?—I didn't mean to."

"Es ef ennything mattahs ez close ez we come tah losin' yo'." And then against her will it came out. "Mary Lou!— Mary Lou! Wot ebbah mek yo' do hit?"

The shadow of the old whimsical smile touched the pale small mouth.

"I didn't, it seems," she said.

For several moments she lay staring straight ahead of her, the smile twisting into a wry little one.

"It's a scream.—If I didn't feel so weak, I'd howl my fool head off. You do your derndest to kick off and then you find you're just where you were when you started.—Makes you think of the funny papers.—You know, the man with the golf club, the one that makes the dandiest, smashing drive, gets chesty and everything, then looks down and the damned [2] little old pill's there just the same?"

"Mary Lou, chile! Ah wish you wudden use such lang-widge."

---

2. In the typescript, Grimké has crossed out {damned}. I have replaced the word to make the next lines comprehensible.

"Perfect ladies wouldn't, would they?" she shrugged her thin small shoulders weakly.

"Dey didn', honey, not in ma day."

"But then I'm thinking, perfect ladies wouldn't try to kick off with gas, would they?—So, after all, what's the dif.—Well, I can waggle my head, it seems, and wiggle my toes and flap my arms about the breathe and my heart—yes, it's beating just the same as ever.—I suppose you and Mr. Paul Brown must know what you're doing—I don't."

"Mahry Lou!"

"Oh they're all very wonderful and admirable accomplishments, I'll acknowledge, but somehow they don't seem to get me anywhere. They don't find me a job, or pay my room rent, or put food in my little 'tummy'."

"But your lettah, Mahry Lou, didn' yo' tay me an' tay me mo' dan onct hit a nice one? Didn't yo'?"

"Oh my yes, very nice; but I was given to understand quite clearly and firmly just where I got off."

"An' knowin' dat, yo' goes out an'—an'—buys coffee and rolls and yams?"

"Well, even the condemned criminal, Miss Lucy, gets one good square feed before he kicks off."

"An' Ah bet yo' ain't got a penny lef' tah yose'f in de worl'.—O, Mahry Lou! Mahry Lou!"

"Quite wrong, my dear Miss Lucy, quite wrong. I wish you to know that I am still the proud and boastful possessor of the astounding sum total of—a dime."

"Ah knew'd hit! Ah knew hit!—Ah kin see hit all, now,—mo' fool me.—Dat's de reason yo' goes tah wuk an' gibs me all yo' pretty t'ings hyah foh ma room.—Yo's gwinetah bre'k ma ole hahrt, dat's wot."

"Come, now, Miss Lucy, you never heard of any one's needing bedspreads and shams and rugs and chairs—where I thought I was going.—Besides I can't figure how I was going to take them with me. Can you?"

Miss Lucy was rocking her huge body back and forth and moaning.

"An' yo' nebbah tole me nuffin, or axe me foh nuffin—jes' goes an'—an' does dis."

"How could I, Miss Lucy?"

"Esy nuff."

"But you were going away and might never come back."

Miss Lucy stopped rocking suddenly.

"Whah Ah gwine?"

"To New York, of course."

"Ah ain't gwine tah no sech a place."

"But you are, Miss Lucy."

"An Ah tays yo' Ah'm not."

"I don't believe you. Don't misunderstand me." She added hurriedly, "I wish you to go, because you wish to."

"Ah doan wish tah go, an' ah ain't gwine."

"You certainly can change your mind quickly."

"No, Ah cayn' change ma mine quickly needah. Ah's been t'inkin' 'bout dis right smahrt—wot yo' say an' all—an' ah sees dat yo's right. Ah cudden go up dataway an' kip mah se'f respec', so—Ah jes ain't gwine, an' dat's all dey is to hit."

"I still don't believe you, Miss Lucy."

"Now, looky hyah, Mahry Lou, ef yo' wuz in ma place, cud *yo'* go?"

"No, I couldn't; but you and I don't see the same."

"Oh we don', don' we? Wall we sees dis hyah de same."

"But—"

"Ah doan wantah hyah no mo' ob yo' 'buts'. Ah guess Ah has ez much right tah ma se'f respec'—ez—ez yo' habs yo'ahs. Dat's settled, now, onct and foh all.—Ah ain't gwine."

She bent over Mary Lou belligerently for several minutes evidently daring her to say anything more, but Mary Lou smiling a little, merely watched her quietly.

"Dat bein' so, in a day or two w'en yo' feels uptah hit, yo's gwinetah staht in dat hahdressin' an' manicurin' co'se; an' tomorrah we's gwinetah pay Miss Robinson foh yo' room rent, an' we ain't gwinetah hab no mo' trouble wid yo' 'bout dis eatin' mattah edah. Unnastan? Ah's got a lottah money, Ah ain't needin', an' weddah yo' laks hit er not, dis somebody right hyah is gwinetah look aftah yo'. So dah."

The small mouth set itself in stubborn lines; the great eyes fairly blazed at the old woman.

"I won't take your money, Miss Lucy.—I won't.—I won't."

"Who's axin ob yo' tah tek hit, Ah'd lak tah know? Ah's lendin' hit tah yo', ain't Ah? An' wot's mo' ef yo' doan come tah time 'bout payin' hit back, w'en Ah say pay, an' payin' me intres' too, (yassah, Ah's gwinetah charge yo' intres'), w'y den Ah—Ah's jes gwinetah natchully grine hit out ob yo'."

"How lovely!" For the first time a genuine smile came into the little face.

"Lubbly! Yo' wait an' see ef Ah is. W'en Ah gits stahted, Ah's a terrible ole woman."

"You're a terrible sweet old woman."

Then all of a sudden the small face puckered up piteously.

"D—don't—be—be—g—good—t—to—m—me, M—Miss Lucy! D—don't! You'll—m—make—m—me—c—cry.—And—I—d—don't—w—want t—to—cry," she wailed. "I—I—c—can't c—cry—l—like—a s—sensible p—person.—I'm a p—perfect—f—fool;—I—I—leak—and—s—spill—all over.—I'm—a—f—flood, I t—tell you, a c—cloud—b—burst!"

"Ez dat so? Wall, Ah's gwinetah see wot we kin do 'bout

dis.—Fustes', Ah's gwinetah close de door—dis away; an'
den Ah's gwinetah wrap yo' all up good an' warm in dis
comfohrtah. An' Ah's gwinetah pick yo' up jes lak dis and
sot down wid yo' hyah; an' hole yo', so; an' den yo's gwinetah
cry jes ez much ez ebbah yo' please."

"B—but—I d—don't w—want to, I t—tell you." The
great tears were already falling steadily in great drops. "I—
I j—just—b—bust over—d—dams an'—an' everything. There
w—won't—b—be a d—dry t—thing—in—t—the—r—
room."

All righty—yo' jes go ahead—an' bus' loose obah all de
dams yo' wantah.—An' Ah wudden be a bit 'sprise ef Ah
didn't fine mase'f bus'in' obah a few ob ma own. Ef we's
gwinetah do dis t'ing, honey, we mought jes ez well—mek a
good big job ob hit an' git hit obah and done wid once an'
foh all.—An' in de mawnin', honey, hit's gwinetah be all
right.—Yassah, hit's gwinetah be all right agin."

* * * * * * * * * *

It was six o'clock of a Wednesday night, two weeks later and
Miss Lucy had just closed the front door behind her and
stood, her back to it. The hall was as inhospitable, as dingy,
as dimly lighted as ever; but as on that former night the air
was laden with the delicious aroma of boiling coffee.

"Dat you, Miss Lucy?" The voice was as sharp as ever,
the difference being that it was no longer muffled but had
regained, to the full, its positive clearness and volume.

"Uh-huh—wot's lef'."

"Yo' soun's—tiahed."

"Ah is—kindah."

"Ah's gittin' mase'f ready tah go tah prayah-meetin'."

"Dat's good," said Miss Lucy politely.

"As Ah allus says—wot wud Ah do widout ma church?
Hit's jes ez good tah me ez medicine. W'en Ah comes out

Ah feels lak a new pusson. As Ah allus says, w'en Ah needs he'p gib me ma church."

"Ah 'specks yo' right, Miss Robinson."

"Uh huh! Yo' bettah come long an' go wid me some ebenin'. Do yo' good."

"Mebbe Ah will—sometime—w'en Ah doan feel so tiahed. Seems lak dese feets of mine gets heabiah an' heabiah an' achin'ah—an' achin'ah—ebry night."

"Dat's too bad.—Dey ain't no mail, Miss Lucy."

"No, Ah wahn't lookin' foh none."

With her hand on the banisters, she looked up with weary eyes. How long the journey ahead of her stretched; but it had to be done—somehow. She began the ascent. It took her longer than ever to gain the first hall. She was just about to climb the second flight, when a voice hailed her from below:

"So long, Miss Lucy! Ah's gone."

"So-long."

"Doan let de house buhn down er nuffin—wile Ah's away." Miss Robinson's laugh rang out staccato and loud, this was her idea of a joke.

"No,—Ah won'."

With the noisy banging of the front door, her own hallway seemed suddenly to blaze with light.

"Mahry Lou!"

"Yes, Miss Lucy," a meek little voice answered just above her head. The old woman craned her head up sideways. She made out what appeared not one head but two, a large one and a small, close together.

"Es dat yo' dah?"

"I think so," said Mary Lou sweetly. "Would you mind pinching me to find out?" The small head said to the big one.

"Yes, Miss Lucy," said a man's deep voice, "whatever this

is beside me answers to that name." The voice was preternaturally grave.

"Who dat wid yo', Mahry Lou?"

"With me? With me?—Why so there is. Now where do you suppose he dropped from? It's Mr. Paul Brown."

"Mister!" the deep voice asked aggrievedly.

"Oh well, then, Paul Brown."

"Ah cayn' say Ah's 'sprised none."

"Now what on earth can she mean by that?" said the small head to the big one, oh! so innocently.

"Sounds deep," said Paul Brown.

"Nebbah mine 'bout all dat.—Wot all dis big light doin' up hyah?"

"Oh for lots and lots and lots of reasons. For one, you're coming, for another, old Long-Nose has gone."

"Mahry Lou!"

"You needn't try to squelch me to-night, for you just can't."

All of a sudden the little figure above began to jump up and down, beating the railing the while with its little hands. A small delightful voice began to chant:

> "Goody! Goody! Goody!
> Old Long-nose has gone.
> Goody! Goody! Goody!
> Old Long-nose has gone."

"Mahry Lou, you'd oughtah be shame' ob yo'se'f. Yo' sho ez scan'lous."

"Scandalous! Scandalous!—You haven't seen me scandalous yet; but wait! wait!

> "Goody! Goody! Goody!
> Old Long-nose has gone."

The beating upon the railing was interspersed by quick tweakings of what seemed to be Mr. Paul Brown's hair and nose and ears. You may not believe it, but the young gentleman did not seem to mind in the least the very rough, rude and unladylike behavior.

"H'm!" grunted Miss Lucy. "Seems lak tah me yo' progressin' right fas', Mr. Paul Brown."

"Fast! Fast! Funny idea you have of fast, I must say."

"O, Miss Lucy dear, can't you, can't you hurry any more than that? We've the most wonderful, scrumptious "duckiest" sur—"

Miss Lucy paused midway the stairs to see what on earth, so mysteriously, so suddenly, could have cut off that little voice. Not that the hall above was noiseless, far from it, one would have needed to be deaf indeed, to have so described it. Sounds abounded, sounds of scuffling feet, struggle and smothered laughter. And then the mystery was explained, she caught a brief glimpse of Mary Lou. The lower part of her face had entirely disappeared and in its place was a man's large and efficient hand. But the hand have belied its appearance—for abruptly a piercing little voice shrieked:

" 'Prise! 'Prise! 'Prise!—So there. And if you put your hand over my mouth again, Paul Brown, I'll—I'll bite it."

"No!—Go as far as you like!—Spleasure'll be all mine."

"I warn you, now, my teeth are as sharp, as sharp—Miss Lu—cy, we've got—chick—"

For a second perhaps there was absolute silence but it was broken suddenly, vehemently by a man's voice:

"Ouch!—You would, would you, you little monkey?"

"Well, you can't say, I didn't warn you."

"Just for that, now, I will muzzle you and no mistake."

There was a rush of feet down the hall and then sounds of scuffling, of struggle and of smothered laughter broke out afresh. Every once and a while Mary Lou's voice must have fought its way free for what Miss Lucy heard was something like this:

"We got cof—" abrupt silence followed by struggle; "and sweet—" abrupt silence followed by struggle; "and fried—" abrupt silence followed by struggle; "and ice—" abrupt silence followed by struggle.

"Huh! Huh! Huh!" In spite of herself Miss Lucy was laughing. By this time she had arrived at the second step from the top and come to a halt. When Mary Lou perceived this fact the battle began to rage in genuine earnest. As soon as Mary [Lou] discovered that all her stratagems would not break the enemy's hold she essayed a new one—she suddenly began to jump up and down on his feet. It worked.

"Help! Murder! I'm killed!" He yelled and released her. Holding his injured foot in one hand, he began to hop around on the other.

"I didn't really mean to hurt you—much."

"Hurt! I'm killed, I tell you. The wretch has heels on her shoes like needles. One went clean straight on through my foot."

"Well, you should have known better than to hold me after Miss Lucy gets there. I always have to take her things from her at the second step from the top."

"You win. It's the first time little Paul ever tried to get up a surprise, but never again. Miss Lucy, I swore that creature there to absolute silence and she promised Honest Injun! Cross her heart! Hope to die and everything, if she'd tell. And you no more than put your foot on the stair there and she has to go yelping all over the place, 'We've got a surprise! We've got a surprise.' "

"Well, we have, haven't we?" said Mary Lou in perfectly matter of fact tones. This seemed to add the finishing touch, for Mr. Paul Brown threw up his hands in pretended disgust and turned away.

Meanwhile Mary Lou had been busy taking the old woman's bag and helping her divest herself of worn hat and coat.

"And it is a surprise that is a surprise," Mary Lou, an impish eye on the gentleman, continued undaunted. "Spiffy's no name for it. Every single thing your 'tummy' ever wanted or dreamed of, we've got. Paul's spent about a million dollars, I guess."

"Absolutely no exaggeration, Miss Lucy, an underestimate if anything." How pleasant, how warming his smile was, the old woman thought.

Meantime so swift had little Mary Lou been that already Miss Lucy's things were on her bed and Mary Lou herself had returned.

"Now, do, do, do hurry, Miss Lucy," she cried.

"Aw right, jes lemme put ma quahtah in ma bank an' ah'll be wid yo'."

In a flash all the joy and the radiance was wiped out of Mary [Lou]'s small face, leaving it ghastly. She went timidly to Miss Lucy and standing on tip-toe put her two little hands on the big shoulders.

"Miss Lucy!"

"W'y, wot's de mattah, honey?"

"Oh, you did tell me the truth—didn't you?—about not going to New York? Miss Lucy, didn't you? I—I—can't bear it, if you didn't. Miss Lucy, please tell it's the truth?"

"Kin yo' ebbah 'membah ma lyin' tah yo'?"

"No, oh, no!"

"Well, den. Co's Ah tole yo' de truf."

"But your quarter in your bank?"

"So dat's hit, ez hit? Wall, Ah reckon Ah's got wot yo' mought call de quahtah habit. Ah's too ole, now, tah brek mase'f ob hit. Ah'll jes hab tah kip on puttin' dem away tell Ah die. Doan mean a t'ing else, honey."

"You're sure, Miss Lucy—You're sure?"

"Ob c'os ah's sho.—You alls run ahlong in.—Ah'll be wid yo' presun'ly."

It was astonishing how light the touch was of that big dark worn hand on the silken curls.

"Yo' all right, now, honey?"

Mary Lou nodded, her brightness a trifle forced, then turned to Mr. Brown, who had been anything but a comfortable spectator.

"Come on Paul," she made herself call gayly.

Paul came on and they disappeared in Mary Lou's room.

And old Miss Lucy dragged her tired old feet along into her own room. Indifferently she took out a quarter from her old pocket book and dropped it into her bank. It fell with as pleasant a clinking sound as ever but, somehow, she did not seem to notice it. Under the sputtering gas light her face had sunken and aged decidedly in the past two weeks. With both hands against the shelf she stood looking and looking at her little grandson's face. The laughter there, in some way, hurt cruelly. And there grew and grew in her old eyes a hunger that was quite hopeless, quite unappeasable. With a little groan, she leaned forward, drew the picture to her, rested her old mouth against the cold of the glass over the small foot and closed her eyes.

* * * *

And from the next room came snatches of talk and laughter.

"What'll I do with this, Mary Lou?"

"What? O, don't put it on yet, we want to keep it hot."

"I see. Where'll I put this butter?"

"That's a good place.—No, put *that* over here.—Really, Paul Brown, I can't see for the life of me, why you have to put your arm the whole way around me like this just to set that down."

"Well, if you will insist in getting right under my feet—"

"Paul, you *are* a fraud."

"Fraud, am I?"

"Oh!"

"What's the matter?"

"Let me put this down first."

A long and utterly inexplicable silence intervened here.

"Now, am I a fraud?"

"Wait till I get my breath and I'll tell you—Yes, yes, yes, and a hundred times bigger, even, than I guessed."

Another inexplicable silence ensued which was followed by sounds of renewed activity in the room.

"Mary Lou!"

"What?"

"Know something?"

"No, what?"

"You *are* rather an old darling."

"Paul Brown!"

"What?"

"Know something?"

"No, what?"

"You're another.—No, you don't.—Miss Lu—cy!"

— / / — — / / — — / / — — / / —

The old eyes opened, the old head raised itself.

"Comin'."

Without looking again at the laughing face, she pushed it gently back against the wall. She lowered the gas carefully and, when the old feet had dragged themselves across the hall to Mary Lou's room, she was smiling.

THE LAUGHING HAND

After four weeks of waiting, the request had finally come; and, in response, just after sunset, Ellen Erroll was walking slowly and rather dejectedly down Elm street. Ordinarily, since she was a singularly diffident creature, the need of her expressed in that joyful, illegible scrawl would have filled her with a swift glowing of joy and wonder as fresh as though experienced for the first time. But now, for no apparent reason, she was afraid. Hands deep in her coat pockets, head thrust forward, and eyes seeing unseeingly the unvarying pattern of the uneven bricks in the sidewalk, she was groping for the cause of that fear. In this attempt she could not help herself: temperament, and habit had made her painstakingly analytical of the motives which governed the actions of herself and other people.

Waning or waxing this fear had been with her for the past five weeks. It had all begun with Phil's failure to keep an engagement and his sending this whimsical letter instead:

"Ellen, dear, I have, so mother says, a bad throat. Frankly I have my own opinion upon that subject. Be that as it may, she has locked the front and back doors and hidden the keys. I could climb out of one of the windows, you say? Ellen Erroll, how can you suggest such a thing? You know perfectly well in what mortal terror I stand of my mother. Consider, too, what a humiliating humiliation (yes, I mean just that) it would be to my self respect and immense pride, after I had

Text was taken from typescript in the Angelina Weld Grimké Collection, MSRC, box 38-12, folder 202.

pushed up the lower sash in a perfectly noiseless manner,
and had slid one leg stealthily over the sill, and was just upon
the point of making a romantic dash to you, to hear my
mother call, 'Philip Grey, what are you doing?'

"Thoughts of what would happen overwhelm me. I find
my teeth chattering. But enough of such a subject.

"At present, I am sitting before a very wonderful log fire
in my studio. I am almost completely swathed in my bathrobe
and a blanket. Necessarily, I am atrociously hot, but do I
dare to remove a single thing? Ah! these little women.
Anyway, I can see your face and your eyes in the fire. A
compensation?

"Ellen, I wish you might be here to see the glorious
entertainment with which mother and I are furnishing each
other. The place is my studio and the time,—every half hour.
To assert my lost manhood, I have determined not to touch
one drop of medicine. I have weakly yielded in everything
else. One must take a stand somewhere, so here I have planted
my stalwart foot. This is my resolution each time, and this is
what happens:

"I hear the footsteps of one, my mother enemy, climbing
the stairs. There is the aggressive tinkle of a spoon against a
glass. In preparation I harden my will and my face. Mother
enters; she smiles wheedlingly.

" 'Dear,' she says in an offhand manner, 'I think it is
about time for your medicine now.'

"At this point the clock on the stair landing booms forth
either the hour or the half hour.

" 'Medicine,' I roar growing purple in the face (O! yes,
but I know I do) 'Begone. I shall not touch a single drop.
Take it away.'

" 'Dear,' mother says in a maddeningly soothing tone, you
must not make so much noise. You will hurt your throat.'

"A long argument now takes place. (By the way, I spend my time between doses thinking up arguments that will be clinchers.) In the end she frowns and turns toward the door. I just can't stand that frown, so I feebly capitulate—until the next dose. She smiles sweetly at me as I struggle to get down the nasty stuff.

" 'Woman,' I say, 'I believe you are a born intriguer. I believe you frown on purpose.'

"Mother opens her eyes innocently. 'Why, dear, what *can* you mean?'

"Isn't she delicious? And aren't we having a hilarious time over my silly throat? Dear, if I can't see you to-night, just remember there is one who is browbeating me almost as thoroughly as you can. I shall see you without fail, a week from to-day."

The next week there was no Phil but this note:

"What a joke! I, who so raged against operations, am to have one to-morrow. On my throat. I am taking it as much for the joke on myself as anything else. Really. I do so love the inconsistent in other people, why not in myself? Don't worry about me, please, for it is truly a very slight operation. And don't come to me. Your eyes would worry me. They would make me talk; and I am not supposed to speak for some little time afterwards. Dear, you are always with me, if not in the body. Remember that, and remember that I shall send for you."

She had waited anxiously five days, and then had written to his mother. A calm, formal little note had arrived promptly. Its gist was, that Phil was doing nicely in every respect, he sent his love, she was not to worry, and please to remember his note.

Another seven days had passed, and then, two or three times a week from that time on, little notes containing a sentence or two, written in his gay manner, and in his gay scrawl (a trifle faint at first) had begun to come. In them he was always better. There was not a single word that was sad, and yet some of them had hurt her past forgetting. One had read:

"There is a good, bright sun to-day, flying clouds, a hustling wind, a lady tree at my side window tapping to gain my attention, the flirt! There are two women in the world who love me as I love them. Dear, my dear, am I not blest?"

Finally, in that morning's mail had come this last: "Ellen, I need you to-day. I shall look for you just after sunset."

And now, knowing that she should be joyful, she was going to him with a heavy heart. When she came to Pumphrey Place, she paused irresolutely, and then, crossing diagonally to the other side, turned westward into it. Instinctively she raised her eyes, and the glory of the street smote her. It was short, only a block in length, running east and west. Before her the straight, slim maiden-hair trees shone goldly, for it was late October. In the gutters, on either side, was a heavy, irregular streak of gold. Splashes of gold spattered the sidewalk and street; and through the vista of touching boughs a gold sky was slowly paling. Gold is an exhilarating, a joy-compelling color.

Ellen smiled. "It is a sign," she said, and straightened and stiffened her back and neck.

Five weeks of wearing anxiety, however, had whitened her healthy skin, sharpened her features, and lined her face. She was thirty-five; and one cannot suffer at that age and quickly efface the traces. When her eyes were curtained, her face was expressionless; unlidded, one experienced a shock. They were astonishing eyes, not for color, shape and size (unimportant details these with some eyes) but for their tremendous power of expression and their vitality. One felt that the soul, that looked through them, had an infinite capacity for all joy and for all sorrow, and for all the shadings of mood, and for all understanding. They were alive, magnetic eyes; and yet withal they held in their depths a sensitive reserve, and an ever elusive mystery.

Ellen necessarily knew there was something unusual about them; but, as she was diffident, and entirely lacking in vanity, she had never consciously tried to exert their power. It had been her eyes that had first attracted the artist in Philip Grey, and then the man. Through them he had risen to fame. His picture of her had been popularly spoken of as "Philip Grey's wonderful portrait of the eyes."

The Grey house was about midway of the block. It was not visible from either end of the street, as it stood far back, up a terrace. On both sides, rising from the very sidewalk and hemming the place in, were dwellings of the usual city type, every one characterless and monotonously the same in outline and color. All that Ellen saw, therefore, as she entered the street was the long, prong-tipped iron fence closing in the wide yard, and in the center, the shut gate. She did not look at the house until her gloved hand was upon the cold iron of that shut gate. Rather timidly then she raised her eyes; and the old fear sprang at her again.

This was the Grey home and yet not the Grey home. Hitherto, day and night, the whole place had breathed of freedom, and joy and unconventionality. There were no frilled and filmy curtains at the windows. After a long dispute, kept up good-humoredly for days between Phil and his mother, yellow shades had been put up; but he never allowed them to be lowered. "What are windows for, anyway," he would say, "if not to let in God's good sun and fresh air and rain if need be. Most people were made to live between solid walls. Mother, I'm weak enough to put up these shades to please you; but don't you ever pull them down." Sometimes, however, when Phil was out of the house, her ingrained, New England austerity and her rather narrow ideas of propriety would grip her; and she would carefully and exactly lower every shade in the house. When Phil returned there was, of course, a most beautiful and heated discussion which always ended in his rushing from room to room and sending each offending curtain up with such a whirring bang that it would often be put out of order forever. "Mother," he would say, laughing at her and shaking a vigorous forefinger the while, "if I didn't love you as much as I do, I should hate you."

Spring, summer, fall, and even late fall, the windows were left open, some from the bottom, some from the top, some from the top and bottom. The two windows of Phil's studio were at the right of the second story. What would appear next at those windows was ever a matter of pleasing conjecture and amusement to Ellen and probably to the few passersby. Sometimes it might be a miscellaneous display of tumblers, a pitcher with a napkin or towel rather ineffectually covering it, a cracked vase holding nothing perhaps, save tree twigs which to his discerning eyes were beautiful. Or it might be his painter's blouse (which, for no very logical reason, he had refused to let anyone wash except himself) that would be billowing in the wind and slapping wetly against the side of the house. Or again, it might be himself in his painter's gear, bedaubed and happy, sitting sideways on the sill, with his knees drawn up, and clasped by his strong and nervous hands. The while he puffed away at an old pipe, his eyes would be watching eagerly some cloud formation, some elusive color of the sky, some swaying tree-top, some winging bird.

At night, he made a light in every room in the house.

When his mother remonstrated with him because of the expense, he would cry out, "Money! Money! What's money? Mother, surely you don't begrudge me a little light." He knew nothing whatever of the value of money and cared less. As no shade was ever lowered, even at night, the place was a blaze of light.

This was the house as it had been. Before her now, the same house rose dark and painstakingly precise. Not a window was open; and every yellow shade was symmetrically lowered half-way. Although lights were beginning to glow dully behind the drawn curtains in the houses across the street, there was not a single gleam here. The lower half of each of the windows was blankly black. The house was colorless, aloof and chilling.

She closed the gate behind her. It clicked noisily as always. Habit was strong within her. She leaned against it, lifted her eyes to the conventionally lowered shades of the studio—and waited. Always before with that click Phil's laughing face, and curly head had appeared at the window. If he were painting, he leaned out, palette and brush in hand. There were never any words of greeting between them. Their eyes spoke. His first words might be:

"I'm in a splendid mood today, working wonders. Ellen, don't move. Do you know sometime I shall paint you just so. You were made for the out-of-doors. You are simply—but don't ask me."

Or it might be:

"I don't like you to-day. I see the little blue devils. Go home."

To which piece of audacity she would answer promptly, making a little move:

"I shan't. I'm bringing them to you. I'm tired of them."

Or it might be, she became a little girl again. Caressed by

his eyes it was often so. Upon such occasions she would cry out joyfully and ungrammatically, "Me first"; and make a dash up the three steps of the terrace, up the rising path, up the steps to the door. Simultaneously with her cry, Phil's head would disappear; there would be a sound of scuffling and noisy scrambling within; and try as Ellen might, flushed and mischievous of face, he always had the door open before she arrived.

"You didn't play fair as usual," she would taunt him, breathlessly sticking out her tongue. "You slid down the banisters. I heard you," and then—

Now there was no response whatever.

Ellen gazed miserably at the house many minutes. If she had done what she most desired, she would have gone away to try to adjust herself somewhat to these new developments; but her pride, her courage, and the fact that Phil was waiting for her, forced her step by step to the front door. She raised the great old-fashioned knocker and let it clang back into place. It was the only bright thing there.

It seemed to her as if fifteen minutes must have elapsed before she heard a fumbling at the knob. The door opened and Mrs. Grey stood upon the threshold. She was a short woman inclining to stoutness. Against the well of darkness within exposed by the open door, the blackness of her dress was scarcely discernible, only the whiteness of her hair, her face, her hands and her apron stood out. She finished a hasty polishing of her spectacles upon the corner of her apron, adjusted them upon her nose, and looked inquiringly at Ellen.

"It's—Ellen?" she asked. Surprise and a faint displeasure made themselves felt in her tone.

"Yes it's I," Ellen heard herself answering rather inanely.

Here, again, she was utterly nonplussed. If there had been one strong trait in Mrs. Grey's character, it had been that of kindliness. The little woman before her was almost openly repellent in manner. Ellen made no steps forward to enter, and Mrs. Grey made no attempt to invite her in.

"You came, I suppose to inquire? Phil is very much better. He, I am sure, will appreciate your interest. He is gaining every day. He walked around the studio this afternoon and considered getting to work again soon. Thank you very much for coming." Mrs. Grey spoke stiffly and monotonously.

As Ellen still made no effort to depart, they faced each other in rather a tense and awkward silence for a moment. Then Ellen said quietly and frankly:

"Mrs. Grey, there is something wrong somewhere, I don't know what or where it is. Phil sent for me that's the reason I am here."

"Phil—sent—for—you? Are you sure?" There was no doubt this time about the surprise.

"Yes. I received a note this morning asking me to come this evening. I shouldn't have troubled you otherwise." Ellen could not drop the hurt note out of her answer.

Rather grudgingly, it seemed, Mrs. Grey made way for her.

"Well—in that case,—why—of course, come in. Er—close the door, please. Thank you. Sit in this chair, here. I'll make a light in a minute. Oh! thank you. Your arms are nice and long. Now turn it—" She stopped abruptly. In the full light of the buzzing gas flame, each had caught a good glimpse of the other's face. The eyes of both softened.

"Ellen," Mrs. Grey said in a kindlier tone, "sit down. I'll light this candle. I meant to tell you not to blow out that match, but never mind. I'll go up, now, and tell Phil you're here. He may not be able to see you; and don't you think that gas just a trifle high? There, thank you, that's better. Now I'm going."

Ellen watched the little woman with the candle making absurd and grotesque caricatures of her upon the wall, until she passed the bend of the stairway and disappeared.

What was the matter with Mrs. Grey? This nervous, awkward creature certainly could not be she. And why her surprise and her repellent attitude? And Phil, would he?— but she refused, at present, to entertain that thought. She had a sense of being a long way off from everything. Nothing or nobody was real, the house, Mrs. Grey, herself.

The footsteps above ceased. A door creaked open and shut slowly. It was the studio door. She knew the sound well.

"She has gone in. She is with him," she thought.

The house, now, was very still. Save for the monotonous, deep-toned ticking of a tall grandfather clock upon the landing of the stairway, nothing was to be heard. Ellen knew that this was so for she found herself listening and listening tensely. What was going on behind that closed studio door?

Suddenly, there was a muffled, spasmodic noise. At first she was startled, and then she remembered. The clock was coughing, as usual, preparatory to striking. There was a pause, and then a deep bell sounded forth the half-hour. Again there was quiet save for that fateful endless ticking. And Ellen, without moving, sat waiting and listening.

Five minutes, ten minutes went by.

The studio door creaked open again and closed. She heard the sound of Mrs. Grey's slow but rather precise footsteps coming towards the stairs. Before she reached the landing Ellen saw the glow and the quivering shadows cast ahead by the candle. She came into view upon the landing; she faced Ellen and came down the remaining steps. The light was full upon her face, and it was very gentle, and sweet and beautiful. This was the Mrs. Grey Ellen remembered.

She placed the candle carefully upon a little side table, and then came straight to Ellen. Ellen rose. Mrs. Grey put out her hands and Ellen placed hers in them.

"My dear," Mrs. Grey said, "I am sorry for the way I treated you when you came. As soon as I went into the studio Phil sensed my displeasure about something, and kept me until he found the reason. Then he explained. I thought, dear, you had deserted Phil and me. The weeks went by, and you did not come. I thought many things. Old people can be bitter. Phil spoke of you but little, and I dared not approach him upon such a subject. Just now he explained why you did not come. Can you forgive an old and foolish woman?"

For answer Ellen put her arms about the little taut form and kissed her. There were tears in the eyes of both.

After a few minutes, Mrs. Grey freed herself and took Ellen's hands in hers again.

She looked long and steadily into Ellen's wonderful eyes. It was an appraisement. Half to herself she said:

"Yes, Phil is right. She is strong and brave."

Then to Ellen:

"Ellen, Phil will see you. Before you go up, however, he wishes me to tell you certain things." Here she paused and gripped Ellen's hands. "You will be brave?"

There was nothing alive in Ellen's face but her eyes.

"I think you can trust me," she said quietly.

"He told you, dear, so I found out tonight, that the trouble was with his throat, and that it was not serious. Well, when he told you that, he was hoping against hope. In his heart he knew better. He was trying to save you. The trouble was not with his throat, and it was serious. It was cancer. They operated. Ellen, my dear, he will never speak again. It was his tongue. The operation was much more complicated than they anticipated. The infection had begun to spread. His face is badly marred."

Ellen closed her eyes. Her strong hands caught and crushed terribly the two hands of the little woman. She did not know what she was doing. Mrs. Grey did not feel the pain.

Slowly, after the first agony, came some understanding: a little of what this would mean to herself, and then, after looking at the little woman before her, what it must mean to her.

Very gently, very tenderly, she put her arms around her and whispered, "Poor little woman."

After a few minutes, Mrs. Grey said:

"Ellen, I want you to know this: I see now what I did not see at first, that is, how much worse it might have been. Phil has taught me this lesson, and we must remember it. He has his eyes and his hands. He can still paint. Don't you see how blest he is? You will hardly believe it, but he is happy. He is just the same. I thought, at first, he was acting to keep me from worrying. I don't think so now. You will see."

"But how—how does he talk?" Ellen asked awkwardly.

"He writes, you get used to it. It's clumsy only at first."

"And—his face? Ellen asked again miserably.

"He wears a mask over the lower part. You get used to that too. He jokes about it as he jokes about everything else. He says he never expected to find himself in the predicament of being ashamed of his own face. He says up until this time, he has been ashamed of plenty of other faces. He declares that he has never looked into a glass since the operation, without the mask. He says his heart is too weak.

"And,—is he cured?"

"The doctors will not say yet. We are hoping for the best. Go up now. He will wonder why I am keeping you so long. Take the candle with you and leave it on that little bracket outside of the studio door. We keep it there now. I brought it down again by mistake. Go, my dear, and be good to my boy."

Ellen smiled bleakly but bravely and started up the stairs. She went up heavily and slowly like an old woman. Before she had mounted three steps, Mrs. Grey called her in a whisper.

"That will never do. He is listening for your footsteps; his hearing is very acute. And your face. That won't do either. You must smile. With him you *must* be yourself. There that it better. Now go."

Ellen walked rapidly up the stairs. She smiled and her head was high. She placed the candle on the little bracket outside of the door. For an instant only she paused; then tapped gently three times, and waited for the summons, her cheek the while against the coolness of the panel. Suddenly the thought stabbed her that Phil could not answer, that, as long as he and she might live, he would never speak to her again. Quickly to avoid more thinking she turned the knob, and the door creaked open. She went in and closed it behind her.

The room was in a half-light, and the sides and corners, therefore, were shadowed. Here and there she made out the blurred shapes of canvases leaning against the wall. One only was upon an easel, and straining her eyes, she saw that it was the portrait of herself. Every window shade was lowered to the sill. Never to her knowledge had this been done before. At her left, in the fireplace set midway of the wall, a purringly cheerful, but rather sleepy fire was burning. Before this and covering the center of the room was a large, delicately beautiful Persian rug, entirely new to her. No vestige of a carpet had ever been seen here before. In the middle of this rug, facing her lengthwise, was a long, very solid-looking table, also new. On the other side of the table was a chair, whether vacant or not, she could not tell, as a large chair with its back to her cut off the view. The back of this nearer chair was high and stood out solidly black against the light. Besides the glow of the fire, the only light in the room came from a student's lamp upon the table at the right of the high-backed chair. The light came through this shade dully green, but poured forth beneath its circle in a brilliant white glare. Here was a great confusion of papers, a brass inkstand, pens and pencils. There seemed to be no one in the room. She was just on the point of turning to the door, when an arm stole forth from the high-backed chair and Phil's strong, beautiful hand appeared within the circle of light,—and his hand was the laughing hand.

It had been a theory of Phil's that the hand showed the individuality of a person as distinctly as the face. Ellen had, at first, been rather doubtful about this. To settle the argument and put his theory to the test, he made this experiment: whenever they were in a public place—a street-car, a theatre, a hall, an art gallery—he let her pick out some face that interested her; then, after she had carefully indicated the position of the person, and he had turned in that direction, he would slowly raise his eyes, which he had kept scrupulously lowered, and look at nothing but the hands. At first, he read so accurately, she accused him of tricking her. One look at his face, however, proved that this was not the case. Sometimes, but very seldom, they found that the hands and the face spoke a different language. There had been indifferent hands, hopeless hands, furtive hands, sensual hands, generous hands, greedy hands, vain hands, hysterical hands, timid hands, determined hands, innocent hands, irritable hands, and sometimes but very rarely, laughing hands—and Phil's hand was the laughing hand.

For several seconds she gazed at it, and then it gayly beckoned her.

It was a very beautiful Ellen who went to him. Her eyes had never been so luminous, so wonderful. She took his hand in both of hers. And then very prettily, very graciously, very reverently, she lifted it to her lips. Two great tears rolled from her eyes, and yet her face was far from sad.

His hand thanked her, and then released itself. It pointed to the chair opposite. Obediently she went around to the other side, drew up the chair, sat down, and rested her elbows upon the table's edge.

Then very slowly, very timidly, she raised her eyes.

At first, because of the glare of light between them, she saw him dimly, and then, little by little, distinctly. He was thinner; and his usually broad and straight shoulders were slightly rounded. A black mask hid the lower part of his face. Above this his forehead and eyes could be seen. He was very white, and there were deep hollows at either side of his forehead. But the laughter was still in his eyes and in his curling irrepressible hair.

For several minutes his eyes and hers spoke together.

At the end, rather slowly, he leaned forward, took up a pencil and began to write on a pad of paper. When he had finished he tore off the sheet and gave it to her.

"For the first time in my life, I am envious," she read and reread.

She raised her great eyes to him questioningly. Instinctively she did not speak. The sound of her own voice would have made her uncomfortable, might even have frightened her. They talked, these two, with eyes and with pencil.

He wrote in explanation.

"It's rather difficult to put into writing. Don't you know what I want—more than anything? Look at me."

For a moment she hesitated, then slowly lifted her eyes. Often before, when they had looked at each other, she had felt as though their spirits rushed forth through their eyes, and met, and mingled; but never, never had she been so intensely certain of this impression, as she was in that long, breathless minute.

In the end, as though by main force, she drew down her lids, and covered her eyes with her hands. She sat thus very quietly for sometime. Across the table, the laughter went out of the man's hands and eyes. A very lonely and hungry soul looked forth. When finally she gave him her eyes again, however, his laughed as ever.

He picked up his pencil and began writing:

"Well, and what do you think of great, strong healthy me now? And the provoking part of the whole matter is, so they tell me, that I couldn't possibly have helped myself. It all goes right straight back to my dad. Now, of all the forms of dying that he had to choose from, what possessed him, do you suppose, to pick out this? If he had to die, why not take heart failure (there is nothing offensive about the sound of that) or apoplexy, or acute indigestion? Why, in the name of all the gods, go out in this way? Of course, now, if I had been here to counsel him, I might have said, 'Dad, dear, I want you, please, to reconsider your decision. I'm going to be perfectly honest with you. You see I'm not entirely unselfish in this matter. Now, you may wish very much to go in this particular way, but please remember me. I know I shall object to this ending when the time comes. I abhor the method.'

"I have no doubt but that he would have said,

" 'Son, there is considerable reason on your side. To please you, I will sacrifice myself, and die with a stroke of paralysis.'

In all probability, I should be here as Phil Grey, at this minute, and not as I am now, Phil Grey—minus.

"This sounds rather irreverent, doesn't it? I don't mean it so. But why should I pretend to love someone I never knew, who dropped out, just before I dropped in? Oh, I know, there are a great many people, most in fact, who pretend, who look very, very sad and woe-begone indeed, when you mention to them, dead fathers and mothers and relatives, they never knew. Some even can squeeze out a few tears. I don't pretend. I love, but I love the living, those I have known and know. Poor old dad, the joke was on him, I guess, just as it is on me now. If you get the right perspective, all life is a huge joke. It's very funny. It's worth more smiles than tears. I'm so glad to talk to you. You always understand."

Ellen read this through rapidly. From time to time, she quickly lifted her eyes to his. The sympathy between them was complete. At the end, she nodded her head and smiled. Then she leaned forward and selected a pencil and a pad of paper from the jumble before him. She wrote for a few seconds and then passed the paper to him.

"It's the same whimsical old Phil, anyway, and I'm so glad."

His eyes smilingly thanked her and he began writing again. She watched the gay, beautiful hand hurrying vigorously down the sheet.

"If I had been a tale bearing, scandal-loving, malicious, old woman, wouldn't this have been a magnificent retribution? Evidently the disposer of all good gifts makes mistakes, now and then, in his journeyings up and down this world. I suppose he is overworked and tired. This careful searching through his pack at each door gets to be a bore. So he says, 'I know I have something for this person, for I remember the name distinctly. It is probably at the bottom of the bag as it generally is. No one is looking, so I'll just slip this little bundle onto his doorstep and ring the bell. It has a very harmless appearance; and I do hope it will prove the useful and proper thing. Anyway, I'll get out of this quickly so they can't put the blame on me, if it isn't.'

"Well, here I am with the old lady's package, and so I must make the best of it. And for some reasons, I really don't mind. I am very much interested in myself, and I am very curious to see just how I am going to behave."

"Phil, dear," Ellen wrote in reply, "you must not forget for one, single instant how blest you are. That little bundle might have held loss of hands, or loss of eyes, or loss of both; and then what would you and the rest of us have done? It doesn't bear thinking of. Your work and those who love you are still left to you, Phil, and it is beautiful."

Phil's eyes were very tender and yet quizzical as he finished reading her words.

"Ellen, I didn't know that I should have to tell *you* that I am not whining. I must have my joke. Yes, I have my work and I have mother and you—three beautiful things in one. I know that I shall work and work as I have never done before. How I know this, I may not tell even you; *but I know*. It will mean unceasing labor. Frankly, I don't know, and the doctors won't say how long I shall be here. That knowledge means that every minute, when I get back my strength, must count. And Ellen, I hate to tell you this: this knowledge means sacrifice. It means I shall have to give you up. There! I didn't mean to break this to you so brutally. Forgive me."

For a moment, after he had finished this, he hesitated. Once he seemed on the point of tearing it up. Then, hastily, as though he feared that he might again reconsider, he passed the sheet to her.

As he watched her face, and saw the quiver of pain that came into it, his eyes yearned over her. For a long time, she sat immovable, eyes hidden, very white of face. Presently, without looking at him she began to write:

"I suppose I ought to have more pride than to write this; but, Phil, you know I should be a help to you and not a hindrance. You know, as well as I do, what the constant doing for you would mean to me. Phil, dear, I am humbling myself to you. Don't give me up. You need me as much as I need you."

Unluckily for her, her shame at what she had done kept her from watching him. If she had seen his eyes then she would have understood. She did not even look at him, when he began to write again. It was not exactly the laughing hand that wrote.

"Ellen, I am not utterly selfish. I have had five long weeks to think this matter out. You couldn't be happy with me. You think you could now; but you will acknowledge that I have the capacity of detaching myself and seeing things just as they are and will be. This little black silk mask that I am wearing—a little insignificant thing like this—would alienate us in the end. I will show you how. In the beginning we would pretend to take it as a joke; but morning, noon and night I should be possessed with the fear that sometime you might see my face; and you, my dear, would be possessed by the same fear. I don't believe it would worry you so much for your own sake as for mine. What a working basis for marriage! We could, you and I, stand a week of it; but marriage might mean weeks, months, perhaps years. Can't you see that that fear would finally become an obsession for both of us? And how much joy or happiness would there be in it for you; and for me, how much accomplished of the work I must do, before I go forth? Dear, don't you see?

Besides, remember that we believe that we belonged to each other in some previous incarnation. To you and me, what should a few hundred years mean? It has been decreed that you are I and I am you. Sometime, again, you and I shall fulfill the purpose for which we were created. And now, don't you think, dear, that, all things considered, you had better not see me again? My time may be short and this work must be finished! I know you understand."

This he passed to her without any hesitation. She read it carefully; and then, for the first time and the last, without let or hindrance, she permitted him to read all of the greatness and beauty of her love for him in her wonderful eyes. And he drank it in, and kept it, for he would have need of it.

At the end, she leaned forward and wrote four words,

"I can wait. Goodbye."

She rose quietly. Their eyes clung together for a long long space, and then she moved to the door. Without looking back, she went forth. The door creaked shut, and she closed it firmly. There was no hesitation, now, in her movements. Pain might come later; at present, she was exalted. Her eyes held a great and beautiful light. Her lips smiled. Thus in triumph, she went down the stairs.

Within the studio, Philip slowly dropped his head into the curve of his left arm. His head and shoulders were entirely revealed within the brilliant circle of light. The laughter was still in his curls. Gradually the laughing hand clenched itself. The noticeable blue veins on the back entirely disappeared. Every vestige of color went out of it. It seemed as though, every second, the knuckles must burst through the shining skin. And thus he sat for hours.

NONFICTION

❧ ❧ ❧

DIARY 1903

Excerpts

July 18, 1903.

This is my first attempt at a diary. Poor little book to bear so great a burden; but one must talk to some one or go mad and so little book I talk to you. You shall be my nearest friend for to you my heart is laid bare.

No answer yet. I shall hope for the best on Monday. I suppose I was a fool and oh how I wish that I had a mother! One to whom I might go and lay my head upon her breast and weep away if possible all the bitterness. But this is the worst there are no tears only the endless ache and endless worry. No wonder the gray hairs are beginning to come.

July 18[1]

Helen Brooks left this morning after a stay of about 2 weeks. She is a fair girl and has learned her lesson of suffering well. I hope that I may become as much of a woman some day, but it is all so new and fresh now and so hard to bear— so very hard.

Dear heart, this is the first time I have written it so and though you are not for me, still—yes, still you are dear to me God knows how dear. How I miss you, dear! Why is it that you must be so much to me? I have tried to crush out all the love but can't. I wonder what you are doing and if you think of me, poor little heart-broken me.

Text is taken from holograph in the Angelina Weld Grimké Collection, MSRC, series G—diaries, box 38-15, folder 248.

1. Repeated date inserted at the top of page 2 of seven-page manuscript, probably repeated because page begins sentence.

{Clarence White was here and arranged to take some of my pains.}[2]

My father and I have been having a hard time to-night over you, dear. I guess he is right and I shall try to give you up. It is raining out of doors to-night and it is late. The skies are lucky to be able to weep, some of us can not. Good-night little book.

Sunday July 19 [1903].

Another dark gloomy day. I was awakened this morning by the endless swish of the rain and rattling gusts of wind. It has rained all day. Somehow to-day has been easier. I have not worried as much although, dear, you are never absent from my thoughts for long. I almost hope to-day that I shall not hear, it will be better for all concerned I know that it worries my father and even, dear, if sometimes in the future you may learn to care for me, for his sake, dear, I ought to give you up. It will be hard to tear out all thought of you. You have been so much to me for over a year now. Yet oh for my father's sake I hope I may get over this madness. The two Johnsons, Jim and Rosamond, and Bob Cole were here this afternoon. Tessa evidently sees little of Rosamond.

I have done nothing all day but read and sleep—and think. I am trying not to think.

I hope that wretched dream I had about you just before you left may mean nothing. Dear, I dreamed you were married. I wonder if you can imagine my anguish even in a dream? It was to someone you never knew or heard of. She is a married woman, the wife of my Principal. What strange

2. This note appears in the left margin of the diary and clearly was written after the journal entry was complete, perhaps to divert attention from Helen Brooks (or some other unnamed woman) as probable cause of Grimké's sorrow.

things happen in dreams. You must have been married in a house across the street, for I have a dim recollection of watching from my window. I heard the Wedding March, dear and it was terrible to hear then somehow I was in the street and I was to see you off. Your little bride came out alone and then you were missing but finally came up. Your bride seemed to me happy, but you were wretched, so wretched my heart ached not only for myself but 10 times more for you. You did not stay with her but stood alone and we, I have forgotten who we were now, stayed with your wife and tried to keep your unhappiness from her. We were waiting for a car, I believe. And then you came and looked within at[3] her or at us and said the car was coming. And then I remember going to a place where I might see you pass. The car passed but neither of you were in it and then suddenly I saw you sitting before me and we looked long into each other's eyes and then he[4] grasped my hand in your agony and crushed and said,

"Nana, it is all a mistake."

And I said,

"Yes, dear, I know it, I cannot stand it. I shall kill myself." And then because my agony was so great I awoke. Dear wasn't that a terrible dream. I hope you will never marry. I can stand it while I know there is no other girl, but—never mind.

Dear, I shall never forget our last day together. We were at Arlington. I would have given anything under Heaven if the little girl you love so well had been yours and mine. Ours: is it not beautiful? I have loved her better ever since

3. Holograph: {and}.
4. Holograph: {he} is difficult to decipher and does not fit in grammatical context; perhaps Grimké wavered between identifying subject as male or female.

and that night, dear, while you were playing whisk downstairs I went up to say "Good night" to the little dears. And inert, I kissed the little girl where you kissed her. I love you a little, don't you think? Goodnight.

July 20 [1903].

Another hard day for me and no letter. I didn't want one last night but to-night I would pray God if I dared to make you write, Oh dear I need some vindication if it be but just one letter. I will never as long as I live, I hope

[End of holograph or remaining pages are missing.]

DIARY 1909

Excerpt

Oct. 28, 1909.

An eventful day,—agreeable and disagreeble. Let me tell the disagreeable part first, and try to forget it. Some time ago, I don't think I told you little book, that Garnet Wilkinson[1] came to me and asked me if I had any verses which I considered suitable for the new magazine, "The School Teacher." Remember this,—*he came to me* and *asked me* for *my verses.* I *didn't go to* him. *I didn't beg him to please take my verses.* I promised to give him some to overlook; and I did give him some. Two he liked, "Surrender" and "A Lullaby."[2] I type wrote them for him nicely, and gave them to him. In the meantime, I had learned that the magazine was an administration magazine. Miss _____s[3] told me so. At the same time she told me not to have too much faith in Mr. Wilkinson. I defended him, for if there was one man that I believed manly and brave and true to his convictions,— it was Garnet Wilkinson. One thing, however, made me uneasy. I knew that the judgement of this lady was well nigh flawless. I have never known it to fail. Nevertheless I crushed down my doubts, or tried to, and continued to believe in the

Text is taken from holograph in the Angelina Weld Grimké Collection, MSRC, series G—Diaries, box 38-15, folder 249.

1. Principal of Dunbar High School, Washington, D.C., while Angelina was teaching there (1907–1926).

2. See two versions of "Surrender" and "Lullaby" in the poetry section of this volume. A third version of "Surrender" follows later in this diary entry.

3. Blank in holograph.

gentleman. My verses were not published in last month's issue. That didn't necessarily mean anything. To-day Garnet came to me and asked if the line, "Let us forget the past unrest" could be misinterpreted. Perhaps I had better write out the verses so you may see them yourself. Here they are;

Surrender [(3)]

We ask for peace. We, at the bound
Of life, are weary of the round
In search of Truth. We know the quest
Is not for us, the vision blest
Is meant for other eyes. Uncrowned,
We go, with heads bowed to the ground,
And old hands gnarled and hard and browned.
Let us forget the past unrest,—
    We ask for peace.
Our strainéd ears are deaf,—no sound
May reach them more; no sight may wound
Our worn-out eyes. We gave our best,
And while we totter down the crest,
Unto that last, that waiting mound,—
    We ask for peace.

Now, little book, what interpretation would you have put upon the action of Mr. Wilkinson? What would you think it meant if anyone came to you and asked you a question like that? You would say as Uncle F[4] said he must be afraid of someone, and if afraid of someone, afraid to publish it for fear of how *he* might be treated as a result. Well, I told him

4. Reverend Francis Grimké, civil rights advocate and minister of the Fifteenth Street Presbyterian Church in Washington, D.C. Angelina lived with Francis and his wife, Charlotte, while teaching at the Armstrong Manual Training School (1902–1907) and at Dunbar High School (1907–1926). They were also her legal guardians from 1894 to 1898 while her father, Archibald, was in Santo Domingo as consul.

that frankly I had no feeling, whatever, if he didn't publish the verses I wanted them any way. He refused to give them to me. I told him that there was no way to change the line. Well, after school, he was standing in the hall at his room door. I went to him again, and asked for my verses. He told me no I couldn't have them; and then he informed me they were on his desk. I made a line for the room; but he got there first. He pulled some of the manuscript out of the envelope and showed me what he considered a fine article by Supt. Maxwell, Superintendent of Public Schools in New York City. While I was glancing it over, Love came into the room and he [Wilkinson] pulled out my verses and gave them to her to read. Strange, wasn't it he should be so careless like with those verses, when he knew I intended to get them if I could? Love read them and gave them to me. I calmly folded them up and stuck them in the waist of my dress. All this was done before him and strange still to say he didn't notice it in the least. Love walked out, and I after her. Then oh so suddenly he discovered the *loss* and came to me to give them back. Naturally I refused. He called me a child and said I was queer. I told him I was no fool that I knew he was afraid to publish them and sometime I hoped to have the pleasure of knowing a real man. He said,

"I suppose that means I am not a man."

I said, "It does."

He said, "Thank you."

I said, "You are welcome."

Just then Love, Haley and Mr. Bailey came in.

Garnet was laughing and making believe the whole thing was a joke. He said,

"Well, I like that, when I first come into the room the young lady treats me as though I am air. When you come in, Doug, she is all smiles."

Haley answered, "Don't mind her, she is sweet. She doesn't mean anything."

Later—

"Doug, what do you think of a lady who would let a little thing break up a friendship?"

Haley,—"Not much."

"Perhaps," I said, "the friendship wasn't worth any thing."

"There you are, Doug. Hear that? That's what you call a friend! a friend! Think of it a friend!"

Then Garnet held out his hand. "Goodbye, Miss Grimké." I refused to take his hand.

Again he offered; and again I refused.

Then they left the room. Love had her things on then. He came out of the room and she locked the door.

Garnet, Haley, and I think Mr. Bailey were in the hall. Garnet all grins offered his hand again. By that time I was near the breaking point. I felt myself getting hot all over. I got a grip on myself, but I guess my eyes were nasty.

"Look here," I said, "you had better let me alone."

"Gentlemen," he said, "you all saw me offer my hand three times."

"And," I flashed back, "you saw me refuse it!"

We left the building. There was a rap on the window of the Gentlemen's Retiring Room. There he was still grinning at us.

Well, wasn't that experience enough to spoil the rest of any one's day, let alone a dinner? And there were Love and I going up to a small dinner that I had ordered yesterday at Martin's. It was come more cold too. It had looked like snow all day; but in the afternoon the sun came out. But a *cold cold* bone-searching wind was blowing. We had ordered dinner for four o'clock. And as it was a trifle late and the wind strong we took a car. We got on an open car and shivered. The whole way up I thought of Garnet and I was all

[Pages missing in holograph here.]

Nita [?] over to me.

"You'd better stop Lincoln. He'll give you a bad name."

"I'm not afraid," I answered.

"Oh, aren't you," she laughed.

They got through before we did.

He said to me jokingly as he went out, "I hope you'll come around to the house soon I have something of great importance to tell you."

I answered, "I am coming to see Anita this evening."

He said, "Good!" We all giggled and they went out. Joe Douglass came in then and spoke to us. He is as crazy as ever. He said to Love,

"You certainly are good looking, Love."

Love blushed, and looked prettier.

Then to me, "You get better looking every time I see you. You'll be as good looking as Love pretty soon."

We giggled.

The waitress came to him and asked him if he would have fish, beef a la mode or lamb. He said he would have some a la mode on the beef. The girl grinned we grinned. Soon, however, we left.

Before then, however, he said "I am going to Boston soon."

I said, "Give my love to my father."

He said, "I thought he had that."

I answered, "He has, but I am sending him a little bit more."

I said, "If you see any one up there that I care for particularly give him my love."

He said, "Is it a gentleman?"

I said, "Yes. There is one up there that I care a lot for."

"Who is it?"

"I can't tell you."

"Go on I won't tell."

"Never."

{Well, I started to put on my coat, and the nice little waiter jumped to help me. I had told him I was sorry he didn't wait on us. He was some manner pleasing. The dinner cost $1.00 I gave Mr. Martin 50¢ and the waitress 25¢ Horrid thing!}[5]

Well, we left and I went to pay Miss Nita the remaining seven dollars on my hat. Five to pay Mrs. Proctor, Nita's land lady, a car ticket for one that she borrowed last night.

Love walked home with me. And we walked briskly. At my house I left my umbrella and papers and walked with her to Dupont Circle. The moonlight was exhilarating and beautiful. I left her at Dupont Circle and started home. I had to turn though and see Dupont Circle and the Lester house again.

The leaves have all turned. Some of the trees were all bare. The soft [?] of their boughs and twigs stood out softly against a golden sky that merged gently into purple. The golden, purple lights lay on the remaining leaves. The Lester house stood out whitely against the sky. It is quite large but simple in structure. In front are four great columns. As I watched the electric light at the top of the column but hidden from sight jumped out. The great columns stood out darkly against the light. Low shrub or evergreen trees hide three sides of the house almost completely to the second story. The house was dark save for a light or two in what seemed to be the

---

5. Passage in braces evidently was inserted in holograph after the entry was complete.

quarters of the servants. The colors were beautiful as I looked. The great quiet white house, the four strong pillars against the soft blue of electric light, the dark outlines of the shrub and trees in this yard, and at the side Dupont Circle with the dimly golden or red leaves quiet against the fading gold and lavender sky. Beautiful! {A great gold moon gleamed at me for a moment.}[6]

Well I came home at a good round clip. Found a fire in the Latrile that heats my room, Joy be! For it was some more cold, told Uncle Frank of my experience with Garnet. (He agreed with me too) was just about to go up-stairs and make my bed, when the pull rang and there was dear Anita Emily Jenifer Taylor. I like her and was glad to see her. With the greatest of brazenness and immodesty I offered to take Emily into my room. My room looked like Sancho too, I can tell you. Well I straightened it out, gave her to eat of the Whitman's Reper sent me, of the Salt water Taffy Harlen sent me, of the Tokay grapes that I bought with my own money.

She seemed to enjoy my informalities, however. And we had a nice cozy chatty time together. Mertel she says is not so well, we made an engagement to go over there and see her Saturday. Poor little kid, she has made such a gallant fight for life, I *do* hope she will pull through. Well about twenty-four minutes of eight Emily left so I prepared myself for bed and you, dear little book. I have written myself to death and you too a guess, my dear, so Good-night.

6. Passage in braces evidently was inserted in holograph after the entry was complete.

DIARY 1912 [1911]

Excerpt

[December 31, 1911]
MY PRAYER FOR THE COMING YEAR

Dear, beautiful God, who art so far away, come thou close to me day by day. My plea is human. I am evil and my ways are evil, and my will is weak. Strengthen thou my will. Teach me the habit of conquering myself. Keep me cheerful in the doing thereof, and keep me brave. Show me my duty clearly, and let me happily perform it. Make me unselfish, quick to do for and help others. Make me charitable in judgement. Help me to see to the good in each and all. Give me the ultimate faith in beauty in truth and goodwill. And yet oh God, too, keep me alive. Let me not grow into a fossil. Let me enjoy all that is worthy for me to enjoy. Let me keep my sense of humor. And when I close my eyes to sleep each night, let me feel I have not lived quite in vain. Amen.

Dec. 31, 1911.

This is my third attempt at a diary. The first lived through a summer, and the second expired shortly after breathing. I hope this new one which will be born to-morrow may show more vitalité. I sincerely hope it may exist one year at least. My faith in myself is not profound. On this the last day of the year 1911 I am brought face to face with myself. I cannot

Text is taken from holograph in the Angelina Weld Grimké Collection, MSRC, series G—diaries, box 38-15, folder 250. The text is labeled Diary 1912, but the entry was written on New Year's Eve, December 31, 1911.

say I am proud. My hands are not clean I suppose no one's hands are entirely clean at the end of the old year. But mine seem much dirtier than necessary. There are so many, many things I could have left undone, some many struggles with myself where I have been not exactly victorious, so many things I could have left undone, unkind thoughts although unkind things unsaid, so many times when I have depressed others unnecessarily because I selfishly was blue, and the shadows black of many other disagreeable and disgusting things. Remorse and regret two unpleasant visitors on the last day yet here clearly beside me hugging me close and I can do nought but entertain them civilly for they are rightful guests. They belong here at my side. The one ray of sunshine on this dark rainy or misty day is, that while they can still come to me there is perhaps some little hope for me. Let's drink to these two uncomfortable guests' lives. May they never die. I do hope at the end of the year 1912, if I am still here at that time that these hands of mine may be cleaner than they are to-day. And yet dear bad suffering old year the tears are in my eyes and throat knowing you're dying. We've suffered terribly together we two. *Three times I have been close to death; twice I have suffered untold agony* and yet I am here still, my back almost as good as new again and hopes no longer rather skeptical of being well again. Suffering, too old year from that horrible searing unfounded scandal. But all these sufferings soon over. Old year, too, you have taught me that the hearts of people are very good after all. You have showed me true and tried friends. You have made me understand the beauty of a family like the Tysons. You have given me Love Percy. Make me to keep the fine noble friendship of this woman with not a spot. Keep me true and patient and kindly always. Help me *never* to forget in some petty quarrel *what* she is. Help me never to forget or lose

my friends. If you have taught me these things you have
taught me much. I am too critical, too impatient about trifles
in my friends. Help me to act the decent part and not be a
cad in the coming year. And now dear old year good-bye,
goodbye. Yes, I am almost there.

I am forgetting, too forgetting, as not the end. My father—
he is so much a part of me he is so all and all so absolutely
necessary that I am taking him, I find as a matter of course.
This is wrong. I wonder, though whether when some people
are as one there maybe for some little excuse. This I know
now and I have always known it and felt it, I have no desire
absolutely for life without him. There is no father like him
and no friend so kind, so patient, so helpful. And I want you
to know that I appreciate him to the full the uttermost. My
happiness and my suffering and his are indissolubly bound
up together. Words cannot do him justice But my greatest
and most beautiful blessing now and always is my father.
Make me worthy of him. I know that I shall never fail him
as I know he will never fail me.

SCRAPBOOK
Excerpt

Here I am all propped up, really "comfy," and doing
something I have absolutely no business doing. What is that?
Why writing to you of course. You say most naturally, "Why
write then?" Here is the answer. It is because you see, dear,
I love—a love for the forbidden clearly the dangerous living
ever attracts me. It has a fascination for me, I find an
exhilaration in the very audacity of being like the moth, I
am like the moth, I love to flutter and dart around the flame.[1]
Don't be afraid though. I shall not get burned nor even
singed. When that is liable to happen I shall rotate myself

Text is taken from a letter in Grimké's scrapbook (in holograph), Angelina
Weld Grimké Collection, MSRC, series D—manuscripts, box 38-14, folder
243. This text is greatly overwritten with phrases crossed out, reinserted,
and changed. In order to present a cohesive text that is faithful to the emotive
sense of the holograph, I have linked Grimké's phrases together, including
many phrases that she crossed out. The oblique references to sexual love and
separation at the ends of both paragraphs, along with the command that the
recipient "cremate" the letter, imply that the recipient is a woman who
engaged in a lesbian affair with Grimké.

1. In her school papers, Grimké included the following anecdote about a
moth:

A man and a woman, one very warm night, went for a car ride. A
gypsy moth blew into the man's lap. Coolly and calmly he pulled its
wings out, and let it go.

"Why did you do that?" Asked the woman.

"The moth is a pest." Answered the man.

"Why not kill it outright, then?"

"That was not necessary. I will do no *more harm.*" The woman leaned
back *and* thought many thoughts. Later the man asked her to marry
him, and she refused.

out through the window again (for the window will be open for me) and fly safely and prettily away. Yes, it is into the night to be sure. No, the idea of going out into the night is not the least unpleasant. The night in many respects is far more beautiful than the day. You understand me, don't you! I hope so.

Here are the verses I promised to let you read. The copy was sent to me by the Editor of the "Listener," himself. It, therefore, means twice as much to me. Be careful of it, won't you. I am trusting you with it. Also remember your promise about returning it. In reading this over it sounds awfully impolite but I don't mean it that way. You know I don't. These verses were born out of great but temporary happiness & great & lasting regret. If I had never known certain people it would have been impossible to have written them. And never mind how far apart the lives of these people and mine shall diverge for diverge more and more they will and never mind all the changes that come into their lives, still don't you think that the memory of these verses may make a pleasant little thread of remembrance in the years to come. I hope so. When you have read all of the life out of this little note, cremate its dead body, won't you? Thank you.

Sincerely your friend.
"The Little Sister"

"RACHEL"
THE PLAY OF THE MONTH

The Reason and Synopsis by the Author

Since it has been understood that "Rachel" preaches race suicide, I would emphasize that that was not my intention. To the contrary, the appeal is not primarily to the colored people, but to the whites.

Because of environment and certain inherent qualities each of us reacts correspondingly and logically to the various forces about us. For example, if these forces be of love we react with love, and if of hate with hate. Very naturally all of us will not react as strongly or in the same manner—that is impossible.

Now the colored people in this country form what may be called the "submerged tenth." From morning until night, week in week out, year in year out, until death ends all, they never know what it means to draw one clean, deep breath free from the contamination of the poison of that enveloping force which we call race prejudice. Of necessity they react to it. Some are embittered, made resentful, belligerent, even dangerous; some are made hopeless, indifferent, submissive, lacking in initiative; some again go to any extreme in a search for temporary pleasures to drown their memory, thought, etc.

Now the purpose was to show how a refined, sensitive, highly-strung girl, a dreamer and an idealist, the strongest instinct in whose nature is a love for children and a desire

Reprinted from the *Competitor* 1 (Jan. 1920): 51–52. Also see Tillie Buffum Chace Wyman's review of *Rachel* in Appendix B of this volume.

some day to be a mother herself—how this girl would react to this force.

The majority of women, everywhere, although they are beginning to awaken, form one of the most conservative elements of society. They are, therefore, opposed to changes. For this reason and for sex reasons the white women of this country are about the worst enemies with which the colored race has to contend. My belief was, then, that if a vulnerable point in their armor could be found, if their hearts could be active or passive enemies, they might become, at least, less inimical and possibly friendly.

Did they have a vulnerable point and, if so, what was it? I believed it to be motherhood. Certainly all the noblest, finest, most sacred things in their lives converge about this. If anything can make all women sisters underneath their skins it is motherhood. If, then, the white women of this country could see, feel, understand just what effect their prejudice and the prejudice of their fathers, brothers, husbands, sons were having on the souls of the colored mothers everywhere, and upon the mothers that are to be, a great power to affect public opinion would be set free and the battle would be half won.

This was the main purpose. There is a subsidiary one as well. Whenever you say "colored person" to a white man he immediately, either through an ignorance that is deliberate or stupid, conjures up in his mind the picture of what he calls "the darkey." In other words, he believes, or says he does, that all colored people are a grinning, white-toothed, shiftless, carefree set, given to chicken-stealing, watermelon-eating, always, under all circumstances, properly obsequious to a white skin and always amusing. Now, it is possible that this type is to be found among the colored people; but if the white man is honest and observant he will have to acknowledge that the same type can be duplicated in his own race. Human nature, after all, is the same. And if the white man only cared to find out he would know that, type for type, he could find the same in both races. Certainly colored people are living in homes that are clean, well-kept with many evidences of taste and refinement about them. They are many of them well educated, cultivated and cultured; they are well-mannered and, in many instance, more moral than the whites; they love beauty; they have ideals and ambitions, and they do not talk—this educated type—in the Negro dialect. All the joys and sorrows and emotions the white people feel they feel; their feelings are as sensitive; they can be hurt as easily; they are as proud. I drew my characters, then, from the best type of colored people.

Now as to the play itself. In the first act Rachel, loving, young, joyous and vital, caring more to be a mother than anything else in the world, comes suddenly and terribly face to face with what motherhood means to the colored woman in the South. Four years elapse between the first and second acts. Rachel has learned much. She is saddened, disillusioned and embittered. She knows now that organized society in the North has decreed that if a colored man or woman is to be an economic factor, then he or she must, with comparatively few exceptions, remain in the menial class. This has been taught her by her own experience, by the experience of her brother, Tom, and by the experience of John Strong, the man she loves. She has learned that she may not go to a theater for an evening's entertainment without having it spoiled for her since, because of her color she must sit as an outcast, a pariah in a segregated section. And yet in spite of all this youth in her dies hard and hope and the desire for motherhood. She loves children, if anything, more than ever. It is in this act that she feels certain, for the first time, that

John Strong loves her. She is made very happy by this knowledge, but in the midst of her joy there comes a knocking at the door. And very terribly and swiftly again it is brought home to her what motherhood means, this time to the colored woman in the North. The lesson comes to her through a little black girl and her own little adopted son, Jimmy. Not content with maiming and marring the lives of colored men and women she learns this baneful thing, race prejudice, strikes at the souls of little colored children. In her anguish and despair at the knowledge she turns against God, believing that He has been mocking at her by implanting in her breast this desire for motherhood, and she swears by the most solemn oath of which she can think never to bring a child here to have its life blighted and ruined.

A week elapses between Acts II, and III. During the time Rachel has been very ill, not in body, but in mind and soul. She is up and about again, but is in a highly overwrought, nervous state. John Strong, whom she has not seen since she has been sick, comes to see her. She knows what his coming means and tries unsuccessfully to ward off his proposal. He pleads so well that, although she feels she is doing a wicked thing she finally yields. Just at the moment of her surrender, however, the sound of little Jimmy's heartbreaking weeping comes to her ears. She changes immediately and leaves him to go to Jimmy. Every night since Jimmy has undergone that searing experience in the previous act he has dreamed of it and awakens weeping. With that sound in her ears and soul she finds that she cannot break her oath. She returns and tells John Strong she cannot marry him. He is inclined, at first, not to take her seriously; but she shows him that this time her answer is final. Although her heart is breaking she sends him away. The play ends in blackness and with the inconsolable sounds of little Jimmy weeping.

LETTER TO THE
ATLANTIC MONTHLY
Reference to the Plot of "Blackness"
and "Goldie"

To the Editors of The Atlantic Monthly
    41 Mt. Vernon Street
       Boston 9, Mass.

Dear Sirs:

    I am sending enclosed a story. It is not a pleasant one but it [is] based on fact. Several years ago, in Georgia, a colored woman quite naturally it would seem became wrought up, because her husband had been lynched. She threatened to bring some of the leaders to justice. The mob, made up of [?] and [?] white were determined to teach her a lesson. She was dragged out by them to a desolate part of the woods and the lesson began. First she was strung up by her feet to the limbs of a tree, next her clothes were saturated with kerosene oil, and then she was set afire. While the woman shrieked and writhed in agony, a man, who had brought with him a knife used in the butchering of animals, ripped her abdomen wide open. Her unborn child fell to the ground at her feet. It emitted one or two little cries but was soon silenced by brutal boots that crushed out the head. Death came at last to the poor woman. The lesson ended.

    Last fall, I think it was you printed an article entitled "Can

Text is taken from a draft holograph attached to a holograph copy of the story "Blackness" in the Angelina Weld Grimké Collection, MSRC, box 38-11, folder 180.

These Things Be?" That was a very brutal [argument on] [1] the Turks. It, of course, did not happen in America.

The facts upon the lynching upon which I based my story happened in the civilized U.S.A. in the 20th Century. Was this woman, I wonder, lynched for the "usual crime?" "Can These Things Be?" Even the Turks have been astounded at the brutality and the ruthlessness of the lynching in this country. Where are these lynchings leading the U.S.A.? In what will they end?

Very truly yours.

1. Holograph partially illegible.

GERTRUDE OF DENMARK
BY TILLIE BUFFUM
CHACE WYMAN

Reviewed by Angelina Weld Grimké

"Gertrude of Denmark," it is true, is not a book dealing with any phase of the race problem; but it is written by a woman rich in the tradition of fair play towards the Negro and of genuine friendship for him. Her great-grandfather, William Buffum, was one of the early abolitionists; her grandfather, Arnold Buffum, was the first president of the first society demanding immediate emancipation; her mother, Elizabeth Buffum Chace, a most remarkable woman, broke first with the Quakers, who, she considered, were not living up to their original principles on the race question and, second, with the Woman Suffrage movement, because the leaders held the opinion that it would be an affront to the white womanhood of the country to pass the Fifteenth Amendment before women received their political rights. There was also an aunt, a sister of Elizabeth Buffum Chace, Rebecca Buffum Spring, by name, who did a most unprecedented and big-hearted thing. In the year 1859, with her nineteen year old son, she went to West Virginia to see John Brown, then awaiting death in his cell. She did not even know him, but so great was her sympathy, she felt it her duty to go to him. After, however, she found she could do nothing to ameliorate conditions either for him or the other prisoners, she returned home and received his wife as an honored guest into her household. Her friendship for these two remained

Reprinted from *Opportunity* 2 (Dec. 1924): 378–79. Citations from Wyman have been set off by indentation rather than with quotation marks as in original. See Wyman's review of Grimké's *Rachel* in Appendix B.

419

steadfast until the end. This may be somewhat beside the point, but the author's husband, John C. Wyman, was a man, himself, of unquestioned courage where Negroes were concerned. Mrs. Wyman, in her "American Chivalry," cites the following of him:

> "Where can such a man go?" asked a doubter of social prerogative when speaking of a colored graduate from Harvard.
> "Into my house," answered John Wyman.

True, then, to her tradition and her surroundings, Mrs. Wyman herself has kept, through a long lifetime, an unfaltering belief in the Negro and has voiced often and courageously her demand, for him, of an equality of opportunity with the white man, politically, educationally, and socially. She is one of the very few fearless enough to push their reasoning to its logical conclusion, for social equality with her means intermarriage.

But Mrs. Wyman, in addition to all this, is a woman with the true literary gift. She has been a contributor to numerous magazines, such as the *Atlantic Monthly*, and is the author of "Poverty Grass," a volume of short stories now unfortunately out of print; "Elizabeth Buffum Chace and Her Environment," a tribute to her mother; "Interludes," a book of poems; and "American Chivalry," (from which I have just quoted) a series of appreciative sketches of value from a historical as well as a literary point of view. William Dean Howells, the "Dean of American Letters," thought so well of Mrs. Wyman's work that he mentions her particularly as one of the remarkable American writers of short story. Whatever, therefore, Mrs. Wyman has to say is well worth listening to.

For many years now, the author of "Gertrude of Denmark"

has been an invalid; but this, the latest book of hers, proves that her brain has lost nothing of its keenness and her pen nothing of its cunning. It has to do with Denmark's tragic queen in the play "Hamlet" and is a mixture of narrative, criticism and interpretation. The point of view is entirely new and the treatment of her subject absolutely original. The style is easy, vigorous and, under her skilful fingers, the characters live and breathe again. Whether you agree with Mrs. Wyman or not, in her interpretation, the book is provocative of thought and is a valuable addition to Shakespearean criticism. It seems to me that this utterly different point of view could have occurred only to a woman and a mother.

According to Mrs. Wyman, Gertrude came to her and begged her to set forth the facts in her life in their true light. Mrs. Wyman listened, became convinced of the entire truthfulness and sincerity of the dead queen, consented, therefore, and with the help of Gertrude, retells, for us, the whole story. Blanks in the action before the play "Hamlet" begins and during its course, are filled in logically and cleverly to prove the queen's case and there is no doubt but that she makes a strong one for Gertrude, the only fault being that often the reader feels that the author is not unbiased in her judgments and that in order to whiten Gertrude's character she has, of necessity, to blacken or change the characters of the others concerned. She is not the judge calmly sifting and weighing evidence, but the able lawyer pleading the case of her client.

Her interpretation of Ophelia is perhaps the only one with which we are familiar. Gertrude is depicted as a woman whose centralizing force is the maternal instinct. She knew nothing, we are told, suspected nothing of the murder of her first husband by her second, was virtuous always, and her overhasty marriage to Claudius, indecorous rather than sinful, was for the purpose mainly of protecting the interests of her son. Claudius, generally regarded as a monster of iniquity, is drawn by her as evil, it is true, but also as a human, suffering tortured soul, never truly repentant but sincere in his love for Gertrude and sincere in the beginning in his wish to befriend Hamlet. Polonius, interpreted usually as a meddling, worldly-wise old man, is pictured as amiable and inoffensive. Guildenstern and Rosencrantz, thought of as spies and tools of the king, are represented as truly friendly to Hamlet, if loyal to their king, and as not for a moment suspecting that they were conducting Hamlet to his death in England. Osric the lightweight, the popinjay, is seen as a true knight worshipping his queen respectfully, at a distance. Horatio, the one true friend, whom the over-suspicious Hamlet trusts implicitly even to the unbosoming of his most private affairs, in Mrs. Wyman's eyes, was capable once, at least, of possible sycophancy. Laertes, she admires through- out. To her he is a noble youth actuated by a desire to mete out justice only to Hamlet. And the unhappy prince himself, how does she see him? He is not the disillusioned idealist, harsh and bitter-tongued as a result of his experiences, but a doubter, suspicious often without a cause, misjudging a good mother, and wantonly brutal to Ophelia because he is innately cruel. There is not a suggestion here of any of the mitigating features that are usually attributed to this strange behavior of his towards a lovely innocent girl whom most of us believe he loved. In Mrs. Wyman's judgment, his doom came upon him not because he was too weak an instrument to carry out his father's commands, but because he deteriorated morally, as all must, who are driven onwards by a desire for vengeance only.

The author is not always consistent, it seems to me, in the

ethical values she attributes to certain actions. For instance, she can pass over the baseness and cowardice exhibited by Laertes in the duelling scene between him and Hamlet with these words:

> Poisoning was then a very gentlemanly method by which high-born folk might commit murder. To use such material as poison, in the compassing of his revenge, really raised young Laertes in social rank and set him among the gentry of the earth.

But when Hamlet, believing Rosencrantz and Guildenstern were leading him knowingly to his death, changes the king's commission so that they shall be killed in his stead, she criticizes the deed in this manner:

> Hamlet had once resolved upon a scheme of vengeance which should send his uncle to his final reckoning, no shriving time allowed. He had now progressed so far on the road towards extreme depravity as to execute a similarly fiendish purpose in relation to the comrades of his boyhood.

However, as I said before, Mrs. Wyman has made out a most interesting and clever case for Gertrude; and those who are not concerned as to whether she is right or wrong will find the book as a story entirely satisfying.

I cannot end this review without paying a tribute to the author for passages of real literary worth to be found throughout the book, passages showing restraint, beauty, and genuine power. I shall quote two of these:

> That night she dreamed of kneeling in the courtyard of the castle and beseeching King Hamlet not to go on some projected journey.
> "It will be cold and lonesome," she cried. "There is snow in the valleys; there is ice on the little river under the willows, and the baby is sick."

The dream king kissed . . . and vanished.

Claudius remained a brief while longer squatting in the alcove, his head nearly sunken on the floor in front of his body.

Finally he rose, stretching himself with a slow movement, betokening muscular difficulty and even physical pain. He stood erect a moment. He looked rather dazed. His lips dropped helplessly apart.

There was an expression of idiotic horror spread over his face.

He had failed to get Heaven on his side . . . and he knew it.

A BIOGRAPHICAL SKETCH
OF ARCHIBALD H. GRIMKÉ

Seventy-five years ago, the seventeenth of last August, my father was born on his father's plantation, "Caneacre," thirteen miles out of Charleston, S.C. He was the oldest of three sons. Henry Grimké, his father, was a member of one of Charleston's aristocratic families; Nancy Weston Grimké, his mother, was a slave by birth, but a most remarkable woman. I knew her for the only time, the last year of her life (she lived to be eighty-four) and though I was a child, then, I can remember her perfectly. She spent her days, sitting in a large rattan rocker in her sunny room on the second floor back of my uncle's Washington home. She moved about seldom and then with the greatest difficulty, leaning on a cane; but there was something unconquerable, indomitable in that bent, gaunt body and in that clean-cut, eagle-like face. If she yielded to age it was only inch by inch. Her keen old eyes could flash and I never heard her speak in uncertain tones. Once she had been beautiful. My father has a picture of her in her early forties, I should say, and there is that in her face and her bearing that is truly regal. Doubters in reincarnation should have known her. Sometime, somewhere, that spirit must have lived in the body of a great queen or an empress. How else explain her? But the most beautiful thing about her was her mother love. It was the guiding passion, the driving force in her long life. There was literally no sacrifice she would not have made for her children. In

Reprinted from *Opportunity* 3 (Feb. 1925): 44–47.

defense of them she would have torn an enemy to pieces. I never saw my uncle John, until I looked down at his dead face in his coffin; but often and often, I have heard both my father and my uncle pay her the highest and finest tribute that can be paid to any woman—that what they are they owe mainly to her, her teachings and her love. A vivid, powerful, unselfish personality!

My father has told me he was born with a caul over his face, the possessors of which, I believe, are supposed to have bestowed upon them two gifts, the seeing of ghosts and the being lucky. One ghost only has he seen, that of an exceedingly disagreeable white sister-in-law, who was very much alive at the time, though sick in bed. She appeared to him while he was chopping wood. This was years ago and he was a mere child, but he is certain of his experience. She gradually disappeared before his eyes as did the Cheshire cat in "Alice in Wonderland," the great difference being that whereas, in the case of the cat, it was the grin that went last, in her case, it was the prying, suspicious eyes. And as for luck. Well, if the getting of things through difficulties by the sweat of the brow and by struggle; if the having of one's share of hardships, of poverty, of suffering; if the sticking to an ideal through the most utter discouragements; if the standing alone, at times, on an unpopular side because one knows oneself to be right; if the refusing to bend the knee or the head for the sake of expediency—if all of these spell luck, then my father has, indeed, been lucky. A kindly Providence has never dropped plump and goodly things into his waiting, quiet lap. In the last analysis, what is luck? Who knows?

When my father was three or four years old, my grandmother moved to a little house on Cummings Street, in Charleston. It was simple, crude even, for they were very poor; but when did poverty ever bother boys much? These were mainly happy years for them, the source, now, of many a pleasant and laugh provoking recollection. Here the little family lived until 1865.

I have never seen a picture of my father as a little boy; but he has been described to me. He was not robust in appearance (he was too sensitive, too highly-strung to be that) but he was wiry and possessed that indispensable quality, vitality. His face framed in auburn curls had the deceiving gentleness, I have been told, of a young angel's. I use the expression "deceiving gentleness" advisedly, as shall soon be seen.

As the years passed, Cummings Street came to know the three Grimké boys. No, not because they loved church and Sunday-school and washed their faces and hands and behind their ears and kept their clothes in spotless condition, but because of all the fighters in the street, they were the greatest. Each was an adept in his line and invincible in it. My uncle John was the champion "butter," my Uncle Frank the champion "biter" and my father the champion "kicker." The trio always fought in unison, an attack upon one being an attack upon all. Against such a versatile Grimké army what could the other boys do? Nothing on the street dared to appear aggressive even. A good many years have passed since then, but the Grimké brothers are fighters to this day, pens and tongues proving as efficient weapons as teeth and feet.

Before the Civil War, the three brothers learnt their "Three R's" in a sedate little school conducted by some white southern gentlemen of Charleston for the children of free colored people. After the war, as was to be expected, a great change came into the lives of the little family. It began in this way. Gilbert Pillsbury, the brother of the famous abolitionist, came to Charleston from the North to be its first mayor during the Reconstruction Period. With him came his wife,

Frances, who opened, for the colored youth of the city, what was known as the Morris Street School. To this school went the three boys. They were good students and successful, but the most important part of this experience was that they gained a lasting and powerful friend in Mrs. Pillsbury. So interested did she become that she finally determined that the two elder boys, Archibald and Francis, should go North to get their education.

My father was sixteen, then, and my uncle Frank fifteen, when after many prayers and much heartbreak and the final consent of the ambitious, self-sacrificing mother, they set their faces towards the North and went eagerly to seek their Great Adventure. There is always something pathetic about confident youth setting forth to conquer the world, their trust in themselves and in their stars is so high and they never, never suspect that sooner or later just around some innocently appearing corner, disappointment is lying in wait. It was "sooner" rather than "later" for the two boys. Mrs. Pillsbury had sent them, as she supposed, into families where in return for work done by them they would be educated. My father spent six months at Peacedale, R. I., in a pleasant enough family and my uncle in Stoneham, Mass., but the longed for opening to their education never appeared. In the meantime, the mother feeling, as it seemed to her, that she had made the sacrifice of separation for nothing, from her children, went to see Mrs. Pillsbury. The result of this visit was, that Mrs. Pillsbury took up the cudgels again for them and, although President Isaac N. Rendall felt they were entirely too young, she was finally instrumental in getting them into Lincoln University.

The four years which followed were happy enough for the two boys. A new universe was theirs, a new outlook on life and lasting friendships. It was not always the easiest matter to make both ends meet. They had to work during their summers either at waiting or teaching little country schools in the South, but all this seemed merely to add a zest to their happiness. They enjoyed their studies to the full; they enjoyed all the school activities and, of course, all the usual horseplay and fun of college boys. Here they had their first lessons in leadership. My father during these early years was very conventionally religious and at the age of eighteen, was ordained an elder in the Presbyterian Church. So religious was he, in fact, that his friends expected him to become the minister and my uncle Frank, the lawyer. At first President Rendall watched the boys from afar. What he saw interested him. Soon interest became love and between them, on the one hand, and the dear old gentleman, on the other, there grew up a most beautiful friendship. Whenever and wherever he could, he helped them. Through him they became student-teachers and my father was made the only colored librarian Lincoln ever had, for Lincoln is the sole colored university with neither a colored professor nor a colored trustee.

A small thing may have an amazing effect. It was during my father's sophomore year that Prof. Bowers wrote a letter to Congressman Shellabarger. In it he spoke of the attainments and the scholarship of a certain young colored boy, Archibald H. Grimké, by name. The congressman, thinking it remarkable that any one with colored blood should have achieved such a reputation for himself sent the letter to the newspapers as a syndicated article and out the news went all over the country. In Hyde Park, Mass., at this time, were living two sisters, Angelina and Sarah Grimké, sisters also of Henry Grimké, the father of these boys. Angelina was married to the brilliant anti-slavery orator, Theodore D. Weld. It has often been said that the life of some people reads like a romance. The life of these two sisters was truly one. In the aristocratic southern blood of Angelina, when she was only a girl, there strangely enough boiled up and over a most violent hatred of slavery. Sarah, the elder sister, felt exactly as she did, and these two utterly inexperienced women, carefully sheltered from birth, broke without a qualm with their traditions and their family, came North and joined themselves to the abolitionists. Courage, it took, tremendous courage. Now, it happened that the syndicated article about my father came to the eyes of Angelina. The name "Grimké" immediately riveted her attention. A correspondence began between her and the boys and, in their junior year, accompanied by her son, Stuart, she came to visit them. She now did a thing that seems well nigh unbelievable. Becoming convinced that these boys were her brother's children, she acknowledged them as her nephews! More, upon their graduation she invited them to visit her and her family in Hyde Park.

They went. They often laugh, now, over the picture they must have presented to the astonished eyes of Weld family that was the simplest of the simple in manner, dress and living. To the boys this was a great occasion, the greatest in all their lives and, cost what it might, they were determined to live up to it. They were virtually penniless, but each carried a cane, wore a high silk hat which had been made to order, and boots that were custom-made. Whatever the aunts and the Welds thought, they were welcomed with wide open arms and hearts and made at home. The simplicity here soon taught them their lesson.

But this Boston experience had a much more far-reaching effect upon the life of my father. At the end of their visit they both returned to Lincoln where my father took both his A.B. and M.A., but a love for Boston and the North had entered into his blood, and he was happy enough when his Aunt Sarah decided in 1872 that he should return and attend the Harvard Law School. His second and last year, for the course then was two years, he won a scholarship. Upon his graduation in 1874 there came a slight rift between him and the aunts over where he should practice. They believed his chances would be much better in the South; but he, knowing what it meant to be, for the first time, a free man, was not a bit inclined to leave Boston. Luckily for him, at this juncture, a Mrs. Walling, with whom he had lived in Cambridge while a student, came to his rescue and interested the well-known lawyer, William I. Bowditch, in him, who, from the goodness and kindness of a big heart, admitted the young man into his office.

During the two preceding years and during the years that were to follow the study of law was to prove a very small part of his education. As I suggested the "Boston experience" was to have a far-reaching effect. If the world of thought at Lincoln was new, how much newer was that world into which he now entered. His whole outlook became changed and vastly different reactions to life came to be his. Boston was indeed the "Hub" in those days. Through the aunts he came to know its cultivated people, its artists, men and women who did the things that were most worth while, who knew and appreciated the best in all the walks of life. He met the Fosters, Lucy Stone, the famous Miss Elizabeth Peabody, his old friends the Pillsburys, Judge Sewell, Dr. Bartol, Garrison, Sumner and Phillips, prominent and great men of his own race, such as Lewis Hayden and Frederick Douglass and more, many more besides, names that stand today for the best in that life of an older Boston. Is it strange, then, that he became a liberal in religion, a radical in the Woman Suffrage Movement, in politics and on the race question?

Those first years, after graduation, were hard ones. The practice of law, at best, for a beginner is not an easy matter.

When richer in knowledge, he left Mr. Bowditch, he made his start in partnership with James H. Wolff. Later on he formed a new alliance with Butler R. Wilson, but it was hard sledding, indeed, those early days. In 1879 he married and beginning with 1883, for two years he published and edited, with the aid of Butler R. Wilson, a colored newspaper called "The Hub." It was in 1884 that he was sent to the Republican National Convention as Henry Cabot Lodge's alternate delegate at large. This was the convention where both Lodge and Roosevelt, as young men, were winning their spurs.

Although a good part of his association had been with the whites, he was always closely identified with his own people. For many years he was president of Boston's famous colored literary society, "The Banneker Club." It is forgotten, now, but the Crispus Attucks Monument to which we point with pride on Boston Common was erected only after a long unpleasant fight on the part of colored people and their white sympathizers. The main glory for this achievement goes to Lewis Hayden; but my father is justly proud of the fact that he had his small part in the battle.

Of all the men that my father has ever known there is none that he has loved as he loved Wendell Phillips. I never saw that benignant and grand old man and yet so vivid is the picture of him that my father has drawn for me, over and over again, that I can hardly believe I never looked upon him in the flesh. He has told me that, many a time, he has met Phillips on the streets of Boston and that the big-hearted, unconventional, beautiful creature has walked along with him holding him by the hand. He died in 1884; and none, I suppose, can estimate the number of people who mourned his death. George William Curtis was chosen by the city to deliver the memorial address at the famous Tremont Temple;

and my father was chosen to make the address for the citizens at the same place.

In 1882, he had moved from Boston and gone to live in Hyde Park, then a suburb, but now a part of greater Boston. It is here that my own memories of my father begin. "Tanglewood" was the name of the modest two-story grey house owned by a couple, in their way as lovable as any I have known. Their name was Leverett. They lived down stairs and we, up. Some of my pleasantest recollections are of what would be called now, our living room—the drawn shades, the yellow lamplight, the big coal stove, the wind or rain or snow without pounding against the six windows and our "reading-time."

It was at the big table in the center of this room that he wrote his articles for "The Boston Herald" and "The Boston Traveller"; and it was here he wrote, for the "True Reformer Series," published by Funk and Wagnalls, his two books, "The Life of William Lloyd Garrison" and "The Life of Charles Sumner."

Once a month, I remember, he used to leave me with the Leveretts or the Welds, who still lived in Hyde Park (although the aunts were dead) while he went to Westborough, Mass. In 1884 Governor Robinson Russell reappointed him, a trustee of the Westborough Insane Asylum. For ten years he served his state not only as a trustee but as the secretary of the board, his duty being to make this monthly visit. In 1894 all these pleasant days came to end, for it was at this time President Cleveland appointed him as Consul to Santo Domingo.

Four years he was in Santo Domingo. Of that time, personally, I know nothing, as I was too young to be taken with him; but I do know that he enjoyed the tropics and that

his days were busy, eventful and happy ones. His one big
achievement was the settling of a law suit over a bridge in
favor of an American citizen named McKay, a suit that had
been pending for years and a source of great annoyance to
this government.

In 1898 he returned to this country and has been here ever
since. At first he lived a part of his time in Boston and a part
in Washington; but, now, with the exception of a few months
in the summer, he makes his home in the capital city. He
has engaged in no paying occupation since his return, but has
given his time and his energies to the writing of addresses
and pamphlets on the race question, to the making of speeches
and to the fighting of race prejudice wherever found. He was
President for many years of the "American Negro Academy"
and is now a President emeritus; he was a President also of
the "Frederick Douglass Memorial and Historical Association" and is still a member of the society. In the "National
Association for the Advancement of Colored People" he has
been a director, is still a vice-president and has been, for
many years, the President of the District of Columbia branch.

In 1919, at Cleveland, he received the "Spingarn Medal,"
awarded him for a long lifetime of service to his race.
President Thwing of Western Reserve University made the
speech and presented the medal and Oswald Garrison Villard
came the whole way to Cleveland to be present, as a friend,
at the ceremony.

As I said in the beginning, he is seventy-five years old
now. He thinks his work is over. I do not agree with him.
Perhaps he may come to agree with me. Many men have
done things and great things after seventy-five. He spends
his days sitting in the sunlight. He reads and he thinks.
Whatever else may be said about him he has the satisfaction
of knowing that his life is open to the inspection of any man;

that he has been a consistent and uncompromising fighter, all his life, for the welfare of his race as he has seen it; that the fight has been a good one, a clean one and above board, unmarred by any pettiness and treachery; that he has never turned a deaf ear to any one who has come to him with a just cause; that as a true friend, himself, he has made true friends; and that if all men do not love him, they respect him. Pleasant, pleasant thoughts these.

As his daughter, it is not for me to say whether what he has said or done or written is going to live—but I know what I think.

REMARKS ON LITERATURE

Madame President, Members Book Lovers, Ladies and Gentlemen: Before reading my little story, I should like, first of all, to thank the members of this club for the honor they have paid me by inviting me here. Your invitation, through your President, was entirely unexpected and a rather beautiful thing to me, beautiful because it seemed so very nice of you to be willing to listen to whatever little message I might have to bring. I appreciate this willingness more probably than you will ever know.

I don't wish to bore you too much, but I should like, if you will permit me, to preface my story by a few remarks. You are studying, this year, I understand, the technique of the short story. Certainly none can gainsay that either to appreciate or to write a short story that an understanding of its technique is absolutely essential. Equally important, if not more so, is the necessity of having something to say, something to write about. If you read the stories in the American magazines of to-day, you must have been impressed very often by at least two things, the staleness of the material and the staleness of the plot. For years the white man has been writing about his own reactions to life. He is about written out. New ground is needed, new harvests. So he is beginning to look about him for new fields from which to get his material. Upon a white man, here and there, the realization

Text is taken from the undated, untitled holograph (loose sheets) in the Spingarn Research Center, Angelina Weld Grimké Collection, MSRC, series D—manuscripts, box 38-15, folder 244.

is beginning to dawn that he need not go far that, in fact, close at hand he has this great unexplored land that he needs, a land virgin almost, and rich even beyond imagined richness—the great field harvested from the lives of colored people. I am not alone in believing that the great American story[1] of the future is to spring from the lives of colored people. Where in just the mere everyday life can you match the humour, the geniality, the pathos, the tragedy even, that is to be found in ours. Some day a genius, white or black is coming and he is going to see us, seize upon us, take us just as we are, no more no less, and make himself immortal through us. I hope he is to be black for certainly, it seems to me, no one can know us as well as one of ourselves. But if he is to be black I do not think the time of his coming is yet, but after all I cannot know this, for a genius is a law unto himself and his coming none can foretell. But before he arrives I most certainly believe there must be a decided change in the attitude of colored people towards themselves as a whole we are still inclined to feel ourselves inferior to white people. We do not consider that what we think or say and feel and suffer interesting or valuable. Some of us are even ashamed of these things. In preparation of the coming of this black genius I believe there must be among us a stronger and a growing feeling of race consciousness, race solidarity, race pride. It means a training of the youth of to-day and of to-morrow in the recognition of the sanctity of all these things. Then perhaps, some day, some where black youth, will come forth, see us clearly, intelligently, sympathetically, and will write about us and then come into his own.

1. Holograph: {short story} with {short} crossed out.

APPENDIXES

APPENDIX A
SELECTED BIBLIOGRAPHY

This bibliography includes the publication history, as much as can be determined at this time, of those works of Angelina Weld Grimké's that have been published.

Adoff, Arnold, ed. *The Poetry of Black America*. New York: Harper and Row, 1973.

"Angelina W. Grimké, Poet, Ex-Teacher, 78" [Obituary]. *New York Times* (11 June 1958).

Ammons, Elizabeth, Comp. *Short Fiction by Black Women, 1900–1920*. New York: Oxford University Press, 1991.

Barksdale, Richard, and Keneth Kinnamon, eds. *Black Writers of America*. New York: MacMillan, 1972.

Bernikow, Louise, ed. *The World Split Open: Four Centuries of Women Poets in England and America, 1552–1950*. New York: Vintage, 1924.

Bontemps, Arna, ed. *American Negro Poetry*. New York: Hill and Wang, 1963.

Bradley, Gerald. "Goodbye, Mister Bones." *Drama Critique* 7 (Spring 1964): 83. Includes critique of *Rachel*.

Brown, Sterling. *Negro Poetry and Drama and The Negro in American Fiction*. New York: Atheneum, 1937. Includes critiques of *Rachel* and of Grimké's poetry.

Brown, Sterling Allen, Arthur P. Davis, and Ulysses Lee, eds. *The Negro Caravan*. New York: Arno Press, 1941.

Christian, Barbara. "No More Buried Lives: The Theme of Lesbianism in Audre Lorde's *Zami*, Gloria Naylor's *The Women of Brewster Place*, and Alice Walker's *The Color Purple*." In *Black Feminist Criticism: Perspectives on Black Women Writers*. New York: Pergamon Press, 1985.

Cooper, Anna Julia. *The Life and Writings of the Grimké Family*. N.p.: self-published, 1951.

Cromwell, Otelia, Lorenzo Dow Turner, and Eva B. Dykes, eds. *Readings From Negro Authors for Schools and Colleges, with a Bibliography of Negro Literature.* New York: Harcourt, Brace and Jovanovich, 1931.

Cullen, Countee, ed. *Caroling Dusk: An Anthology of Verse By Negro Poets.* Harper and Brothers: New York, 1927.

Davis, Arthur Paul. *From the Dark Tower: Afro-American Writers.* Washington: Howard University Press, 1974. Includes critique of *Rachel*.

———, ed. *The New Negro Renaissance.* New York: Holt, Rinehart and Winston, 1975.

Edmonds, Randolph. "The Blacks in the American Theatre, 1700–1969." *Pan-African Journal*, no. 7 (Winter 1974): 302. Includes critique of *Rachel*.

Grimké, Angelina Weld. "At April." In Bernikow, 1924: Stetson, 1981.

———. "At the Spring Dawn." In Kerlin, 1923.

———. "Beware Lest He Awakes [Beware When He Awakes (3)]." *Pilot* (10 May 1902).

———. "A Biographical Sketch of Archibald H. Grimké. *Opportunity* 3 (Feb. 1925): 44. Also in Brown et al., 1941.

———. "The Black Finger." *Opportunity* 1 (Nov. 1923): 343; rpt. *Opportunity* 5 (Apr. 1927): 110. Also in Locke, 1925; Hughes, vol. 1, 1949; Bontemps, 1963; Adoff, 1973; Davis, 1975.

———. "Black Is, As Black Does." *Colored American Magazine* 1 (Aug. 1900): 160. Also in Ammons, 1991.

———. "Blue Cycle." In Johnson, 1971.

———. "Brown Girl." In Johnson, 1971.

———. "The Closing Door." *Birth Control Review*, special number (Sept. 1919): 10; 3 (Oct. 1919).

———. "Dawn [(2)]." In Kerlin, 1923; Cromwell et al., 1931.

———. "Death [(1)]." *Opportunity* 3 (March 1925).

———. "Dusk." *Opportunity* 2 (Apr. 1924): 99. Also in Cullen, 1927.

———. "El Beso." *Boston Transcript* (27 Oct. 1909). Also in Kerlin, 1923.

————. "The Eyes of My Regret." In Cullen, 1927.

————. "For the Candle-Light." *Opportunity* 3 (Sept. 1925): 263. Also in Cullen, 1927; Hughes, vols. 1 and 2, 1949; Stetson, 1981.

————. *"Gertrude of Denmark* by Tillie Buffum Chase Wyman" [review]. *Opportunity* 2 (Dec. 1924): 378.

————. "Grass Fingers." In Cullen, 1927; Cromwell et al., 1931; Barksdale and Kinnamon, 1972; Davis, 1975.

————. "The Grave in the Corner." *Norfolk County Gazette* (27 May 1893). (Juvenile poem not included in this volume.)

————. "Greenness." In Cullen, 1927.

————. "Goldie." *Birth Control Review* 4 (Nov.–Dec. 1920).

————. "Hushed by the Hands of Sleep." In Cullen, 1927.

————. "I Weep." *Opportunity* 2 (July 1924): 196. Also in Cullen, 1927; Patterson, 1973.

————. "Little Grey Dreams." *Opportunity* 2 (July 1924): 196.

————. "Longing." *Boston Transcript* (16 Apr. 1901).

————. "May." *Boston Transcript* (7 May 1901).

————. "A Mona Lisa." In Cullen, 1927; Barksdale and Kinnamon, 1972; Stetson, 1981.

————. "Paradox." In Cullen, 1927.

————. "The Puppet-Player." In Kerlin, 1923; Cullen, 1927.

————. *Rachel: A Play in Three Acts.* Boston: Cornhill Company, 1920; rpt. College Park, MD: McGrath Publishing Company, 1969.

————. " 'Rachel' The Play of the Month: The Reason and Synopsis by the Author." *Competitor* 1 (Jan. 1920): 51.

————. "Street Echoes." *Boston Sunday Globe* (22 July 1894). (Juvenile poem not included in this volume.)

————. "Surrender [(2)]." In Cullen, 1927; Cromwell et al., 1931; Brown et al., 1941.

————. "Tenebris." In Bernikow, 1924; Cullen, 1927; Hughes, vols. 1 and 2, 1949; Adoff, 1973.

————. "Then and Now." In Kerlin, 1923. (This poem was originally titled "Written for the Fiftieth Anniversary Celebration At Dunbar High School.")

————. "To Clarissa Scott Delaney." In Bontemps, 1963; Johnson, 1971.

————. "To the Dunbar High School." *Crisis* 13 (1917): 222. Also in Cromwell et al., 1931; Bontemps, 1963.

————. "To Joseph Lee." *Boston Evening Transcript* (11 Nov. 1908).

————. "To Keep the Memory of Charlotte Forten Grimké [(2)]." *Crisis* 9 (1915): 134; 38 (1931): 380. Also in Kerlin, 1923; *Opportunity* 3 (March 1925); *Negro History Bulletin* (Jan. 1947): 79, 95; and Stetson, 1981.

————. "To Theodore D. Weld—On His 90th Birthday." *Norfolk County Gazette* (25 Nov. 1893). (Juvenile poem not included in this volume.)

————. "The Want of You." In Kerlin, 1923.

————. "The Ways O' Men." In Cullen, 1927.

————. "When the Green Lies Over the Earth." In Cullen, 1927; Brown et al., 1941; Hughes, vols. 1 and 2, 1949.

————. "Where Phillis Sleeps." *Boston Transcript* (31 July 1901).

————. "A Winter Twilight." In Kerlin, 1923; Bernikow, 1924; Cullen, 1927; Brown et al., 1941; Hughes, vols. 1 and 2, 1949; Adoff, 1973.

————. "Your Hands." In Cullen, 1927; Cromwell et al., 1931; Adoff, 1973; Patterson, 1973; Davis, 1975.

Grimké, Charlotte Forten. *The Journals of Charlotte Forten Grimké*. Edited by Brenda Stevenson. New York: Oxford University Press, 1988.

Hartnoll, Phyllis. *The Oxford Companion to Theater*. London: Oxford University Press, 1967. Includes critique of *Rachel*.

Hicklin, Fannie Ella Frazier. *The American Negro Playwright, 1920–1964*. Ann Arbor: University Microfilms, 1974. Includes critique of *Rachel*.

Hughes, Langston, ed. *The Poetry of the Negro: 1746–1949*. Garden City: Doubleday, 1949.

Hull, Gloria. *Color, Sex, and Poetry: Three Women Writers of the Harlem Renaissance*. Bloomington: Indiana University Press, 1987.

————. "Under the Days,: The Buried Life and Poetry of Angelina Weld Grimké." In *Conditions, 5, The Black Woman's Issue*. Edited by Lorraine Bethel and Barbara Smith. New York, 1979, p. 17. Rpt. *Home Girls: A Black Feminist Anthology*. Edited by Barbara Smith. New York: Kitchen Table: Women of Color Press, 1983, p. 73.

————. "Women Poets of the Harlem Renaissance." In *Shakespeare's Daughters*. Edited by Sandra Gilbert and Susan Gubar. Bloomington: Indiana University Press, 1979.

Johnson, Charles, ed. *Ebony and Topaz*. New York: Books for Libraries Press, 1971.

Jones, Anne Goodwyn. *Tomorrow Is Another Day: Women Writers in the South, 1859–1936*. Baton Rouge: Louisiana State University Press, 1981.

Lampkind, Katherine DuPre. *The Emancipation of Angelina Grimké [Weld]*. Chapel Hill: University of North Carolina Press, 1984, p. xv. (Angelina Weld Grimké comments on being namesake of Angelina Grimké Weld.)

Lerner, Gerda. *The Grimké Sisters From South Carolina*. Boston: Houghton Mifflin, 1967.

Keller, Phyllis. "Mary Porter Tileston Hemenway." In *Notable American Women: 1607–1950*. Cambridge, MA: Harvard University Press, 1971. (Subject of Grimké's memorial poem "Two sonnets to Mrs. Hemenway ["On Seeing Her Picture"].)

Kerlin, Robert T., ed. *Negro Poets and Their Poems*. Washington, D.C.: Associated Publishers, Inc., 1923.

Locke, Alain, ed. *The New Negro*. New York: Albert & Charles Bone, Inc., 1925.

————, ed. *Plays of Negro Life*. New York: Harper and Brothers, 1927.

McKinney, Ernest Rice. "Rachel: A Play by Angelina Weld Grimké" [review]. *Competitor* 3 (Apr. 1921): 35.

Miller, Jeanne-Marie A. "Images of Black Women in Plays by Black Playwrights." *CLA Journal* (June 1977): 494. Includes critique of *Rachel*.

Molette, Barbara. "Black Women Playwrights: They Speak: Who

Listens?" *Black World* (Apr. 1976): 30. Includes critique of *Rachel*.

Patterson, Lindsay, ed. *A Rock Against the Wind: Black Love Poems: An Anthology*. New York: Dodd, Mead & Co., 1973.

Play program for *Rachel*. *Washington Post* (19 March 1917).

Review of Rachel. *Buffalo [New York] Courier* (3 Oct. 1920).

————. *Catholic World* (Dec. 1920).

————. *Columbus [Ohio] Dispatch* (26 Sept. 1920).

————. *Grinnell Review* (Jan. 1921).

————. *Rochester [New York] Post Express* (14 Sept. 1920).

————. *Utica [New York] Daily Press* (8 Oct. 1920)

————. *Washington [D.C.] Star* (5 Dec. 1920).

————. *Wilmington [Delaware] Every Evening* (4 Sept. 1920).

Segrist, Mab. *My Momma's Dead Squirrel: Lesbian Essays on Southern Culture*. Ithaca, NY: Firebrand Books, 1985.

Stetson, Erlene, ed. *Black Sister*. Bloomington: Indiana University Press, 1981.

Stevenson, Robert Louis. "The Image of the White Man as Projected in the Published Plays of Black Americans, 1847–1973." Ph.D. Dissertation, Indiana University, 1976. Includes critique of *Rachel*.

Wyman, Tillie Buffum Chace. "Review of *Rachel*." *Journal of Negro History* 6 (Apr. 1921): 248.

APPENDIX B
REVIEW OF *RACHEL*
BY TILLIE BUFFUM
CHACE WYMAN

Miss Grimké's drama of Rachel is a beautiful and poetic creation. She has produced this effect by a literary instinct which is fine and mainly cultivated. Its native vigor carries the reader past an occasional crudity, which it would seem to be hypocritical to notice. The sweep of passion in the drama is elemental. She has connected the story of a girl-woman with the most woeful of earthly tragedies, namely the crime of a great nation against one of its component parts.

The feelings expressed in the drama, though elemental, are uttered in the terms of modernity. The structure of the drama is modern, and yet there is something in the figure and movement of Rachel herself which reminds the present writer of Antigone. We do not see Antigone before the hour when she has chosen to meet the doom that man's law has decreed should she perform the task that human love and religious faith have enjoined upon her. Antigone goes to the death of her body declaring that in the Infinite there is a longer time for love than there is on earth.

But we do see Rachel before the ultimate choice has come to her. She is a gay and happy girl. The drama proceeds to the hour when she too must choose between the issues of earthly love and those which reach into eternity. She learns from her mother, Mrs. Loving, that ten years before, they all lived in the South and her father and her half brother were lynched. Briefly summarized, this is Mrs. Loving's story. As a young widow with a boy seven years old, she had married an educated man of color. She was a person of color herself. Mr. Loving owned and edited a paper in which he wrote on behalf of the people of color. A Negro innocent of all crime was murdered by a mob in that region. Mr. Loving de-

Reprinted from the *Journal of Negro History* 6 (Apr. 1921): 248–54.

nounced the murder and the murderers in his paper. He received an anonymous letter apparently written by an educated person, threatening him with death, if he did not retract what he had said. In the next issue of his paper he published an equally stern arraignment of the lynchers and their crime.

That night a dozen masked men broke into his house. Mr. Loving had a revolver. He defended his life and his home. Mrs. Loving tried to close her eyes. She could not. She saw all that happened in her bedroom. Four of the masked assailants fell. "They did not move any more . . . after a little while." Then she saw her husband dragged out of the room. Her older boy, George, tried to help his stepfather. He was dragged out also. She went to the bedside of her two younger children. They were asleep. Rachel was smiling. The mother knelt down and covered her ears. When at last she let herself listen, she heard only the tapping of the branch of a pine tree against the side of the house. She did not know at first that it was *the tree*.

She fled with her two little children to the North. Those children had never before this day of revelation known how their father had died. The shadow of white cruelty to the body and souls of black folks had darkened somewhat over their lives in the North, but still they had been frolicsome and loving young creatures. Now they begin to realize the full significance of "race prejudice."

Rachel speaks to her mother: "Then, everywhere, everywhere throughout the South, there are hundreds of dark mothers who live in fear, terrible, suffocating fear, . . . whose joy in their babies . . . is three parts pain. . . . The South is full of . . . thousands of little boys who one day may be, and some of whom will be lynched." "And the babies, the dear, little, helpless babies . . . have *that* sooner or later to look to. They will laugh and play and sing and grow up, and perhaps be ambitious,—just for that."

"Yes, Rachel," answers her mother. The girl is one of those rare, feminine creatures whose soul and body are framed for maternity. In one swift rush of realization and of premonition, she comprehends all that the doom upon her race must eventually mean to her; she utters the cry of Africa's heart in America. "It would be more merciful to strangle the little things at birth. . . . This white Christian nation has set its curse upon the most beautiful, . . . the most holy thing on earth . . . motherhood."